BLURRED LINES

BLURRED LINES

RETHINKING SEX, POWER, AND CONSENT ON CAMPUS

VANESSA GRIGORIADIS

An Eamon Dolan Book
Houghton Mifflin Harcourt
BOSTON   NEW YORK   2017

For information about permission to reproduce selections from
this book, write to trade.permissions@hmhco.com or to Permissions,
Houghton Mifflin Harcourt Publishing Company, 3 Park Avenue,
19th Floor, New York, New York 10016.

www.hmhco.com

Library of Congress Cataloging-in-Publication Data is available.
ISBN 978-0-544-70255-4

Book design by Rachel Newborn

Printed in the United States of America
DOC 10 9 8 7 6 5 4 3 2 1

For my father

CONTENTS

AUTHOR'S NOTE

Composite and imaginary characters do not appear in this book. In most cases, I have identified people by their real names. Pseudonyms are noted with asterisks.

"MATTRESS GIRL"

I met Emma Sulkowicz on a hot day in August 2014, a month before Columbia University was back in session. We were having tea at a café in Manhattan's Greenwich Village, and she was listing all the ways she felt her university had failed her by what she perceived as a combination of incompetence and malevolence. Suddenly, she brought up her plan: she was going to carry a mattress around the campus every day until the school expelled the student she said had raped her. It was so crystalline and simple, such perfect payback. I laughed, not because schlepping a fifty-pound mattress around campus sounded insane, though it did — and if Nungesser wasn't ejected, she vowed to carry it for the entire school year — but because it was an act brilliantly conceived to capture the attention of our outrageously performative, meme-happy, absurdist age.

Sulkowicz herself laughed too at first, because she has a good sense of humor, but then she abruptly stopped. One of several students I was meeting for age-appropriate drinks to talk about sexual assault at Columbia, she sat in a square of sunshine, her black T-shirt hanging loosely over her lean, athletic frame, her eyes eight-ball black, her shoulder-length hair dyed at the tips in a Monet-at-dusk palette. She spoke slowly and deliberately, her words punctuated by an occasional nervous giggle at a perceived error or ill-phrased statement. When she didn't like what I'd said, she became severe and cold.

Japanese and Chinese on her mother's side and the granddaughter of Holocaust survivors on her father's, Sulkowicz seemed a few years older than a college senior, if you ignored her Invisalign braces. Her self-assured bearing was likely a product of being raised by two psychiatrist parents, one of whom is now a leadership consultant for corporate executives. Her scholarly focus toggled between science and art — specifically, mechanical physics, which she expected to major in, and fine art, which she chose instead. When

I asked her to describe her own personality, she said "an older sister." She was even-keeled. In charge. "In high school, people always said, 'Emma never cries, Emma's very Zen,'" she explained. "I'm stoic in many ways, and the one who isn't going to be emotional or dramatic—unless something really bad is happening."

In high school, Sulkowicz floated around cliques—not a nerd, not a jock, but an individual, a fencer who scarfed down six eggs each morning to build muscle, and an artist so talented she helped other students in drawing class. She was quiet. She had her first kiss at fourteen, but when she entered college, and even on the night at the beginning of sophomore year when she says she was assaulted, she had yet to have a boyfriend. Like most students, she was casual with those in whom she was romantically interested, and over the course of some months, hooking up was what she'd been doing with a German architecture student, Paul Nungesser.

On the night in question, they'd started kissing in an ivy-covered courtyard, then retired to her dorm room, where they had extensive intercourse—oral, vaginal, anal. The first two, they agree, were consensual. But Sulkowicz insists the last was not. Many months later, she reported the incident to the school, and many months after this, a Columbia disciplinary panel, operating in a confusing manner, ruled against her. They left Nungesser unpunished, a decision that made her angrier, perhaps, than anything else had in the course of her short life.

This was the bad thing that happened, and it not only turned Sulkowicz's Zenned-out world upside down but changed the collegiate experience of a generation. Until a few years ago, an Ivy League student who went public about a rape was a rare bird. But soon after our chat at the café, Sulkowicz inverted the typical public roles of rape cases, the long tradition of a Kobe Bryant or William Kennedy Smith declaring his innocence at a bank of microphones while the victim began her offstage downfall—became depressed, dishonored, maybe even suicidal. A sexual assault victim's anonymity, ostensibly for her own protection, was a precept of the old system. Now victims—or, in the current parlance, *survivors*—stepped into the spotlight, and the accused tried to hide in the shadows. Now Sulkowicz pointed one of her neon-painted fingers at the university as an enabler. Now she insisted, despite scant evidence, that the public believe her story (there was no smoking gun here; in campus cases, there almost never is). Most important, now she called into question the definition of *consent* in teeny-tiny, linoleum-floored dorm rooms across the country.

For Nungesser, Sulkowicz, or her image — which were not quite the same — going viral was a horrifying experience. Before she was a victim and he was an alleged rapist, they were both star students on a straight path to success. Nungesser was on a full-ride merit scholarship to this refuge of solemn urban quads that was founded as King's College in 1754 and today is so competitive it accepts only 7 percent of applicants. Sulkowicz, unbelievably, hadn't stepped foot on campus before she was accepted (Columbia was something of a safety school for her). Now her life was completely upended, and his was too. He claimed to be terrified of Sulkowicz, whom he perceived as a vengeful ex-fling. He provided context for their relationship by making old messages between them public — messages that many took as proof of his innocence. "People were like, maybe this is a misunderstanding," Nungesser declared. "But the matter of the fact [*sic*] is it's not a misunderstanding." He said she was the villain in this story, not him.

The situation outraged both sets of parents, and parents, more than their children, are the university's true customers, the ones paying the increasingly astronomic bills. "You know, you send your kid off to school, and like all kids that age, they have that special mix of competence and vulnerability and yet need to prove themselves and be grown-up and independent," Sulkowicz's mother, Sandra Leong, told me. "So they rely on the school. The idealization and trust in the school as an institution is crucial as a place that can provide safety, support, and guidance along with the necessary freedoms and introduction to the world. And when the institution betrays them, it's devastating." Nungesser's parents were shaken to the core too. In a letter, they desperately appealed to Columbia's president, Lee "PrezBo" Bollinger: "We have just learned that our son was ambushed outside his residence by two reporters," they wrote. "Do we have to wait until Paul is beaten up, severely wounded or even killed? . . . We just talked to Paul on the phone and found him devastated, depressed and without any support . . . You are again massively worsening our son's situation . . . Shame on you, Mr. President!"

The mattress meme soon spread beyond Columbia, becoming an embodiment of all the confusion, righteousness, and anger that roils around sexual assault, the most complex topic on college campuses today. Sulkowicz was transformed into "Mattress Girl" (a nickname she found offensive, but it stuck), a modern curiosity that, in an era in which sensations as varied as the "Leave Britney Alone" guy to biologically Caucasian NAACP activist Rachel Dolezal to the dress that half the population saw as blue and black and half as white and gold, suddenly became one of the biggest stories in America. She flew in and out of America's inboxes and web tabs, making news everywhere from the *New York Times* to MSNBC to a podium beside Senator Kirsten Gillibrand at President Obama's 2015 State of the Union address. Coverage went from the lowbrow—"Do 'Bedder,' Columbia U," screamed a *New York Post* headline—to Hillary Clinton; in a bright yellow Mao-style jacket, she told the Democratic National Committee's Women's Leadership Forum about Sulkowicz's slight, sinewy form struggling through campus under the mattress's weight, adding, "That image should haunt all of us."

Not all the coverage was positive. In May 2015, during graduation ceremonies at Columbia, anonymous bandits pasted concert-bill-size posters of Sulkowicz on buildings around campus. In the picture, she was leaning against the mattress—she usually carried it as one would carry a large framed poster, not like Jesus's cross on her back—with a look of determination and resolve. It was a photo I recognized. It was the one from the *New York* magazine cover story that I'd written about sexual assault at Columbia weeks after my tea with Sulkowicz entitled "A Very Different Kind of Sexual Revolution on Campus." She was presented as a hero for my magazine, but now she was used in another way. Our headline had been replaced by capitalized words in old-timey typewriter font: PRETTY LITTLE LIAR.

Still, the mattress branded the conflict, gave the issue a visual signifier imbued with emotional responses and concerns. Or perhaps it's better to say that, like good activist iconography—such as a coat hanger or, more recently, a safety pin—it absorbed and made manifest many people's meanings and concerns. The mattress also spurred a quantum leap in the discussion of college sexual assault, going straight to the limbic system by using a few charged terms that elided the complexity of the issue: *Sex. Rape. Fear. College Girl.* It had become about much more than one individual.

INTRODUCTION: ORIENTATION

Two generations into coeducation, college is a strange planet, and sex on this planet is complicated. It's characterized at many colleges by female exploration and empowerment, the frontline of sex-positive feminism, and it's driven by a pop culture where sexual appetite is a crucial aspect of female strength; the Kardashians, Beyoncé, and Rihanna stand as heroes. Bragging about sexual conquest over a hungover coffee at the dining hall is part of the weekly routine for many girls, a gender reversal of the stereotypical conquistador. But Planet College is also dotted with bastions of traditional masculinity—bigtime sports, fraternities, and round-the-clock Grand Theft Auto or YouPorn—where sex can be a dehumanizing pursuit, and young men learn questionable lessons about their emerging adulthood. These cultures exist around the same quads, sometimes in the same dorm rooms.

It's a planet unlike planet Earth. Here, few are surprised if a girl gets her butt grabbed at a frat party, but if someone grabbed my butt on the sidewalk in my neighborhood, I would be outraged. It's a planet on which a girl who passes out in a frat basement isn't brought a glass of water with a straw, as she would be at a mall or an airport, but has a decent chance of being poked and prodded and jeered at by her classmates, who draw penises on her face with Magic Marker. It's a planet on which a dorm mate with whom one has a nodding acquaintance might slither into one's bedroom and attempt a hookup with one's sleeping body—this happened to me in school, and to some of my friends too. The response has long been not to call 911 but rather to push the other student off and go back to sleep.

But the gravitational field on Planet College is shifting. The story of Emma Sulkowicz and Paul Nungesser—in all its complexities and ambiguities, and in all its cultural heat—anticipated a revolution. The sex act in dispute may not fit everyone's standard definition of *rape*. The couple was, initially, having consensual sex. But at this moment, twenty-year-old students, middle-aged college administrators, and even the federal government are overturning preconceived notions of what constitutes sex and sexual assault among college kids today.

The line is, indeed, blurry, but it is moving in a distinct direction. The old frat-boy syllogism "no means yes" that justified countless intimate coercions is being discredited, as are the attitudes and gender roles that underlie it. More and more sexual acts that previous generations might have filed under "Terrible College Experience" are being reclassified as offenses that can earn banishment from the Ivory Tower. And the legions of young men and women who have and will come forward to speak on this topic are caught up in one of the greatest cultural shifts to happen on American campuses in decades: a reframing of sexual dynamics.

It's Complicated

I was inspired by Sulkowicz and her peers, but in these women's impressive march into the nation's consciousness, they've left questions in their wake. Many, many questions — some of which call the finer points of their ideology and tactics into doubt.

This book starts from the proven phenomenon that sexual assault is rampant on college campuses. But it does not end there. What type of student is assaulted in college? Can we figure that out and use this to guide our efforts to combat this problem? How many offenders are there? Who are they? Do they do it once over the course of their college careers or many times? By the way, what is *it*, exactly? Is sexual assault like pornography — you know it when you see it — or does it have many definitions, some in the eye of the beholder? And what does all of this have to do with a new national consensus among universities about consent?

These are hard questions to answer because on Planet College, paradoxes around sex and sexual assault abound. Today's college students aren't actually having more sex, or more sexual partners, than students in previous decades — sociological studies show that they aren't. But they are having it more casually, and that's the type of sex that one doesn't always feel good about afterward — or, often, at the time — and during which women, particularly, have a difficult time expressing what they want. Add to this the influence of hardcore Internet porn, which has operated as a form of sex ed for today's college students, and it's clear that some girls are having worse sex than a generation before. (A surprising number of the rape cases I learned about for this book, for instance, involved unwanted anal sex.) The normalization of binge drinking makes navigating all this even harder.

The biggest paradox, of course, is that universities, which sell parents the myth that their campuses are a halfway house between childhood and adulthood, crisscrossed by SafeBuses and with dorms protected by magnetic swipe cards, have some of the highest rates of sexual assault in the country, with one in five female undergrads surveyed reporting that she has been sexually assaulted at some time in college. The number is creeping even higher. In one study, 30 percent of female undergraduates at two of our nation's top schools — the University of Michigan and the University of Southern California — checked boxes for yes.

I'm a bit skeptical of upward trend lines in victimization. There's enough fire here that we don't need to fan the flames. The words *rape* and *assault* may have surged in our culture and on campus, but there's little clarity about their meanings. Definitions have multiplied, often controversially, to cover a wide variety of problematic sexual behavior, from luring a classmate into an apartment and locking the door from the inside to a time-tested dodge ("I'll only put in the tip") to even a sexist, objectifying remark ("Nice ass!").

We're better off focusing on what is largely causing sexual assault: the number of times that one comes into contact with acquaintances or, in particular, what sociologists call "in-network strangers," often at a party or at an off-campus apartment. An in-network stranger is the friend of a friend from the next dorm over, someone's brother visiting for the weekend, a guy who strikes up a conversation with you in the library stacks. In other words, many of the individuals a student might encounter on campus, because at college, although students perceive themselves as being among peers, they are actually surrounded by strangers. The risk is college itself, as defined in the popular imagination, those heavenly expanses of pretty quads, homecoming games, and rowdy frats.

There are a few other characteristics of modern universities and modern students that are deeply intertwined with the sexual-assault phenomenon.

The first is partying, and that's something that universities have become expert at providing for their students, structuring higher education to push students away from professorial oversight and toward engagement with peers. A small cohort of students used to spend their college years in a YOLO haze; sociologists now think many undergrads do so. Given this environment, the term *acquaintance rape,* which replaced *date rape* in colloquial language long ago—*date rape* sounded too romantic—has been shifted to the side by some experts by another, more specific phrase: *party rape.* This means the assault comes after a social, sexualized atmosphere, even if it doesn't happen between a girl and a guy she likes. "You go to college and you have no idea who you are, and the most important thing in the world is frat boys and sorority girls and who is popular—it's not that different than being in a cult," a recent University of Southern California grad told me, a bunch of colored bangles clacking on her wrist. "And the same way if you're in the Mob you might get killed, or if you hang out in a heroin trap house you might get HIV, if you're at a crazy college party, you might have sex that's somewhere between consensual and rape. Everyone's getting really, really drunk or on sixteen hits of Molly and having sex, and maybe not wanting to have sex but too fucked up to say what they want."

The second factor, as cheesy as it sounds, is social media. It's created a great deal of pressure on students to craft sexualized identities—some aggressively hetero, some fluid, but all more bawdy. They're certainly more public. The complex web of display, desire, and emotion that make up post-adolescent sexuality—enacted for decades in bathroom mirrors—have been turned into publicly shared global performances. Our digital age's instant, immersive space flattens us into avatars and demands constant attention to one's attractiveness and sex appeal.

And yet, in college, these formless, endless nights and carefully crafted erotic identities are on a collision course with the unyielding edifice of teenage morality. As they always have been, college students are particularly prone to the third consideration: black-and-white views on moral issues that their elders see in more grayscale terms. Though eighteen is seen as the gateway to adulthood, girls in college are still very much adolescents, and boys are even farther behind developmentally. Their cognitive faculties are actually as robust as any adult's. The problem is that these faculties are only sometimes in control of their socioemotional systems. They are also developmentally driven to intensely mirror and deeply care about the opinions of one extremely exclusive set of people on this planet: their friends. If you don't remember feeling this way, you don't remember being nineteen.

Let's not forget, too, that many college kids consider the specific kinds of behaviors that lead to a risk of sexual assault to be positive. After all, isn't indulging in boundless freedom, a mind-numbing amount of alcohol (or the right amount of mind-expanding drugs), and sexual experimentation what our society calls pleasure?

The Silver Bullet: Consent

Even if life in college, for girls, has always meant playing by sexual rules that no one else in society has to play by, the contest was considered a game of sorts and a learning experience, part of what makes a naive girl into an adult. But now, the rules are open to debate and the contest is becoming a battle. A modern buzzword, *consent*, is being loaded with as much new meaning as *rape*, part of the larger project: to define a new sexual standard for all students, one in which nonconsensual sex is no longer what it has been historically: a property crime, the woman's fault, or a man's privilege.

Consent is a powerful lever, one that many regard as a cure-all for dysfunctional sexual culture on campuses. Among students that I interviewed for this book, the majority claimed to establish *verbal consent* for each sexual encounter, which is quite the reframing of sexual dynamics indeed. Kevin Carty, Brown University '15, was amazed by the change he witnessed at the school during his time there. In Carty's frat, "the younger the pledge classes, the more amenable they were to focusing on sexual assault and consent," he says. "I got to see an evolution. The idea of consent got genuinely popular. Guys who hook up a lot, guys who I wouldn't necessarily expect to be feminist guys, were super-down with the concept of consent, and not only because the concept was everywhere on campus, impossible to avoid." Carty says none of them wanted to be "that kind of sexist guy" who wouldn't get consent. *Woke*—a slang word that means "highly attuned to injustices and inequalities, racial, sexual, or otherwise"—has become a desirable adjective, at least at Brown and, as time goes on, more broadly.

A straight male University of North Carolina at Chapel Hill student, majoring in history and active in the campus ministry, agrees. He talks about finding a new group of friends his junior year who wanted to stay up late with him "having these conversations that I had always wanted to have but never had [with old friends], my brain filling with information." They discussed sex with girls—what was fair, what was not. "It got me reflecting on my life experiences, asking, Do I know what consent looks like? Do I ask for consent?" He realized he hadn't asked for it in the past and mentions his freshman-year girlfriend; both of them were religious, and sometimes it was okay to finger her, and sometimes she'd move his hand away. Realizing that in those situations he had pressured and guilt-tripped her "was tough for me to accept. I was only thinking in terms of *I don't know if we should do this, because, you know, God*, and she was thinking, *I don't know if I want to do this tonight.*"

This UNC student was among the first to absorb the new paradigm before losing his virginity. "When I did have sex for the first time, [it was] with this new way of thinking about sex and consent," he says. He awkwardly stumbled his way through it, "but it happened. And now, one of my big turn-ons is knowing that someone wants to be with *me*." Not that he's not tempted to take other types of sex too. "You're in the moment, you want something to happen, you're horny . . . and it can be frustrating to talk. Not everyone is comfortable having that conversation with someone we don't know that well but want to fuck."

As this student's comments suggest, wokeness entails an awareness of nuances in one's own thinking about how some sexual situations can simultaneously embody differing degrees of wokeness. I thought about this when I read a 2016 online article titled "10 Men on What a Blow Job Feels Like." There were the usual pros and cons (pro: sex's ne plus ultra; con: teeth), but there was also this take on fellatio from an interviewee: "To me, in a twisted way, it seems like one of the few things that couldn't secretly still be rape. It's clearly her choice, and the more clearly it seems like her choice, the better it is for me. On her knees seems submissive, but to me it's the perfect balance. I'm dominant but she's making the choice for herself. It's the wokest sex act masquerading as the most degrading."

Yet for all these students' efforts to feel and sound comfortable with the new attitude toward sex and assault, many of the guys I interviewed were frankly scared. Allegations of sexual abuse can be a nuclear option in the war between the sexes, and the terror of being falsely accused was intense and primal. And while few women lie, some do exaggerate, and this probably happens more often among students than in the larger culture. Admitting this was difficult for me—like many women, I feel like these thoughts are a betrayal of womankind. If boys are being punished unfairly or for minor offenses or for offenses where the behavior of all parties was ambiguous, then how can we reconcile this injustice with the greater good of banishing sexual assault from universities?

These complexities and more are why this book is called *Blurred Lines*. I know that's the title of a 2013 Robin Thicke song, the one with the video of naked dancing girls and a blinking red sign reading #THICKE, a double-entendre hard to miss (if you did, helpful metallic balloons spelled out ROBIN THICKE HAS A BIG DICK). Perhaps you recall Thicke's performance of the song at the MTV Video Music Awards, during which a nude-bodysuited Miley Cyrus twerked on his black-and-white-striped suit and did unmentionable things with one of those foam fingers used to show school spirit at football games. The blurred line to which Thicke was referring was summed up by the song's chorus: "I know you want it, but you're a good girl."

After the VMAs, criticism of Thicke and Cyrus became deafening. Even in 2013, the lines around sexual assault weren't so blurry that a star could defend lyrics implying that *no* means *yes* and that girls mean the second when they say the first. At Liberty University, the Christian school in Virginia founded by televangelist Jerry Falwell Sr., a visiting minister's comments on this subject were greeted with silence. "I want to say a word to the young ladies: stop making it so easy for the young men," the minister had lectured. "God has designed us to be the pursuers, and you to be the pursuees." According to a report, the last line didn't meet with audience approval. "Sometimes the truth doesn't get a lot of claps," he later shot back.

In the wake of the "Blurred Lines" debacle, as with many media stories that involve sexual assault, finger-pointing began. The female video director said the message conveyed by the song wasn't her fault because she'd offset the misogynist lyrics by telling the naked girls to stare straight into the camera, thus telegraphing that they were more powerful than Thicke and his collaborators, producer Pharrell and rap star T.I. The lead dancing girl said it wasn't her fault because she was a feminist and had done her best to come off as annoyed in the video; she later called the song "the bane of my existence." T.I. said it wasn't his fault because "if you perceive it as negative because you have negative thoughts of yourself, that's on you," but his rap, which included a line about giving a girl something big enough to tear her ass in two, was cut from televised versions of the song. Pharrell, a spacy genius, said it wasn't his fault because the song was actually about the power of God.

Despite all this, "Blurred Lines" became the number-one song of the summer of 2013.

Syllabus

Young women are driving this awakening, so accordingly the book begins mostly with their points of view before weaving in portraits of boys (woke ones and extremely unwoke ones). On the most superficial level, no one can miss that many girls embracing new sexual standards today dress and behave quite differently than the revolutionaries of the past. In the 1970s, some feminists wore overalls and were none too impressed by Gloria Steinem's miniskirts and aviator shades. In the 1990s, when date rape briefly appeared on the national agenda, young survivors weren't stylish icons to emulate; an Antioch University student of that era describes the perception of her friends as a "borg of shrill, kiss-legislating feminists with shaved heads, ethnic vests, and Doc Martens, and nobody took our picture." But today's young women embrace a pornified look of short-shorts and half shirts, depilated everywhere, accessorized with more piercings and tattoos than boys. One minute, they're throwing down the most radical feminist rhetoric heard in nearly fifty years, and the next they're posting about #waxing #goals. They see no reason to align their self-presentation with their politics. (And they're right; as I said, the risk of sexual assault in college is higher not because of the way women dress but, largely, because they're spending more time socializing with friends and acquaintances than older or younger people do.)

This book appears in three parts: Consensual, Nonconsensual, and the Man. I begin by describing college life and consensual sex before moving on to material that will be gnarly and hard to read. And by *the Man*, I mean universities, a reluctant third point in this triangle.

From the universities' perspective, sexual assault is a problem from hell. The days of open doors and one foot on the floor are long gone, but college administrators have been deeply confused about how to police their charges in parietal matters. Columbia president Lee "PrezBo" Bollinger told me that he'd spent "as much time on this issue" — meaning sexual assault on campus — "as any issue" over the year that Sulkowicz carried her mattress, and that year included Columbia's largest expansion in nearly a century, a $6.3 billion, seventeen-acre satellite campus in West Harlem. Yet it's also true that when I checked out the yearbook for Sulkowicz's class, I was surprised to not find one picture of her mattress in the hundred-odd glossy pages — not among the candid shots, not on the page entitled "Campus and Community," not even on the page headed "Political / Activist."

In 2016, Harvard Business School published a remarkable working paper analyzing four types of scandals — sexual assault, murders, cheating scandals, and hazing — at the top one hundred U.S. universities between 2001 and 2013. When scandals attracted a high level of coverage, applications to the school were significantly reduced — for example, a scandal worthy of a long magazine article translated to a 10 percent drop in applications to the university the following year. This was the same impact that losing ten spots in the *U.S. News and World Report* college rankings had.

The bind that universities find themselves in is not merely one of public perception. Universities are bound by legal interpretations of Title IX, a federal statute that prohibits gender discrimination in educational institutions. The logic is that sexual assault is a form of discrimination and denies the victim an equal education. Unfortunately, the resulting system is flawed; it requires the colleges to adjudicate disputes and levy punishments, but the institutions lack the powers that a court has to gather evidence, subpoena witnesses, and so forth. And even a flawless system would be hobbled by the fact that often there are no witnesses or reliable testimony to be had. Sexual assault can be impossible to prove. Somehow, amid these impediments, colleges are charged to find the truth, punish the guilty, and avenge the survivors. An impossible task, it would seem.

But universities may be able to solve this hellish problem. Not only is the campus judiciary system getting better year by year but, prominent psychologist Charlene Senn tells me, experts are hopeful that a large group of college men who are assaulting today might not down the line. "The research is new, but I think we're going to find out more about these men and how strongly influenced they are by the social norms, by the communities they're in," she says. She's speaking specifically about guys who start offending when they get to college but never have before, a number some sociologists peg at 8 percent of the male student body. University communities that shift social norms about sex and assault may be the most successful in this endeavor. There are other proven measures that students, administrators, and even parents can take to reduce the risk, and we'll examine them throughout this book. Some —like changing rules around alcohol and banning Greek culture, where fraternities dominate the social scene—would meet with forceful opposition but nonetheless deserve serious examination.

Universities also need to decide what to do about an even trickier situation. In the new system, believing that one has been raped is usually interpreted as meaning that one has been raped. "In all the years I've been doing investigations, I believe I've only had one person bring a case intentionally falsely, and that's a case without merit," a top college investigator tells me. "In every other case that I've had, there's been something the person *feels* was inappropriate."

There is never going to be a simple answer to this big issue. Yet the knottiness of the problem is no excuse for not tackling it. Anyone with children at or near college age, anyone who cares about the future of sex or about issues of gender equality in our society, has a significant stake in solving this dilemma.

Welcome to the Panopticon

Though colleges are populated by students of different genders and sexualities, I'm focusing on heterosexual experiences between students, and concentrating on the way young women are connecting dots between self-esteem, self-expression, and sexual autonomy. Of course women can be sexually aggressive too, but if you scour prisons for a female rapist, you'll come up nearly empty-handed. Most studies using the loosest definition of *sexual assault* have not picked up female assaulters, though emerging research on gay and trans relationships may change this. Male-on-male sexual assault is a complex world unto itself and beyond the scope of this book, partly because of timing. A study has shown that men take, on average, two decades before disclosing their childhood assaults, and while some college boys have been part of the current movement, it remains female-driven.

Those limitations aside, this book will strive to be panoptic, examining how sex and sexual assault on campus affects all of those involved (one should also keep in mind the intensely panoptic nature of social media and the college campus itself, with young people constantly semi-surreptitiously observing one another). In this way, it will differ markedly from the media coverage of this topic to date. I interviewed survivors as well as survivors' friends, families, and sorority sisters; accused students and their own mothers and fraternity brothers. I also studied the collegiate activist network —"the largest undergraduate sorority that no one knows about," as Landen Gambill, a UNC survivor, put it — and a powerful force for change in colleges nationwide.

Sulkowicz's story may seem strange to you, but across the country, the same elements pop up over and over again: A stubborn student who defies a culturally defined shame to stand up for what she believes to be morally right. An aggrieved boy who insists his accuser isn't telling the whole story. An incident in which, often, things started out friendly. One that, even more often, involved alcohol (Nungesser had been drinking). A university that must judge the matter behind a veil of secrecy. And the horde of female students, as well as a few males, who step out of the shadows to say that they've experienced similar harm.

These people — many of them larger than life, charismatic, quotable — are telling the real unfolding narratives of sexual assault at universities today, not the stories about predators gang-raping defenseless students that always rise to the top of the news. There are no strangers and no ski masks in this book. Some of these stories will seem atypical, but they are the norm in college sexual assault. Many resemble the famous Steubenville, Ohio, case where two high-school boys brought home a passed-out girl and fingered her on a base-

ment couch. They're not deeply pathological sex crimes so much as immature ones, not *Fatal Attraction* so much as *The Rules of Attraction,* not *The
Accused* so much as *Fast Times at Ridgemont High.* I found them strangely
boring much of the time.

I interviewed one hundred and twenty students from about twenty universities — from Yale to Michigan State to the University of Tennessee at
Chattanooga — spoke with nearly eighty administrators and experts, and
combed through dozens of case reports. I traveled widely exploring the subject, interviewing a complex cast of characters ranging from women who
think the issue of sexual assault has been overblown to men who have devoted their lives to helping other men realize the role they play in perpetuating it. Much of my research was conducted at Wesleyan University in Connecticut, my alma mater, host to one of the most radical student populations
in the nation, and a school that took a surprising stance against sexual assault
during the time I was reporting. A smaller portion of my research occurred
at Syracuse University, a large Division I school in Upstate New York with
an entrenched Greek population. While I was reporting there, the state enacted its new affirmative-consent policy. This means students on all New
York campuses, public and private, must receive consent, either in the way
that Brown's Kevin Carty describes it (verbally) or, as the legalese puts it,
by actions creating "clear permission regarding willingness to engage in the
sexual activity" (moans, screams of pleasure, pulling down one's own pants)
for each escalating sex act. In 2016, Connecticut adopted much the same law.

My work took me to university administrators who have wrestled with
their own demons when dealing with rape cases and to members of the network of highly paid consultants and lawyers who advise colleges on sexual-
assault policies. I also considered the role of some exceedingly important
players over the past few years, ones who have been on both sides: journalists.
I spent time listening to civil libertarians who slam our nanny-state government for encroaching on college students' due-process rights, and I learned
about men's rights activists and conservative writers who call survivors neo-
Victorians or Munchausen syndrome victims.

Most of my reporting was conducted at prestigious universities, the front-
lines and flash points of campus sexual assault for decades. Brick-and-mortar

schools, the kind with residence halls, frats, and sports teams, are also the only institutions that have demonstrated a significant problem with student-on-student sexual assault. Commuter and community colleges don't register on this scale. I spoke to students with diverse racial and ethnic backgrounds, though most studies indicate that black, Latina, and white women share similar victimization rates; American Indians' are much higher, and Asians' much lower. Most of these students are social types, engaged in the collegiate party lifestyle because they want to be and because universities encourage them to be. Most hail from middle-class families. Class might matter or it might not in terms of who is assaulted in college; the data is conflicting.

A note on reporting: I'm five foot two, partial to jeans and sneakers, and as much as I sound like an asshole saying this, I really do still get carded for drinks — all of which made it relatively easy for me to blend in on campus. Then again, when I began this project, I was a forty-year-old with a husband, a mortgage, and a toddler. I was generationally and developmentally distant from my subjects. As they were turning from adolescents into young adults, I was moving from adulthood to midlife, with its attendant physical frailties, joys, and losses.

Did this gap in age and authority make me feel like a creep at times? Yes, a thousand times yes. But the hyperverbal, curious, smart students with whom I struck up conversations while on the road put me at ease. I'd estimate that half of them called me "ma'am" and began scanning the room for the exits; the other half treated me like a peer, innocently asking, "What year are you?" Disabused of this notion, they'd ask when I'd graduated. "Ugh, you don't want to know," I'd say sometimes. Other times I'd answer, point-blank, "In 1995." "But that's the year I was born," the student would respond, shocked and confused.

I'll now issue a trigger warning. I know that's a fraught term, but some readers, particularly young ones, may want to know they will encounter vis-cerally upsetting material ahead. The stories I will share in this book have heavy emotional ballast; they're weighted by fear, trauma, depression, and white-hot anger. Students are perforated consensually and nonconsensually, by fingers, penises, and a water bottle. Liquids — semen, blood, urine, vomit, tears — flow from orifices.

Coming to terms with one's own bodily vulnerability while reading these stories might be, on a core level, terrifying. Casting back to one's memories, perhaps long repressed, of sexual assault in college might be as well.

Personal to Political

I followed this story for nearly three years, from 2014 to 2017, a period of significant turmoil, and finished my reporting as the subject became more charged than ever. The battle over assault at schools was joining the ones that Americans have fought over sexual topics (contraception, abortion, homosexuality, same-sex marriage) in the postwar era. Stanford swimmer Brock Turner, who was caught assaulting an unconscious woman behind a dumpster—two Swedish grad students cycling by at the moment witnessed the event and restrained him until police arrived—received a light criminal sentence, which created a furor throughout the nation. America was taking the subject more seriously than ever before. Yet its citizens also managed to elect a president who not only bragged about grabbing women "by the pussy" without seeking their consent but also was accused of assault by over a dozen women.

The modern college campus is billed as a charmed world where students are insulated from what comes before and after. It has its own rules—or no rules. Wild experiments can be safely tried because it's not the real world; that frat boy grabbing your ass or pushing your head down or even introducing you to a cuddly and consensual threesome is a biochem major who sits two rows down from you in the lecture hall, not a strange predator. But thanks to the Internet, what goes on in college doesn't stay in college. Students not only are more connected to the real world, they're actively changing it.

Universities are one of many previously inviolable institutions that have been rocked by revelations about sex and corruption lately; others include the Catholic Church, the military, Fox News, and northeastern prep schools, which were revealed as hideouts for an assortment of Humbert Humberts only a generation ago. Historians might eventually credit the seismic upheaval of these bedrock establishments with changing the culture of silence around sexual assault, but the truth is that it was the cultural change on college campuses—already in motion, in some cases—that triggered the shift.

The refrain of "believe women," so closely tied to campus rape activism and the media apparatus that supports it, is what allowed accusers to come forward and tell their stories for the whole nation to hear.

This gradual revolution was part of a larger awakening. It was a sister movement to Black Lives Matter and a relative of Occupy Wall Street and the millennial crusade that drove the Bernie Sanders campaign. Catalyzed by social media, these movements share a political vocabulary as well as some of the same weaknesses.

Much of the gleeful, angry energy of Breitbart News, whence came Trump's alt-right Svengali Steve Bannon, has been directed at campus politics in general and the sexual-assault movement in particular. In the view of many conservatives, colleges are in the grip of what they call "rape-culture panic" and a culture of grievance and coddling that is seeping out of the campus bubble and infecting the whole country.

To sexual-assault victims, Trump's presidency is a macroaggression. If Trump were a college student under pre-2017 rules, he undoubtedly would have been expelled. As it stands now, given that he appointed Betsy DeVos, who is the most important religious-right supporter in America, secretary of education, a college student who acted like Trump may have a better chance of getting away with it. DeVos might do her damnedest — not that she would use that word — to roll back as much of what young collegiate women consider progress against university sexual assault as she can.

DeVos could stymie parts of the campus court system, which is critical to the anti-sexual-assault movement. In another paradox, even the most fervent college social justice warriors, as much as they complain about universities, are not interested in *Law & Order: SVU*–type cops hustling male students to prison. I see their goals as rewriting the rules of consensual and nonconsensual sex, overcoming deeply ingrained attitudes and making young men respect women and their bodies. These fierce, thoughtful, determined, and ruthless young activists want nothing less than new power dynamics in the bedroom, an area where feminism has previously not been able to reach.

The details of how to fairly punish sexual assault at universities will be hammered out in the coming years. And the rejection by Trump voters, a large subset of Americans, of the concerns and values of the allied movements that have defined modern college politics will shape our culture's future. The permanency of the changes young women have wrought hangs in the balance. We will soon see if they heralded a new age or if they are just another modern curiosity like the "Leave Britney Alone" guy, a spectacle portending little and soon to be replaced by another.

A Movement Rising

I'll return to Sulkowicz's unfolding story periodically throughout this book for a couple of reasons. First, her mattress project might fairly be considered the chief catalyst for campus anti-assault activism in its current form. Second, her story parallels the larger saga of sex and assault on campus in key ways, as we'll see. The next time I saw her was a bluebird fall day a couple of weeks after tea, when she gathered with her friends on the steps of Columbia's Low Memorial Library, built in 1895 and designed to resemble the Pantheon. Below the dome, a large engraving explained that the university is to be "maintained and cherished from generation to generation for the advancement of the public good and the glory of almighty God."

Sulkowicz was less enthusiastic about the attention directed toward her mattress than she'd seemed earlier, though she had a sense of humor about the fracas it had engendered. Laughing, she told me so many reporters were calling her that "my phone keeps dying so I have to be constantly plugged into a wall . . . and I feel like my brain has fallen to the floor." But she was also serious, sharing her typically thoughtful ideas about her project with others. She was carrying her mattress to make her private suffering public, to bear witness, to demand accountability — and to initiate change. "I feel like, hopefully, if we can't educate the old men who are controlling Columbia, at least we can educate the fresh minds that are going to own the world once PrezBo — um — dies, you know?" she said. "I think, in the long term, things will be different."

Today, her mattress had company. Dozens of students had made their way out of Columbia's high-rise dorms with their own mattresses, which they dumped on Low's steps; the area looked like a plush spot for somersaulting at a kiddie gym. They cut up cardboard for signs using glitter scissors, talking as they worked. ("Can someone write *With* and *Survivors*?" asked a woman with a sign reading STAND.) Camerapeople showed up, and the women looked around warily, and then excitedly. One asked another, "Do you want to model for the press?" She put her hand on her hip and walked forward with a swagger. "It's kind of like a red carpet — give them what they want!"

Sulkowicz threw an arm around her little sister, still in high school, and shouted: "I have an announcement — my sister wants everyone to know she brought snacks." An organizer added, "And there are juice boxes, if you're feeling triggered or hot or emotional in the heat. Let's prioritize the survivors when we hand out the juice boxes."

Now they hoisted signs: COLUMBIA UNIVERSITY PROTECTS RAPISTS; YES MEANS YES; FUCK RAPE CULTURE; FUCK YOUR FAKE CONCERN; DON'T GET RAPED, with the GET and the second D crossed out.

This was billed as a campus speak-out, a gathering where students shared their opinions, experiences, anxieties, and battle cries. These orators took turns talking, passing a bullhorn, and I found this event to be remarkable, simultaneously an encounter group, a show, and a three-hour flood of personal disclosure, secrets that were instantly transformed into a new kind of politics. The point was not only to shed light on what was happening at the university, and it was not only about victims' rights, about who should be listened to, though that was part of it. It was also to overthrow a whole culture — the rape culture, a set of ideas that Sulkowicz and her allies believe is hidden in plain sight of many students and ignored by college administrators. In this way, there was a positivity, even a joyfulness, to the crusade. Here was a moment where progress could be made.

At the same time, the traumatic stories shared by students (mostly female, black and white, gay and straight and in between) were crushing. A male student in salmon-colored shirt and khaki shorts, a transfer from Amherst, talked about a good friend who had been expelled for rape there last year. The speaker hadn't defended his friend's actions, and he'd been ostracized by his peers. "For something about which we're right and they're wrong," he says. "Rape culture is what's wrong."

Each speaker brought the rhetoric to a higher pitch: the alum who said she was assaulted the first day of her freshman year twenty-two years ago and the crop-top-wearing freshman who said she had been assaulted six days ago; the heavyset woman who described the campus's response to stories of sexual assault as "when a pretty girl is raped, it's a tragedy, and when a fat woman is raped, she should be grateful" and a blonde from Barnard who screamed, "We are objectified every day, we are told we are not as good, our bodies are dirty. I want the administration to do something—just fucking do something!"

Subjectivity—not only an opposition to being objectified but the demand to have one's subjective experience believed—was integral to the message. "Once I was young and I was silent, and then I was a little older and I was silent, and now I'm twenty-one and kind of tired of being silent," said a third-year engineering student as the crowd pulled in close. "I know what it feels like to be the person in these crowds who doesn't know how to hold this bullhorn yet, and I want to say something for those who are not going to come up here, who were me, who are me. We believe you."

There were moments in reporting this book when I felt that boys had been unfairly punished, that accusations were unreliable—but not at this moment. Right now, I was deeply moved and wiping away tears. No longer would a college student traumatized by a sexual experience—so young! Barely able to vote!—have to endure that trauma alone. A raising of demons and a mass healing was at hand.

When Sulkowicz finally took the bullhorn, her hair pulled back in a bun and her feet planted firmly on the ground, she reinforced the sense that something special was happening. "This isn't a shouting speech, but I have to shout anyway," she said; her words were not as poetic as the others'—she's a visual thinker, not an orator—but they were powerful nonetheless. "Your e-mails, your thank-yous, and your help carrying my mattress has shown me that we really do care. We are more determined than ever to end sexual assault on this campus. Across the nation, a movement is rising."

She prophesied correctly. Soon, students across America—from Kennesaw State University to George Washington University, from Indiana's Goshen College to Belmont University in Tennessee—brought out their mattresses, sometimes even air mattresses, to show solidarity with this burgeoning cause.

After the rally, I asked Sulkowicz about her specific struggle—about actually, physically carrying the mattress every day, each day. She told me it was good to have help. "For the record," she said, "the best arrangement is four people carrying the mattress, because we each take a corner. Then it's really light."

Part I

CONSENSUAL

1

Planet College, Millennial Edition

T wenty years ago, I drove to my final year at Wesleyan University in my parents' station wagon, a microwave-size computer and a dot-matrix printer in the trunk. The name of this school may ring a distant bell. I've corrected those who think I mean Ohio Wesleyan or Wellesley, the women's college west of Boston that Hillary Clinton attended, too many times to count. But among the northern elite, this tiny liberal arts college in Connecticut is equally renowned for its academics and its social life, which revolves around stupendous student musicians who have included Santigold, Le1f, the members of MGMT and Das Racist, and Hamilton's Lin-Manuel Miranda. It's also where the cool kids are, which means it's a bastion of radical politics on par with UC Santa Cruz and Oberlin. In fact, Wesleyan inspired a mid-1990s Jeremy Piven comedy, a film long since forgotten but whose first two letters are on the lips of all Americans today: PCU.

I've rarely been back, but my own alma mater was a natural first stop on my quest to learn about students' perceptions of sex and sexual assault at universities throughout the country. Set on a hill above the crumbling Colonial city of Middletown, which peaked as a port of call during the Civil War, the school has never *looked* all that progressive. The center of campus is made up of churchy buildings in muted Protestant ocher from its founding as a Methodist college in 1831. Extending from that core are green lawns dotted with a hodgepodge of weird modern structures as well as pretty pastel mansions that resemble sturdy wedding cakes.

When I arrived at Wesleyan in the 1990s, our flying-saucer-shaped cafeteria, an architectural semi-marvel, still had a smoking section. My freshman year was the first year the university recycled. The cartoon strip in the *Wesleyan Argus* — our newspaper, named after the hundred-eyed monster of

Greek myth—was about a listless student with messy Debbie Harry bangs who loved the Smiths. Above her head, thought bubbles read *The world reeks of emptiness and angst.* College fun in my student years was DIY. Warm beer from a keg; a Tom Collins at the townie restaurant with a lax ID policy. The university provided a few extracurriculars each week: a vegetarian potluck, an African drumming troupe, an origami-making meeting for a new campus sorority. In my mind, my time there plays like slo-mo Jim Jarmusch, but with dinners of microwaved quesadillas and Dunkin' Donuts.

My Wesleyan was a little planet spinning on its own axis, its students protected from real-world hassles and public scrutiny and not that different from the college planet of one generation prior. My friends and I rallied to free Tibet and worked at the library, sliding books across the circulation desk, to make a dent in student loans. We traveled with Phish and read Kurt Vonnegut novels; we played Hacky Sack and memorized Tennessee Williams dialogue under maple trees. We never talked to administrators, whom we perceived as narcs; we rarely called our parents, and when we did, we revealed nothing. We weren't concerned with our digital or public images because we had no digital or public images—we barely had e-mail accounts.

Today's students are living on a planet I hardly recognize. Other than the dorms, which remain nostalgically hideous, Wesleyan has been spit-shined to brochure-readiness and seems to be playing in fast-forward in iridescent Pixar colors. A sprawling, triangular $47 million student center has landed in the center of campus, anchoring a proper quad. Far on the edge, near a highway artery, there's only dirt where the spacecraft-cafeteria used to be.

The new, ultramodern student center's soaring main dining room, with parallax views of a new baseball diamond, now offers not a main course of microwaved quesadillas but cuisine that PETA calls among the finest. A set of documents resting on a table near the cashier detail the guilt-free dining options, like sustainably harvested local cod and pasture-raised heritage pork from a farm in Vermont. "These happy pigs," a fact sheet explains, "graze leisurely on rolling hill pastures with scenic vistas and are fed grain, grass, hay, and organic veggie."

It's funny to see ye olde alma mater looking so different when the students look almost exactly the same as we did. Youth culture's twenty-year nostalgia cycle is coming back around to my time right as I arrive on campus, and the school is awash in Doc Martens boots, velvet chokers, Converse high-tops, plaid flannel shirts, and shoulder-slung mini-backpacks. Sonic Youth patches are no longer sewn to backpacks' front pockets; instead, since plastic water bottles are banned around these parts, those pockets often dangle a carabinered steel canteen.

Not only do these students look the same, they also talk, urgently, about many of the same issues, in particular sexual assault.

Radical Chic

One drab gray morning, wearing her stick-straight brown hair in a bob like *Divergent* starlet Shailene Woodley, Chloe, a senior, waves me into a small, gingerbread-style house that she shares with friends on a quiet street behind the science library. Wesleyan residential life has always been unique; students who don't live in dorms reside in small homes on the perimeter of campus.

When Chloe and I start talking, I imagine her as the brassy yet sensitive punk in the John Hughes version of college — smart, funny, and stubborn, with strict definitions of right and wrong and an appealing self-awareness and insecurity revealed in frequent jokes at her own expense. In her living room — pastel balloons from a housemate's party deflating in a corner, a synthesizer keyboard holding a sheet-music book that's open to Simon and Garfunkel's "Bridge Over Troubled Water" (one imagines the late-night chortling) — she takes a seat on a couch and describes growing up in middle-class New Jersey with loving parents. In high school, she even sometimes watched right-wing pundit Bill O'Reilly with her dad, who worked in finance. In other words, her environment was no breeding ground for radicalism. Entering Wesleyan as an "art-history-major-slash-maybe-a-doctor," she became a neuroscience major with an economics minor. She's active in student government and even ran for president once, but lost, which she tells me about with jokes and giggles — she didn't hold a grudge.

Though she may not sound like it, Chloe's one of the most radical students on campus — and that means she's plenty radical. As progressive as Wesleyan was during my student years, identifying with a certain band or genre of film back then was what made you cool. Now those markers are subordinate to a cause, a purpose. Much of the fun at Wesleyan has always been politics, but it's now more central to a college student's social identity than any time since the sixties, more vocation than avocation.

Economic inequality, destabilization in the Middle East, access to guns? No, students here don't talk about that much. Racism, sexism, gay rights, trans rights, and sexual assault? These topics are constant, and guidelines about how to discuss them abound. On one trip, I see a ton of instructional flyers entitled "Halloween Checklist," decorated with festive pictures of witches and pumpkins, the sort of holiday advice that's now a staple at universities across the country. *Is Your Costume Offensive?* it says, followed by a bunch of thought bubbles that look like clouds. *Ask: Does this costume mock cultural or religious symbols such as dreadlocks, headdresses, afros, geishas, etc.? Attempt to represent an entire culture or ethnicity? Trivialize human suffering, oppression and marginalization?*

The kinds of free-speech issues that were in their infancy in my era are now in full flower. In 2015, after the *Argus* published an opinion piece criticizing Black Lives Matter, some protested that the article shouldn't have appeared at all, and Wesleyan's student government preliminarily voted to reorganize and severely defund the paper.

Chloe and her friends' cause is sexual assault. They carried a mattress in solidarity with Sulkowicz the same day that the students from George Washington and Belmont did. To coordinate, they posted a schedule of where the mattress would be at each point during the day and designated carrying shifts. Their talent for frictionless organization through the web separates today's Wesleyan students from my generation and indeed is a hallmark of activism on campus generally now, as I would discover. Debates about what is consensual and what is not, what type of sex is ethical and what is immoral, are essential to life here today. "There's a difference between illegal and unethical," Chloe told me. "Life is not about doing whatever you can do. It's about *not* doing what is traumatic to another person."

As we're walking around, some of her friends nod meaningfully at various guys going by on Wesleyan's leafy paths. "Aw, there are so many rapists on this campus, and you never know who is one — people are multifaceted, man" is the way one of them put it to me.

So many rapists? That's not the kind of thing we'd have said in the 1990s, even back when we had our own anti-sexual-assault moment. As I passed yet another of the campus's somber ocher buildings, I thought about my sophomore year when some of my classmates started scrawling a list on a bathroom stall of guys to stay away from. It was an underground thing. I don't recall Wesleyan's administration responding. They certainly didn't do as Brown University had in 1990 after students posted names of thirty guys in bathroom stalls. A Brown administrator smeared them as "Magic Marker terrorists" and threatened the women with expulsion if caught.

Crouching in the Wesleyan bathroom stall back then to see the list for myself, I was shocked when I came upon the name of a student I'd dated. He wore his pants low and listened exclusively to rap—we used to call these guys *wiggers*, a term appropriately scrubbed from today's lexicon—and liked to kiss for so long and with such force that my lips would become raw from rubbing against the stubble around his mouth. One night at a backyard party, he spied a yellow excavator the next lawn over. He had me climb into it, and then he came in after me, and we ended up in the cab making out for an uncomfortably long time. I didn't like being in there because I thought the people at the party could probably see us. I didn't voice that I wasn't into it— didn't want him to think I was a prude, didn't want to come off as rude, didn't want a confrontation. I didn't know how to get away.

Was that an assault? There were radicals on campus back then who would answer yes, but I never considered it. To me, that guy was pushy. But Chloe and her friends today are unafraid to stand up to sexual behavior that my friends and I called only gross and creepy. And they're not so impressed by my Take Back the Night march stories, which I'm a bit wounded to sense they deem lame. "We don't want to change one night, we want to change every night," one of them tells me.

The Gas Giant

I'd like to pull back for one moment and talk about what you may already be thinking: this is quite a bit of radicalism for such an affluent school. At Wesleyan, 18 percent of recent grads hail from the bottom 60 percent of America's income scale (high for an elite school), but the exact same percentage comes from the 1 percent. That's a hell of a lot of millionaires' children.

Under the aegis of president Michael Roth, a wiry, perma-grinned scholar with a focus on interdisciplinary learning, this turbocharged version of the old Methodist city on a hill is streamlined, richer, and, as an institution, vastly more ambitious. With the skills of an ace brander, Roth, who is also an alum, models a folksy Wesleyan identity while emphasizing academic excellence. "This is such a goofy, wonderful, eclectic community that if it strikes you that way, it's probably the right place. If it strikes you as too disparate, heterogeneous, too uncertain, then Williams is probably right," he's said.

Goofiness, though, does not come cheap. Tuition is nearly fifty thousand dollars a year, one of the highest in the country, and admissions are no longer need-blind but *need-aware*, an odd term ("We're aware that you *need* aid, but . . ."). Like most universities that cater to elite students, it is ever more elite. The university accepted nearly 40 percent of applicants when I was admitted; it accepted 17 percent to the class of 2020. The endowment, which languished in the 1980s, has been mightily repaired, and the campus bureaucracy runs efficiently. Departments are regrouped into interdisciplinary learning centers: College of the Environment, College of Film and the Moving Image, and College of Integrative Sciences. Administrators are attentive — affirmative-action specialist, civic engagement fellow, equity compliance director, sustainability coordinator.

Today's university has transformed itself from an isolated little planet into a seething gas giant. The bidding-up I've described has been happening at American universities since the 1970s, when "both public and private colleges were driven to constantly one-up one another, buying more famous scholars on the job market, building fancier buildings, and passing the cost along to students and parents," writes Kevin Carey in *The End of College*. "When you're in the status business, nothing is ever enough if your competitor has more." American universities today, these nominally nonprofit institutions, are now corporate behemoths, and many of them much more so than Wesleyan (the university has prioritized its rigorous academics and intimate classes); they pay the utmost attention to the marketing and public relations of their "products" and have middle managers to "facilitate" the health and well-being of everyone involved.

Scholars are no longer as important as they once were. The share of full-time tenure-track positions has fallen 50 percent in the past forty years as adjunct salaries push the professoriate to the breadline. Money flows disproportionately toward two quarters: plant and facility construction (such as new gyms with state-of-the-art pools, slides, and hot tubs), and salaries in the ever-expanding administrative departments (one tentacle of which handles sexual assault cases). Salaries of these administrators are way out of line with middle management at other nonprofits. The dean in charge of sexual assault at the University of Virginia when *Rolling Stone* reported its fateful story about rape on campus — or not-rape on campus — made $113,000 a year, a third more than a similarly ranked professional at another nonprofit.

Students — or, in a current term of art, *education consumers* — are in an incredibly weird place vis-à-vis colleges today. Tuition has risen much faster than the rate of inflation and is now the highest in history while financial aid packages remain inadequate. Yet in this unequal power balance, they do hold one card — they are potential donors, a future revenue source. This is a fact hardly lost on campus anti-rape protesters, whose cardboard signs at rallies include messages like #NEVERDONATING, #LIKEEVER.

Are kids suspicious about what they're paying for? I think they may be. No longer does a degree ensure a pleasant middle-class future, and so, in this age of economic anxiety, the stakes are higher and the stress more extreme. Many years after the end of in loco parentis, they want to know the institution protects them. They want to know the institution cares about them. They are concerned that the moral education this suspicious corporation is providing may not be moral enough. The fact that Wesleyan students largely live in their own small houses on the perimeter of campus isn't the only reason the school has the feeling of a topsy-turvy Hogwarts where students live like teachers. You try to give the kids a moral education, and they school you.

Walking through campus, I meet a bunch of Bernie bros knocking around, boys with a macho take on politics and psychological complexes about Hillary Clinton — or at least a need to topple old idols and representations of the past. "I'm all for a vagina sitting on chair in the Oval Office, but not Hillary," one of them, who's quite possibly a little high, tells me. "Republicans may be scared sheeple who will vote themselves into concentration camps if you tell them it's their neighbor's fault, but Hillary is high on her own farts!"

Let's be frank that drugs are everywhere on this campus and others, a millennial brew of Molly, cocaine, prescription pills, and marijuana, though you wouldn't pick up on the last, since bongs and joints have largely been replaced by incognito, smokeless vapes. Guys who approach hot-button topics more thoughtfully also seem like they could be high. One, sporting long blond locks, reveals his discomfort with being a straight white man while simultaneously vaping. "I feel privileged, and I have a privilege," he explains. "And I'm fine with girls on campus saying I have a privilege! I apologize that I was born into this form, but I am living the best I can." He chuckles, but then looks genuinely pained. "I'm not afraid to be me, but I don't want to come across as being insensitive."

Another senior, in an unguarded moment, puts it differently. "It's hard to be a white male on this campus," he grumbles. "Which is completely ridiculous."

These folks are not part of Chloe's radical crowd. Her people hang out at one of Wesleyan's themed residential houses: Art House, a sprawling, yellow-painted program house, for students who are artists and musicians. It's an emblematic institution at a college where, as one student puts it, "Everyone is trying to out-crazy each other," fitting in by standing out. In the band MGMT's day, Art House was known for its naked parties, which were supposedly about freedom, not sex, but there was sex anyway. "Art House was taken away back then, but the art kids got it back," says Chloe. Students petitioned the administration. "They said, 'Oh no, this is a different house, this is *Studio House.*' But now it's called Art House again, and whatever."

In the downstairs common room, lined with bay windows, there's a craft fair in progress. The students here are smart, sweet, and goofy, as Roth described; vibrating with excitement at just being alive, porous to new ideas and strong emotions. (I must admit I loved hanging out with these students, as much as they presented me with philosophies not totally in line with my own beliefs and some eerily unchanged from the ones I encountered here in the 1990s, both in analysis and poetics. Like many alums, I felt giddy at my alma mater, like I'd entered a time machine instantly making me twenty years younger.)

A student puts a couple children's books—*I Am a Bunny* and *Oliver's*

High-Flying Adventure — next to a yellow sweater she knit. "My grandma got some yarn from a woman who died, and then she didn't know what to do with the yarn, so she gave it to me," she says to a group of students. "Whoa, a possessed sweater," one of them says, nodding.

Most of the art is under ten dollars, and some sellers will barter for the items. One is going for A HUG OR A SMILE, reads a sign. Tess, Chloe's friend, a jovial, intense Chicagoan who hosts a popular radio show, has laid out a bunch of handmade black choker necklaces, tiny colorful beads spelling out BITCH, LOL, FUCK, CUM, POOP. About a dozen have only one word — NO — except the O in NO is made out of a heart. "I want a wrist full of bracelets that say *no, no, no*," declares Chloe — an incantation of the consent era.

On another table there's a selection of tiny, painstakingly made paper zines, like one entitled *Self Love, Self Care*, covered in pictures of hearts and trees. *We live in a society that has normalized self-hate and self-harm*, it says. *Fuck society! Practice self-love as a means of resistance.* Inside a squiggly thought bubble: *Fight the man! Fall in love with yourself!* Self-care tips include *sleep, drink water, eat fruits and vegetables, and surround yourself with people you feel safe with.* When I ask to purchase one, the student who has made it, in a turtleneck and thick glasses, tells me that she only wants to barter. "I don't want money; what I was kind of envisioning is, I want you to read it and e-mail me, and you can e-mail me about anything . . ."

There are a few guys at the craft fair, but not many. A student talks about breaking up with a boyfriend: "He's nice but we fought too much," she says. "I said, 'You are patriarch-ing me right now,' and then he shushed me. I was like, 'You let *me* speak.' Damn."

While I'm holding the self-care zine, a male student in a green T-shirt reading VERMONT ORGANICS walks up. "Those are called zines," he says, rhyming *zines* with *pines*. "I just learned about them today, when I heard someone say she'd made a zine, and I was like, 'What's that?'" He chuckles and walks away.

Tess shakes her head. "He's said, 'Let me mansplain zines to you,'" she says huskily.

"Come on, this is our domain," says Chloe, giving a light, tinkly laugh.

Sexual Truth

Even if the dude in the green shirt is a mansplainer, the traditional male-female divide that animated so much activism in my student days has given way to a diverse and fluid take on gender and sexual preference on both individual and cultural levels. Our Take Back the Night marches, hundreds of students strong down frat row, featured chants like "Hey, mister, get off my sister," and I don't recall students giving the mike to men at speak-outs, since female victims were the ones who mattered. But today, I ask a student if many students at Wesleyan are gay. "Um, one hundred percent," she answers. "When I go out into the world, I'm like, 'Oh, you're not even, like, queer? Oh, you think you're one hundred percent straight, awww, that's so cute.'"

Today, the word *gay* is completely out, as it connotes old-school binaries and stodgy *Modern Family* stereotypes of married Gen Xers. Though Wesleyan isn't quite the walking app store of psychosexual Bitmoji that one might imagine—despite that answer I got, there are plenty of straights around these parts too—the students who want to play with their gender and sexuality play hard. To the sexually insecure eighteen-year-old—which is all eighteen-year-olds—it's irresistible to learn, via Tumblr-influenced Internet culture, that there's a whole planet of gender possibilities out there and you aren't bound by what's on your birth certificate or in your pants. Empathy with the trans community is an essential part of the new take on gender on campus. Everyone's on the spectrum, so we should be in awe of the people who take the step toward their heartfelt identity (a small slice of the American population; researchers put the trans population at about seven hundred thousand, or a quarter of 1 percent of the nation). And when describing the entire smorgasbord of gender, LGBTQIA (the last two letters stand for *intersex* and either *asexual* or *allies*, meaning friends to the cause) has been joined by TGQN—for *transgender, genderqueer, questioning, not listed*.

The spectrum of new genders is head-spinning. It goes way beyond *cisgender*, meaning that one identifies with the gender one was assigned at birth, and *nonbinary*, describing those who reject the notion of male and female as the only options. There's also *agender*, someone who intentionally has no recognizable gender presentation, and *bigender*, where one's gender is a combination of two genders. The two most common terms are *gender-fluid*, wherein an individual's gender can change from month to month or even day to day, and *genderqueer*, an umbrella term for genders outside the binary that has been claimed by Miley Cyrus, who said, "I don't relate to being a boy or a girl."

Also, being uninterested in sex is okay. "Why is sex the be all and end all of every relationship?" asks a student at another university who identifies herself as "the asexual in the room." "This is a stupid, stupid model that we've been operating on, that sex is the biggest deal in life. I get it — reproduction." She rolls her eyes. "One person not having sex is not going to F up the foundation of the human race. So especially if it's not for reproduction, why is sex the biggest source of pleasure of our lives?" This is something I heard from several students. "I spent high school with sex being so built up and hyped as the craziest, raciest, coolest thing, and then I did it, and I was like, 'That's it?'" says a recent Princeton grad. "I feel sex should be *less hyped.*"

But it is majorly hyped at Wesleyan, and not only among students. Sexuality and gender are here intertwined as subjects of study — if not in the classroom, then outside. Bulletin boards are papered with flyers advertising events like an upcoming queer-theory conference called "Queer Art & Poetics" and a concert called the "exHOTic other," a burlesque revue purporting to go "from exposing skin to exposing the depths of the soul." Many bathrooms are all-gender, with signs declaring ANYONE CAN USE THIS RESTROOM REGARDLESS OF GENDER IDENTITY OR EXPRESSION. When a security guard walks over to stop a young woman with an oversize poodle from entering one, she breezes past, tells him it's an "emotional support animal," and closes the door.

That bathroom stuff is pretty passé; Wesleyan's had gender-neutral bathrooms for some time. And while kids take these topics seriously, they poke fun too. One day, I walked by a freestanding chalkboard put up by Wesleyan's wellness center announcing LOVE YOUR BODY DAY! A small cup with pastel chalk was provided for students to answer the question *How will you love your body?* Answers: *Masturbating; Sex; By eating a burger every day; By giving it no sleep to write an essay.* Then I noticed someone had crossed out the BODY part of LOVE YOUR BODY and written next to it, *This is ableist.* At first I thought that line was serious, but then I laughed heartily. Attitudes may change, but the humor stays the same.

Feminist Fight Club

Leaving aside the guys for a second, a new type of feminine icon is very present at Wesleyan: the loud, proud, somewhat emo, not totally straight, perhaps not even cis-gendered, defiantly sexy collegiate radical. They call themselves girls, thus aligned with larger pop culture (*Girls, Two Broke Girls, The Girl on the Train,* et cetera); they don't insist on being called women, the way we did in the 1990s, or womyn, to remove reference to men from the gender, even as a phantasm. Upon graduating, they expect not only to smash glass ceilings in a progressive-friendly field but to smash them while celebrating girl power. They'll do this with an eye to denigrating girl power's enemy: the dumb, uncaring, hookup-happy fuckboy, a term that has replaced Gen X's pejorative *fucktoy*, which was used mostly to refer to women.

Today's college women grew up when feminism was a zombie movement — not fully dead, but far from alive (and far from cool). This era of activism is a reaction to their preteen years in the deeply conflicted early 2000s, when Dubya-era family values like abstinence education, a federal ban on late-term abortion, and a proposed constitutional ban on gay marriage were the talk of the land. Teens had conquered pop, with ex–Disney stars leading the way. Before Britney Spears, a teen star could gyrate like Elvis and proto-twerk with eyes crossed like Josephine Baker, but a contralto-voiced seventeen-year-old couldn't put her hair in puffy pigtails and dress up in the exact kind of midriff-baring Catholic-schoolgirl outfit that a porn star playing a Catholic schoolgirl would wear and purr, "Hit me, baby, one more time" into the camera. Spears did, yet she was still required to toe the party line about her supposed innocence. Like the other stars of her era, she wore a purity ring and insisted that she was a virgin.

By the time the students enrolled at Wesleyan hit puberty, the focus in pop culture was almost entirely on the low, the crass, and the raunchy. *Girls Gone Wild* was burning up the TV, and stars like Jessica Simpson had learned that playing dumb on reality shows would make you rich if singing didn't. Airheaded sex symbols like Paris Hilton and Jenny McCarthy and uber-masculine tropes like hitting strip clubs and smoking cigars ruled even as social conservatism spread across the land.

Clarity was needed. And what I think we could call a backlash began in the late 2000s, near the start of Obama's tenure. Pop feminism dawned, bringing with it a slew of girl-power-branded female stars (now, it seemed, you could be a pop star only if you were female), from Beyoncé to Taylor Swift to Lady Gaga. In the real world, abortion rights were under attack by the states; in the imaginary pop realm, these totemic figures strode the earth, conquering platforms and metamorphizing from entertainers to one-woman entertainment conglomerates. As much as their feminism could be vague and shallow, it cannot be said to be anything but an improvement on what came directly before.

As they grew up, today's students embraced pop feminism and began looking with some skepticism at the earlier sex symbols, like Spears, and advertisements that sold them commercialized hetero-sex culture with every product. It's even possible that the current chic around queerness and gender fluidity is in part a reaction to this. As one bisexual woman put it to me, "If I have to see tits sell a watch on a billboard or [see] a naked woman in Guess jeans and that means I'm supposed to buy Guess jeans, I should be able to speak *my* own sexual truth."

These students also stepped into a vastly different time in terms of gender equality. By the time they finished high school, girls were surpassing boys in test scores, college-admission rates, and even pay, at least when they were all under the age of thirty or so. Equal, of course, except in that most intimate of spaces. Jessie Ford, a New York University doctoral student who is analyzing sex and sexual assault in American colleges, puts it this way: "What you have is young women today saying, 'I feel equal growing up, I feel equal in school, I feel equal everywhere — but then I had sex. And I do not feel equal. I felt that my body was used. I suddenly felt like an object, like I've never felt before.'"

The anti-rape movement is, at least in part, these girls' sexual empowerment movement — it's their way of compensating for the culture sexualizing them. At the same time, they don't want to let go of their sexiness. One of the most radical and prominent Columbia activists adores Kim Kardashian for what the star has accomplished on her own terms. In a world where women's sexuality has been thrust upon them, Kardashian has mastered it as a form of self-expression and profit.

It is symbolically appropriate that Ke$ha, the last pop star of the 2000s — a party girl whose style could best be described as "walk of shame" and who rapped about "brushing my teeth with a bottle of Jack"—has more recently become a survivor icon, declaring that Dr. Luke, the producer who orchestrated her success, abused her emotionally and raped her at least once. Pop impresarios have done the same and worse from time immemorial; it was once called a casting couch. But when Kesha (she dropped the $ when she came out of rehab for an eating disorder, a disease she says was partially caused by Dr. Luke's abuse) told her story, the public embraced her.

The clothes most women wear have changed little since Kesha was Ke$ha, but the women wearing those clothes are thinking differently about the bodies beneath them. Objectification is okay as long it's processed as self-gratification, and in fact it may even negate the power of the male gaze ("If I do it first, you can't do it at all"). Play out desires on your own terms, place limits and boundaries on what once seemed like a sexual free-for-all, and, most important, exercise the right to say that a sexual experience went down the wrong way, and say that loud and proud. Middle-aged handwringing about young women denigrating themselves as sexual playthings misses that *this* is their answer: Wearing whatever they want, talking and acting as raunchy as they want, but also establishing new rules about sex and calling out boys who don't treat them right. They strive to take charge on all fronts.

Some among you may find this new brand of young woman offensive and annoying; thoughts on them may also be culturally informed. "If there's anything the nation feels more anxiety about than sexually empowered adult women, it's sexually active girls in their late teens and early twenties, the women who are preparing to head into the world not necessarily to become wives, but to become people," author Rebecca Traister wrote.

What's the favored word to communicate this new feminine ideal? *Bitch* isn't only on bracelets. That's a word women didn't use in the 1990s, a similarly linguistic convulsive period—not about each other, not about themselves, not about any woman under discussion. Leona Helmsley was difficult, Glenn Close's *Fatal Attraction* character was dysfunctional, Bosnian ethnic-cleansing enthusiast Biljana Plavšić was a product of postimperial tribalism. Resistance begins with language and we didn't need Orwell to tell us that *bitch* had to be left behind.

We authored seminar papers delineating the word's cruel history, as described in the *Oxford English Dictionary*—a female dog, perhaps associated with Artemis, goddess of the hunt — and listened to Queen Latifah, who said, "Every time I hear a brother call a girl a bitch or a ho . . . You know all that gots to go." On *Ill Communication*'s opening track, the Beastie Boys publicly apologized for their earlier misogyny — "I want to say a little something that's long overdue / the disrespect to women has got to be through" — then refused to take the stage with the Prodigy because of its 1997 hit "Smack My Bitch Up."

The reclamation of *bitch* began soon after, with otherwise forgettable alt-rock singer Meredith Brooks's hit "I'm a Bitch": "I'm a bitch, I'm a lover / I'm a child, I'm a mother" (sinner, saint, et cetera), and these days, *bitch* is a way of declaring control and dominance. The word is like *faggot* for gay men, empowering and problematic at the same time. For a young woman, *bitch* is satisfying to say because of those dynamic opposing forces. Tina Fey victoriously proclaimed in 2008, "Bitch is the new black." Female stars like Nicki Minaj in many a track and Madonna in "Bitch, I'm Madonna" tell us they're bosses, or bitches, or boss bitches, which seems to be contradictory or redundant but is rarely said with irony.

Unlike *fag*, *bitch* is still used openly by those who should perhaps not use it. It's a slur in hip-hop — Kanye West told us, "I made that bitch famous," in reference Taylor Swift, who certainly needed no help — and in society at large. Every woman knows that the first thing that comes out of a furious road-rager on the highway is "Get out of my way, bitch!" Every woman knows that when she has a miserable fight with a male lover, his usual parry is "You're such a bitch!" Every woman who has called out the random guy harassing her on the sidewalk knows that "You're pretty, baby doll" quickly turns into "Screw you, bitch!" All of this makes me wonder if womankind should even allow men to use the word *bitch*.

Anyway, that's the flip side. In our pop culture today, a bitch is crazy, cool, maybe even goes off sometimes at a system that's stacked against her. The girls I met on my travels called themselves bitches all the time. When they said it, part of what they were saying was that they weren't nice girls, and they were good with that. They were dark destroyers, Lady Macbeths, Medeas, Delilahs, twisted sisters with backpacks dangling carabiners, here to initiate change. And don't for a moment think they didn't use another word for themselves, one that girls who buck the system have appropriated for ages: *witch*.

A bitch is 180 degrees removed from her opposite, the basic bitch. The bitch can't be pinned down, but the basic bitch is boilerplate. Though the term originated in rap, with the white female rapper Kreayshawn boasting about separating herself from basics by refusing to wear clothing with designer labels, now it refers to a typical middle-class white girl in Uggs and leggings moving through a midsize American city carrying a pumpkin-spice latte in a manicured hand. She's eager to do or say or wear or shave anything, not for her own gratification, but to please a man. (A subtle point, to be sure, and one some older feminists see as evidence of a new generation's unknowing subjugation to male norms.) The basic bitch, in the eyes of young radical women, is a victim of the culture that the radicals are trying to overthrow, the culture that keeps the balance of sexual power permanently tipped toward men.

But how do you keep from talking crap about men while fighting their power? Well, maybe you don't, as I found out when I attended a meeting at Wesleyan for a play some students were putting on.

In the small kitchen of another home near campus, they make a dinner of chicken and pesto spaghetti as they chat about the production.

"I don't see any forks," says one girl, rustling around in the drawers.

"Um, shit, are we out of forks?"

The first girl picks up a doll-size cup and fills it with wine. "I like these tiny cups, though."

Moving to the living room, the play's crew, made up of a half dozen girls and one guy, sit in a circle, pulling up an old Papa Bear chair and small couch. One of the students from the craft fair sits in a rocker. They discuss a *Vagina Monologues* performance soon to take place. In this era of gender plasticity, the show — based on playwright Eve Ensler's interviews of two hundred women, many of whom were ashamed of their vaginas, including septuagenarians who confessed they'd never taken a mirror to their undercarriage — has been criticized by younger feminists as cis-sexist. Mount Holyoke students, declaring that "gender is a wide and varied experience, one that cannot simply be reduced to biological or anatomical distinctions," refused to put it on. So students at Wesleyan are preparing to follow a performance of *The Vagina Monologues* with an updated play about transgendered, queer, and women's empowerment: *The Shmagina Monologues*.

"Why don't the Vag and the Shmadge work together more?" asks the dude.

A student answers that they are this year, then explains that the director of *Shmagina* is appearing in *Vagina*, and the director of *Vagina* is in *Shmagina*. She describes the plays with intensity, her hands arcing in the air. *The Vagina Monologues* is historically important, though outdated, and we also need to hear a super new perspective on sex and sexuality, she says.

A housemate in running gear comes down the stairs. "Wear a headlamp so you stay safe. I wear my flashing bike vest when I run at night," someone calls out.

The door slams.

"Every time you leave this house, eight people comment on what you're doing," the play's director says. She announces that the group should have an icebreaker activity, some sort of game where they all say their names and give fun facts about themselves.

"What about the age you discovered masturbation?"

She cocks her head and suggests some activist improv instead; everyone should announce his or her favorite famous white male to hate.

A voice calls from upstairs: "Woody Allen!"

Who else makes the cut? Andrew Jackson. George W. Bush. Jesus — but was He white?

The guy says, "I think a good white male to hate is Pat Robertson, though originally I was going to say Harold Bloom."

The student in the rocking chair chooses Sigmund Freud, whom she knew she was going to hate because of the sex stuff, she says, but when she started reading him for class she realized his prefaces are "so self-congratulatory and about how the reader won't believe his psychoanalysis because 'you're stupid and I'm smart.'"

Someone opts for Robin Thicke of "Blurred Lines" — a whole song about how it's okay when men want what a woman is saying she doesn't want. The girls note that it's a catchy song, and it's frustrating that it's catchy.

Last to go is a curly-haired girl who climbs on the couch and announces: "My favorite white male to hate is Michael Roth." Then she makes an (ironic) heart with her hands like a Belieber and pushes it in and out while saying: "Michael Roth is *the* patriarch." Later, she unpacks this statement while we're talking. "He is the patriarch, because he perpetuates," she says.

2

Number-One Party School

You hear them before you see them, several hundred shouting college girls descending on the skylighted atrium of Syracuse University's brick octopus of a student center; they're about to enter doors located in too many corners to count. Cheers and shrieks at various pitches mingle into a single earsplitting tone that sounds like an express subway whizzing by a station. Doors slam open as the volume leaps by thirty decibels, and a second later, they're in view.

Hands raised, sporting hairstyles as varied as you'd find in a hundred-page fashion magazine, the girls wear Mardi Gras beads and sparkly metallic vests, backward baseball caps and neon boas that drop feathers as they go. Some of them carry Greek letters the length of sandwich boards, one with a *zeta* slung around her neck for easy transport. One after the other, they walk-jog through the atrium to the student center's fifteen-hundred-seat auditorium: Tri-Delt blondes with the glittery fake eyelashes, brunettes with flower crowns of interlocking daisies, a group dressed as football players with black paint striped across cheeks and the words BID DAY stenciled on mesh T-shirts.

This is, indeed, Bid Day, an annual tradition dubbed "the running of the girls" at this university of twenty-one thousand—an institution to which the Princeton Review had months earlier awarded the distinction of the nation's "Number One Party School," mostly because Syracuse has a beloved, high-ranked Division I basketball team and a more entrenched Greek system than nearly any college in the Northeast. The school's location makes it either surprising or inevitable that it should be touted as party central. Syracuse, New York, is in the running for the nation's snowiest city, and it is in any season a drab, postindustrial shell with Dickensian city corners. But as at most American universities, the fewer cultural offerings nearby, the more hard-partying the campus scene becomes.

A typically dismal January afternoon isn't enough to dissuade these girls from running, slipping and sliding, along ice-covered paths. Syracuse is half *Game of Thrones'* forbidding, gothic Winterfell, half squat utilitarian brick DMV. Soon they'll head onward and upward over the campus hills to their new roosts in Syracuse's sorority houses, sprawling mansions between big frat houses that add an aristocratic touch to the landscape. They overlook the campus like a dozen marooned cruise ships.

For now, the students fill the campus center's auditorium. On the orchestra level, the uninitiated, not yet in full plumage, mill about with slightly dazed expressions. Moments ago, they were all in university classrooms with upper-class chaperones standing by to ensure that each girl sat on her square white envelope and didn't sneak a peek at the card inside, which told her fate. Then, at the strike of a clock synched to Time.gov, every girl had reached under her butt, and, in unison, they'd all ripped open the envelopes. One chaperone filmed the mass revelation with a cell phone, hoping, she told me, to preserve an "awesome" moment for posterity, but posterity would have to settle for a much more bittersweet scene. Those who didn't get their first, second, or third choices collapsed. One girl burst into tears. "I'm having a lot of emotions right now," she said, fanning her face with the fateful white square. "I'm not happy at all."

Now, though, most of the initiates keep their eyes raised heavenward, or at least toward the auditorium's mezzanine, where the older sisters have gathered and are whooping and screaming, as crazy and power-mad as a bunch of Greek goddesses on Mount Olympus, shaking boas, videotaping themselves with selfie sticks, throwing chapter hand symbols like gang signs.

"Take a seat, you are a fire hazard," yells a middle-aged buzzkill who's stalking the stage below and pointing up at them. "Do not throw anything from the balcony up there onto the school, thank you. If you drop anything off the balcony, I will find your chapter!" Two Thetas back against a banister and pucker their lips for duck-faced selfies. "Stop hanging off that banister," yells the woman. "No! Stop!"

They will not stop. The girls-only pep rally segues into a girls-only dance party, older sisters running onstage to shake their butts, wave their arms, sing along to house tracks. The new ones send eager text updates (*My roommate's going to be a Delphi too; The girl next to me is crying and laughing at the same time, take a chill pill*) while clutching cards bearing messages like *The Sisters of Alpha Xi Delta Cordially Invite ____ to Become a New Member of the Eta Chapter.*

Soon enough, the spangled migration will pour out a wide set of doors, go past Syracuse's impressive quad, and head up toward their new nests. But for now, two lone male students stand by the auditorium doors. "C'mon, we've been creepy enough," says one, jerking his thumb back toward the campus.

"I just wanted to check out the talent—the new talent in the freshman class," the other says with a leer.

"Du-u-u-de," chides the first, chucking a rolled-up piece of paper at him and shaking his head.

Why are so many female students drawn to this ritual? To hear participants tell it, Bid Day is the christening of a lifelong sisterhood, one that elevates the character, provides a sense of purpose and belonging, and molds girls into women who, as one house creed's challenging syntax says, "without bitterness or defeat may encounter misfortune and with humility meet success." But that's not all. It's also a well-designed vehicle for postadolescent identity creation, for a desire to try out a new self, and for that self to be surrounded by and eagerly embraced by one's peers. At the same time, siloing students in a certain kind of sorority or a certain kind of fraternity carries the risk of cementing those identities before these young men and women have a chance to decide if they want to become those people. It puts even greater emphasis on following social norms and the wisdom of the flock.

Go 'Cuse!

Universities sell parents the myth that campuses are the only place in America where children can be molded into happy, well-rounded, and gainfully employed adults. Nothing can be allowed to undermine this, and Kent Syverud, the chancellor of Syracuse University, was not happy about the Princeton Review ranking. "It is not a good thing for a school to be labeled as number one in partying," he wrote in a tense memo to his Orange Friends (Syracuse's original mascot, an American Indian warrior, had been replaced by a base-ball-cap-wearing orange in the 1990s). "We have to pay even more attention than our peers to the aspects of student life—and parties—that get in the way of students succeeding," he continued. "My belief, which I hope some of you share, is that to be labeled the number-one party school is to be told those boundaries need more attention. With your help, they will get it this year."

Parents may look for a university with great career-oriented departments —of which Syracuse has several—but for many eighteen-year-olds, particu-larly males, there's one reaction to the dreamscape conjured by a who-gives-a-shit orange as a mascot and the phrase "number-one party school in Amer-ica": Enroll now. They see a sweaty dance floor and a steady stream of the sickly sweet drinks that college kids these days favor (strawberitas, limeritas, whatever combines beer or hard liquor with many tablespoons of sugar). A gang of friends with whom to roam the campus at night, performing minor acts of vandalism. Forget freshman orientation, with its dreary anti-binge-drinking seminars and pizza-party gatherings in cinder-block dorms—at Syracuse, the PG-rated bacchanal of Bid Day is the real orientation. Formals, semiformals, *Little Mermaid*–themed parties, space-themed parties, ABC parties (anything but clothes), charity events, pregames, bar nights, wine nights—the typical sorority girl at Syracuse is invited to three or four social events each week, and as the newbies slipping through the snow soon find, the sisterhood expects full attendance.

If Wesleyan represents the vanguard of activism at American schools, Syr-acuse embodies the norm—a large institution whose social life is dominated by Greek culture and whose famous alums are broadly acceptable icons: Dick Clark, Megyn Kelly, and the dreamboat member of the wildly successful mid-2010s pop EDM duo the Chainsmokers (though I would be remiss if I did not note that Lou Reed was also an alum). At the same time, a few months before the 2015 Bid Day that I attended, students staged the university's second sit-in in forty years. For eighteen days, dozens of students camped out on the ground floor of a brick octopus across from the Bid Day brick octopus, rail-ing against multifarious ills like racism, xenophobia, and transphobia, as well as the chancellor's abrupt shuttering of their standalone rape-crisis center. Syracuse has fewer radicals than Wesleyan and more than Oklahoma State, but activism exerts its influence on all campuses today. Sulkowicz's name and cause are familiar at 'Cuse, and indeed students took part in a mattress rally just as they did at George Washington and Belmont University. The sheet that covered the mattress at Syracuse was later displayed in the campus center. Students wrote Sharpied phrases on it, including, in orange, *I will carry the weight we both share, mom*, and, in black, *It's heavier than you know.*

The two schools are also more alike than they are different in terms of rites of sex if not in how they *think* about sex. As sociologist Lisa Wade writes in *American Hookup: The New Culture of Sex on Campus*, a study analyzing 101 college students' private journals about their intimate lives, "No matter the size of the college, how heavy a Greek or athletic presence it boasts, its exclusivity, its religious affiliation, or whether it's public or private—hookup culture is there. We find it in all regions of the country, from the Sunshine State of Florida to the sunny state of California." By hookup culture, Wade means a climate where sex is largely decoupled from romantic relationships, at least during underclassman years. Her conclusion? Hookup culture "is college." Places like Wesleyan are exporting their culture to places like Syracuse, but the reverse is happening too. Even if you're not in a frat or a sorority, the assumption is that you will, at least occasionally, party like you are.

After all, at universities, and especially in Greek culture, nights are about sex hovering in the near-middle distance as a possibility; rituals are built around it, toward it, lurching always in the direction of it. "Guys in frats at Syracuse are in it for the opportunity to hook up with girls, period," one Kappa Alpha Theta sister told me firmly. "If that's what you want your Syracuse experience to be about, you join a frat."

Or a sorority: "Girls in Greek life at Syracuse have much more sex than people who aren't in Greek life," said another sister from that sorority. "We have so much exposure to so many different kinds of guys. Sex doesn't feel like that big a deal here. You might know the guy already, or know his friends. It's not like after college, where I think if you meet a guy in a bar it would be weird to go home with him, because he's a real stranger."

Male students had the same inkling—that after college, women wouldn't be as easy to land—but they linked this to a more even playing field after graduation. "I think the whole hookup culture outside of school will be different," a Wesleyan senior said. "If I get a date a month, I'll be lucky. Whereas here, there are boundless women. College is a weird four-year period where you learn how to be you, you get to experiment . . . Then you leave, and it's all expunged, gone, 'Oh yeah, that thing I did in college.' You're in the workforce, and you call it a day."

Blackout Blonde

To learn more about what Syracuse's planet is like for women on a daily (or nightly) basis, I went out for pizza and a glass of wine with a pretty, petite twenty-three-year-old who in her senior year wrote a column for Syracuse's alternative newspaper under the evocative nom de plume Blackout Blonde. She was older than most of the women at Bid Day but had a similar precision to her appearance, with a small, upturned nose, neatly applied lip gloss, and pale, slender arms and legs. Despite her willingness to talk frankly about sex, she held a defiant posture throughout our conversation. It felt as if she was only half opening up — to me or to herself or perhaps to both of us, displaying a braggadocio that sounded similar to the girl who told me about "so many rapists." Her opinions, though, were diametrically opposed.

Hookups on Planet College are fun, Blackout Blonde tells me. After all, if they weren't, why would so many people have them? At a time when every type of music has been discovered and every pierced and tattooed subculture brought into the commercial fold, semi-anonymous or mostly anonymous sex with someone you barely know is a wild experience, one of the few forms of rebellion left for youth in America.

Blackout Blonde says she is just being honest about what she saw around her, though as with sex columnists since time immemorial, I think we can assume she exaggerates here and there. "Our timelines on Twitter are scattered with blurry, dark Instagram photos of our friends and peers passed out in the grass the night before; filled with tweets with hashtags that sound like they belong in Katy Perry's 'Last Friday Night,'" she wrote in a column. I hoped she was referring to the more benign lyrics of that song, the ones about riding pink flamingos in the pool, not the ones about finding a stranger in one's bed, and a "pounding in my head . . . Is this a hickey or a bruise?" The morning-after quarterbacking with friends is part of the fun too, like the actresses on the old HBO show *Sex and the City* gossiping about the previous night's encounters over brunch — except these girls talk mostly through oblique, or overt, references to hookups on social media, this generation's version of talking to your girlfriends over brunch (though they often eat brunch together too). "You walk through the dining hall on any given Friday, Saturday and Sunday morning and the only words heard while standing in line for eggs are, 'I was literally so drunk last night, literally,'" she wrote.

At least on the surface, Blackout Blonde is pro-girl, admonishing frat brothers for being cheap and serving warm Keystone beer at parties because they know girls will "dry hump each other on the speaker system" no matter how little they spend on liquor. She parsed the difference between a good and bad "sexcuse" — being on one's period, good; "Aww, roommate's home," questionable — and tells girls to have sex whenever it's offered because "sex is like pizza, even when it's bad, it's still 'pizza.'" Men needed to accept that women were sexual beings too. "College is the land of the drunken hookups and in today's society females are on the prowl for hookups just as much as guys are," she wrote. "You may think that we text or call you asking what your plans are for the evening out of pure interest, or because we are a 'crazy,' 'overly-attached' species that craves connection after a few rolls in the hay, but that's simply untrue . . . Drunk, sober, late at night, midday between classes, why not? We enjoy sex just as much, duh, and also find it fun and interesting having something, and frankly someone, to do." She added, "Don't be surprised if you are to us what we have always been to you, a toy, an object."

There's some support for Blackout Blonde's contentions. The most comprehensive analysis of sex in college, performed by New York University sociologist Paula England and based on an online survey that has grown to encompass twenty thousand students at twenty-one universities and colleges, has shown that in heterosexual hookups, men and women's enjoyment is nearly equivalent, though men reach orgasm far, far more often. College women get something out of a casual sex life, whether they come or not, some combination of affection, attention, emotional satisfaction, ego boost, exercise, peer approval, the satisfaction of having the kind of crazy experience every American college girl is supposed to have.

Blackout Blonde sees this clearly. When we meet for pizza, she tells me, "Guys are not that rapey, and girls want the D" — shorthand for *dick*. "The problem with Syracuse girls is they want to be nice girls. They don't want to admit that they want to have sex, because they think it makes them look like sluts. But in private you can hear the same girls talk about how they give such amazing blow jobs. 'I'm the queen of blow jobs, ooh, it's the top of my priority list.'"

As she takes minuscule bites of pizza, she does ultimately recount some experiences that belie her pro-hookup line. One time when she was making out with a Sigma Alpha Epsilon brother in an alleyway behind a frat party, he started to squeeze and manhandle her too aggressively. She took off a heel with one hand and hit him on the head with it, then ran down the stairs. As she descended, she called a friend and yelled into the receiver: "I'm like fucking Cinderella escaping the prince!"

Another night had a murkier, more troubling denouement. She was hanging out with a fifth-year senior, a hockey player, at his house — but all she can remember is doing keg stands to a Taylor Swift song. "I was a sophomore, and he was so much older, so that made me really like him and think he was really cool, but I don't know what happened that night," she says. In the morning, she woke up in bed with him wearing his boxers. She couldn't find her clothes at first and then she looked between the mattress and the wall and saw her outfit sandwiched there. That was a weird place for her clothes to be unless the two of them had hooked up, she thought; clothes didn't usually get smashed between a mattress and wall unless someone pushed them hard off the bed in the middle of sex.

"The guy kept saying, 'Don't worry. I was too drunk last night to fuck Blake Lively, okay?' Acting all 'Don't flatter yourself.' Well, (a) I appreciate the comparison to Blake Lively, but (b) I think he at least tried." She grimaces. "After a ton of searching, I found my phone and I was out of there. I was in such a rush I even forgot one of my layers at his house." She smirks. "And I was pissed, because that was a nice top from Urban Outfitters."

I ask if she thinks of herself as a rape survivor. "Fuck no," she says, taking a swig of wine. "As far as I'm concerned, there's only one person to blame in that situation, and his name is Jose Cuervo."

Super-Casual Sex

The girl at Wesleyan told me rapists lurked everywhere on campus. Blackout Blonde told me that Syracuse students just like to party. There had to be a middle ground. As I traversed the snowy campus, interviewing about a half a dozen sorority sisters in person and on the phone, I found their attitudes about sex more nuanced and conflicted than either of those two women would have had me think.

Much of what I heard about sexual politics from the other girls at Syracuse — and they were as obsessed as the students at Wesleyan, although gender fluidity tended not to enter the picture — was complicated. These girls, most with hair as long and sleek as Afghan hounds and waists smaller than possible without extreme calorie restriction (the new euphemism for anorexia), loved to talk about the ins and outs of hooking up and dating, though none of them had been on more than a few dates, the kind involving dinner or a movie, in their college careers. Regarding sexual assault, though, they sounded much like I did when I was a student uncomfortably confronted with the guy in the cab of the yellow excavator. They identified certain guys as "weird," "disrespectful," "icky." They didn't call them rapists. But many had had nights like the one with the Taylor Swift keg stand that Blackout Blonde described.

Broad similarities notwithstanding, Syracuse and Wesleyan would never be mistaken for each other. Again, 'Cuse is closer to the American mean. It's larger, it's less elite and demanding academically, the food in their cafeterias is inedible, and its students have a dramatically different idea of what constitutes fun. They consume a heroic amount of beer and weed; I wondered at times if the two drugs had become equivalently legal in their minds. And they're generally focused on a different type of fun than most Wesleyan students — silly and risqué costumes, selfie-snapping/selfie-reflecting ("Oh my God, my teeth are shining way too bright in that picture, my teeth are weird"), dancing until dawn. On Bid Day, the song playing at the sororities' grand mansions was a David Bowie–derived house track "Heroes (We Could Be)." "'Spin around and round for hours,'" they sing. "'You and me, we got the world in our hands'" — a cookie-cutter call to superheroes who run the streets at night and seize life's fleeting joys.

Wesleyan students project childlike-innocence-slash-hipster affect on their dorm-room doors (HI! reads one sign, explaining the resident hails from California. MY BIRTHDAY IS ON BASTILLE DAY. THAT'S THE DAY THE FRENCH PRISONERS BECAME A MOB AGAINST FRENCH

ROYALTY. I THINK. STILL DON'T KNOW IF I NEED TO BUY SNOW-
SHOES). Syracuse's dorm-room doors are covered with pop-culture posters like a printed-out photo of all the Kardashians with the student's friends'
faces Photoshopped on the bodies. Even though most of the women I spoke
with at Syracuse were warm, kind, and funny, Wesleyan students might de-
ride them as basic bitches, and the Syracuse girls would not like that. "Just
because you like to work out, like avocado toast, and get your nails done
doesn't mean you're a basic bitch," one says to me somewhat mournfully.
"That's not all you're about."

At Syracuse, the university gym is filled with girls plucked and waxed to
perfection watching Melissa McCarthy comedies on the ellipticals. The pressure to look hot comes from inside and out. One sister confided in me that
she selected her particular sorority because "it's one of the few where you
don't feel like you have to put on makeup before going to the house." Not long
after my visit, a senior from Bethesda, Maryland, posted a video that went viral revealing why she'd left her sorority. She claimed that her Syracuse sisters
had told her, "We don't want any FUPAs in the house" (translation: "fat upper
pussy area"), advised the girls to "dress sluttier at the next formal, so the guys
like us," and even threatened to put a bottle of the weight-loss supplement
Hydroxycut in the handbag of a plump little sister.

Yet the obsessive precision with which these girls handled their own lives,
their schoolwork, their social media profiles, their waistlines, and their never-
stained sweatshirts with Greek letters decorating the front disappeared when
guys were involved. In fact, they resisted putting labels on anything to do
with sex. Compared to the rigidity of their social lives, which were organized
around events in the Greek system, their sex lives were completely casual
— and, for many, chaotic. "I know it's backwards from generations before us,
but we see a cute guy at a party, figure out his name, hook up, and then
you get each other's number, and you're texting every day until you hook up
again," says a Syracuse sorority sister. "Honestly, I don't know how you would
get someone's number and show interest if you hadn't hooked up with him
first." Even the casual term *hook up* isn't the most popular slang anymore. If
one student is sexually active with another, the two tell friends that they are
"talking," an even more casual label.

The attitude toward protection is casual too; fear of AIDS has diminished,

STDs are usually treatable, and guys care even less than they used to about contraception, say these girls. "All my friends are on the pill, but I had problems with it, and IUDs gave me cramping," says a sister from another sorority. "A few weeks ago I went home with someone and asked him to wear a condom, and he rolled over and went to bed. I left the house. It was so rude. And that's not the first time it's happened to me at 'Cuse. I don't get it — don't you not want a baby too?"

These students are right that no romance begins in any way other than the hookup at most colleges today — or, for that matter, in most urban areas with Gen Xers and Boomers, many of whom begin relationships with no-strings sex. Even students from Tennessee's Freed-Hardeman University, a Churches of Christ school of fewer than two thousand students where sex before marriage is a sin, daily chapel is a requirement, and there are social clubs in lieu of a Greek scene, say there's a fair amount of hooking up — though most of them wouldn't engage in intercourse. "When you go on a date, you go wherever the guy takes you, but there's nothing to do in the city except go to Taco Bell," a sophomore with blue eyes and wavy hair tells me. Instead, the kids go "boogin'," their silly name for that venerable practice of necking in a car. "Me and my friends go boog-busting, which is looking for people who are boogin, and then flash our lights on them to scare the crap out of them." She laughs. "All the teachers know about it — they'll say, 'All right, who's been boog-busting this week?'" However, the college doesn't look the other way when kids of the opposite genders are in the same bedroom. "My friend was living on the first floor of our dorm, and she got caught with a guy in her room. The school made her move up to the fourth floor and told her next time she'd be suspended."

Good Sex and No Sex

Here and elsewhere, though, kids aren't hooking up as much as one might think. First of all, they're losing their virginity later than teenagers have since the 1950s; the average age of deflowering in the 1990s was fifteen, and it's seventeen and a half today. Second, NYU sociologist Paula England found that about 80 percent of students were hooking up, on average, less than once per semester (*hooking up* was defined as any sort of casual sexual activity, from making out to penetration). England says the average number of hookups was eight over four years of college; 28 percent of the students she surveyed never hooked up. But 20 percent hooked up a lot, reporting ten or more hookups by senior year.

I talked about ever-more-casual sex (and no sex) on campus with Deborah Singer, the head of marketing and communications for Lulu, a dating app for women — specifically, college women. Lulu was popular with millions of female students at big party schools, particularly in the South, from 2013 to 2015, after which it went the way of so many apps. One of its prime gimmicks was having girls assign hashtags to guys that their friends might want to date, like #PornEducated, #KinkyintheRightWays, and #NeverSleepsOver, but guys did not appreciate this, and the waters became rough for the company.

In a spiffy conference room at the company's headquarters (before they closed shop), Singer shares what she learned about college women from catering to their romantic needs. "When we initially launched, we had categories for guys that were pretty traditional — *he's an ex, he's a crush, he's a friend, he's a hookup*," says Singer. "And one of the first things we heard back from girls was 'We need more categories because our relationships with guys aren't like that: I want *friends with benefits*, I want *we're talking*, I want *rather not say*, I want a lot more flexibility in defining these relationships.'"

Lulu polled its users about sex, racking up over a million respondents to a set of questions, and Singer shares some of their responses with me. I'm not sure how scientific this data is, but many of these girls' answers are remarkably close to some of England's findings.

When I looked over a spreadsheet, I immediately realized that the users were women from the millennial generation, the tail end of which is in college now, because when they were asked about what they most wanted to know when meeting a new guy, 54 percent said "his relationship with his family," 26 percent "his last girlfriend," 9 percent "his ding-dong," and only 3 percent "his bank account." These are women who know they don't need a man to support them financially. They also exhibited the typical millennial dedication to amplified sexiness. Asked if they wore makeup, over half said "never leave home without it," and for "What kind of garden do you grow?" the same proportion ticked the box for "scorched earth policy, here."

On sexual matters, their responses were similarly fascinating. Once upon a time, you didn't want your partner to know you were very sexually experienced. Once upon a time, you might also have kept this from your friends. Even in the 1990s, it was important not to get a reputation as easy. But in Lulu's survey, college women refused to assume the sexual shame of prior generations. Over three-quarters answered the question "How many hookups make you a slut?" by ticking one of two boxes: "I don't believe in sluts" and "Fuck you, my sex life is my damn business."

And yet, at the same time, England found that nearly 20 percent of college seniors were virgins. You might assume that virgins are the girls who aren't on Lulu or who aren't participating in Syracuse sororities, but you might not be right about that. In Lulu's million-girl survey, in answer to a question about how women feel about their parents knowing that they have sex, about half the women responded that their parents didn't know they had sex. Singer also tells me that Lulu, trying to catch the popularity of apps like Whisper and Secret — which allow users to anonymously share their deepest secrets with the world and which were briefly popular in the early to mid-2010s — once created a similar feature for its app, called Truth Bombs. And the most popular truth bomb dropped by college women who were on this racy dating app? They were virgins.

Most of the female students that I interviewed said that they lost their virginity around seventeen, in their junior or senior year of high school. They also implied that they were hooking up all the time, and on this score, I could never figure out if this was because they were simply part of England's hookup-happy 20 percent cohort or if they were exaggerating because they wanted other people to think they were having a lot of sex — wild and satisfying sex, I might add.

"The way that girls talk at school makes it hard for me to talk candidly about sex," says a Brown student. "We're in the cafeteria, and it's like other girls almost *pity* you if you aren't having orgasms — like it's part of your duty as a strong woman. I hadn't even been in a real relationship freshman year, and it felt hard for me to admit that there was so much stuff I didn't know. And it felt like the only way to learn about that stuff was to try to have a weird sexual experience. But then, you're having sex with someone you don't know, and you also don't want that person to *know* you don't know everything about sex, so the experience is . . . strange." In other words, there's subtle (feminist!)

cultural pressure to at least appear to be in control of the situation as a college woman having sex—even if you're not feeling that way. And it's easy to see how that would become confusing for both partners.

Beyond this, both England's and Lulu's surveys demonstrate that there's a five-alarm-fire problem with Blackout Blonde's stance. As we all know, she isn't telling the whole truth about heterosexual sex. When I wrote earlier about England's survey demonstrating that the genders were equivalent in pleasure in hookups, I didn't mean *sexual* pleasure. The dirty secret is that heterosexual sex is often not pleasurable for the female in the equation, with a large percentage of these empowered, expecting-to-be-financially-independent college women admitting they fake orgasms. And for all the acceptance of super-casual sex culture, a study of six hundred undergrads led by a sexuality scholar at the Kinsey Institute found that women were nearly twice as likely to reach orgasm in a serious relationship as in a hookup.

This doesn't even consider the effects of the types of sex that's becoming more popular among young students—unreciprocated oral and anal sex. Blowjobs haven't been shocking for years (unless they happened in the Oval Office), but anal sex used to strike most women as a fetish or a sign of male contempt. Today, for a generation deeply familiar with porn, it's within the usual bounds of experimentation. A 2010 national study conducted by Indiana University says 20 percent of eighteen- to nineteen-year-old women had tried anal sex, and the number increases to 40 percent by ages twenty to twenty-four.

I don't want to be judgmental about anal sex—it can certainly be pleasurable for women, although that usually involves having it with someone experienced in the art. A sign of its normalization—recently, Elite Daily, a skeevy website with *Cosmo* aspirations targeting young women, ran an article entitled "11 Reasons You Should Give the Gift of Anal This Holiday Season": "Because anal is reserved for only the most special people. You wouldn't go on a colon cleanse for just anyone"; "because he really doesn't need another tie or a Vitamix. Guaranteed usage upon receipt"; "because it's more a gift for you than for him. You're the one in control here."

Despite Elite Daily's suggestion of empowerment and control, the fact is that during college years, oral sex isn't reciprocated by men too often, and most girls aren't hiding strap-ons in bedside-table drawers. And when the women in Lulu's survey were asked "What sex acts make you really uncomfortable?" 56 percent of them passed over tit-fucking, giving head, getting head, and asshole-licking to select anal sex. So not only are women already dealing with the unfortunate anatomical reality that the clitoris is not in the orifice where the penis goes in, but they're also being asked to engage in some types of sex they may find, a priori, unappealing. As I mentioned earlier, many of the contentious campus rape cases that I heard about involved anal sex. On a mattress, no matter how much we may want them to be, the genders are not equivalent.

Fresh Meat

Lianna, a tall blond Kappa Alpha Theta sister and a talented writer, talks to me about these contradictions and the way she felt about the sex life that Syracuse handed her. On Bid Day, as girls raced about the auditorium bursting into tears and hysteria over their sorority decisions, she was filled with a mix of nostalgia and horror, thinking back to her own freshman year. She loves her sorority but never liked the way that guys at fraternities looked at her, the way they didn't treat her as an equal or a friend unless they were expressly introduced to her by a frat guy she was already friends with. "I was fresh meat," she explains. "Essentially a newborn baby living in a giant pool of giant drunk babies who are, to put it eloquently, trying their best to get their 'willies' wet ASAP."

Lianna is five foot nine — "Five foot nine and a half if we're being technical," she adds solemnly, in the way that postadolescents talk about half-inch additions to their stature — and has always been a little insecure about her height, though she has a sense of humor about it. "Please don't ask me, or any girl for that matter, why they're tall," she's written, addressing a male in absentia. "We don't ask why your penises are so small." She's also struggled with her weight, which rose to a very reasonable one hundred and seventy pounds her freshman year at 'Cuse. Still, she worried, because so many of the other sorority sisters were so thin and so small. *Giants in paradise,* reads the caption on a Facebook picture of her and her current boyfriend standing in front of Buckingham Palace, the upward angle of the camera making them appear nearly as tall as the roof of the castle.

Whereas Blackout Blonde came out swinging, Lianna, whom I speak to late one weekday morning—"My schedule is epic," she says, telling me that she doesn't have class until 12:30—offers a quieter account of her sex life. She starts off by underlining some sisters' earlier points: "There are a lot of girls at Syracuse who are having sex because they want to have sex, but there are a lot of girls who are having sex just because they want someone to talk to them," she explains. "Here's the main problem with our generation, hookup culture, and college: Guys are resistant to giving girls a chance, or even getting to know you, unless you have sex with them. But once you have sex with them, most of them are done with you! They want nothing else to do with you! It makes absolutely no sense."

This has been a problem for far longer than Lianna's generation, but still, her conflation of the word *talking* in collegiate colloquial usage—to mean hooking up—and the way that she uses it here, to imply an emotional need, is what gets my attention. This is another alternate reality in college: "It's a war of who gives a shit less," one student tells me about nascent relationships. Today, to be seen swooning, crushing, "catching feelings," is to be seen as weak. But for many women, love and sex are connected, even if, like Blackout Blonde, they say they are not.

Despite Lianna's trip to Buckingham Palace with her boyfriend, her romantic life didn't sound like a fairy tale, though it was not as gory as Cinderella bashing her heel over a prince's head. "There are only a few kinds of relationships at Syracuse, and I've had all of them," she says. "I've had a boyfriend, which is hard to do, because you're looking for a gem in a bunch of really crappy stones. Then I've had the two- or three-month fling where the guy texts you on Thursday or Friday night, you have sex, and that's it, and when you ask, 'What's going on here,' he flees. I've had the short relationship where I dated a guy for two months and then it was summer, and when we came back, he freaked out. I've had one-night stands. I've dipped my toes in all of it. But not because I wanted to"—only because that's what is available at 'Cuse.

Lianna's keen perception of the hookup game on campus had yet to encompass rape. "I've never felt scared [with a guy]," she says, slowing down a bit to make her point. "I've definitely felt pressured. My problem has always been that I didn't know how to say no. I didn't know when I wanted to say no. And I didn't know how to. And I felt bad saying no." She sighs. "Which is so stupid." She pauses for a minute, and then puts a finer point on her comments. "I guess I should say that it wasn't even that I wanted to say no. It's just that I didn't want to say yes. It's not like I was totally opposed! I was thinking, *I don't want him to think I'm not interested at all, but I'm not in the mood, and I'm kind of drunk. Let's just get it over with, because I'd rather be watching TV.*"

I came away from Syracuse with answers to some questions. Is there more sex on campus today than in the past? No. Are there pockets of heavy hookup scenes? Yes. Do these heavy hookup scenes include more sexual assault? Yes, they have to, because if 20 percent of college seniors are virgins and a large slice of female students are raped when they're students, that simply doesn't leave enough sexually active students to account for the high rate of penetrative assault. Can we blame the sexual assault problem on the hookup scene? Not exactly, but we can't ignore it.

The Red Zone

Whether these girls' blunt talk about sex was performance or truth is unknowable; whether in bed, too, they felt like they were performing, like the Brown student, is also unknowable. But what did become clear to me as I talked with these women was that their casual, flexible attitudes about sex extended to the way they thought about sexual assault. They either didn't think sexual assault was a big deal à la Blackout Blonde, or they didn't think it was a big deal à la women voters for Trump, rolling their eyes at his mundane male boorishness. They might even have had vestigial worry that they would be labeled sluts (as the old saying goes, good girls don't get raped, and Blackout Blonde told me they secretly want to be good girls). They definitely didn't want guys to perceive them as *unfun.*

What they did mention time and again was that "weird things" had happened to them at the beginning of freshman year. They'd had nights like the one the USC grad told me about (the woman with the bangles who drew comparisons to the Mob and trap houses), nights that were supposed to be sex but might have been rape. As freshmen, they were newbies, ready to party but with nowhere to go. No invitations to cool off-campus parties or upperclassmen's tiki-torch-lit backyards. The invitations for freshmen during orientation, and for weeks after, are only from the frats. So you go, decked out in your high-school best — slinky pastel dress, high heels, push-up bra — and see where the night will take you.

Sociologists who study sexual assault call the beginning of freshman year the red zone — the riskiest period of a college woman's life. She'll be at a strange frat or a new dormitory, or she'll be hanging out with a guy she wouldn't invite to her room if she already had a strong clique, or she'll be getting stinking drunk, possibly because she's had little drinking experience in the past. Jessie Ford, the New York University doctoral student working under the aegis of Paula England, says studies show an unaffiliated female freshman (such as a student before she enters a sorority) is the most at risk for assault.

United Educators, America's largest collegiate insurance company, puts out a report to their university clientele to help them better address risk populations. It has some interesting data on this point. In their analysis of two years of sexual assault claims across the United States, 73 percent of victims were freshmen or sophomores, and 88 percent of gang-rape victims were freshmen. A stunning number of claims were party rape or, more specifically, rapes that happened after the victim and perpetrator attended the same off-campus gathering and then together headed back to a residence, where the sexual assault occurred.

There might even be data specifically supporting danger for young women in the first year of college at Syracuse, or possibly at a university nearby. In 2015, Kate Carey, a Brown University professor of behavioral and social sciences who'd previously taught at Syracuse, published a survey about the sexual assault experiences of 483 freshman women, 26 percent of the class at a "private university in upstate New York." I whipped out a calculator. If 483 women is 26 percent of the freshman class in Syracuse's approximately 15,000 undergrads, and Syracuse is 55 percent female and 45 percent male, that's, well, right on target. (When I e-mailed Carey to confirm my suspicions, she declined to comment.)

Wherever this institution is, her results are shocking. One in six freshman women surveyed was a victim of either rape or attempted rape, often while she was heavily intoxicated or "incapacitated" from drugs and alcohol, *by the end of freshman year.* That's one in six freshmen who checked yes for one or more of the following three parameters.

1. Has anyone threatened to physically harm you or someone close to you in order to . . .
2. Has anyone ever used physical force (such as holding you down) in order to . . .
3. [Did anyone ever], when you were incapacitated (e.g., by drugs or alcohol) and unable to object or consent . . .
    A. . . . try to have sexual intercourse with you (but it did not happen) when you indicated that you didn't want to?
    B. Succeed in making you have sexual intercourse when you indicated that you didn't want to?
    C. Make you do oral sex or have it done to you when you indicated that you didn't want to?
    D. Make you have anal sex or penetrate you with a finger or objects when you indicated you didn't want to?

I don't find anything other than the syntax unclear in these questions. Still, I mention the criteria in Carey's study for a specific reason. As in all studies of sexual assault, her study doesn't ask if someone is a victim, only if she has been subjected to the behaviors above, behaviors that meet the definition of rape and sexual assault. Usually, about half the women who meet these criteria will say no if asked whether they have been assaulted. Some proportion of these women will also say that they didn't feel the experience was a serious one. They just woke up half naked and didn't remember anything beyond doing keg stands to Taylor Swift songs. They don't know quite what to call it.

3

A Boy's Life

Today is the era of the playful player. By that term I mean to include guys who have physical prowess, good game with girls, and an arrogant attitude toward women that falls short of overt misogyny. Their idols are sports stars like Tom Brady and Cam Newton, with their cavalier attitudes and gorgeous wives or girlfriends. Delivering Justin Bieber from his post-child-star crisis—he adopted a monkey as a pet and then left him at an airport, chucked eggs at a neighbor's house, performed all manner of misdeeds in a white Lamborghini—has meant transforming him into a worked-out hunk too. Crossing this Rubicon, Bieber swaggered (from which the colloquialism *swag* is derived) his way to becoming a double-sleeve-tattooed thug, a gold-chain-bedecked hood able to sell Calvin Klein tighty-whities like Marky Mark, even if someone did leak alleged before-and-after-Photoshop photos of his bulge.

The rock band is over for now; few Americans care about the feelings of a foursome of dapper dudes. The number of solo male pop stars can be counted on one hand, with men mostly scripted as young good old boys, singing pickup-truck country music or house, or electronic DJs, laying out throbbing beats; they're all party, no emotion. If they want to express deepish feelings in mainstream radio hits, it must be as part of a duo (the Chainsmokers, Twenty-One Pilots). Big-budget films haven't produced a major leading man in a decade, preferring to rely on interchangeable handsome actors like Chris Evans and Chris Pratt and comic-book adaptations from *The Avengers* to *Batman v. Superman*. Young actors who threaten to be interesting—Shia LaBeouf, Miles Teller, Joaquin Phoenix—seem to go nuts with varying degrees of artistic intentionality.

These are not Brando, McQueen, Dean; they do not embody boys' hopes and dreams. College guys are much more enticed by the icons of comedy, particularly this moment's regime of the ripped, the two poles of which are Zac Efron and his six-pack and Dwayne "the Rock" Johnson and his billion-pack, both of whom are *also* excellent at sending up the kitsch value of their own extreme bodies.

"I think the James Dean era is over," a lacrosse player who transferred to Syracuse from the University of Alabama tells me. "It's no longer enough to look the mysterious, quiet role of the stoic male. My favorite male stars, and I think a lot of my friends would agree, are the ones who *parody* the traditional, dated values of masculinity. There's a certain awareness Efron, Johnson, Paul Rudd, and Chris Hemsworth can pull off that says: 'I'm intelligent. I know things have changed, are changing, and *should* continue to change.'" He adds, "The stars I respect are the ones that play on vestigial values of manhood, like Efron mocking his own physique and Charlie Day playing the role of the bumbling anti-male."

Being a playful player is a way of coping with the changing cultural script provided to young American men, now asked to be both sensitive and strong, as well as a subtle way of maintaining power; you can't mock your own masculinity if you're not supremely confident in it, after all. It's arguably more difficult than the old-fashioned version of maleness, and so perhaps it's unsurprising that some young men have retreated, angrily, from these new norms. Where do they go? To the deep-ironic, nihilistic humor of culture's other major offering for young men — adult cartoons like *Robot Chicken* on Adult Swim, an entire network devoted to male-centric animated shows, and online bulletin boards like 4chan and the Reddit-sphere, both of which could be said to have birthed the millennial alt-right (but more on this later).

The hook-heavy Spotify list booming out of most of the dorms and parties I attended was dominated not only by EDM but by a crop of post–Lil Wayne, post-2014-mainstream-fame rappers, some of whom may denigrate women but who generally follow Kanye West's emotive lead. At parties, kids are listening to Childish Gambino, the rap name of multiplatform cutie Donald Glover; the polymathic Chance the Rapper; Frank Ocean, who has come out as gay; dreamy Future, whose 2016 album is *Evol*, or *love* spelled backward; slurring, vulnerable Post Malone; even more slurry Young Thug, who likes to wear dresses on occasion; and one-eyed Fetty Wap, who rhymes love stories about the girl who is his trap queen, the two of them counting opiates and money side by side.

Then there's Drake, godfather to the family. Drake is the woke guy who is still dudely — seductive, horny, obsessive, scornful, lonely, working on getting huge muscles. A Canadian Jewish half-black guy who starred on *Degrassi: The Next Generation,* he knows exactly how to bring humor to the complexity of being a playful player, shuffling across the stage with moves that he might imagine are sexy but that come off as grandpa and telling girls that he respects them but then, somewhat cluelessly, asking them to move their thang "like you getting money for college / break it down like you're working for tuition at Howard!" He reminds me of the Syracuse guy hanging out at the Bid Day event, the one who wasn't quite so woke that he didn't eyeball a new crop of freshman girls but was self-aware enough to check his friend who called them "the talent." "Drake's not some pious guy saying, 'Oh, I support survivors,'" a Georgetown grad tells me. "You can see Drake aggressively going after a girl but also saying, 'Uh, is this okay?'"

Drake claims that women are the master race, yet he doesn't like it when they're not good girls or when they're "wearing less and going out more," as he puts it. Lips on the mike, he testifies about subjects on men's minds. He simultaneously is intimidated by women and needs to dominate them. "Why do I want an independent woman to feel like she needs me?" he asks poignantly.

"I Love College"

American culture provides a sketch of appropriate sexual conduct for today's young women — be perfect and sexy at all times, particularly in Instagram photos, while also hiding sexual desire, except when hammered and on the dance floor — and it's created similar rules for college boys. From the moment he's conscious to his high-school graduation, the average U.S. male has been fed a broadband message through every medium: sex is everything, and real men make sure they get as much as they can.

One more message: Get as much as you can in college, because it'll never be as good as it is then. As lackadaisical-voiced rapper Asher Roth puts it in his hit "I Love College," about the succession of keg parties, wet-T-shirt contests, and celebrated moronism: "I love women, man, I love college." In the song's video, Roth, who is wearing a copy of the sweatshirt John Belushi wore in *Animal House*, wakes up on a couch next to two sleeping beauties, then casts his mind back to the night before, an evening that included a student throwing a mattress off a second-floor porch, beer pong, chest bumps, pizza, a frog mascot humping a keg, someone shaving the head of a passed-out student, vomiting, hot girls finger-painting, two guys chugging gallons of milk, and random kissing that led to Roth's waking up to the two beauties.

"I Love College" was meant to be a joke, but college kids didn't take it that way, putting it in spring-break rotation. After all, it highlighted that culture's main appeal to the psyche of the eighteen-year-old male recently released from what one student calls the "cage" of high school and helicopter parents. When I discuss university life with a Southern Methodist University student, he lifts a fist and pumps it. "Fun! Good grades! Hot girls! Parties all the time! No problems! Eat lunch at seven p.m.!" He stabs a finger at his chest. "This is my schedule, my time — not my parents' time." A different male student, this one studying postmodernism, makes a similar point with more highfalutin language: "Sex is an activity that constitutes your public personhood . . . Sex makes you into an adult, collegiate subject. Less abstractly, it helps you fit in."

Our culture tells boys that all girls want to sleep with them. The girls themselves often don't feel the same way. Negotiating this misunderstanding is a complex process that frequently involves subtle and blatant displays of male power and domination, much of it manifest on Planet College: The playful player (who is a hair removed from the fuckboy, a similarly hookup-focused guy but one who is unfeeling and manipulative). A boy's need to make an independent woman feel like she needs him. The introduction of feminist radicals — who insist they don't need boys — into social circles. A remarkable generational frankness about sex and a refusal to be ashamed by having it — *and* little actual, IRL experience with sex. We've talked about all that. But I haven't mentioned the overtly sexual aspects of youth culture today: rave/EDM culture, which privileges bodies over brains, plus a childhood and adolescence with easy access to porn. This is the stuff at the bottom of the stew of newly fluid gender identities at Wesleyan and rigid hetero ones at Syracuse.

To begin unpacking this dense cultural baggage, let's start on yet another bone-chilling night at Syracuse, this time at the annual revue put on by Syracuse's Sigma Alpha Epsilon, with the wittingly or unwittingly hilarious name of *The Penis Monologues*. A collection of skits and parody songs on a phallic theme, it is, in title at least, an extremely left-handed homage to Ensler's *The Vagina Monologues*, those classic soliloquies that are roundly dismissed by some millennial feminists, who decry their blindness to transgender women. But that play gets no such critique at Syracuse. Students consider it outré and still find in it what it purports to offer: an exploration of cis-women's complex feelings about their own body parts.

To say the least, no such ambivalence appears in frat brothers' contemplation of the analogous male organ at this event. Held in the Gifford Auditorium, far smaller in size than the Syracuse theater that hosted Bid Day and usually the place for honors societies' induction ceremonies and overseas-job fairs, *The Penis Monologues* begin with the assembly of a dozen guys resembling network sitcom stars (a few of them as handsome as the Syracuse alum in the Chainsmokers). With dark, well-cut hair and black sweatshirts sporting a bright yellow ΣAE, they take the stage to fervent claps and high-pitched squeals from an audience of about sixty sorority sisters, few males. After all, what guys on campus will turn out in the cold to listen to other guys boast about their penises?

If *The Vagina Monologues* struggles with the awkward, shameful associations of its eponymous body part, tonight's monologues are by contrast Keatsian odes, loving, reverent paeans to what even Blackout Blonde would admit is, even more than girls, man's most treasured toy. These treasures are ideally *serviced* by girls, a discovery another brother recalls like a novitiate's epiphany: "Girls can do this for me? You've got to absolutely be kidding me. And holy shit, they can use their mouths too?"

Before tonight's show, I loaded videos of ΣAE's *Penis Monologues* performances from years past, like one where a brother crooned, "Baby, baby, baby, oh! Sigma Alpha Epsilon penises are so damn fine!" to the tune of Justin Bieber's "Baby." Over the years, the most popular standup bits have been on failings in the art of the hand job. Soberly, one man stood center stage and, like William Jennings Bryan, declared the three things no man should endure: "One, getting drafted for war; two, seeing his dog die; three, receiving a hand job by some girl pulling at your cock like she's in a tug-of-war championship."

Another ΣAE brother warned girls against inducing the (spurious) medical condition of "blue balls," which he described as "menstrual cramps inside your ball sack," a "true disaster to society," and a "serious tragedy." That this was a guilt-trip tactic used to pressure girls to bring guys to orgasm didn't seem to register with the crowd.

Some years they told some jokes at their own expense and showed a series of hand-drawn cartoons of their own penises one by one, like a PowerPoint presentation. One boy talked about the time a girl "laughed in my face and asked, 'Is your penis wearing Harry Potter's invisible cloak?'" Another shared a poem told from the point of view of a penis. The penis was conflicted about grinding, an awesome dance "that is quite frankly centered around me," but that left him trapped between denim and underwear, "subject to pounding."

This year, the best moment happens after two guys begin fiddling with a malfunctioning music system. "Turn that shit up," a brother catcalls. "Make it louder than the porn you play!" At last, speakers emit the swirling orchestral opening to the Grammy-winning "Let It Go," from *Frozen*, Disney's animated fairy tale about enchanted and braided princesses who save each other from black magic and lame guys, a powerful product in the new Disney regime of wokeness. In place of the epic chorus Idina Menzel propelled to the top of the charts and the toddler hit parade, this retasked "Let It Go," titled "Let It Grow," portrays a male's state of enthrallment, with rhyming lines such as "I'm going to puncture that ho" and "I'm about to blow."

This may be a good time to mention that *The Penis Monologues* is a benefit for Syracuse's rape-crisis center. That cause got a bit more stage time in previous years' performances, such as when two ΣAE brothers asked the crowd, "When both people are drunk, who thinks they can consent to sex?" They asked for a show of hands, chided those who raised theirs, and closed the topic: "Okay, that's about as educational as we're going to get."

Tonight's crew doesn't even get that educational. "Let It Grow" crashes to a hammy finish, accompanied by whoops and giggles throughout the hall. As the girls file out, they sing the retrofitted lyrics to Disney's soaring female-empowerment hit, their voices echoing through the auditorium. They sway and laugh, push through the exit doors, and head out into the cold night, on the way to the next party.

Privilege

A playful player isn't a man-child, that lovable nebbish who adores his bros and not his hos, popularized in last decade's films like *The Forty-Year-Old Virgin* and *Knocked Up*. His look is casual even if the big red earphones attached to his iPhone match the red swoosh of his Nikes and the tiny bit of red lining the inside of his black hoodie. Social media, buttressed by cultural gender norms, may be PCP for young women, leading them to shell out crazy amounts of money on contouring makeup, constantly check if their Snapchats are hot, and tie their looks and flirting skills to future earnings potential. They're financially independent from men but slaves to style (Zara sells a shirt playing off this, with the phrase CAN'T AFFORD TO BE PLAIN printed on its back). But guys have a different online reality.

Boys send fewer texts, take fewer pictures — "How you girls always manage to have your cameras on you is mind-blowing, everything is documented from every fucking angle, girls are the historians of one of the most depressing and disappointing generations ever," a Syracuse frat brother joked — and their tropes on social media and dating apps are not about pure hotness but rather their mastery of activities: dude hiking with his friends, dude about to jump from a cliff into the deep blue sea, and, of course, dude on date with a super-hot girl, to telegraph to girls who might be interested that other girls see him as dateable.

Even when the playful player wants to work on behalf of women — say, by organizing benefits for the rape-crisis center — he has to show he's a real man (that is, talk about his penis). Sex, and sexual culture, is the most visible of ways male privilege manifests. "There is no more gender equal institution in the United States today than the American college campus, and yet . . . [it] is also marked by dramatic gender inequality," Michael Kimmel, a Stony Brook University professor and author of *Guyland,* a seminal sociological study of this age group, said. "You may call it daytime and nighttime."

Power dynamics can be subtle, as they are with the playful player, or they can be explicit, and Kimmel is right that some at college, America's supposedly most egalitarian environment, are blaringly explicit. Guys buy the kegs. Guys have the drugs. Guys play the sports that students flock to see on weekends. Guys rent the frat houses, and don't think that when they have parties they're desperate to get a bunch of guys they don't know in. Some frats remind the brother manning the door to maintain a two-to-one ratio of girls to guys for the evening.

None of this has changed much in the past twenty years, even as the world around it has, and this has implications for sexual assault at universities. Scholars in this field say that hierarchies matter. "Rape takes place most often when there is social hierarchy — among men in prison, by men in marriage, by soldiers at war, by those who have enslaved another group, by adults who control children, and by those preying upon people with physical or mental disabilities," explains an essay. It's absolutely true — and absolutely absurd — that we could add the modern residential college to that list.

It's particularly absurd at a moment when so much of youth culture is based on ideas of sexual liberation. Today's college guy grew up with EDM culture, which is supposed to be a free-love culture, although a true free-love culture in America is as real as the unicorn; for all the rhetoric, the 1960s were choked with abusive relationships, sexual assault, and people being jealous and hurt. Beginning in 2010, commercialized rave culture — an update to the 1990s (when else?) uncommercialized rave culture — spread quickly through the country. Many kids in college today spent their formative years desperate to be part of this, splurging on tickets for the new spate of drug-filled free-loving raves rebranded as dance music festivals, fueled by the easy availability of Molly, a cheap drug that is supposed to be pure MDMA (old people call that Ecstasy). Molly, which usually comes as a white powder, combines the properties of stimulants and hallucinogens, but most of what's being passed around in folded envelopes today is weird science shipped here from labs in China, and it can be dangerous. A rave culture doesn't have any truck with danger, though — at least, not until someone is hauled off to the medical tent.

A rave culture, in theory, is the opposite of a rape culture; it's about PLUR, or "peace, love, unity, and respect." The main event is dancing, bonding, and camping in vast tent cities with your friends. For sizzurp-slurping guys, there's also the option of joining a crowd of shirtless dudes midway back from the stage slam-dancing to un-slam-danceable music. I'm not saying that people on Molly don't want to have sex — that would not be the correct description of the drug's biodynamic profile. But what happens at festivals is yet another culturally mediated problem between boys and girls, because boys often go to festivals expecting to hook up and, their minds appropriately tweaked, are disappointed when it doesn't happen, or they may push boundaries with that expectation in mind.

Then there's the excess of the ages: alcohol. Year after year, studies demonstrate that students' binge drinking — defined as five drinks in two hours for guys, and four drinks in two hours for women — is widespread and has risen particularly for women. Blackouts in college are common. In a 2002 study of drinkers at Duke University, over half of the students said they'd had at least one blackout. But what state of consciousness they augur and the responsibility each individual has — to himself and to others (unless they're blaming Jose Cuervo) — during this period is a question colleges wish to avoid.

Many universities today try to regulate alcohol. Syracuse does. A friend of mine who was a Sig Ep brother in the early 1990s tells me, chortling, about the one hundred and twenty kegs he and his brothers lined up outside the house for their annual Barbarian party. Today, kegs are banned in frat houses, and a third-party vendor has to pour drinks. Syracuse students who don't have wristbands — meaning that they're under twenty-one — aren't supposed to drink, but they do anyway. "We have a security guard called Ron, and when he comes to the door, everyone screams, 'Ron's here, drop your cup!' And we slap each other's cups out of the other person's hand," says Lianna, giggling. "It's not a real system. It doesn't make sense."

You can't be surprised that I'm talking about alcohol, even though a book about sexual assault isn't supposed to, but you may be surprised to hear that the federal government has an express rule not to provide a majority of grants to sexual-assault programs that focus primarily on alcohol. The hesitation to link drinking with sexual assault makes sense. No one wants to blame drunk victims for assaults. But it's impossible to talk honestly about the situation without acknowledging the issue.

"Over and over, young men and women knock back drinks together only to find themselves on the slurry side of an evening with very different ideas about how things should end," explained Sarah Hepola, author of *Blackout*, a memoir about her young adulthood as a drinker, in an excellent *Texas Monthly* essay about campus assault. While Hepola was reporting her story, the fact that universities didn't want to talk about sex and sexual assault while students were drunk upset her. "I felt frustrated that the larger conversation didn't include more nuance and complexity about alcohol: how it changes us, lowers our inhibitions, warps what we remember, torques what we will say and do," she wrote. "It's true that consent is golden. But what if you drink your consent away?" Later in the essay, she put a finer point on this comment. "The reason I liked getting drunk was because it altered my consent: it changed what I would say yes to."

For a young person exploring freedom, sexual and otherwise, this can be thrilling — until it isn't, of course.

Porn

PLUR is a strange part of the gender norms that a college man must navigate today, and it might have given some of them the idea that women are more sexually available than those women mean to be. It also exists alongside binge drinking (mind off) and old-fashioned male competitiveness (mind on). Even if there's a lot less sex going on at college than boys would have us believe — the relationship with the hand seems the central one — it's important that other boys view them as confident swordsmen. Girls' bodies are often the prize in rivalries between guys, either unofficially — sizing up who's the biggest player on the dorm floor, who has more pictures of himself with girls on his Instagram page — or officially, like minor fraternity pledge tasks that require boys to "get nudes" to qualify for the brotherhood.

At the University of California at San Diego, a ΣAE brother was told to wheedle a girl into e-mailing him topless pictures with Greek letters written in marker across her chest, but things went spectacularly wrong. "Rachel!!! I need your help," Spenser Cornett wrote to the girl. "Lol funny story, so I'm in a frat now and we have to get 'rush boobs' if you or any of your friends can help me out I would really appreciate it," he continued. "I don't need faces just topless pics with 'Rush ΣAE' written on their chests."

Unfortunately for Cornett, Rachel proved a poor choice for his campaign. She may have been one of the college women influenced by Sulkowicz and her peers, and his text to her soon made its way to local news organizations. Suspended from his now-humiliated chapter, Cornett protested that he had a reason for reaching out to Rachel, whom he knew had marched topless a year earlier in a Free the Nipple protest of state regulations of women's bare chests; he'd merely failed to discern the difference between that public semi-nudity and the one he'd been obliged to seek. To women, the ideological underpinnings of such third-wave acts of protest are obvious. To some young men, the only obvious things are nipples.

Cornett's mistake may be one of the world's most boneheaded flubs, but he's not wrong that women's bodies are presented for consumption more today than ever before, and it's easy for boys to skip over the feminist justifications for it. Modern culture has been fully pornified, and people's understanding of sex appeal has changed with it. Instead of subtle flirtations, sex appeal now involves enhanced body parts, skimpy clothing, and overt come-ons. Some Kardashians have waxed each other's private parts on camera, and the middle sister, Khloé, has named her camel toe Camille the Camel. *Seventeen* magazine, which is read by twelve-year-olds, has featured a cover story on Iggy Azalea talking about her new boob job and how confident it makes her feel. The current emphasis on butts in pop culture and fashion—I recently received an e-mail about a new brand of yoga pants sold with instructions about how to take an appealing "butt selfie"; for example, "give a little tricep flex LOL"—doesn't mean that breasts are no longer sexualized, only that more body parts are sexual hot zones. The pink eye shadow that became ubiquitous in spring 2017 looked to me like vagina eyes.

As anyone who has turned on a computer in the past decade knows, porn's content has also changed considerably. We're light years from the early 2000s Jenna Jameson world, where porn stars "start slow, baby, and make them pay you more for each thing you do," as she told me on her back patio in Scottsdale, Arizona, when I interviewed her in 2004 (I was primarily a pop-culture reporter then, and porn was part of the beat). Over a decade, Jameson shot fewer than fifty films, recutting old video into new DVDs and pocketing checks. She controlled the kind of sex she had and never had anal sex on camera. "I look at these new girls today, taking on six guys and doing bukkakes, and I think, what the hell are they doing?'" she said, stubbing out a cigarette. "In my day you hardly had to have sex, let alone two dicks up your ass."

Jameson was an innocent. But the influence of today's porn on collegiate sex lives—and, possibly, on sexual assault—cannot be underestimated. A British study of college students found that 60 percent considered porn akin to an instruction manual for sex. In a 2015 *Harvard Crimson* survey of 760 graduating seniors, 45 percent of male students said they watched porn multiple times a week while in college. "It's amusing, for me, now that I've had a girlfriend, that I know what *really* happens when a girl gets semen on her face—she's like, 'You dick!' and then I'm running around looking for a towel," a Syracuse ΣAE brother said at *The Penis Monologues.* Another brother said, "It is simply impossible to sit at a computer writing a final paper or drafting a study and not stop every paragraph to whack it . . . I'm sure our inability to keep our pistols holstered is why we score lower on exams than girls."

It's not common to walk into a frat house and find house members sitting with their female guests before a plasma TV screening porn, but guys don't hide their usage either. "Girls in my sorority don't sext pictures of ourselves to guys, because we know that those pictures will get around frats way too quickly—that was more of a thing in high school, before we were older and wiser," a sorority sister tells me. Her friend adds, "But when I go to my boyfriend's house, it's not weird to see a guy or two watching porn."

Another recent female grad from Georgetown talks to me about her complex relationship with porn. When she was younger, she spied on her dad using it, a habit of his she found disturbing and processed as his cheating on her mom. Would it break up their marriage? She was genuinely frightened. In college, she started watching porn herself, and she consumes it once a month or so now. "I don't feel negatively about hardcore porn, and I like the idea of legalized and empowered sex work, but . . . it does feel to me that in porn the more it feels like you're doing something to her that she might not want what's done to her; *that's* what's arousing," she says. "It's 'You're going to be anally fucked or shove my cock in your mouth and choke on it,' plus not having a consensual conversation. And that's how guys are assuming sex should go."

I tell her that I've started to think that young women today are expected to have sex in a way that previous generations weren't. The data sets showing that they're giving more blowjobs and engaging in more anal sex are evidence not only that intercourse is less important, but that acts that aren't exactly the ne plus ultra of feminine pleasure have been prioritized. Do you feel that way about your personal experience? I ask. "I know the way that I interact with sex has a lot to do with what I've seen done," she says, nodding. "I like enacting those things — making men happy, making them feel like they're in a porno. It's problematic, but it's what turns me on. This is how I've grown up . . . How many women's first sexual experience today is giving a blowjob? 'He wanted a blowjob, so I gave him a blowjob.' Did you want to? Did it give you pleasure? Probably not, but you wanted him to be satisfied and happy."

Handing over the reins in sex, letting a guy do what he wants to her, and "hearing his pleasure" when she does is also a self-esteem boost. "In the moment, it's 'This guy thinks I'm hot, this guy thinks I'm special,' because the attention that a man gives you when he wants to have sex with you is the most singular and focused you can get him to be on you. Sort of like your wedding day." An odd comparison, but everyone knows it feels good to be wanted. She adds, "Lusting and objectifying you in a way for sexual pleasure — I've been raised to know this is my source of power. So maybe all sex is about power."

Once hotly debated in feminist circles, pornography is a dead issue now. There are only a few anti-porn voices in the wilderness, like comedian Tina Fey, who said in a *Saturday Night Live* skit about *Playboy* models: "These women aren't doing it for the money — they're doing it because they were molested by a family friend." Young Mormons in Salt Lake City have created a thriving Porn Kills Love movement that has gathered admirers like Elizabeth Smart and bad-boy-gone-straight Russell Brand. That's about it. When I ask a radical feminist Wesleyan student about her feelings on porn, she whispers, "No, no, I don't think it's good at all." She puts a finger to her mouth, and says, "Shh. You're not supposed to say you feel that way."

Henry

My views on porn — that it might have links to sexual assault — weren't shared by students I interviewed. When I ask Henry,* a redheaded student from Vermont majoring in philosophy, about it, he e-mails back an answer quickly. "I know how I'm supposed to answer this question," he declares. "I'm supposed to explain the egregious implications of pornography, or how watching such material inspired erroneous sexual expectations or unhealthy perceptions of femininity and masculinity, and how I'm a worse person for having engaged in such content—that it is vile, or dirty, or whatever." (This interview, along with some others with male students, was conducted via e-mail, though we met in person afterward. I found that boys were more comfortable confessing genuine thoughts this way, though the reverse was true of girls.)

This is obviously not what Henry wanted to say. I told him to speak his mind. He talks about going to a Catholic high school. He didn't watch porn until college, not only because he was afraid of getting caught but because he'd been taught it was a sin. That meant it would evoke shame along with feelings of baseness and reprehensibility. His teachers taught him abstinence; they told him condoms broke almost all the time, and women could get pregnant three weeks out of the month. "Sex was basically analogous to playing a game of Russian roulette, 'you have five bullets and you're bound to lose,'" he says of his Catholic education. "That's not only not how a pregnancy works. It isn't even how you play Russian roulette."

Henry looks like a gym rat, but he's the most serious student I interviewed, weaving class texts into conversation (Hannah Arendt, Albert Camus, Zadie Smith). He has a heart-shaped face and amply worked-out pecs that peek out from sleeves of his V-neck T-shirt, and he likes to play video games like Super Smash Brothers and NBA with his friends alongside other social activities like smoking and drinking. He's always been masculine in the traditional sense of the word. "I'm athletic, I'm competitive, I look like I belong in a fraternity, I tell my barber 'short on the side, long on the top'" is the way he sums up his look.

In high school, he wanted to become a cop. "Growing up, my brother and I were always treated as boys—in the traditional way: we were given weapon-like toys, we were read action books, we were enrolled in sports. And we behaved like boys—in the traditional way: we wanted to see violent movies, we played aggressively, we enacted war games." During the invasion of Iraq, the most recent one, they traced and cut out cardboard M-16s, put on life vests and helmets, and pretended to be soldiers. "But we also did other activities during childhood: we took art classes, we had gymnastics lessons, we worked on our handwriting in little booklets," he says. "Had one of us preferred cooking toys over dump trucks, I'm sure our parents would have allowed us the less-boy-like experience." Though gender roles weren't forced on Henry, as he grew, he took them on himself. "I wanted to be bigger and stronger than other kids," he explains. "I wanted to beat them at games. I wanted to be seen as tough and capable and emotionally consistent."

As he broke out of his high-school cloister, Henry says porn helped him develop a realistic depiction of sexuality. "I came to understand just how normative the practice was—and that, ironically, you were probably deviant if you weren't watching it," he states. He ticks off criticisms against the industry: "(1) Porn fails to convey reciprocity in sexual acts (it's from the male perspective and satisfies the male's desire, all we see is penetration from the beginning of the video, etc.). Answer: here are videos in which the entire shoot is foreplay; here are videos in which the woman's pleasure is the essential feature of the porn-watching experience. (2) Porn shows rough sex and pretends such behavior is always pleasurable . . . Answer: here are very slow, gentle representations of the sexual act—in fact, here are thousands of such examples. (3) Porn elicits a kind of sexual promiscuity that fails to incorporate the intimacy of human connection and love. Answer: here's an entire porn community in which couples post videos of themselves, replete with pillow talk and genuine affection." This is a counternarrative that does not get enough attention. "For every irresponsible porn video, there is a responsible one," he continues. "For every video of two people fucking, there is one of two people making love."

This is not a completely fair assessment of what the average porn consumer is watching—*teen* is the number-one search term in porn, not *genuine affection*—but Henry's right that in the current porn climate, everyone can find whatever's to his or her liking. He likes silly porn, he tells me. "I've seen extended commentary below a video discussing the football game playing in the background as a couple has sex—the football game!" he declares. "I've seen a discussion on the best way to make waffles beneath a video depicting some kitchen fantasy. The mainstream porn community is not as serious as one might be led to believe." He continues, "I think this kind of transparency, and humor and irony, is in fact very healthy. And much needed. It has certainly allowed me to loosen up and find within sexuality something more natural and enjoyable."

Ideology Over Biology

Henry told me he had engaged in conversations on campus about the nature of sexual consent, and when I asked him what the difference was between sexual assault and a bad sexual experience — the line that Blackout Blonde and the others from Syracuse hadn't explored — he gave one of his typically cogent, if long-winded, answers. He began by explaining that he never has one-night stands because the true desire of his partner is usually unknowable.

"Maybe she's putting herself in this situation where control is taken from her — by alcohol, by the pressure of her friends to get out and forget the boyfriend who just dumped her," he says. "Besides, I take sexual activity to be a more intimate expression of affection (I guess not all was lost from Catholic school) and one I would have to actually care about my partner to engage in. And so I'll always let her initiate when she's ready."

What's sexual assault and what's bad sex, then? I ask. Henry gives me the current university and feminist interpretation, which is a good one. "Sexual assault is when sexual activity is not in accordance with vocalized expectations, and is not initiated by both parties in a consensual manner, and is a decision made while not lucid and uncoerced by external pressures," he explains. "Bad sex is the opposite of the above, but where pleasure is not satisfactorily fulfilled. I think this is a pretty clear line — between not wanting it, and wanting it but not being satisfied."

I've spent a fair amount of time in this chapter convincing you that today's college man is not a stock villain. He's dealing with cultural pressures that are almost as harmful as the ones girls are dealing with; they may be more pervasive, and they're certainly less flexible. At Vanderbilt, a poster bringing attention to these narrow choices sums up the message to guys at the school: DON'T CRY, HAVE SEX, MAJOR IN BUSINESS, PLAY SPORTS, MAN UP.

This is a partial explanation, if not an excuse, for the wide streak of cruel misogyny on campuses, the chatter about "puncturing hoes." Here are a few jokes allegedly overheard at the Stanford chapter of Sigma Alpha Epsilon's Roman bath party: "What do you tell a woman with two black eyes? Nothing, you've already told her twice." "What do you call the useless skin around a vagina? A woman." "What do a woman's orgasm and her opinion have in common? No one cares about either."

Most "jokes" on campus are more benign, but still, guys find them funny, and girls—and their parents—just don't. During freshman orientation, spray-painted banners drape the fronts of frat houses: HOPE YOUR BABY GIRL IS READY FOR A GOOD TIME (Old Dominion University); 21 TO DRINK, 18ISH TO SLEEPOVER (Ohio University). And this gem: SHE CALLED YOU DADDY FOR 18 YRS, NOW IT'S OUR TURN (West Virginia University). And of course, the anxiety that underlies these jokes—about being unable to control sexual urges—is real. In studies, young men answer yes to "I think about sex more than I would like" and "I must fight to keep my sexual thoughts and behavior under control" more often than women do.

Yet we know from science that some women can feel the same amount of desire as men, even if women tend to feel desire after they become physically aroused, whereas men feel desire beforehand. So there's a difference here: the readiness for sex. But we're animals who sit at laptops and fly to far-flung lands in aluminum cans; we've socialized our natures, and I don't have too much sympathy for the multiple college guys who emphasized their *need* to have sex, or at least to ejaculate (the blue balls again). A Cornell grad told me about how a girl he'd slept with once who'd asked if she could take erotic photos of him with her friend for a photography class. He showed up at the dorm thinking he might even have sex with both girls, but she took some black-and-white photos of them naked and then announced that the session was over. "I did these pictures for that girl and then I even didn't get off," he complained. "I was so mad that I snatched the camera and ran off with it."

A silly move on his part, but excusable. Some episodes aren't. I'll share a brief version of what I heard when I went to talk to college guys late at night, something I did not enjoy doing but felt was necessary. Here's the consent conversation at two a.m. at a dive bar with several bros, clad in sweatshirts in various shades of blue, who'd had a few drinks too many.

They noticed, first, that I had olive-colored skin. "Is it true that, for the white man, the more liquid exchange he has with dark women, the darker skin he gets?" one slurred. This gathered some hearty laughs.

I began to ask about consent. Is consent like a vampire, "I've invited you to my room," or does sex require explicit permission?

"Last night I should've gone to jail!" was the first thing one of them said. (Guys made this joke a lot when I asked about consent.) When asked for clarification, he laughed. "Oh, you know, just booty-grinding on the dance floor," he said, then winked. "Everybody does it."

When I approached knots of guys during the day, they usually made earnest stabs at defining consent. A University of Texas at Austin student kept up a running monologue for ten minutes professing his bona fides: "I always stop when I hear no," "I ask what she wants," and "My mom brought me up well." But that night, three sheets to the wind, these men delivered, perhaps, more honest answers. Women *want* nonconsensual sex, they explained. "I, like every male, feel that a woman is very happy when she has sex in a gray-zone way," said blue sweatshirt number two.

"What's a 'gray-zone way'?" I asked.

"Well, when a girl says yes when you ask her to come over, that's the permit. *She came over, I'm going to fuck the shit out of her.* And the girl is still thinking, *Maybe I want to have sex, maybe I don't.* But the male system is like a water system. You open a valve, water's going to spread everywhere!"

"Come on, that is not true," I said. "And even if it was, if she doesn't want to have sex, you can go to the bathroom and jerk off."

"Noooo," they declared, almost in a chorus. Number two, in particular, became agitated. "You can't, because the girl already started it! So she says you can lick here and lick here, but you can't put it in? I mean, come on!"

"You know you're describing rape right now," I said.

He shrugged and said something that was meant to be ironic, or at least jokey, though it didn't quite come off that way. "Bitch, I'm going to slit your throat," he said, then he pointed to the dirty floor. "Lay down and spread your legs. I'm going to pour hot metal in your vagina."

At this, I took a step back, collected my belongings, and walked quickly out of the bar. At Wesleyan, boys told me they completely understood what their classmates were going on about in terms of sexual assault. "You won't find anyone on this campus who isn't pro-survivor," one of them told me. Another one even offered the example of castration anxiety to explain how women's rape fantasies are probably not real, since men don't want their penises cut off but dream about it anyway. Henry told me he knew the line too.

Now, horrified, I wasn't sure what to think. On the street, I dialed my husband on my cell phone and told him what happened. "That guy is obviously sick in the head," he said. "No one has that little humanity." Later, I told a female friend about it. "Yeah, of course," she said. "That's what guys want to say but will only say when drunk."

You don't need a PhD in the philosophy of rape to know that this spectrum of comments are evidence that cultural gender norms about boys and girls are at the heart of sexual assault. Male sexual assertiveness in college isn't all biological — boys will be boys — but learned behavior, a reaction to context. And the most important cultural change that's happened in the past decade is girls have gotten more power, better grades, and so forth. What if it's not a coincidence that BJs have gotten so popular in middle and high school? What if it's not Bill Clinton and Monica Lewinsky's fault but a way men try to keep control of women, at least in the bedroom? Sexual assault, even though it has been around for quite a while, could be interpreted as a compensatory backlash to the prevailing cultural norms of the day. This is one area that, despite the work of feminists, seems to be staying tipped toward men. Guys might be asserting themselves in the bedroom because they can't in other places.

The bottom line is that gender norms, enhanced by putting boys in charge of social life at college, create the playful player, or much worse.

Let's Be Acquaintances

College in America is a cherished secular space, unlike anywhere else in the world, where most students live with their parents and go to school for a career, not a party. It's a place for students to try on new selves — personal, intellectual, political, sexual. In the past couple of decades, echoing the cultural explosions of the 1960s, the university has taken on utopian overtones, a community where the adult world is continually reimagined as what it could — or should — be. But utopia means something different to all these students. To some, it's a place to go crazy; for others, it's a place to develop a solidarity-forming, illusion-shattering political life. To still others, it's a place for mastering a sport, for finding a career and achieving academic enlightenment, or for perusing the campus-wide drug bazaar. But they've all been taught by a shared American culture that, whatever else it is, it's a place to get laid as often as humanly possible.

Yes, colleges are cliquey institutions, but there are still many more chances for mixing socially with an assortment of people you don't know here than anywhere else in America, a country of socioeconomic silos and suburban cul-de-sacs. College kids are joiners, generally; they love clubs and events (and not being alone). Most campuses now offer easily two to three times as many social and cultural offerings as they did in my day. Participation in athletics and extracurricular clubs are way up. Today's students have been marinated in the notion that downtime is an evil since they were kids, and now they themselves have banished slacking from college life.

Let's think about the concept of the in-network stranger for a moment, and the way it relates to millennial culture, not only in college but in social media. Social media, after all, *is* an acquaintance culture — a culture in which strangers are converted into acquaintances. Through it, one is constantly in touch with ex-teammates of one's last boyfriend, the kids who sat behind you in homeroom in high school, a friend's buddy from out of town whom you met tailgating at a game. Social media has not only changed the way college kids relate to old friends — they now feel fairly close with those they haven't actually spoken to in years — but also exponentially widened their social circles. "Millennials have the power of acquaintances, not friends," says Gary Vaynerchuk, the digital advertising entrepreneur and social media analyst. "Everybody still has six or eight friends. But the millennial generation is able to maintain and hold on to dramatically more acquaintances, and that's powerful. It's a big deal. And it's a permanent shift."

This is America's largest generation, and the most racially diverse. The average millennial has attended or attends a four-year college for which he or she carries, or will carry, thirty thousand dollars in debt. They want to get married, but not until shockingly late (thirty years old); they want to live close to family and friends instead of flinging themselves to outposts around the country; and they don't identify with a political party. They want to be famous. They already feel famous, with their friends on social media applauding every step they take.

Past this, op-ed takes on millennials stride in two different directions: to some, they're the next greatest generation of do-gooders, with studies showing they're committed to donating their time and money to causes they care about; to others, they're enslaved techno-narcissists destined to live in their mothers' basements for the remainder of their days, their greatest satisfaction coming from making their cell phones, those handheld robots, spit out what their friends are saying about them. "This generation loves and cares about their phones more than they care about their cars," Tony Conrad, the Boomer Silicon Valley investor and founder of about.me, told me. "Do you know how crazy that is for my generation to comprehend?"

These trends sound contradictory, but they go hand in hand. Growing up glued to the Internet — or, for young millennials, the cusp group featured in this book, almost exclusively to their phones — hasn't made millennials antisocial, though it's clearly made them a certain kind of narcissist, meaning that the concerns of the individual and what others think of that individual are very much front and center; we could dub them "Generation Like Me." At the same time, tunneling through the web's magical portal to encounter different kinds of people and ways of looking at the world has, perhaps, made them more empathetic, able to relate to the marginalized and downtrodden in society. This doesn't mean that they'll lead society to a new golden age, and it should be noted that when it comes to traditional forms of civic engagement, like voting, millennials still lag behind.

What it does mean, though, is that they have a front-row seat to acquaintances going through transitional periods — changing gender identities, sexualities, posting on Facebook about experiencing a rape — which is part of why they take social issues from transphobia to rape seriously. They've all had an acquaintance or two or more who have gone through these experiences, and they've issued their Likes, beaming them across the digital airspace like a protective veil of love.

But it's possible that social media's insertion of more acquaintances into their lives has implications for their risk of sexual assault as well. If you're comfortable sharing your life online with acquaintances, then you might not have your guard up when you're at a party and a guy whom you "met" on Facebook or in bio class asks you to go back to his apartment with him to get the beer he has stored there. It might mean that you accept a ride back to campus from a student you run into at the lake and then accept his invitation to go upstairs when you get to his off-campus apartment.

Although the twenty-one thousand Syracuse students creating a temporary community in this snowy college town were described by a Kappa

Alpha Theta sorority sister as not "real strangers," they are strangers, or acquaintances, particularly in the red zone. The fact that universities themselves encourage their students to mix with new people — usually with much alcohol involved — has vast implications for college sex, both consensual and not.

Part II

NONCONSENSUAL

Interlude 1

Pallas Athena

On a stormy day in late October, two months after the intimate rally of a few dozen Columbia students I attended on that bluebird September day, several hundred of Sulkowicz's classmates protested against sexual violence at the school. This was perhaps the biggest campus rally of its kind in our era, beginning on New York's Broadway, a multilane street full of urban hubbub. A strange sight met passersby: not one mattress, not two mattresses, but twenty-eight mattresses, meant to represent the twenty-eight students who had recently come forward to complain about Columbia to the federal government. On the top of each mattress, students had formed the names of various campus groups here today in support: the justice-for-Palestine kids, the Queer Army, the school swing club, the King's Crown Shakespeare Troupe, which also used the occasion to advertise its upcoming performances of *Titus Andronicus*.

Backpacks bulging, ballet flats and Converse sneakers slapping on the wet pavement, the students lifted the twenty-eight mattresses over their heads. Then they paraded across Broadway, passing satellite trucks, and wound their way to the long, wide granite steps of Low Library, the grand building where the first rally had taken place. They gathered around what has long been Columbia's symbol, *Alma Mater*, an enormous bronze sculpture of Athena, the Greek goddess of wisdom. Wearing academic robes, she holds in her right hand a scepter made of four sheaves of wheat topped by a tiny version of the original crown of King's College. Her left hand is outstretched, welcoming new freshmen. A tiny owl is hidden in the folds of her skirt, a symbol of how difficult knowledge can be to find.

This four-ton, eight-foot-tall mother soul is the focal point of Columbia's sprawling campus, though the concept of alma mater began with the first

Western university in 1088, which took *Alma mater studiorum*, or "Nourishing mother of studies," as its motto. It's been here since 1903, when the university commissioned it from Daniel Chester French, the artist behind John Harvard's statue at Harvard University and the Emancipator at the Lincoln Memorial in DC. Students love to screw with it: In 1970, as antiwar protests convulsed universities across the nation, especially Columbia, a bomb exploded under her throne; in the 1980s, Cornell students ran away with her scepter. And these contemporary students transformed her into a piece of powerful agitprop vandalism. At most of their anti-sexual-assault rallies, they scrambled up her side, climbed into her enormous lap, and fixed a strip of red tape to her lips.

Nourishing mother of studies? No to that. The worldview that includes women giving succor to ascending young sons isn't one to which today's students subscribe. Gagged *Alma Mater* symbolized the silencing of rape victims through millennia, from Greek myth's Tereus cutting out Philomela's tongue after he raped her to the university silencing Sulkowicz. I thought it might also represent the desire to silence the university itself, an announcement that it was the students' turn to speak.

Taking a position in front of Athena, student leader Zoe Ridolfi-Starr—an enthusiastic and experienced political organizer who was brought up by two moms who co-founded the Northern California Innocence Project and who calls herself a "second-generation queer woman"—began to heat up the crowd. "Mama, Mama, can't you see / what Columbia has done to me. / Rape culture is all around. / There's no safety to be found!" chanted the students. Raising the pitch higher, she introduced Sulkowicz: "Our amazing, the fearless, the powerful, the strong, brave, courageous leader!"

Calm, charismatic, smiling solemnly, Sulkowicz standing in front of *Alma Mater* looked to me like a sculpture standing in front of a sculpture. She was a star now, not only an obsession for mainstream news and the center of a "bizarre cult of personality," as she put it, but also a new arrival to the art world's highest tier, and this before a single solo show. She won the number-one slot in *New York* magazine's art critic Jerry Saltz's annual compilation of the best art in the city; he praised her performance as "clear, to the point, insistent, adamant . . . pure radical vulnerability." The *New York Times'* Roberta Smith compared the project to performing the Stations of the Cross and an "extra-heavy" version of Hester Prynne's scarlet letter. When performance-art giant Marina Abramović spoke of her, she sounded more like a fan than a peer, telling a reporter, "I really want to meet her . . . Many people don't have the willpower to stick to something no matter what, and that's what she's doing." Her project was genius, but still, it started to get a little over the top.

As the crowd erupted in cheers, Sulkowicz pulled down her windbreaker's hood to reveal hair dyed dark purple. "Better with the hood off?" she joked, then she began reading from a piece of paper, becoming again the girl I'd first met — funny, precise, a perfectionist, not one to give a passionate off-the-cuff speech, though she departed from the script once: "My serial rapist is still on this campus! You know who I'm talking about — I don't need to say his name. If you Google-image-search *Emma Sulkowicz attacker*, his name is the first related search."

Another chant, this time Rodney King–era — "No justice, no peace!" — and then these hundreds of students set off through Columbia's campus in a long, straightish line, some carrying pieces of plastic that they struggle to throw over their mattresses in the rain. Like their predecessors taking part in '60s free-speech marches, they go from the university plaza to Columbia president Bollinger's elegant home in Morningside Heights. When they arrived, they dumped their twenty-eight mattresses on PrezBo's front lawn as one of them, following Martin Luther, tacked a manifesto to his elaborately carved front door.

A bright rainbow poked out of the horizon as I moved closer. Instead of ninety-five theses, there were ten here, mostly about administrative procedures but ending with a chief objective: Nungesser's retrial and, they hoped, immediate expulsion.

Today's rally was a show of raw power, a victory lap — not one mattress, but proliferating mattresses, and about a seventh of Columbia's undergraduates thinking, *Screw the rain, this is a cause I need to get out and support.*

But quietly, behind the scenes, Nungesser was plotting. He might have viewed these crowds of protesters as a mob carrying not cardboard signs, but torches and pitchforks. "They're practicing extralegal justice against Paul," said a friend solemnly. "They're shooting at him in the town square. This is the Ivy League as the Wild West."

4

Carnal Knowledge

*R*ape has been defined and redefined for centuries. Greeks portrayed it as heroic conquest, as in Zeus in the guise of a swan enveloping Leda. For Romans, it was a narrative pivot point in the history of their kings, particularly the rape of Lucretia, the virtuous wife of a Roman prince whose rape led to the formation of a new Roman republic. They called it *raptus*, derived from the Latin verb *rapere*, meaning to forcibly seize and carry off — it was kidnapping more than violation, women as the spoils of war.

According to *The Encyclopedia of Rape*, a comprehensive history edited by scholar Merril Smith, in Hammurabi's ancient code from 1780 BC, virgins who were raped were considered innocent while their offenders were executed; however, if a married woman was raped, she was considered an adulteress, and both she and her rapist were thrown in the river unless her husband bestowed mercy. In the Middle Ages, the rape of a virgin was a crime against a woman's family, because her virginity had to be protected in order for her to make a prosperous marriage. If a woman who claimed she was raped became pregnant, she was often considered a liar; a woman's orgasm was thought to be necessary to conceive, and she couldn't have had an orgasm if sex was forced on her.

Legal and linguistic shifts continued well into the twentieth century. In 1940 an American husband was still legally free to force himself on his wife, and some states retained this law into the 1990s. The FBI's definition of *rape*, formulated in 1927 — "carnal knowledge of a female forcibly and against her will" — did not waver.

Eighty-five years later, the definition shifted and finally began to include male and trans victims. Today, our law calls *rape* "penetration, no matter how slight, of the vagina or anus with any body part or object, or oral penetration by a sex organ of another person, without the consent of the victim." Reasons consent cannot be given include the use of force, the threat of force, or incapacitation. Though universities have messed with the definition of *incapacitation*, in criminal law, those who can't give consent are those who are unconscious due to drinking or drugs, asleep, physically or mentally disabled, or underage.

To qualify as *sexual assault*, an umbrella term that includes penetrative rape and nonpenetrative acts (the latter is, in law, sexual battery), definitions are much broader and can be far less carnal—basically, touching any sexual part of another person. The example of a guy grabbing my butt on the street in my neighborhood—the one I gave in this book's introduction—counts. But most people don't know this. Some people use *sexual assault* as a synonym for penetrative rape; some call anything that's not penetrative *groping*, not sexual assault.

Bringing common usage in line with the legal definition is an advance of the past few years. "Sexual assault is no longer about having a penis penetrate you—now it's about being frisked, being touched, saying no, and still having a guy aggressively put his body on you," Ariel Bershadskaya, a visual art and art history student, tells me in the café at Columbia's exquisitely renovated main library (cost: $110 million). Wearing a mod look of silver hoop earrings and severely pulled back hair, she tells me she adores the 1960s—she's even painted a picture of her idol, sex symbol Twiggy, directly on her Mac laptop, the apple glowing in the center of Twiggy's face—though she's talking about behavior that no one blinked an eye at back then. "The line has moved," she continues. "We know now that sexual assault doesn't mean that you were raped, doesn't mean genitals pushing together. Personally, for me, that's a change. Five years ago if a friend told me a guy groped her I wouldn't necessarily have called that sexual assault."

A wider scope of harm—like stalking and domestic sexual abuse, updated to the term *intimate partner violence* or *dating violence* to incorporate non-cohabitating partners—usually enters the discussion. Most of these behaviors, including assault and rape, are sexual violence, which is the term activists both young and old use to describe them. In fact, using *sexual assault* instead of *sexual violence* immediately defines the speaker as unaligned with the radical cause. I have chosen to focus only on sexual assault in this book, though I agree that *sexual violence* is a useful broader term.

Rape

I shouldn't pretend, though, that my ideas about assault fall entirely within the bounds of millennial feminist thought. I like that girls have expanded their zone of safety and redefined crude collegiate predation often enabled by massive amounts of alcohol. I also like that a smack on the butt, a grab and kiss, denigration, and subjection to coercive speech like "I can't feel anything with a condom on" and "just a couple strokes" is being taken seriously — much of it for the first time in history. Five years ago, I wouldn't have necessarily called some of this assault either. Even today, not everyone in America would agree.

Rape is a problem of definitions, and sexual standards have long been mutable. My mother's generation, coming of age in the 1970s, imagined that when a woman went to a man's apartment, she'd signaled her intent to have intercourse. Twenty years later, I thought I could walk out of that apartment without an obligatory kiss, but I would never have lain down on a mattress with someone with whom I didn't plan to hook up. Today, inviting someone into your bed is "cuddling," usually but not always sexual, and certainly does not have to lead to intercourse. A girl who invites a guy friend to sleep over in her bed with her and then wakes up in the middle of the night to find him groping her can report him for assault. This is rare, but it happens. Usually, he'll get suspended from school.

The types of college assault can be divided into four general categories. There's penetration — intercourse, oral sex, and fingering (so much fingering in college) — that involves a guy shoving someone up against the wall, or twisting an arm behind a back, or pushing a girl down on a bed. He rarely brandishes a gun or a knife or a makeshift weapon. We're talking about something similar to what St. Paul's boarding-school student Chessy Prout says Owen Labrie, a bespectacled, popular, Harvard-bound senior, did to her, that he overpowered her even as she was frantically pulling her underwear up to avoid escalating the encounter.

The next category, with exceptions, is largely particular to the college environment. That's "incapacitated rape," meaning sex that happens when the victim is unconscious. In United Educators' report for insured universities, sexual assault of a zonked-out college victim was more frequent than any other type of assault.

A loss of consciousness is the general standard for this category. But many schools have erred on the side of caution to include very drunk students in this group. This is a wild shift from the past, when no one thought much about very drunk sex. In 2005's *The Forty-Year-Old Virgin*, a strikingly gentle comedy of sex manners, Steve Carell's virgin is counseled by one of his amiably supportive work colleagues at a nightclub when the topic comes up. "You about to go run down some drunk chicks, all right?" the wingman advises. "And don't confuse that with tipsy . . . I want vomit in the hair, bruised-up knees. A broken heel is a plus." When Carell demurs, he says, "A tiger knows he's got to tackle a gazelle. There's a code written in his DNA . . . and believe it or not, in every man, there's a code written that says, 'Tackle drunk bitches.'"

The third bin is anything that doesn't involve penetration—for example, a grabbing of a boob or a butt—while the victim is simultaneously experiencing physical violence or the threat of violence or while he or she is unconscious. And the grabbing itself, "aggressively putting his body on you," of course can be force. Grinding on a girl on a dance floor without asking may or may not count.

The fourth is a case that doesn't explicitly involve force, the threat of force, or incapacitation, but it also doesn't involve consent. This is the vast middle ground and causes a lot of confusion. College students today may have engaged in the push-pull of high-school encounters, but they now understand that Robin Thicke is wrong—that *no* does not mean *yes*. Lines aren't so blurry these days that young women often pretend they don't want to have sex, believing that doing otherwise makes them seem like sluts. The usual contemporary scenario in this category involves a guy ignoring a girl's "Let's wait" and "I don't think so" until she gives up, whether because she panics and is afraid the situation will escalate to physical violence or, like Lianna, because she figures it's easier to have sex than a confrontation ("I didn't want to be rude" is a common sentiment).

I've also heard quite a few stories, despite the clean line that Henry described dividing sex and rape, that sound to me like . . . bad sex. The most typical one involves a guy who's there just to get off, whether that means not reading her body language to discern what she wants or forgoing post-coital cuddling to immediately pick up his phone and scroll through Snapchat, looking at all the other hot girls he knows. A bunch of girls talked about guys guiding their heads down to give them blowjobs while they were in the middle of foreplay; not great, but no one used to call it assault. And do any of us think that the norms of *The Penis Monologues* don't teach boys that prioritizing a guy's pleasure is the way a real man has sex? "Guys don't care about women in hookups," a recent Princeton grad tells me emphatically. "They know girls will continue to have unsatisfying sex and still go down the rabbit hole of 'Why doesn't he care?' 'Does he not like me?'"

She goes on to analyze Sulkowicz's saga in this context. "To me, Emma's story is about control and communication. She felt out of control: 'Why didn't he ask me [about anal sex], does that mean he doesn't really respect me?' Women don't have words to say what we want in that moment." This was an interesting take on Sulkowicz and Nungesser, and believe me, everyone on campus has a take. The truth is that female students largely believe Sulkowicz, and male students largely don't. "Oops, I slipped and put it in your ass, what's the big deal, we did it before" is the way a Duke grad characterizes Nungesser's actions to me. "Don't talk to me the next day. Don't invite me to your party. But now you want me thrown out of school?"

Beyond this, I must admit that some of the stories that I ran down for this book were, frankly, bizarre. An old girlfriend accusing an ex of assault began bringing tangentially related people to the attention of the university, claiming they were harassing her when it sounded like the other way around. A drunken hookup that took place after a girl puked into a wastebasket began with intercourse, which she agrees was consensual, and then, an hour later, another episode of intercourse, which she says was not. Another United Educators' study analyzing one thousand sexual-assault cases says that 21 percent of them involved a victim or aggressor with mental-health issues, defined as a personal or family history of suicide attempts, eating disorders, or trauma from sexual assaults in the past.

Stories were sometimes operatic, but when I looked into the circumstances of a case, the facts began to blow away. It strained credulity to imagine the sex wasn't consensual at the time; it seemed more likely that later one partner wished he or she hadn't had it. And with the new framework embraced by college students, it was easier for this behavior to be recalled as assault. In some cases, this made sense; in others, it did not.

Sometimes I felt like I had found myself on the set of a Bravo reality show. There was a small truth in each story, but so many layers of semi-truths and misperceptions, amplified by the reactions of one's friends and peers, were wrapped in that kernel, I couldn't tell fact from fiction. Never underestimate the collegiate gossip mill, which runs overtime where sexual assault is concerned.

Title IX

This decade's changes around the definition of sexual assault didn't simply happen on their own. They are due, in large part, to the work of a small group of students — heroines, if occasionally flawed heroines, with tactical minds and political nous. Part of their genius was overstating the case and conflating lesser slights with forcible rapes. Actually, they insisted, assault should not be placed on a spectrum. "It's all violence," one of them told me passionately. They were focused on one overarching goal: tipping the balance from believing boys to believing survivors.

The groundwork for this change was laid far before these young activists arrived at college. The essential shift that led to the current fervor about campus rape may owe little to parsing the meaning of sexual assault, but it does have a great deal to do with calling a college president a "perpetuating patriarch," as the curly-haired student at Wesleyan did, and with flamboyant activism of the kind devised to silence Columbia's *Alma Mater,* performed by 1970s forerunners of Sulkowicz and Ridolfi-Starr.

Betty Friedan, the suburban wife and author who in 1963 published *The Feminine Mystique,* a manifesto against housewifery, began second-wave feminism. She didn't talk about rape much back then, though in her 2006 autobiography, she elaborated on the violence she said was in her own marriage. By the end of the 1960s, radical women's speak-outs in New York City — similar to the early rally I attended at Columbia, with riveting and heartrending personal testimony — led feminists to reject the prevailing Freudian view of the time that rapists couldn't control their passionate urges. They recast rape as a crime of violence, not sex, and made it political. As Susan Brownmiller wrote in *Against Our Will*, a thrillingly comprehensive book about women's rapes through history published in 1975, rape was "nothing more or less than a conscious process of intimidation by which all men keep all women in a state of fear."

This group was successful on many fronts: they attacked the marital exception for rape, the law's corroboration requirement (that someone must corroborate a woman's story or she must have physical injuries that support her accusation), the resistance requirement (that she must have physically resisted), the notion that delayed reports are false, and the myth that most rapes involve black men attacking white women. America soon had rape shield laws, preventing (to varying degrees) portions of a woman's past sexual history from being presented at trial, and a new social service: rape-crisis centers, slowly established through the nation.

In the educational realm, change didn't occur until 1972. That's when Title IX began. The law was a response not to sexual assault but to sexism within academia, sparked by Bernice "Bunny" Sandler, a mother of two finishing the University of Maryland's doctoral program in educational counseling in 1969. Sandler worked hard and was well liked in the department, but she was rebuffed when she tried to secure a faculty appointment. "Let's face it," a faculty member told her, "you come on too strong for a woman."

At the time, Title VII of the Civil Rights Act prohibited employment discrimination based on gender and other categories, but its umbrella didn't cover academia. Working in conjunction with activist attorneys, Sandler crusaded for a new law. She filed complaints against over two hundred and fifty colleges and universities, claiming that they were violating an executive order that prohibited federal contractors from discriminating on the basis of gender, then mailed copies to Congress. One of her letters landed in the hands of Edith Green, a congresswoman from Oregon, who introduced the legislation that eventually became Title IX, slipped into the Education Amendments of 1972 as a forgettable footnote. She even discouraged Sandler from lobbying for the bill, declaring the less attention it got, the better.

President Richard Nixon didn't want to support Title IX, but he planned to sign the statute in which it was included, one that postponed court orders to integrate racially segregated schools by busing. It's a short statute: "No person in the United States shall, on the basis of sex, be excluded from participation in, be denied the benefits of, or be subjected to discrimination under any education program or activity receiving Federal financial assistance." Few imagined its ultimate reach and transformative power — it would protect equal rights for women in sports and act as a shield against sexual harassment and assault, becoming both tool and totem. These days, the *IX* can be tattooed on the bodies of those most devoted to the cause.

The first flash point occurred in 1976 at Yale University, an institution that would become a perennial proving ground for Title IX issues. Yale's women's crew team lacked bunkhouse showers and rowed dilapidated shells while the men's team had better facilities and flew by in better boats. Staging a dramatic piece of protest theater, the women's team stormed the office of Yale's director of Physical Education. There, some doffed their sweats and stood nude in a graphic demonstration of human fragility as one of them clarified their intent. "These are the bodies Yale is exploiting," she said. "We are not just healthy young things in blue and white uniforms who perform feats of strength for Yale in the nice spring weather; we are not just statistics on your win column. We're human and being treated as less than such." And in black marker on their naked backs, they wrote the symbol of the equal treatment they were legally guaranteed as Yale students: IX.

A year later, another university insider sought a more radical application of the statute. At the time, Catharine MacKinnon was a newly minted Yale Law graduate, not yet a prominent feminist legal scholar, a woman who later cut a dashing figure with her white hair styled in a bouffant, a dark stripe running from her forelock. An electric speaker, MacKinnon was part of late-stage second-wave feminism, and some of her ideas departed from the movement's mainstream. She not only changed Americans' understanding of sexual harassment but argued forcefully against pornography. MacKinnon worked with *Deep Throat* star Linda Lovelace (who spoke out against the film years after release, saying "virtually every time someone watches that movie, they are watching me being raped"), and co-drafted a Minneapolis ordinance that would have allowed women to sue pornographers on the basis of a direct link between husbands' domestic abuse and their porn usage. When Friedan and fifty feminists successfully argued that this would "reinforce rather than undercut the central sexist stereotypes in our society," she shot back that they were "fronting for male supremacists."

MacKinnon was similarly blunt about rape. She said that in a gender-imbalanced society, rape was regulated rather than impermissible. "Hostility and contempt, or arousal of master to slave, together with awe and vulnerability, or arousal of slave to master—these are the emotions of this sexuality's excitement," she wrote. "Pressure, gender socialization, withholding benefits, extending indulgences, the how-to books, the sex therapy are the soft end; the fuck, the fist, the street, the chains, the poverty are the hard end."

The important 1977 Title IX case, involving undergraduates at Yale, was *Alexander v. Yale.* The argument arose from a report the students, led by Ann Olivarius, had compiled about the status of women on campus a decade after coeducation hit, and it included damning accusations of Yale professors sexually harassing students, fondling and even raping them. "If the student actually worked up the courage to tell her residential college dean or master, the usual reaction was to express sympathy, but to advise her that this was 'all part of life,'" Olivarius explained. Taking their story to the media, Olivarius claimed Yale played hardball. She said administrators threatened to arrest her for libel (not that anyone can be arrested for libel) plus gossiped to a *Time* magazine reporter that she "was flunking out (I graduated summa cum laude, a soon-to-be Rhodes Scholar), and was a lesbian (I'm glad for people who are, but I'm not)."

As a law student, MacKinnon had written a paper that recast superiors who offered workplace subordinates sexual quid pro quos as sexual harassers. Now she and the plaintiffs argued that sexual harassment in universities was a violation of Title IX. A judge dismissed the specific charges as "tenuous" and decided that the plaintiff, having graduated, didn't have standing as a student, but he seemed to support the broader argument. This was a major moment in the statute's evolution. And in 1980, courts decided that a professor's offer of a sexual quid pro quo to a specific student was considered a violation of *all* female students' rights to an equal education free from discrimination, even if what that meant in practice was left unclear.

The Nineties, Again

In the 1980s and 1990s, there wasn't a lot of talk about sexual assault and Title IX outside of the courts, but date rape briefly rose to the level of a national issue when I reached Wesleyan. Then it quickly fell back to earth. In 1993, toward the end of the cycle, a *Saturday Night Live* skit summarized the general feeling about it at the time, which was that it was preposterous. The sketch made fun of Ohio's Antioch University's affirmative-consent policy — a policy similar to the one being implemented across the country today. They used a *Jeopardy!*-like game show called *Is It Date Rape?* to accomplish this, with the categories "Halter Top," "She Was Drunk," "I Was Drunk," "Kegger," "Off-Campus Kegger," "She Led Me On," "I Paid for Dinner," and "Ragin' Kegger." The host, a "dean of intergender relations," asks the contestants — Chris Farley playing a clueless male student, and Shannen Doherty as a too-clued-in "major in Victimization Studies" — to put labels on answers such as "The last day of school, a female student asks a male student to move her futon." "Date rape!" yells Doherty. The dean then calls on a new bunch of comedians in roles as "the Antioch date-rape players" to dramatize consent-worthy encounters: "May I elevate the level of sexual intimacy by feeling your buttocks?"

In 1990s intellectual circles, date rape was treated more as a philosophical koan of sex relations than an important social issue. In David Mamet's *Oleanna*, a play about a feminist student whom he called a "frightened, repressed, confused . . . abandoned young thing of some doubtful sexuality who wants power and revenge," the main character irrationally categorizes a professor's arrogant comments as the exploitation of a "'paternal prerogative,' and what is that but rape; I swear to God!" Controversial academic Camille Paglia argued that masculine sexual aggression was normal, and a woman's only choice was to protect herself; to say otherwise, she declared later, was to join a brigade of "fanatical sex phobes." And the same year as the *SNL* skit, Katie Roiphe, a young Harvard graduate, made a large splash with *The Morning After*, a damning manifesto about her classmates in which she argued that sex that didn't involve physical force was, ipso facto, not rape. "Allowing verbal coercion to constitute rape is a sign of tolerance toward the ultra feminine stance of passivity," she wrote. "Imagine men sitting around in a circle talking about how she called him impotent and how she manipulated him into sex, how violated and dirty he felt afterward, how coercive she was, how she got him drunk first, how he hated his body and he couldn't eat for three weeks afterward. Imagine him calling this rape."

Roiphe became a target of feminist attacks but over time her view became one pole in a frozen, static debate. On the surface, the issue barely budged over a generation. But there was movement beneath.

Incremental change led the Supreme Court to take a case considering student-on-student harassment in 1999. A fifth-grader in Monroe County, Georgia, had attempted to touch the private parts of a fellow student and made comments like "I want to feel your boobs" and "I want to get in bed with you" for several months, without the school intervening. The Court broke 5 to 4 in its decision for the student (Justice Sandra Day O'Connor was the deciding vote between liberals for and conservatives against). Student-on-student abuse was now a violation of Title IX, putting schools on the hook for curbing it.

In the law, sexual assault fell under the umbrella of sexual harassment, which might appear to minimize it, but there was a specific logic at work. "Title IX is about contact, targeted at somebody because of gender, that is unwelcome, and severe and pervasive enough that it becomes a condition of one's school life—the same way it would be in a place of employment," explains Christina Brandt-Young, a former senior staff attorney at Legal Momentum, the oldest legal advocacy group for women in the United States. Harassment requires repeated incidences. "An offhand comment doesn't change conditions of employment. But if somebody had to go to his workplace and there was a burning cross on the desk, and a noose, and people using the N-word all over the place, that's objectively severe, and would change the conditions of employment for black people working there." Assault doesn't require more than one incident. "Sexual assault is really darn severe, so it only has to happen once to be considered sexual harassment."

Though universities now bore responsibility for policing assault, some were slow to take on their new role. Defensive postures included encouraging survivors not to report the crime, arguing it would exacerbate their trauma, and filing forms and convening hearings in superficial compliance while failing to address the pressing needs of counseling, treatment, and relocating offenders from dorms and classrooms. Many times, victims weren't even told of the outcome of the complaints they'd brought. "For a very long time, there was no due process for victims. Victims were told to withdraw from school. Victims were told to take the semester off," Colby Bruno, senior legal counsel with the Victim Rights Law Center, explained.

There is also reason to believe that some schools dissuaded survivors from reaching out to law enforcement. The 1990 Clery Act, named after Jeanne Clery, a nineteen-year-old Lehigh University student who was raped and murdered in her dorm room, requires colleges to keep a daily log of crimes, notify students of crimes in a timely manner, and publish an easy-to-find report each year. But publicizing these statistics runs in direct opposition to a university's interest in luring prospective students, and some universities may have fudged numbers over the course of many years.

Dear Colleague

When President Obama took office in 2008, the tone and terminology surrounding the issue of campus sexual assault differed from what it had been in the 1990s. It wasn't about the patriarchy but about civil rights. "There's a reason the story of the civil rights movement was written in our schools," Obama said at an NAACP Centennial Convention. "It's because there is no stronger weapon against inequality and no better path to opportunity than an education that can unlock a child's God-given potential."

For Obama, the father of two teenage girls, combating sexual violence in schools was a priority, and he also had a deep interest in challenging gender stereotypes. "When you're the father of two daughters, you become even more aware of how gender stereotypes pervade our society," he wrote in *Glamour* magazine. "You see the subtle and not-so-subtle social cues transmitted through culture. You feel the enormous pressure girls are under to look and behave and even think a certain way." This wasn't mere paternalism. Obama felt the negative effects of gender stereotypes when he grew up without a dad around. "It's easy to absorb all kinds of messages from society about masculinity and come to believe there's a right way and a wrong man to be a man," he wrote. "But as I got older, I realized that my ideas about being a tough guy or cool guy just weren't me . . . Life became a lot easier when

I simply started being myself." In the same essay, he called himself a feminist, the first sitting president to do so.

Radical legal thinkers like MacKinnon and the Yale plaintiffs had changed the course of Title IX; Obama, a Harvard-trained attorney cut from progressive cloth, knew that it could be pushed even further. Prior to Obama's election, Title IX's chief enforcer, the Department of Education's Office for Civil Rights (OCR), was a backwater. Clarence Thomas ran it in the 1980s, assisted by young attorney Anita Hill, who would famously raise charges of sexual harassment against him when he was nominated for the Supreme Court. Its attempts to correct inequality were less than vigorous.

Obama emboldened the OCR. Following an influential Center for Public Integrity report that featured survivor and attorney Laura Dunn, he linked college sexual assault to education's overt and subtle forms of discrimination. "If we could get this right . . . then so many of the 'isms' that we face as adults would go away," emphasized Russlynn Ali, his OCR assistant secretary. Vice President Joe Biden — who, while he may not have stood up for Anita Hill during Thomas's confirmation hearings, did champion 1994's Violence Against Women Act, which contributed to great gains in domestic violence protections — accompanied Obama on this quest, hoping to cement this legacy.

In April 2011, Obama's administration released the era's seminal text on college sexual violence. This Dear Colleague letter — government correspondence that functions like a position paper — didn't have the force of law. It was considered a preview of how the agency planned to use its existing authority, and this time it had strong recommendations with respect to guidelines and responsibilities that most universities hoped they didn't have. And for the first time in history, the American government called sexual assault a civil rights issue.

Over time, Obama's administration provided a list of universities' Title IX responsibilities. Every school had to create a process for resolving cases of sexual assault that students brought to them, period. And they had to resolve most cases within sixty days. Every school had to hire a Title IX coordinator (this had been in the regulations since 1975, but schools kept forgetting about it). Every school had to publish information about its disciplinary processes and distribute it widely. As soon as a student filed a report of sexual violence — not upon a decision of culpability — the university had to immediately move dorm rooms and offer accommodations on missed papers and exams if necessary. Perhaps most important, universities were told that their tribunals couldn't apply the same standard that a criminal court uses to impose prison terms, guilt beyond a reasonable doubt. The standard had to be the civil court's "preponderance of the evidence." To be found guilty or, in the university's milquetoast term, "responsible," the accused need only be more likely than not to have committed the offense — that is, 51 percent likely.

These shifts required justification. When it offered a rationale, Obama's administration was sloppy. It lobbed an eye-popping statistic: "about 1 in 5 women are victims of completed or attempted sexual assault while in college." This number — since cited widely — was based on the misreading of a 2007 study of sexual assault on two campuses, and when asked, the author of the study refused to agree with the claim that his survey was nationally representative. The White House also later pointed to a buzzy study that found that 4 percent of college men were responsible for more than 90 percent of rapes and attempted rapes on campus — indicating, as one of the study's authors, retired University of Massachusetts Boston clinical psychologist David Lisak, said, that "every report should be viewed and treated as an opportunity to identify a serial rapist." That study would also come in for intense criticism down the line.

Nevertheless, the penalties for universities that failed to enforce these new Title IX standards were severe: denial of federal funding for the entire university. Nearly every American university, private or public, relies on taxpayer dollars in the form of grants, and many students rely on federally funded Pell Grants and Stafford Loans. Only the tippy-top of the university food chain, the institutions with billion-dollar endowments, could possibly operate without these funds. The stakes were high indeed.

In a move that might seem to run counter to common sense, Obama's administration said that law enforcement could be called in to deal with a victim — but only if the victim wanted that. And anti-rape advocates agree with this position. "The thing about sexual assault is that it takes away your ability to make decisions for yourself and makes the victim feel helpless about the most basic thing, i.e., what enters his or her body," says Brandt-Young. "It does not help anyone to throw a rape victim into a police situation, if he or she does not want to be there. Not everybody can handle it. At the level of the individual victim, whether to report to the police should absolutely be his or her decision only. There is no other blanket category of crime in the United States for which anyone is trying to take away the right of adults with full mental capacity to decide for themselves whether they want to be involved in that system."

This stipulation makes sense. Why wouldn't a victim want to report the crime to the police? Well, lots of reasons—not wanting to relive the incident or experience the indignity of a rape test, maybe even guilt about locking the other party in prison. But let's start with the fact that the police have a terrible track record with rape, and so does the criminal justice system, though there are indications that these law and order components are trying to remedy this (for example, well-funded grants to teach cops new ways to solve rape cases are being distributed throughout the nation).

Still, they have a long way to go. The Rape, Abuse, and Incest National Network (RAINN), America's largest anti-sexual-violence organization, estimates that out of one thousand rapes, only three hundred and ten are reported to the police. Fifty-seven of these lead to an arrest, of which eleven end up in the hands of a prosecutor, seven lead to a felony conviction, and six offenders serve time in prison. That's a conviction rate of 0.6 percent. Given these shortcomings, a university's passing along responsibility for adjudicating sexual assault looks a lot like an abdication of its duty and an injustice to survivors.

Student Uprising

In the Dear Colleague letter, advocates found a powerful new set of standards, and campus administrators found overdue reforms. As one salty ex-Vanderbilt officer told me, "This is the shift that was brought to us, because for so long we didn't give a rat's ass." Still, at first it wasn't clear that *enforcement* of these new standards would move forward swimmingly. In fact, quiet avoidance is the way things normally went where universities and the Office for Civil Rights were concerned. "Think about Title IX's application to athletics —there have been more than eight interpretations, clarifications, and Dear Colleague letters on that, and there are still so many compliance problems," says Erin Buzuvis, a Western New England University law professor whose influential blog tracks Title IX developments. "Nobody cares. Athletic directors aren't wringing their hands and forming new organizations to address how they're going to support each other in reaching compliance. 'Oh well, we're not in compliance. The governments never revoked anyone's federal funding yet, so we don't expect we'll be the first.'" But assault proved to be different for one specific reason: "The missing ingredient was student activists . . . creating a tipping point of cases that demonstrated to the thinking public that this was a problem that needed a response."

In the early 2010s, a new wave rose once again at Yale. Student Alexandra Brodsky, the public face of a student-activist group, said that when she reported her attempted rape to Yale's Grievance Board, they dissuaded her from pressing ahead, making statements along the lines of "'I shouldn't pursue anything formal, because I would be retaliated against'; 'he would tell people about me,' as though the damaged reputation would be mine rather than his; and 'this was clearly just a case of a young man being so madly in love with me.'" This tactic struck her as ethically fishy at the time. But as she learned about Title IX, she began to think it was illegal.

Olivarius's daughters were enrolled at Yale, and they spread the word about the 1977 case and the subsequent history. This new generation understood that sexual assault could be connected to a larger trend of Yale's stupid frat tricks, all of it creating an academic environment hostile to women. And what a list of these behaviors Yale was generating. Twelve Zeta Psi pledges had posed for a photo in front of the Yale Women's Center holding a sign reading WE LOVE YALE SLUTS. A "Preseason Scouting Report," by an anonymous author, listed fifty-three first-year students by name and dorm and ranked each by the degree of drunkenness required before a man would deign to screw them ("sobriety," "five beers," "blackout"). And, most famous, pledges from Delta Kappa Epsilon, the frat at which George W. Bush was once president, in a march on campus yelled, "My name is Jack, I'm a necrophiliac; I fuck dead women" and "No means yes! Yes means anal!" They were jokes, but not funny ones. Of the rankings, which seemed deadly serious, Brodsky declared, "I can't imagine being a freshman. You got in because of your 4.0 GPA and 1600 SATs, and suddenly you're being told you're worth three beers."

The DKE faux march was the last straw. At the Office for Civil Rights,

Brodsky and her cohort filed what is considered the key Title IX complaint of this era, which had many more to come. These can be easy to write. Typically, they're first-person accounts of survivors' experiences plus a grab bag of details about university treatment that might have violated the statute. But they are a potent way to terrify universities with federal action, generate media attention, and give students a sense of their own power.

Yale began shifting policies around sexual assault and publicly disclosed a new punishment for DKE's banner-holding pledges—a nonnegotiable, five-year revocation of their charter. "We had been banging on about what was happening at Yale for a long time, and then we said it in the right way with a signature at the bottom, and they changed," Brodsky tells me. "It was tremendous." The university's actions, however, won them an extremely soft landing with the OCR, which fined Yale a total of $165,000 for misreporting forcible sex offenses earlier that decade, a violation of the Clery Act, which had been uncovered by journalist Emily Bazelon years before.

Remarkably, this sum—a pittance when compared to Yale's $3 billion operating budget and $25 billion endowment—remains one of the highest fines (other than Penn State's $2.4 million post–Jerry Sandusky fee) against any university for Clery Act violations. What about violations of Title IX? The government says that the only fee that can be levied is pulling funding from the entire school, which it can't do, because it would be catastrophic.

The only sense one can make of this puzzle is that the Obama administration had initiated a political dance: they promulgated a new set of standards and then didn't enforce them, perhaps to avoid infuriating colleges. College students, though, are optimists, and they refused to let cynicism infect them. A new collegiate activist network radiating out from Yale would form a shockingly effective organization. Brodsky joined with Amherst's Dana Bolger to found Know Your IX, an influential organization bringing Title IX law, direct-action skills, and movement history to students around the country. They were invited to Capitol Hill and also spent, in Brodsky's telling, "a truly tremendous amount of time" convincing lawmakers that university cases should not be automatically referred to the police. "It's to a lot of legislators' credit that they've listened to students," says Brodsky.

For these radical students, campus rape was not just a cause but also a forum, a foundation upon which to build and share a new vision of the world.

Most of them rallied around the serial-predator theory, though some would later change their minds. They cast off the old language of victimhood, rejected the conventions that advised them to stand down and not cause too much trouble, and upended the old worldview wherein those who feared rape were taught to carry cans of mace and enroll in self-defense classes. Preventing rape wasn't a woman's responsibility, the new wave argued. It was the culture — "rape culture" — that had to change.

Girls Take Over Media

Students on their own couldn't spread these ideas widely; they learned from and were supported by blogs, particularly women's blogs. These blogs ramped up a few years before 2011, beginning with *Jezebel*, a *Sassy* magazine for the millennial era and a middle finger to the banal, bourgeois "feminism" of mainstream women's magazines. Founded by Anna Holmes in the late 2000s, *Jezebel* was a small revolution; before it, marketers thought that women wanted their sugar separate from their spice. Holmes was brewing a *Bitch*-mag-inspired mix of feminist theory, pop culture, and righteous anger over a fashion and beauty industry that prodded young girls into buying overpriced makeup and developing eating disorders. *Jezebel* made its name with a clever gimmick: It offered $10,000 to any magazine employee who leaked an unretouched magazine-cover photo. Faith Hill was the first victim.

In America, girls are not generally taught about feminism in high school, at least not any feminism more recent than Susan B. Anthony and the suffragettes. But *Jezebel* schooled them with addictively fun-to-read posts about what they were up against. It quickly became canon for a generation of young women, and the model was copied across the Internet. Tumblr, in particular, became a hotbed of feminist, and emo, radical thought. Cool kids swapped out *Zen and the Art of Motorcycle Maintenance* for Audre Lorde's theories on Tumblr in one-hundred-fifty-word chunks.

But even *Jezebel* found it difficult to navigate between the shoals of sex-positivity and fighting the patriarchy. The old standards would not hold, but what should the new ones be? This conundrum emerged most vividly at an event called Thinking and Drinking, moderated by comedian Lizz Winstead and featuring two rebellious, talented *Jezebel* writers, Moe and Tracie, third-wave feminists with slacker personas and hard shells. They were talking about sex and drinking beers onstage—as advertised in the event's title—when Winstead shifted in her seat.

"You're focusing on sexual freedom, I mean, there's just not—it's not always safe," she stammered. "It's not always safe to have a free, one hundred percent total sexual life."

"What's going to happen?" asked Moe nonchalantly.

Winstead shot back: "You could get raped."

"But that's happened too," she said. "You live through that, you know."

"Sometimes you don't," said Winstead. Tracie then tried to argue that the men in her neighborhood were too cowed to be rapists.

"I live in Williamsburg and there are only pussies—" she began.

Winstead sat up straight. "What the fuck!" she exclaimed.

Later in the conversation, Moe appeared to consider the issue more seriously.

"I guess the third guy I ever had sex with date-raped me. I got very mad at him. But I wasn't going to turn him in to the police and fucking go through shit," she said. "It's a load of trouble, and I have better things to do. Like drinking more."

Tracie, agreeing with her colleague, said, "I hate talking about rape, honestly. I mean, I know it's a thing. I know it's real, and this one," she said, referring to Moe. "But I've never, ever been in that situation, and I have had lots and lots and lots of sex."

The two women continued in this vein for a while. When Tracie suggested no one should emulate people in the media, particularly writers for *Jezebel*, Winstead bristled with anger. "Your whole blog is based on people emulating you," she said. "Regardless of whether you think they should. That's like when football players say, 'I'm not a role model.' They are—you are. You're de facto role models."

It didn't take long for the two writers to regret what they'd said, and over time, *Jezebel* wrote more about sexual assault, even if it wasn't its original mission. "At the beginning, I'll admit that I had a bit of trepidation about writing about rape," Holmes tells me now. "I thought maybe readers wouldn't want to hear about it." She was surprised at the reaction she got. "The posts on rape were actually the most commented upon of all our articles. Now, I don't mean they were the most well read. But there were four hundred or five hundred comments on each story we wrote about sexual assault. And since readers responded so well, we wrote more and more about it."

The pump had been primed. The term *rape culture*, used in the 1970s, was revived, and dots were connected between an American society that turned a blind eye to sexual assault and the ways it affected the real life of girls. A rape culture is one in which rape myths — for instance, that a woman's outfit or alcohol consumption caused her rape — dominated. No one questioned prevalent attitudes that boxed in the victim: blaming her for her motives or sexual history; trivializing sexual assault because if you've had sex before, what's one more penis; assuming women lie about rape; tolerating TV shows and music where a woman's position is presented as "no means yes," as in "Blurred Lines." And male sexual aggression went unchallenged because, as the "hot metal" guy claimed, "boys will be boys," and they couldn't help themselves once they were aroused.

Many young activists grew up reading blogs. They may have written that they wanted to talk more about sexual assault in those blogs' comments sections. But they also adopted theory percolating in other areas of the Internet, one that students would decide was more important than some of *Jezebel*'s ideas, and MacKinnon's too. As much as they admired MacKinnon, they left part of message — her laserlike anti-porn focus and her male/female binary — in the past. From the sex-positive perspective of the current moment, she could seem a bit prudish.

Instead, they promoted a theory of intersectionality, rape victims as one strand in a larger web of people oppressed by society's systemic injustice. They drew attention to the way each individual in the web wasn't a one-dimensional figure — "rape victim," or "Latina," or "queer" — but could possess overlapping minority identities. This theory, a kind of multiculturalism on speed, came from Kimberlé Crenshaw, a professor at Columbia and the University of California at Los Angeles's law schools. Concerned about racial and gender discrimination and the "profound invisibility" those who pulled the short straw suffer in relation to the law, she named the problem in the 1980s. As part of Anita Hill's legal team during Clarence Thomas's confirmation hearings, Crenshaw watched white women supporting Hill while African Americans defended Thomas. This rift hinted at a larger problem with the feminism of that time: it had failed to unite the causes espoused by white middle-class women with those of their poorer, darker sisters. In that rift, Anita Hill's complex, intersectional identity — a black woman — was lost.

Intersectionality did not become a popular topic in the 2010s because of the academy. It was popularized by Tumblr, blogs, and students themselves. They called for allyship, meaning solidarity, while practicing resistance to the crossbred evils of sexism, racism, homophobia, classism, ableism, and every other hegemonic exertion. I understood now why Ridolfi-Starr and her clan had been so focused on the Palestinian group and the queer group and even the Shakespeare troupe carrying those mattresses; she was after a great wave rising up against Columbia.

The violations can be tiny — microaggressions, in the favored term, like a white girl asking to touch her black classmate's hair. And they can be large, up to cops' slaughter of innocent African Americans on the streets of Ferguson. And there are a wide variety of villains: Straight white men. The U.S. prison system. Israel. Don't make the mistake, as I did, of inviting an intersectional campus activist to lunch at an Israeli restaurant. "It says Israeli pickles on this menu," I was told. "If they're Israeli pickles, they're Palestinian pickles too." Teach For America was a point of contention too. "Is it deprofessionalizing teaching, is it a colonial practice?" a student mused.

And even women can be creeps. There are "corporate feminists," like *Lean In*'s Sheryl Sandberg, and "neo-liberal feminists," whom the activists faulted for ignoring class. Then there are "white feminists," which includes feminists who prioritize local issues like pay equity and subsidized childcare over human rights and social justice. In other words, white women who are subsumed in the previous era's feminist debates, the type of debates I thought Sulkowicz and her friends would want to hear about before I learned that they wanted to talk about intersectionality. In other words, women like me. Indeed, I'm aware that for most of them, I am not a figure to be admired. Even Sulkowicz and I exchanged cross words, some through an intermediary; she liked me and then didn't, calling me narrow-minded among other criticisms, some of which were fair. To many of these students, my middle-aged, middle-class point of view is considered hopelessly retro, insufficiently woke.

To me, intersectionality carries a tinge of implausibility — none of us can get anywhere until everyone can get everywhere. But I understand how it can also be inspiring in its full-throated diversity and visionary utopianism and meaningful for young activists in a period of vast social upheaval. Over coffee in a shoebox-size café, Marybeth Seitz-Brown, a Columbia graduate and a Know Your IX activist who is the daughter of a Lutheran pastor, spoke to me about "sociological imagination" and Octavia Butler, one of her favorite writers. "As activists, we need to be sci-fi, or even fantasy writers [like Butler] — we can be that imaginative," she said. "We can create the world we want, if we have the guts to do it. It might take a long time. The first abolitionists didn't see slavery go away, but they laid the groundwork for the next generation."

Seitz-Brown said one shouldn't try to fix sexual assault without also trying to fix racism. This was a matter of ethics. "If you are only connected to or care about issues that you're related to by blood, we are all fucked," she explained, her voice soft but determined.

Front-Page News

There was a powerful mashup happening here: feminist attorneys' arguments, the widening scope of Title IX based on the emerging view of rape as a violent crime and a civil rights issue, and students' embrace of the merging of academic theory and enlightened, defiant, entertaining youth-oriented media. Soon, the characterization of rape culture became broader. "Rape culture is an attitude toward women in particular, but I think not even just to women — to treating all people as sexual objects," Anna Bahr, a recent Columbia graduate and former editor of the school magazine, explained to me. "It's about thinking of people as being nothing more than the opportunity for sex."

Starting in 2012, following a heartbreaking personal essay by an Amherst student, college girls began sharing their stories online. Each generation has a seminal tract about the difficulties of young womanhood — Sylvia Plath's *The Bell Jar*, Elizabeth Wurtzel's *Prozac Nation*. In our era, the web-based confessional essay moves mountains. And personal testimonies about college sexual assault, a form that reached its apogee in the eloquent, heart-wrenching letter written by Brock Turner's victim in 2016, spread activists' message even wider. A personal blog, a Facebook post, a Tumblr page, a college newspaper — wherever survivors could share their stories, they were suddenly doing so. The confessions were real, beating hearts. And as hundreds of these stories filled the feeds of students across the country, they began thinking more deeply about their own sexual experiences, the ones in the dark, on their mattresses.

In general, to put radical political ideas into our culture, one needs a political machine: think tanks, academic programs, AstroTurf groups, lobbyists. But young collegiate activists found that they could accomplish many goals simply through having the girls who were sharing their stories on Tumblr share them with the media too. In the digital age, journalists are easily contactable — e-mails listed online, DM-able Twitter accounts. Most journalists are millennials themselves or Gen Xers fervent about women's rights. Other media players have a different motivation. They're eager to trade emotionally disturbing stories for clicks — another log on the raging fire of American fear, burning alongside terrorism, mass shootings, extremist rhetoric, and natural disasters. This arbitrage proved lucrative.

I learned about the vanguard of this change on a sizzling summer morning when I sat down in Los Angeles with Andrea Pino and Annie Clark, two petite recent University of North Carolina at Chapel Hill graduates with degrees in political science. We'd set breakfast for ten a.m. at a small café near their tiny one-bedroom Craigslist rental in Silver Lake, a hip neighborhood on the east side of the city, but when I arrived, Clark e-mailed me in a panic, explaining they'd slept through the alarm because they'd stayed up late the night before counseling survivors on the phone.

Apologizing profusely, they rush into the café minutes later with a rescue poodle owned by Danielle Dirks, the Occidental College sociology professor with whom they've formed an advocacy organization for survivors. We take seats al fresco, the dog panting on the ground nearby. Pino, a Cuban American scholarship student from Miami who said she's the first member of her family to go to college, is curt and hyperintellectual, whereas Clark is Raleigh-born sweetness, freckles, and EQ. They're dressed similarly, in purple tops, precisely applied black eyeliner, and a surfeit of tiny sparkling earrings.

Activism is a difficult way to make a living. They eat their breakfast burritos with gusto. A few months ago, after running out of money, Clark and Pino lived in their car, later in a tent. We stop by their Craigslist rental after the meal, and the place is so makeshift and spare that they're using a cardboard box for a desk. But this tiny apartment is also an anti-sexual-assault

Death Star. A map of the United States hangs on a wall; colored pushpins mark colleges they are targeting to call out for sexual assault. Because it's August, they're starting to teach journalists about the red zone and its dangers for freshman students.

Within a year of this breakfast, Clark and Pino would supersede Sulkowicz as the nation's most famous campus survivors. They were cast as the protagonists in *The Hunting Ground,* a cult documentary about college sexual assault, and also became the movement's most effective behind-the-scenes power brokers. Though multimedia projects like Ali Safran's Surviving in Numbers, which depicted survivors holding cardboard signs with parts of their stories, sparked public conversation, Clark and Pino were key to broadening the national discussion to include schools across the country. Clark talks about their ideas in the context of Penn State's Jerry Sandusky scandal. "Like at Penn State, when things aren't connected, it's so easy to say, 'Okay, here are four people doing things wrong. We'll fire them, and the issue goes away.' We reframed the debate as 'What's happening at one school is a microcosm of what's happening everywhere.'" And on their ankles, the duo would get matching tattoos with Roman numerals: IX.

Their organization is called End Rape on Campus, and in an example of their savvy, they secured the first Google hit for *campus rape* for their website. They not only helped bring students' stories to the media; they also helped students file complaints like the one Brodsky and her group brought against Yale. End Rape on Campus collaborated with students at American University, Bard, Dartmouth, Emerson, Hobart and William Smith, Iowa State, Northeastern, Pace, Swarthmore, the University of Texas–Pan American, the University of Utah. They also worked with Columbia student leaders Ridolfi-Starr and Seitz-Brown to help those twenty-eight individuals, represented by the mattress carried to the *Alma Mater* sculpture, file claims.

In 2013, the Office for Civil Rights received thirty-two complaints about Title IX violations involving sexual violence and college students. One year later, there were a hundred and two. By spring 2017, about three hundred and twenty investigations were pending. The headlines in major newspapers about these investigations killed.

Much of that dramatic increase was due to the labor of a small group of activists, not only EROC but also activist attorneys and professors. For example

Michele Dauber, a Stanford law professor, sent the tip about Brock Turner's victim's letter to a *Hunting Ground* producer, who brought it to *BuzzFeed*, where it got eighteen million views. "Schools only care about media and money," says an activist who was engaged in this work. "I tell survivors, 'I'm sorry, don't even bother talking to your administrator. Just go straight to the national media. You'll spin your wheels, waste your time.'" She adds, "This is a highly orchestrated social movement, even though it may look spontaneous—'Here's a survivor story, here's another one.' We're pairing people with the right reporters, we're giving reporters the angles." They asked students who wanted to go public, "What are the key quotes from administrators that will make news? What are the crazy, off-the-wall punishments for rape, like a five-page book report, at your school?"

Dumping news to journalists and hoping that a story will explode when published can be a rickety strategy. But media has kept this topic hot, kept girls talking about it, kept university administrators paying attention. (I attended some campus rallies where reporters, searching desperately for a story, outnumbered students.) A school can truly be damaged by the wrong kind of coverage. Scandals have direct effects on corporate bottom lines. Nike's golf-ball sales initially sank after the Tiger Woods scandal, and the stock price of his corporate sponsors dropped too. And schools, of course, are businesses more than ever.

With stakes high—a ten-spot drop in the *U.S. News and World Report* college rankings was no small matter—universities began to panic. Media power was squarely the province of the activists, and now universities were the silenced party. Many news stories included student claims of "institutional betrayal," survivors' favored catch phrase for administrative neglect. Victims were devastated, as Sulkowicz's mother explained at this book's outset, to learn that their universities, which their parents had taught them represented the pinnacle of educational experiences and which were meant to act in a quasi-parental role, had cast them aside.

But what schools had actually done remained hard to find out. The same law that had given universities cover from public scrutiny when they shirked their responsibilities to investigate sexual assault now worked against them. Colleges are prohibited from making substantive comments about individual disciplinary cases by a 1974 law, the Family Educational Rights and Privacy Act (FERPA). For example, a Williams College student who said she was assaulted wrote in the student newspaper at the school, "In one instance, [members of the offender's athletic team] surrounded me, threw full beer cans at my head and chanted that I should have kept my mouth shut. When I spoke to the deans about the incident, I was told that everyone was 'exhausted' from dealing with the case and that perhaps it would be better if we all just 'took a little break.'" Bound by FERPA, Williams said only that it was "very confident" it had followed proper policies and procedures.

West Coast media-savvy leaders were every bit as radical as earlier activists, intersectional feminists determined to combat patriarchy wherever they found it. "Violence is entrenched in our culture; it manifests in transphobia, racism, ableism, homophobia, and misogyny" is the way Clark and Pino put it in their 2016 book *We Believe You.* But journalists wanted stories that hewed to their tropes — white, "straight-presenting" damsels in distress. The activists were revolted by the notion of reinforcing bad old ideas about virtuous victims (white, young, middle class) while looking away from the wrongs committed against the poor, the queer, and minorities — but they had goals.

One activist puts it this way: "If you look around yourself, there are colonial practices and state violence that gets enacted every day. But then we lose our audience, who is like, 'What? We're going to talk about heteropatriarchy now? And I don't know what *cis-gender* means.'" The conversation could be kept sharply focused. "*If* you don't question state violence, *if* you make people feel uncomfortable about not helping the white ladies who happen to be at the wrong place at the wrong time, *if* you talk about predators who we can all get behind and hate, *if* we get rid of them with harsh penalties and punitive actions that Americans love . . ." She trails off, but I get the gist — there are gains to be had here.

This networked clan of activists, some connected through a secret Facebook group, communicated at a length and frequency different from their forebears'. In fact, they were among the first advocacy groups to harness the power of the MSM/social media nexus, which became so important to the success of groups from Black Lives Matter to the alt-right. The play went like this: The young activists contributed to new media outlets like *BuzzFeed, HuffPo,* and *xoJane.* They gathered followers for these stories on Twitter. They retweeted one another and allies. This loose army then policed the topic, reinforcing their talking points and belligerently calling out those who didn't toe the line.

Unleashing humiliation — the humiliation that universities, and boys, had made victims feel — was key. Some delivered a reputation-tarnishing naming and shaming for "rape denialists," like writer Emily Yoffe, who suggested binge drinking might be at fault for the campus rape problem ("There's a special place in hell" for her, tweeted Brodsky); George Will, who called victimhood "a coveted status that confers privileges"; and Richard Dawkins, who tweeted, "Date rape is bad. Stranger rape at knifepoint is worse." Of the last two, University of Southern California activist Tucker Reed wrote that they "think they're being clever when they perpetuate these victim-blaming, predominantly woman-hating stereotypes. Like everyone else is drinking the Kool-Aid and they're fucking Sherlock Holmes — some cynic-genius breaking ground. Um, no . . . You don't come across as smart. In fact, not only do you reek of being the opposite of smart — but you are simultaneously telegraphing to the world at large that you are a self-centered, inconsiderate subhuman shit."

By 2014, Americans, tethered to their smartphones, began to be showered with stories about rape on campus. News delivered via cell phone, a far more intimate medium than print or the TV, gathers clicks only if it connects on a deep, emotional level with the reader's own identity. Genocide in Syria doesn't jolt one's system like a mugging or break-in down the block. These stories allowed readers to connect with their own pasts in college. Or their friends' pasts. Or what their teenagers might experience.

Fear spread, and it was the deepest kind of fear — fear for the safety of one's children. One day, my chiropractor, a peppy, aerobicized mom of a teenage daughter, began a monologue about her thirteen-year-old and the news about campus rape. I lay on her magenta table, staring up at her matching magenta lamp. "When I think about my daughter in college without me there to protect her," she said in words that came out in a torrent, "it makes me so scared I want to vomit."

I steeled myself for a neck crack.

5

"Rape Girls"

Memes, like Sulkowicz's mattress, viral survivors' tales, and the brilliant and merciless tactics of young activists started to turn a tide that had, for decades, flowed only one way. On Planet College, sexual-assault charges used to create cliquey rifts and furors resulting in the ostracism of the accusing girl. Accusations are so hard to prove, and so damning, that the accused boy almost always has an amen corner, friends who will invariably proclaim his innocence. This is part of why a cool girl in previous generations brushed off anything untoward, knowing there was no percentage in calling a boy out because even if a few of her friends believed her, the rest of the campus would not. And it's a two-step—disbelief and shame, leading to self-blame. The assaulted girl takes others' doubt to heart, analyzes every detail of the night, then berates herself for the way her one-shouldered dress showed skin or for her decision to have that fifth vodka shot.

As college-assault testimonies and news reports began to be consumed in nighttime dorm rooms, a smartphone's backlit screen shining beneath a fleur-de-lis duvet, this dynamic began to flip. The power of web-based sharing met the power of belief, creating an epistemic certainty among girls about the frequency of assault, not only at schools like Columbia and Wesleyan, where the classification of sex acts as assault went wide and wider, but at Syracuse, where a few lone sorority sisters stood up for themselves. Girls did this even though refusing to bury what they said happened to them required going from sunny campus life (the studying and talking urgently, the YOLO nights) to a land of emotional instability and depression. In some cases, the trauma of the assault had already put them there.

I would be remiss not to mention that this new up-swelling—all rape talk, all the time — makes some survivors uncomfortable, and they're unimpressed by activists' in-your-face tactics and heated rhetoric. "I'm not in the women's empowerment movement — I think those people have no idea what the fuck they're doing," says Liz,* twenty-one. "These girls should be seeing therapists, not shouting their experiences from a megaphone in the middle of campus. That whole group has the wrong idea. I think they're going to hurt people."

Liz says she was raped multiple times before she reached college, beginning in eighth grade when an eighteen-year-old from her youth group offered to drive her home from a church fair. "In the car, he told me he thought I was beautiful, and I'd never heard a guy ever say that before," she says. He kissed her. "It was my first kiss. I had no idea what I was doing, and things really progressed. I'd say, 'I don't want to,' and he'd say, 'Okay, that's fine, let's go home,' and then he would pull over again." He was older, and much stronger. She was afraid he might become violent, so she gave in. "When he finally dropped me off, he made me recite to him that it was consensual, and I was so young I believed it."

Afterward, she fantasized about him. "I thought, *He loves me, he wouldn't do this unless he loved me, he's going to leave his girlfriend because he loves me*," she says. Concerned about Liz's depression, her parents transferred her to a new school. "I hated everybody, and then I found another girl at school who hated everybody — you know how that is when you're a teenager — and we became friends," she says. They went out with guys in their twenties, smoking weed, drinking to blackout, snorting Xanax, hanging out at the mall wearing heavy eyeliner. "Basically, every cliché in the book," she says dryly. "Sleeping with lots of guys. And it was not pleasurable, the sex. I don't think I was even interested in boys until I was seventeen, and by that point I had been fucking people for three years just because they were there and they wanted me to. The sex was very painful. I felt very degraded all the time, [even though I thought] I should be getting something good out of it because I knew you were supposed to — that sex is supposed to make you feel good."

At a friend's sweet sixteen, she followed a group of guys into the woods to smoke weed. "I was so fucked up I couldn't stand, and they were like, 'Let's take turns with this one.' They were propping me up on trees and shit. Nothing I said mattered." When Liz told her friend what happened, she didn't believe her. "She said, 'Those are my guy friends from the neighborhood, I'm sure they didn't want to hurt you.'"

This was Liz's nadir. "I thought, I don't know if I could feel any shittier about myself than this," she says. "And I pulled myself out of it. I was like, 'You're smart, you could get into an Ivy League if you studied.' I got into an honors society. I studied for the SATs. And I did get into two Ivy League schools."

At college, Liz attended a meeting of student anti-rape activists but was turned off. "These people are going to their weekly meetings and it's 'I hate men and let's talk about our rape again,'" she declares. "It's a pity party. I think they need to be seeing therapists, especially a girl who walks in there with my experience, but new." They were failing to turn themselves around as she had, and she worried about them. "But I can't speak out against the women's group on campus, or even say something like 'their methodology for talking about sexual assault isn't as good as it could be,'" she says.

Liz has no interest in speaking out publicly; she's so concerned about her anonymity that she asks me not to even mention her university. She's proud of herself for the way she's handled her experiences. "When this happens to you for real, it is a huge part of your identity, and then it becomes a smaller and smaller part," she says. "Today, what happened feels like a dream."

How much sharing is too much? Some survivors' families think they're getting carried away too. Ti'Air Riggins, a PhD student studying biomedical engineering at Purdue University, says another student raped her but went unpunished. At first, she tried to move on. But she began having nightmares and lost ten pounds. "I had to go to counseling, because I was very angry," she explains. A beauty-pageant contestant at the time, she told her coach about her assault experience. "He said, 'Wow, this is very powerful. You have to go with this because many women will relate to you.'" These instincts were correct; wearing a clingy white gown, a bouquet of flowers clasped her hands, she was crowned Miss Indiana United States 2015. "The main thing about being a title holder is that the people you meet give you the benefit of the doubt," Riggins says. "They see the crown and the sash, and they think, 'This one has something important to say.'"

But Riggins's mom told her that she felt she was overdoing it. "When I first told her what happened, she cried and said she would pray for me, but I guess she doesn't understand [why I am] so passionate," she says. "She once said to me, 'You are kind of making yourself into a victim. You are obsessed with this.'" Riggins explained, and her mother ultimately supported her. "I told her that I don't agree. I told her my speaking out has helped other people speak out."

A New Frame

Liz has some good points. But at the risk of being insensitive, we could call her off trend, because once I stopped speaking with students about consensual sex and began to talk to them about assault, I received a flood of disclosure of all kinds — rape and assault, repressed memories and newly bleeding wounds.

Let's talk about old memories first. Many seniors discussed coming back to memories from freshman year with a new understanding of what constituted assault. This was happening in the wider culture too, even among women who went to college before rape was redefined. Lena Dunham, who graduated from Oberlin in 2008, wrote in her 2014 memoir *Not That Kind of Girl* about an experience that she now understands as rape: drunk and high, she had "terribly aggressive" sex with another student who'd removed the condom without telling her. When she tells a friend, "she clutches my hand and, in a voice reserved for moms in Lifetime movies, whispers, 'You were raped.' I burst out laughing."

Dunham was in college in an era, recent as it was, when her friend's attitude wasn't the norm, not even at a school like Oberlin. Women bonded over their most risky sexual exploits back then in much the same way today's students find community in supporting one another as survivors for incidents that sometimes don't sound that different from what previous generations of girls would have considered just an especially slutty night, even if those nights didn't exactly sit right with them in their heart of hearts.

In 2016, Jessica Knoll, author of the best-selling *Luckiest Girl Alive*, an anti-chick-lit novel about a brooding twenty-eight-year-old big-city magazine editor, made an announcement. In a scene similar to one described by her book's protagonist, Knoll explained that when she was fifteen years old, at a party populated almost exclusively by high-school boys, she drank too much, stripped from the waist down, and passed out. She woke up in the morning with the vague memory of three boys and the MSG taste of ejaculate in her mouth.

Knoll's high-school buddies called it an epic hookup and defined her as a ho. She kept the secret for many years, channeling her trauma into her novel. Now she was ready to tell the truth. "I've been running and I've been ducking and I've been dodging because I'm scared," she explained. "I'm scared people won't call what happened to me rape because for a long time, no one did. But . . . I've come to a simple, powerful revelation: *everyone* is calling it rape now."

Some students described coming to terms with memories that weren't redefined, as Dunham's had been, or denied, as Knoll's, but that popped suddenly into their consciousness. Karmenife is an outspoken senior at Wesleyan with a soft, delicate face framed by a mass of curls. In her closet, she has an opalescent jumpsuit that goes with the opals in her septum ring and a wool skirt-suit ensemble patterned with a million tiny Bart Simpsons; she describes her sartorial choices as "Rihanna meets Jimi Hendrix" and "extraterrestrial dominatrix." She's a student who can monologue at length about the island queens she idolizes for their attitudes, accomplishments, or self-regard. Specifically, there's Dominican revolutionary Mamá Tingó and Haitian queen Anacaona, who resisted Spanish rule, plus Nicki Minaj (from Trinidad) and Rihanna (from Barbados). "I love Rihanna because she's assertive and confident in herself," she says. "She's always fighting for body rights. She wore this incredible see-through Swarovski crystal dress, posted pictures of it on Instagram, then Instagram took it down because you could see her nipples." That Rihanna is from the islands was part of why that happened, she says. "The problem is not only women showing nudity but black women."

When Karmenife and I meet at an Indian restaurant, she's in platform shoes, which makes her Amazon-size. At one point, she tells me a story about carrying a male classmate knocked out on ketamine home from a party. "And he's a tall, lanky string-bean motherfucker, so it was a lot." But I'm surprised to hear a romanticism about sex that's at odds with her bravado.

Her story begins early in freshman year, the red zone. A male student was drunk and kissing her on a frat's dance floor, squeezing her face in his hands, after which they went to the laundry room and had what she describes as nonconsensual sex on the floor. As we're talking, she starts to cry. "Sex is a beautiful thing, a chance to connect with someone else, and here someone had taken my body that I live in, that I've grown up in all my life, and used it against me," she says, casting her body as both a weapon and a stolen possession. "To have something that's so purely yours be taken from you is devastating."

Karmenife says this was only the second time she'd had sex and she buried the memory, but it came back two years later while she was walking by the frat on her way from class. "I saw snippets of different things—the tiles [in the laundry room], the drain, his vomit in the corner, the way his chest looked, his socks, and they kept colliding and colliding until I felt like I was going to die," she says. Everything was throbbing. And it's weird how it activated her sense of smell—that disgusting smell he had of alcohol. (The boy did not respond to a request for an interview.)

Karmenife also says she didn't recognize the alleged rape for years because of societal factors. "You know, women of color, particularly black and Latino women, are often categorized as unrapable because we're hypersexualized," she says, nodding. "Supposedly, we're always asking for it. So when this happens to you as a woman of color, you have all this institutionalized oppressive shit in your mind going, 'Oh, you were asking for it because of your body, the way you're shaped. This is just how it is.' Plus, I think part of me didn't report for years because I was afraid to call the guy a rapist, because that's reinforcing a stereotype for all black men. How can I say I love black men if I turn this person in? It forced me into silence."

When the night came flooding back, she took the gray wool sweater she'd worn, put it in a plastic bag, and then threw that bag in a garbage can. "Somehow even though it had been years, just seeing the sweater evoked all these senses," says Karmenife, addressing me in a quiet tone. Then she considered what to do. "I wouldn't go to the police, because I'm a woman of color, and I don't do that—that is not a safe thing for me," she explains. "Growing up as a black kid, you learn that the police are not there to help you . . . Anytime people of color call the police for help, they either get discriminated against —or they die."

Soon she's talking about how she'd used a picture of Sulkowicz and her mattress as her computer's background so she could see it every time she sat down to her homework. "Emma is a hero to me," she says. "I have two twin mattresses in my room, set up to look like a couch, and one time I even tried to carry one of them to see what it was like. How much does this shit weigh?"

Variations of Rape

At Wesleyan, I received other confessions besides Karmenife's. I talked to sophomores at a house party that turned into what felt like a therapy session, and a girl who told me about her rape while we were standing in the gym. I received a disclosure from Anna,* a young woman whom I'd approached in a lounge area. I'd wanted to borrow the phone charger she had plugged into a bank of red-and-black outlets (those are Wesleyan's school colors), and she was hanging out, designing props for an upcoming play between posting on Instagram. Now she told me about a night when she wore a dress under a parka. She was sitting next to a guy she was friendly with but whom she wasn't interested in romantically, and he stuck his hand up her skirt. No one could see what was happening because of the parka, and she didn't know what to do, so she didn't say anything.

Anna told her parents she was going to report the boy for sexual assault. "I looked in the Wesleyan handbook, and it said that even unwanted kissing is sexual assault," and this was way worse than that, she says. Her parents were dismayed by the idea, which they regarded as drastic. "My mom said, 'You know, an old man tried to kiss me when I was six, and that's something I went through,'" she says, rolling her eyes. (This boy was not contacted for comment.)

Anna decided not to press charges, but she wasn't ashamed. She told others what had happened, and her story quickly spread through the tiny campus. "We're all pretty high-strung, and everyone's on some sort of cocktail of meds for anxiety or depression, but no one knew how to deal with feeling really afraid," says a friend. One of her friends went to a Take Back the Night demonstration and realized that he had been assaulted as a child. Another student tells me, "Every time I was in my dorm, I felt scared and unsafe and confused as to why there weren't more adults on campus who could tell me everything is okay."

The stories I've told you may seem odd: a recovered memory, a hand under a parka in front of a group of classmates, the way the hand under the parka became terrifying for other students on campus. I assure you that these stories are not unique. But why do some women tell stories about these odd, horrible things and not others?

Often a target of sexual assault is vulnerable in some clear way: she's a freshman, or she's drunk, or she may be some specific kind of vulnerable loner who has experienced assault before, the type of loner not dissimilar to the kid a pedophile picks out in the playground. She seems sad. Some guys like that. I'll add a bit of testimony here. No matter my age, I'm rarely able to walk more than a mile in a big city without a guy harassing me on the street. In the months before my father passed away, men began stopping me much more. I hadn't suddenly become hotter but, rather, viscerally emotionally wounded, and hence more vulnerable in their eyes. This supports the theory that sexual assault is a violent crime more than it is a crime of passion, because attackers may home in on women they believe they can overpower.

I'm not just speculating about those types of victims. They're the likeliest at universities, according to sociologists. But the real clincher for who is assaulted and who is not is opportunity.

Golden Gophers

Let's recall the earlier section of this book, the party-culture part, when we discuss another assault that happened in the early fall, the alleged rape of a female student by multiple University of Minnesota Golden Gophers' football players. This incident made big news across the country because after the University of Minnesota suspended some players, the Gophers threatened to boycott the 2016 Holiday Bowl, a major revenue generator for the school. Soon, press conferences, daily coverage, and midnight meetings took over practice time. The resistance was strong until the university's meticulous, eighty-two-page investigation document about what might have happened was leaked to local news stations. Then the defiant football players backed off.

According to this investigative report, which forms the basis for the coming paragraphs, the scene was set at a large dorm after the first football game of the year. Group messages among the Gophers earlier in the evening indicate a goal-directed Friday night: *Party at my crib 331 invite hoes!!, I got 4 hoes where the party at,* and, as victory was achieved, *Go to the rail hella hoes.*

It's unclear if the victim was one of those hella hoes, but we know she showed up at the football players' apartment complex at two a.m. along with eight girlfriends. Parties were raging on various floors, and this crew went from one to the next before the girl started flirting with two guys, eventually lying down on a couch beside them. One of the guys asked her if she wanted to see his apartment—the apartments had different floor plans; it was interesting, he said—and she played along. The second guy joined them. When they got there, though, the boys took her straight to the bedroom instead of showing her the interesting floor plan.

She excused herself to go to the bathroom; she had her period and took out her tampon, which most women know could mean that she was planning to have sex, though she later explained that she did so because her flow was light at that time and she was planning to head home soon. In any case, one of the guys—the other was a high-school recruit in Minnesota for the weekend—was already undressing in the room. They had another idea: *Me and the recruit finna double team this bitch,* the player messaged the group.

After the guys allegedly unzipped her bodysuit, the three of them had what might have been consensual sex. There's video of the girl being penetrated from behind as she gives the other guy a blowjob, in between saying, "Okay, I have to throw out my gum, where do I put it." The player seems to have messaged the group again (*Lol we forreal going brazy lol,* then *I took good videos*). Then, disappointed the recruit couldn't ejaculate, the player left him alone with the girl in case he'd have better luck solo. Afterward, he had sex with her himself. Then he told some other guys they could have their turns with her. (The players denied some details, including this one.)

What happened from here is in dispute, but it seems that the victim stayed on that mattress while somewhere between four and six other guys came into the room. She says she wrapped herself in a blanket because her clothes were in a pile across the room and she didn't want them to see her naked. Her phone, a key part of all our identities, was over with her clothes, but the guys didn't give it to her. In fact, they allegedly used it, adding themselves to her Snapchat and Instagram accounts. The victim didn't know how to get her clothes on or her phone back, so she sat wrapped in the blanket until one of the guys said something like, "You are too sexy, I need my turn," and forced himself on her.

At times she focused on the ceiling and the blank, black television screen, confused about what was happening. She recalls saying things like "I hate you." One of them — she knew him a little because they'd matched on Tinder — allegedly grabbed her hair and pushed her down to his penis; she told him she was going to throw up. Though the evidence gathered by the university indicates that a handful of men were present, she imagined that ten to twenty men had sex with her while others chanted and jostled for position in a line waiting for turns. She remembers a guy saying, "You have a lot more to go."

The Minnesota investigator summarized the woman's account of the end of the assault this way: "The approximately two-foot strip of floor between the bed and television stand was covered with yellow/gold condom wrappers and used condoms. There was a pile of around 12 used condoms on top of a white plastic set of drawers next to the television stand. Semen was dripping down the drawers . . . She had no sense of how long she had been in [the] bedroom or of how many men had had sex with her. She remembers wondering, oh my god, how can I not remember what just happened." She allegedly watched the last man swear under his breath as he, too, took in the scene, then turned his attention to cleaning up. While he was distracted, she grabbed her clothes from the floor and fled the apartment.

Back in her own bedroom on the dorm's sixth floor, she scribbled some notes.

Hello it's after the 1st game I need help . . .

Help I'm scared & hate everyone I need help this isn't okay

Where is everyone

PS Help

Who are they

Despite these sentiments, an even stranger — yet common — event occurred after this: she messaged a friend that she'd been in a scary situation with twelve men, but she wasn't sure if it was rape. I'll repeat that: *She wasn't sure if it was rape.*

And she was not unique in this reaction. Jennifer Marsh, the vice president of special projects at RAINN, the national support service for abuse victims founded by singer Tori Amos that I mentioned earlier, tells me that trained staffers at their 24/7 hotline, the largest in the nation, take about 266 calls a day and conduct 130 online counseling sessions. "One of the first things that our users say is 'I don't know what happened to me,'" says Marsh. "It's not uncommon for them to say things like, 'I woke up the next morning and cooked him breakfast.'"

Proof

You may have read this far in this book wondering why rape is so traumatic. Obviously, what Karmenife says is part of it—you've had something taken away from you, something essentially yours. And what Liz and the Gophers' victim mentioned is true also; you're left so confused that you're not sure it wasn't consensual. But there's another reason as well. Most of the time, the victim can't prove rape. For a lot of survivors, speaking out isn't a way to raise consciousness or get attention (I recalled the Columbia student at the early rally who jokingly put her hand on her hip and swaggered down a fake red carpet). It's the only way for them to feel they've attained a measure of justice.

The difficulty of proving what happened perhaps struck the Gophers' victim when, the next day, she drove herself to the hospital for a forensic exam and a rape kit, in which a bathroom drawer's worth of tools for collecting fibers and DNA—comb, nail pick, swabs—is run over one's entire body. Here, she encountered yet another paradox in the world of sexual assault.

Thousands of rape kits across America, some decades old, haven't been processed by police departments, possibly because cops don't want to take on these cases, which they know are hard to solve, or because they have a tendency to disbelieve victims, or because there are vague policies about rape-kit testing (not unconnected to the fact that kits are expensive to process, upward of a thousand dollars each). This is a national disgrace. It's also bad policing. DNA identifies serial rapists, and it could resolve open cases.

But if you already know who was there, DNA doesn't tell you what happened. That's the first problem of rape kits and of most rapes at universities. Here's the second: Kits tend to be administered too late. Victims are slow to take in what happened—*was it rape?* If they head to the hospital, they usually go after a few days, but most evidence is lost by seventy-two hours after the incident. Few victims will arrive for medical care without having taken a shower, which means that even if they go to the hospital quickly, hair and semen and rug fibers might already have gone down the drain.

If that's not complex enough, here's problem number three: sexual-assault exams frequently do not show evidence of injury, even when rape has occurred. The victim in the Gophers case told the university that her sexual-assault examiner did not find evidence of "significant" injury. "The truth is that rape doesn't leave a whole lot of physical evidence — the idea that rape leaves a ton of injuries is a great big myth," says attorney Christina Brandt-Young. "The fact that you can't see trauma doesn't mean that sexual assault didn't happen. That part of the body is built to withstand a baby coming out of it." (She adds that one must do a proper investigation to arrive at the heart of the matter; more on this later.)

I spoke with Randall Brown, a Baton Rouge gynecologist and medical director of his local rape crisis center, about this. "The vagina doesn't always show trauma, and what it does show depends a lot on the prior sexual activity of the victim," he tells me. "A woman who has had three children vaginally, good-sized children — well, you wouldn't expect to see trauma unless it's been a very long time since she's had intercourse. A woman who is virginal — well, that's different. We'd see signs of intercourse. But we still wouldn't necessarily know if it was forced."

College women tend not to fall on either end of this spectrum — they generally haven't had children, but they're not virginal — so there's little vaginal evidence of trauma, though there may be bruising on the rest of the body. But if physical force wasn't used, there's typically no evidence at all. "Today, we have the phenomenal ability to get a [stranger-rape] conviction or secure a plea because of DNA: doctors are trained, the public is enlightened, police officers are enlightened, and when we get that DNA, we often find the same guy has committed ten [rapes], and he's going to take his twenty to twenty-five years," Brown continues. "But with acquaintance rape, we don't have eyewitnesses. Plus we have conflicting testimony over consent." He sighs. "This is a crime that's very, very difficult to prove."

Other experts sum it up this way: the perfect crime.

Totally My Fault

In a move that you may find shocking, local Minneapolis law enforcement declined to take the Gophers' victim's case. Why? They might have thought that she didn't have enough evidence; they might even have thought her account of events was untrue. They definitely knew prosecutors wouldn't win. Not only do rape victims often wait too long to go to the hospital, thus losing critical physical evidence, but they pose substantial problems for cops and attorneys owing to a host of counterintuitive reactions they have to the event, some of which are due to posttraumatic stress disorder.

On the college lecture circuit, Michigan State professor of psychology Rebecca Campbell, a funny and engaging speaker, has a knack for elucidating these difficulties by putting science in layperson's terms. At one of her talks, she began by showing a slide of a brain and saying, "This is your brain," then adding, "Actually, it's not *your* brain, your brain is in your head." She waits a beat. "Folks, these are the jokes!"

Campbell tells groups that over the past decade, scientists have begun to understand the neurobiology of trauma, and these findings explain the major problem that cops have when they encounter rape victims: "The stuff they say makes no sense." Trauma puts the brain's prefrontal cortex, key to decision-making and memory, on the fritz. This means the way victims are typically interviewed by authorities — asked to tell a story over and over in a logical fashion — is an ineffective method to determine if they're telling the truth. Instead, we should recognize that victims' memories are fragmented, like a series of Post-it notes on the "world's messiest desk." Campbell observes that when officers are involved in a shooting, police departments allow them to sleep one or two cycles before interviews, because sleep consolidates memory, and she recommends that survivors be afforded the same accommodations.

Anyone who's been through a trauma knows it not only scrambles one's memory but can produce seemingly inexplicable reactions. The hormonal soup that victims experience in the aftermath of a rape makes them act in ways one wouldn't expect — they're not necessarily crying and sobbing; they're sometimes not cooperative or even nice. During a traumatic event, the body releases oxytocin, natural opiates, and various other hormones, which means that some victims may exhibit a lack of emotion or may laugh inappropriately when they talk about the assault. They may even talk about the other party in loving terms. All of these responses are the result of the body's attempt to deal with the trauma one has just endured.

Other reactions are also common. A pedestrian in the path of an oncoming car may freeze. Flight, fright, freeze — these are normal responses. That victims might experience this sort of paralysis mid-assault seems logical; that they'd continue to have what might look to others like consensual sex, perhaps less so. Victims testify often about "frozen fright," and though people could use this as an excuse for morning-after regret, Campbell believes many rape victims experience tonic immobility — that is, they are aware of events but physically cannot move.

When these characteristics of genuine victims aren't recognized, authorities, including those at universities, may turn their backs. And let's not forget that victims already have a hard time saying they're victims — *was it rape?* The two-step of disbelief and shame culminating in self-blame that I described at the beginning of the chapter can become particularly frenzied when authorities doubt them. Campbell says that 80 percent of victims report that they don't want to continue requesting help from authorities after an initial meeting, partly because they are made to feel even more disbelieved and ashamed than they felt at the outset.

"Needless to say, rape, the most heinous crime imaginable. Seems it's a comic's dream, though," says Sarah Silverman in the lead-up to her widely heralded rape joke (and diametrically opposed to Daniel Tosh's infamous heckle of a female audience member: "Wouldn't it be funny if that girl got raped by, like, five guys right now?"). In her trademark dumb-girl-who-is-sometimes-a-genius drawl, Silverman continues, "The truth is, it's like the safest area to talk about in comedy. 'Cause who's going to complain about a rape joke? Rape victims? They don't even report rape. I mean, they're traditionally not complainers. The worst maybe thing that could happen — and I would feel terrible — is like after a show maybe somebody comes up to you and is like, 'Look, I'm a victim of rape, and as a victim of rape I just want to say I thought that joke was inappropriate and insensitive and totally my fault and I am so sorry.'"

LOL?

Syracuse Speak-Out

With myriad barriers—from not acting "victim enough" to inconclusive rape kits; from the societal injustice that Karmenife described to proving some acts as "true sexual assault"; from being shamed by one's peers to the way the Gophers' victim was doubtlessly embarrassed by the week of national news about her experience, during which America hotly debated whether she'd truly been raped and if the team should proceed to the Holiday Bowl or not, and even to my own hesitation—it's understandable that many victims stay silent.

At Wesleyan, with all the hubbub about assault, it became easier to speak out. Survivors were not only supported by peers. They also learned their Title IX rights and began bringing complaints against the boys to the university. From 2010 to 2013, only one or two cases per year were reported to the school. However, when Chloe, the student I met at her gingerbread home behind the science library, put her mind to addressing the issue in 2014, that changed. When we discuss the action she took on this front, she says, semi-sarcastically, "I know all the rape girls on campus."

In the spring of 2014, Wesleyan had twenty-three reports of rape. This made the school the *number two* university in America for rate of sexual assaults reported per student. Which you would think, from reading the various "I'm shocked!" headlines, such as "These Are the Schools with the Most Rape Reports," might mean it was the *worst* university to send your daughter to. But actually, this distinction meant Wesleyan was getting safer. Did it also mean that there was a bit of contagion on campus that grew to encompass some students who weren't really assaulted? Perhaps. But what it definitely meant was that women felt more comfortable speaking up.

At Syracuse, the situation was very different. In fact, public records at the time showed that for the same period, out of twenty-one thousand students (about fifteen thousand undergraduates), one student reported a rape. If I haven't made this clear, this is not something to be proud of.

That Syracuse student may not be a sorority sister, but there were a couple of sisters around who decided that it was worth speaking out, that they wanted to change the scene at school. And on a frigid afternoon, I sat down with two Alpha Xi Delta sisters, Jacqueline Reilly and Caroline Heres, at a coffee-shop-slash-vintage-clothing-store on campus to talk about their experiences.

They weren't radicals. Reilly, who was studying graphic design, made clear at various points in our conversation that she didn't want to be perceived as anti-administration, militaristic, negative — "Negativity is easy to spread and turns me off," she said. A pretty Irish brunette with porcelain skin and a pragmatic nature who's also "a little bit of a control freak," in her words, she grew up in Boston, where her family was active in the Catholic Church until disillusioned by the pedophile-priest scandal. As a kid, she loved Disney princesses, dreamed of becoming Britney Spears (in her "pre-haircut days"); she now enjoys futurism (books like *Brave New World,* movies like *The Hunger Games*).

At our meeting, she shows off a claddagh ring — a traditional piece of Irish jewelry — that her parents gave her for Christmas half a dozen years ago and that she's worn every day since. She explains, "If the heart is pointed towards you, you're in a relationship, and if it's out, I'm looking for love." The ring is turned in now; she has a boyfriend, and she's happy at 'Cuse.

Heres and Reilly, now juniors, met when they were in AXiD's pledge class. Reilly always knew she wanted to be in a sorority. Heres, not as much. They talk to each other in the call-and-response pattern of close college girlfriends, one friend summing up, the other affirming, and then a compare-and-contrast. "I didn't burst into tears of joy when I opened my bid — I was more just 'Yay,'" says Heres.

"That's also not you, to burst into tears," says Reilly.

"Yeah, I don't cry a lot," says Heres. She smiles a little, enjoying her essential self being recognized. "I'm like a robot, I don't know."

At the beginning of sophomore year, Reilly says she was lured into a fraternity brother's bedroom, and Heres and her AXiD sisters weren't around. She was working as a peer adviser in the red-zone period at the start of the fall semester, that time when female underclassmen are most vulnerable to sexual assault. Some girls she didn't know well invited her to a frat party—not even a party, just a handful of students hanging out in a room. A brother "separated" her from this group. The girls who'd been with her earlier banged on his bedroom door to make sure Reilly was okay, or so they said. They took off down the stairs in their heels.

In the morning, she woke with no memory of the night before other than drinking from a Styrofoam cup, the contents of which she did not pour herself. "I was terrified, but I tried to play it off like I wasn't," she says. She didn't call it rape at first. "It had been taught to me all my life that rape happened with a stranger in a dark alley, and there wasn't much wiggle room around that," she continues. As quickly as she could, she headed for home, where she found her roommate concerned about where she'd been. She stared at herself in the mirror. "On my neck, I had fingerprint bruises," she says. "That was the moment I knew this shouldn't have happened, that I didn't consent." When she took a shower, scrubbing her body to erase the boy's unwanted touch, she walked herself right into problem number two.

Reilly covered the marks on her neck with concealer and headed to the university's main drag, Marshall Street. Near the Starbucks, she bumped into Heres, who saw the marks on her neck and assumed they were hickeys. "I pretended to whip out a microphone like a newscaster, saying, 'Tell our viewers who you hooked up with last night!'" Heres tells me. Reilly took her hands in her own and looked her straight in the eye. "'No, no, Caroline, come back to earth,'" Heres recalls her saying. (Though Reilly's account was confirmed by Heres and another friend who spoke with her after the assault, the alleged offending party was not contacted for comment.)

Reilly, who says she felt afraid that the boy or his friends were going to come hurt her again, called her parents, who had just dropped her in Syracuse for the new semester. She told them something had happened, something that wasn't "the usual night in college," and they rushed back to campus. They weren't expecting to see the guy, but while they were walking to dinner, he suddenly appeared on a path. "My whole body froze," says Reilly. "I lost all feeling. I don't know how my dad didn't jump and kill him."

The real problem was her own trauma—figuring out how to sit with it, metabolize it. Speaking out became a way to assuage it. Heres, who says she was in an abusive relationship in high school, sat with Reilly one afternoon in a dorm common room — vending machines in the corner, uncomfortable couches, one table for studying, fluorescent lighting. They sat on folding chairs, "and we did not move from those chairs for four hours," says Heres, as they discussed what to do.

A couple of years earlier, few in Greek life at Syracuse talked openly about sexual assault. Gabriela, a progressive sister, says most women didn't take it seriously. "Once, a girl was 'forcibly touched' behind the library, meaning, I guess, some guy groped her," says Gabriela. "It was a buzzword on campus — 'Hey, do you mind if I forcibly touch you?' It was treated as a joke." But now sorority sisters began to swap stories with a clearer framing on what had happened. One of the women that I interviewed on Bid Day told me that she realized that during the red zone, she'd had an experience similar to Reilly's that she redefined as rape rather than another crazy college night, "blame it on Jose Cuervo," which was the way she'd originally processed it.

Some sisters made their own rules about alcohol at parties. "When I ask a guy at the party for a beer, I want to control what I'm drinking," says Heres. "I'm not taking it if it's open. If it is, I put it to the side, and then I say, 'Can I have an unopened one?' If they turn me down, 'Okay, I'll leave.'" They're nervous about drinks being very strong or possibly even dosed with Xanax or Robitussin to loosen people up. "Usually, each girl in our sorority keeps an eye out, and if you're at a party you might get a listserv e-mail saying, 'Don't drink it, it's gross. It tastes like cough syrup. I think there's something in there,'" says Heres.

Doctors I've interviewed about college rape say that victims often think they're drugged when they're very drunk. The doctors repeat, almost as a mantra, "The number one date-rape drug is alcohol." At Syracuse, it's hard to know whether drinks are dosed — it's an oft-repeated part of campus lore. To my knowledge, no Syracuse fraternity drugged drinks, but a sorority sister in a leadership position says she thinks differently. "We've told the frats to stop putting things in the drinks, and they'll either say they've never done that or they'll say, 'Well, some sororities request that we put it in the drinks, because they like the feeling of it,'" she explains. "Other frats will say, 'No, we pour energy drinks into jungle juice, and that's why girls feel sick in the morning.'"

(When I contacted Syracuse University to ask about this, along with a larger list of questions, they did not comment on this subject.)

The changes at Syracuse came largely from girls following Reilly and Heres's lead, sloughing off shame and speaking out. At AXiD, there's a tradition: During pledging, the dozens of new recruits sit down in the sorority's graciously appointed living room and share their secrets—parents' divorces, siblings' deaths. This is consciousness-raising, sorority-style. This voyage is the one that led to Heres realizing how abusive her high-school relationship had been. "As I was listening to my friend talk about her experience with being abused by her boyfriend, I was seizing up inside—*Oh my God, this happened to me too*," says Heres.

Now, more and more, the secrets were about rape and sexual assault. "We reveal ourselves to each other, peel off the layers, tell each other our deepest scars, trust these girls with stories you've barely told," says Heres. Afterward, they cry and pledge to support one another.

"It's a really special night," says Reilly, then adds in her pragmatic way, "Our sorority always sees results out of that night."

6

Rape Theory 101

As more students spoke out across the country, a casting-out of spirits — or a totting-up of results, as Jacqueline Reilly of Alpha Xi Delta calls them — began to take place. At the same time, statistics around sexual assault started shifting in a complex way. From 1995 to 2005, national data indicates that the total rate of sexual violence against American women twelve or older declined by 64 percent, part of the enormous reduction in crime in this country over the past twenty years (although the mid-2010s had a slight uptick). Not so at colleges. You've heard that one in five American women enrolled at universities were sexually assaulted by graduation. This is true. But the nuances involve expanded definitions of *sexual assault* and whether the victim chooses that phrase to categorize what happened to her.

Until recently, academic research into sexual violence was dominated by true believers. Many came from an ideological standpoint similar to activists' today: sexual violence occurs on a vast continuum, and all of it is equally important because it's evidence of patriarchal structures in society. The grants to study the problem were small. Few took notice of the work that was done. Yet the numbers the research generated were staggering, beginning with Kent State psychology professor Mary Koss's survey of six thousand students at thirty-two colleges in 1985. Koss came up with a one-in-four stat for rape and attempted rape, though critics argued that she'd inflated results by including a somewhat ambiguous question: "Have you had sexual intercourse when you didn't want to because a man gave you alcohol or drugs?"

Poring over dozens of these surveys made me sweat. Some included attempted assaults, some only completed ones; some asked about postpuberty sexual experiences, some didn't; many tweaked the definition of sexual assault. (I should note that the rate of penetrative rape seemed to fall dramatically over time, though when I brought this up, researchers told me it was impossible to know this for sure.)

Deep in the rabbit hole, I called two top victimization experts. One was Christopher Krebs, a senior researcher at the nonprofit group RTI International in North Carolina (who looks like a young Harrison Ford in the photo that accompanies his online bio); he's the scientist who designed the 2007 survey that the White House touted as evidence of its one-in-five statistic. The other was Callie Rennison, co-director of the Criminology and Criminal Justice Research Initiative at the University of Colorado Denver's School of Public Affairs.

Krebs and Rennison agreed on one point that raises a serious question about the one-in-five statistic from the jump. Both said there are few, if any, representative national numbers about college sexual assault. All numbers are not only school-specific but also tend to represent only a small percentage of each university's students because surveys aren't typically mandatory. It's possible that students who choose to take sexual assault surveys are drawn in not merely by the promise of a twenty-dollar gift card to Chili's but because they have experiences with sexual assault, thus skewing a supposedly random sample.

On other topics, the two experts' opinions diverged. Krebs perceives a widespread problem at college. In fact, after he explained that his original survey, cited by the Obama White House, was not a nationally representative statistic due to its small sample size — only two schools — the Bureau of Justice Statistics funded him to study twenty-three thousand students at nine universities. In 2016, Krebs found that the rates of sexual assault at these schools were variable, of course, and some universities were off the charts (he won't say which). Taking them all into account, he came up with the one-in-five statistic again, or even somewhat higher.

Reading the survey questions for Krebs's new study, I don't believe that he's making mountains out of molehills. His definition of *unwanted sexual contact*, for example, is hard to misinterpret: "Unwanted sexual contact often occurs when someone uses force against you, such as holding you down with his or her body weight, pinning your arms, hitting or kicking you; someone threatens to hurt you or someone close to you; or you are unable to provide consent or stop what is happening because you are passed out, drugged, drunk, incapacitated, or asleep. This could happen after you voluntarily use alcohol or drugs, or after you are given a drug without your knowledge or consent." Perhaps a student could focus on the word *drunk* and answer affirmatively even if she wasn't truly incapacitated, not truly scared, but it's hard to imagine anyone interpreting this question as being about drunk sex.

There is a thornier problem here, though. About half of the women who click a box for behavior that meets the definition of rape or sexual assault will say no when they're asked point blank if they've experienced rape or sexual assault. When questioned further, they sometimes say that they didn't think what happened to them was a big deal. "Very often their conception of what rape is—'The stranger jumped out from behind a bush or a parked car, hit me over the head, I fought back but I couldn't fight him off, I screamed *no*'—does not map well onto the legal definition of rape," Krebs told me. "But when you start to say that if a woman didn't think what happened to her was rape then it's not a rape, you're really, truly missing something." Then he passionately answered a question I hadn't asked. "And if you're saying that because she didn't report it to the police it wasn't a crime, then you're missing that this is the most underreported crime in the world."

When I talked to Rennison, I heard a different perspective. A quick-witted woman with Joni Mitchell hair and a rock-climbing hobby, she said that her niche in victimization research was proving that "pretty much everything we think we know isn't right. If you saw it on TV, it's probably a hundred and eighty degrees from the truth." The new focus on college sexual assault drew Rennison's attention; it's the "crime du jour," she said dryly. Lecturing at various universities, she's met parents who have told her they're too worried to send their daughters to college. "How horrifying!" she exclaimed, then added out of the side of her mouth, "And when the topic gets big you always get invited places, 'Hey, would you write a chapter,' and you know you've got eight or ten publications in it."

Rennison told me that we should not be calling the problem a campus crime because most assaults occur off campus *and* only at a small percentage of American universities—at residential schools, not community colleges, which have harassment and stalking but whose low-income and nonnative-English speakers are unlikely to confide in authorities. (It's also worth noting that "one in five by graduation" includes the many months students spend away from campus, like summer vacation.) Sixteen- to twenty-year-old women are, indeed, more at risk for sex assault than anyone else in America, but according to Rennison's research, those who are not in college (again, when *college* includes two-year colleges as well as online schools) actually face *more* risk than those in college.

Krebs and young activists do not separate butt grabs from physically violent rape because it's all part of rape culture. Rennison disagrees. She's said that when she sees posters touting the one-in-five stat, she wants to rip them down. "I'm not saying rape never happens — that's not my position," Rennison said to me. "But in victimization there's an idea that everything has to be an epidemic, and it drives me crazy." She's aghast at the breadth with which sexual violence is now being defined. "I'm finding what [social scientists] are studying is getting broader and broader and broader," she said. "As a field, we need to say, 'What do we mean by rape? What do we mean by sexual assault? What do we mean by sexual battery?' . . . This is how Krebs's one-in-five gets thrown around, and no one has any idea what it means."

The only reliable measure of sexual assault of college women over time, said Rennison, is the U.S. National Crime Victimization Survey, which demonstrates that over a six-month period, about six in one thousand women in any type of college experienced sexual assault *on campus*. Rennison agreed that these numbers are low, and the way the information is gathered — in person, sometimes with parents present; over the phone; and by expressly asking if someone is a victim of sexual assault, not if she's experienced behavior *equivalent* to assault, *and* not asking about incapacitated rape — is flawed. Still, she added, "Butt grabbing? It happens a lot. Rape? It happens, happens way too much, but it's super-hard to measure."

Rennison felt the need to finish our conversation by explaining that she was not trying to shut down conversations about sexual assault with her data. But, she said, "something about the way it's being done isn't healthy. I was talking to [a young woman] who was very good with her survivor language, but it came down to her being groped once in a public place. And I was — I am old — I was, 'You're calling yourself a survivor? I'd like to introduce you to my friend who was kidnapped, raped, and her throat was cut. She is a *survivor.'"* She sighed. "I do struggle with this. It would also be nice to live in a world where you could be somewhere in public and not get your butt grabbed."

She doesn't have kids, but she has teenage nieces who plan to attend college. I asked her what she told them. "I say, 'It's not around every corner, not everyone's bad,'" she said. She tells them that they should feel safe on campus but to take a friend along if they go to an off-campus house, to leave with that friend, and to understand that wherever there's alcohol, there can be trouble. "I explain that boys have a different culture, the go-get-'em-tiger culture, which is alive and well off and on campus: 'Tell her this, tell her you love her, give her some alcohol, then have sex with her.'" Rennison paused. "I don't know if that resonates. I remember my mom telling me that when I was young, and I said, 'Nah, Mom!'"

Rennison and Krebs draw dramatically different conclusions from similar studies because of their own divergent opinions of what should be considered sexual assault. I thought I might find more clarity by looking beyond their realm, the study of crime, to experts in another field, one we might call hookup studies.

Elizabeth Armstrong, a University of Michigan professor of sociology and organizational studies (aka Planet College Studies) and author of *Paying for the Party*, a renowned book about the lives of girls on one dorm floor at a large midwestern university, agreed that these stats are confusing. "The family demographers in the U.S., the people who are best equipped to engage in prevalence and incidence measurements like this, didn't take it on as one of their agendas," said Armstrong. "The only people who did take it on systematically are the NCVS, and their measurements are disastrously wrong."

Armstrong accepted the one-in-five numbers, but she doesn't go for the "it's all violence" principle. "It's incredibly important to define things very clearly, and indicate, 'Okay, if we're going to define *sexual assault* as someone grabs a body part in public at a party, and also a vaginal rape, those are different things,'" she said. We discussed the fact that the number of students penetrated, or raped, is smaller than the number of those assaulted; it's 1 in 7 or 1 in 10, maybe 1 in 14. And if we know that 20 percent of American college students are virgins at graduation, wowza, that is a lot of rape.

Jessie Ford at NYU agreed with Armstrong on most points. Ford, a thirty-one-year-old graduate of Brown University, is an intriguing new voice in this space and a far younger one than most in the field. Her scholarly focus has long been sexual pleasure, and when she was at Brown a decade ago, sexual assault wasn't a pressing issue. But like Rennison, as the campus-assault topic blew up, she was drawn to it. "Communication around sex is so interesting, and confusing, when you're starting to have sex moving on from adolescence, and I've found that the same things that I was interested in in terms of pleasure and learning how to have good sex are also relevant with bad sex and dangerous sex," she told me.

Ford and I talked about Paula England's work measuring the rate of hookups on college campuses over time. "I don't think the number of hookups has changed today," Ford said. "What's changed is the number of women who have realized that what was a bad night historically is *actually* sexual assault. More women are realizing that they might have been sexually assaulted than they would have in the past."

I asked what Ford thought about so many women checking the box indicating they've suffered behavior that *is* sexual assault and simultaneously saying they don't think they've been assaulted. A majority of those women, when asked why they didn't report the incident, say that they didn't consider it serious enough. "This is super-interesting," Ford said, and talked about a study she's doing of one hundred students whose responses classify them as victims. She's looking specifically at students who check the box for having sex they didn't want to have. "They say things like 'I might have wanted to have sex with him down the road, but I didn't want to have sex with him that night,'" she told me. "'I was really drunk, so it happened, and I was upset it happened, but in theory, if the circumstances were different, I might have slept with that person.' And other people will say, 'Well, I wanted to have sex with someone but I didn't want to have sex with that person, and I got drunk, so it ended up happening with that person.' It can cross into a gray area."

I thought the next thing that Ford would say was that assaults were happening because of hooking up. The culprit was super-casual sex after all. But neither she nor Armstrong said that. "It's not the hookup, per se," that's creating all of these scenarios (rape, assault, public-place butt grab), said Armstrong. "It's the gender inequality."

Consent

Suzanne Goldberg is Columbia University's new head liaison on sexual assault, appointed in 2014 to revise Columbia's policies around issues raised by Emma Sulkowicz, Zoe Ridolfi-Starr, and allies. A law professor who was co-counsel on the Supreme Court case reversing Texas's sodomy law, her office faces the Wien Hall dormitory, in whose courtyard Nungesser and Sulkowicz began kissing that fateful night. While I was there, we peered at the view together. "You know, not my favorite [thing] when students stand in front of the windows . . ." She trailed off as I conjured images of jockstrapped boys backlit by Ikea lamps.

Goldberg began a monologue about Columbia's new sexual-assault policies, then added, "It's hard for most people to navigate sexual relationships, and particularly challenging for young adults." She clicked on her computer screen to show me a poster hanging in undergraduate dorms with red, yellow, and green lights. Red means stop — someone is drunk, asleep, or passed out, or one person doesn't want to have sex. Yellow is pause — mixed signals. Green — a mutual decision has been made about how far to go and "all partners are excited and enthusiastic!" Goldberg, who was wearing a black suit and pearls, looked pleased. "A traffic light is useful," she said. "It gives people a vocabulary for having what can be an awkward conversation in a congenial way." She printed out and gave me a copy of the poster, which I tucked in my handbag.

Consent is both the answer to the question of how to reduce those terrifying statistics and part of the reason those stats are climbing (you may have noticed that Krebs's question about unwanted sex includes "unable to provide consent," and some newer surveys ask this more baldly, without connecting it to force or incapacitation). Colloquially called "yes means yes," affirmative consent is a new doctrine that shifts standards for consensual sex.

Silence isn't consent. "No means no" misses the important question. Getting busy must include a verbal *yes* or some type of totally-impossible-to-misinterpret moan or groan or high-pitched scream of pleasure. That must be secured *before* every sexual act, from smooching to touching breasts to anal sex, which means Nungesser, in Sulkowicz's telling, clearly trespassed. Planet College hasn't evolved so swiftly in this arena since coeducation. This is now the Ivy League standard and the standard for at least half of the other universities in the country, say experts (though, oddly, no one's keeping a national database). It's law in California, New York, Illinois, and Connecticut for all students at public *and* private universities.

In 2015, Obama's White House began promoting the word *consent*. Just that: *consent*. In a celebrity PSA, the camera cuts from one fresh-faced, millennial-friendly celeb to another as together, finishing each other's sentences, they don't exactly define *consent*, but they express its importance.

The Vampire Diaries' Nina Dobrev: "Sex without it . . ."

". . . isn't sex," says *Gossip Girl's* Jessica Szohr.

"It's rape," says *The Hunger Games'* Josh Hutcherson.

Zoe Saldana, *Avatar's* blue alien hunter Neytiri, finishes the round robin. "Consent," she says. "If you don't get it, you don't get it." She gives a slight, yet definite, shake of her head.

Who gets consent? When do you get it? How do you get it? What is it, exactly? The PSA doesn't say, and that may be intentional. Philosophers and, more recently, law professors have written many thousands of pages on this topic, and even they can't say for sure what it means. It might have something to do with engaging in behavior in such a way that a reasonable person would conclude you agreed or assented to it. What was evident to both parties in that moment? Would both have reasonably inferred that there was an agreement? As an internal, psychological matter, consent has something to do with desire, but not everything. Gideon Yaffe, a Yale Law professor studying consent, offers me the example of drilling a tooth. One consents to it, but one doesn't desire it. And we all know sex isn't only desire; it's attraction and revulsion, desire and shame, domination and submission, often all at the same time.

Universities tend to proclaim their adherence to a "yes means yes" standard in student-conduct handbooks and leave it at that, but in 2013, Yale clarified terms for students by offering "Sexual Misconduct Scenarios," a four-page guide listing the ways that sexual consent could be established between students and noting which failures to do so would be punished by the college. "Talking with sexual partners about desires and limits may seem awkward," Yale explains in a policy document, "but serves as the basis for positive sexual experiences shaped by mutual willingness and respect."

The students in these hypothetical scenarios were given notably gender-neutral names. "Jessie and Vic have been flirting all semester, and agree to meet at a party. After dancing closely together for a while, Vic proposes going to one of their rooms and Jessie agrees . . . Once in the room, they begin touching. Each is interested in hearing what the other wants, and each is paying attention to the other's signals. They reach and sustain clear agreement upon mutually desired sexual activities."

Like the rest of the scenarios, Yale next presented a correct answer about which category of consent was met. In the case of Vic and Jessie, "This is consensual sex: Vic and Jessie reached positive, voluntary, unambiguous agreement to engage in sexual conduct together."

Another scenario: "Devin and Ansley are engaging in a consensual sexual encounter, which Devin begins to intensify. Ansley responds by pulling away slightly, moving Devin's hands and saying 'not so fast; I'm not sure.' Devin cooperates briefly but then intensifies the contact once more. Ansley inches backwards and then becomes still. Nonetheless, Devin has sex with Ansley." Answer: "While the initial sexual activity was consensual, that consent was not sustained." Penalty is anything from multi-semester suspension to expulsion.

One more: "Ryo and Casey are dating. Casey is uncertain about whether they should have sex, but Ryo is persuasive and finally obtains Casey's voluntary agreement. As they engage in sex, Casey says 'wait — stop — that hurts.' Ryo nonetheless continues for several more minutes, restraining Casey. Afterwards, Casey is upset. Ryo apologizes, but says they were past the point of interruption." Answer: "While there was initial consent, that consent was withdrawn." Penalty is expulsion.

I'd guess that, like me, you got most of those right. I'd also bet you'll struggle a bit more with this last one. "Morgan and Kai . . . go to Kai's room. They undress each other and begin touching each other. Morgan moves as if to engage in oral sex and looks up at Kai questioningly. Kai nods in agreement and Morgan proceeds. Subsequently, without pausing to check for further agreement, Kai begins to perform oral sex on Morgan. Morgan lies still for a few minutes, then moves away, saying it is late and they should sleep."

Answer: "There was initial agreement, but the bounds of that agreement were not clear. Kai may have thought that Morgan had consented to reciprocal oral sex, but took no steps to obtain unambiguous agreement." Penalty is a reprimand.

The Moral Mind

At some universities, this way of having sex is still considered ludicrous — screw what it says in the student handbook. At others, students take it seriously. The moral mind, particularly the postadolescent one, wants to sort the world into good and bad, locating aggressive certainties and incorporating them into his or her worldview. Presented with the blurry lines of sexual assault, students are open to imposing ethics on what they regard as a confusing situation. "I guess in my head, [I thought,] *My mom raised me well . . . good people treat other people well, and bad people are the ones who assault others, but good people don't,*" J. D. Laurence-Chasen, a Brown student who has served as a student adjudicator of sexual-assault cases, says. "*I'm a good person and I'm friends with good people.* And yeah, I think pretty immediately [at Brown] it became very clear to me that there's no black and white like that."

Edgier colleges have rallied around the idea; this may even be the standard for American society down the line (when PrezBo — um — dies). If you think about it, consent and trigger warnings are two sides of one phenomenon. They're both connected to the developing adult's desire to control the environment, to create a closed subculture of one's peers, and to express oneself differently than the generation before (don't think for a second students don't know much trigger warnings drive parents and some professors nuts). They're also probably born of millennials' minds having been formed by the Internet. What we may view as ludicrous and presumptuous and entitled — the right not only to trigger warnings, but to censure someone who said something that offended or triggered them and, ideally, make it/them go away — reflects the technologically mediated culture in which they were raised. One swipe and a person is gone forever. Blocked. Which is actually a perfect word for the way they're inhibiting and shutting off contrary ideas — ideas that piss them off, and probably also terrify them, for reasons that may be worth examining.

This may also have to do with growing up bullied, which many of them were; in middle school, the Internet is a who's-in who's-out bullying machine, often based on who is a different color and who is fat less than who is genuinely cool. By the time they're in college, the cusp millennial group I'm studying in this book has been mean enough to peers for a lifetime.

At the same time, I should note that the existence of these things on campus has been overplayed. When I came across safe spaces, which didn't happen as much as you might expect, they were largely akin to the Columbia's mattress-rally organizer casually offering juice boxes, not preplanned cuddles and cry-ins. And a safe space is not that different from what we used to call it in the 1990s — an alternative space, a coffee shop. Yes, sometimes they have coloring books, which are also popular among adults searching for quiet meditation.

I'm not saying that campuses aren't more radical than ever; some definitely are, and the video of what David Brooks has called "fragile thugs," and conservative publisher Roger Kimball calls "crybullies" denouncing and, yes, silencing conservative speakers like Heather MacDonald and Ann Coulter is troublesome, to say the least. I'm saying that rubrics like safe spaces are presented on campus more organically and less stridently — and far more optimistically. The moral mind wants life to have rules, and these kids strive to be moral.

Trigger warnings are about a reader giving consent. They are about extending a hand to others, about an ethics of caring and kindness. And consent standards are about making sure that the desire of the other is present when gratifying oneself, an attunement to gratifying the other too. They're also, of course, about the ever-present undergraduate elimination of ambiguity. The need to communicate constantly — very millennial — may also be a naive belief in explicitness. Nothing should be beyond words, no liminal realms of discomfort can be allowed to exist.

Yes Means Yes

In the past few chapters, and in world history, we've progressed from rape that results in pregnancy as punishable by drowning the victim and her attacker in a river to a check-in during reciprocated oral sex. Given America's countrywide neuroses about sex, at least among older generations — taught not to discuss sex but inundated with cultural artifacts that force them to think about it — these new rules about consent amount to a stunning demand. How many college kids' parents live by them, or even communicate during sex? The self-help aisle at Barnes and Noble isn't stuffed with books about sexual communication for no reason.

Still, I like "yes means yes." "No means no" is logical in some ways. It makes the line between sex and assault crystal clear. If you didn't say no, you were not assaulted. But "yes means yes" may better suit not only those learning about intimacy for the first time, but modern sex, with its hookups and online acquaintances, its faux promiscuity and lack of boundaries.

"Yes means yes" merely extends to sex the same rights assumed for other acts of volition. No one can take your purse without your consent. No one can trespass on your property. In exchanges like these, you're not obliged to say no. Looked at in this light, it's odd that "no means no" is our nation's law. "Right now, America's legal theory on assault says every person is consenting to have sex with any other person at any time and in any place until he or she says no," says a top sexual assault researcher who asks not to be named. "You have to *prove* that you didn't want to have sex with that person in that moment. And if you can't, well, all good."

One hopes "yes means yes" can solve cases. Students passed out from drinking — people who can't say yes — would be safe, and witnesses could testify to their grasp of the English language in the moments before the closing of the bedroom door. In practice, this isn't quite as easy as it should be.

One of the most prominent affirmative-consent dustups happened at the University of Tennessee at Chattanooga: Molly Morris, a psychology major, said she was raped by Corey Mock, a nationally ranked wrestler whom she'd right-swiped on the dating app Tinder but in whom she was not sexually interested. I meet her at her parents' home in Albuquerque's foothills, in a neighborhood awash in pink stucco. She's just returned from teaching a preschool dance class and is still clad in a toddler-friendly tank top made of bright blue sequins. Her Ford 150 truck, parked in the driveway, has a peeling bumper sticker on the back window: SILLY BOYS, TRUCKS ARE FOR GIRLS!

A Christian who says she planned to stay a virgin until marriage, Morris speaks intensely. When the alleged assault occurred, she'd recently arrived at UTC. Coincidentally, she and the guy from Tinder ended up in the same sociology class. Mock recognized Morris and began sitting behind her. "I'd always come to sociology from my dance class, so I was always wearing yoga pants. And you know . . ." She trails off. "Guys and girls in yoga pants, it is what it is."

Taking a seat at a table in her living room, surrounded by pictures of pensive clowns that her parents like to buy on vacation (it's a family tradition), she shows me the texts between the two of them. It doesn't seem to me that Morris led Mock on. She didn't want to go out with him, but she agreed to have breakfast once. There, she accepted his invitation to attend a wrestling party later that night, after she finished her job as a cocktail waitress. When she arrived around two a.m., she says he met her outside the house, where they exchanged "a little side-hug."

Inside, he handed her a strawberita from the fridge, then introduced her to some guys from the team. Morris started playing beer pong—not drinking beer, but sipping her own strawberita. One of his buddies gave her a flask of Jack Daniel's, and she mixed that with Coke. Someone offered her a bottle of fireball whiskey. There wasn't much in it. "It had a teeny, tiny bit left in the bottom, and I rejected it, because I thought it'd be nasty and weird to drink the remainder of someone's whiskey," says Morris. But the next drink she had tasted of cinnamon.

These events are generally agreed upon, as is what happened afterward: Morris threw up in the bathroom. But after that, the scenario becomes murky. The two of them ended up in Mock's friend's bedroom, where they had intercourse. Was she conscious at that time? She says no and believes the cinnamon whiskey may have been drugged. He says yes, according to news outlets, although not one word was exchanged between them. "Everything was like a normal kind of hookup," he told a reporter. The next day, after waking up curled at the bottom of a bed, Morris raced out of town to confab with her roommate, who was spending the weekend at her parents' home. They didn't go to the police or the hospital because they were worried about upsetting the roommate's parents.

To believe Mock, you'd have to accept that a woman who declined dates in favor of breakfast and who says she was a virgin would, shortly after arriving at a party and throwing up in a bathroom, have decided to have sex with him. At the same time, a witness said he heard a woman's moans coming out of the bedroom. Plus, there's the issue of Morris arriving after two a.m. It shouldn't matter. But the late hour could introduce doubt.

It doesn't seem like UTC could figure this out, so they eventually reminded both parties of the school's affirmative-consent standard and expelled Mock for violating it. But on appeal, a Tennessee court overturned the decision in a complex reading of burdens. The judge wasn't so sure affirmative consent was lawful, and she noted that Morris didn't claim that she'd said no. UTC readmitted Mock.

Boyfriend Material

The strongest argument for affirmative consent, to my mind, is that it frees American girls from the cage of socialized politeness that has historically led them to surrender their sexual agency. Victims often don't say no because they don't want to offend a guy or be rude. There's also an angle to this that's less gender-specific and more linguistic: In America, we simply don't say no often in our personal relationships, and a guy who is macked on by a girl he doesn't like won't generally push her away and issue a strict no either. "I have a girlfriend" and "I don't think we should do this" are his way of conveying what he is afraid to say.

This is a very gendered book, and it is this way because I believe that gender norms, and the fact that women are afraid of being physically hurt by men, who have strength and usually size, are the primary contributors to heterosexual college assault. But God knows there are guys who can testify about the sloppy female cokehead at the college bar who wordlessly drags them into a bathroom for hookups; the notion that girls are never interested in sex that's quick and risqué is simply not true. Everyone will lose some of that freedom — if you'd rather call it that than "unhealthy behavior" — if we impose these rules.

It's also true that women will benefit more than men from a "yes means yes" standard. As much as guys aren't always thrilled to be dragged into the bathroom, they don't perceive it as a traumatic event. "I've interviewed at least five men who were blackout drunk and came to with a woman on top of them, and some of their stories, if you role-reversed, it would be crazy," Jessie

Ford tells me about one of her studies. "But because they're men, they don't call it sexual assault."

The same girls who won't say no don't always want to say yes, as Syracuse student Lianna explained. And when universities started making noises that female students should be asked for a yes, college girls mostly liked this, seeing it as a sign of kindness and potential "boyfriend material"—even perhaps a way of making sex more pleasurable instead of less. "I've been seeing a guy for a year and a half because I think the best sex I've ever had is with him, because he'll ask me, 'Hey, do you like this,' 'How does this feel,'" says Wesleyan's Karmenife when I talk to her after our lunch at the Indian restaurant. "That's attractive to me because he's showing me that he thinks I'm a person. I'm not this receptacle. I'm not supposed to lay there and be his object. This is something that we're doing together." She adds, "Of course you're going to feel uncomfortable talking about your sexuality when the whole time [in America] you're being told you should be quiet about it, and that we're not supposed to [like it]—of course that's going to be the way. But if you actually start practicing this, you realize, 'Hey, sex is about me too and I'm supposed to be enjoying this too, not just you. It's not all about you.'"

Other students said the situation wasn't so simple. "Sometimes I think it's nice when guys ask more questions, sometimes it's weird," says a twenty-one-year-old female student. "Some men in college are way too scared now of potentially assaulting people. I hooked up with a friend who was very drunk, and I was not very drunk. I liked him. Afterwards he didn't like me. So I said, 'I'm upset, I liked you.'" The boy reeled back, worrying that she was about to accuse him of assaulting her, not understanding that she was saying she was bummed he regarded the night as a drunken hookup and nothing more. "He was very upset about his level of drunkenness, and 'Did I take advantage of you?' I said, 'I'm not saying it was nonconsensual! I *liked* you. You don't get to be the one, all worried *Did I rape you.* I'm upset about you passing the friendship line, and you're hyperventilating about [your] level of drunkenness!'"

Of course Kai's situation in the sexual-misconduct scenario is ridiculous. Of course far too literal escalating stages of affirmative consent, from kissing to "May I elevate the level of sexual intimacy by feeling your buttocks?" won't catch on. But a question here and there seems like the millennial version of the Gen X precoital check-in "Should I get a condom?" It's a question that's always been about more than safe-sex protection, and over time, no one freaked out about it as an unrealistic stricture on a natural act.

But right now, the situation about what consent is and isn't is chaos. Students inhabiting Planet College have wildly varying opinions about what constitutes consent. In 2015, *Washington Post*/Kaiser Family Foundation polled one thousand current or recent four-year college students about their opinions on the definition of sexual assault. Nearly half considered sex when "both people have not given clear agreement" to be assault; 20 percent said the same of sex when "both people are under the influence of alcohol or drugs." Only 34 percent of them thought that sex should require a yes.

7

The Accused

After learning about the broadening definition of terms that qualify as sexual assault, the raised consciousness, the reclassification of old encounters, and the new definition of *consent*, I began to set up interviews with perhaps the most aggrieved population: those who have been accused of assault at school. Inevitably, their ranks have swelled.

I can't say I was surprised that not one of the accused boys I met admitted guilt. Instead, they said they were confused by what had happened. Confused because women acted like they wanted it when they were on the mattress, then later cried rape. And they believed the new rules I've described might have been designed to ensnare not only the guilty but the innocent too.

It's the oldest trick in the book — *she wanted it*. But after listening to these boys, I was surprised to find they had a point. When I talked to Oliver,* a freshman at a state school in the vast midwestern plains, he told me a story that crushed me.

He was a virgin, he said, even though he'd had a couple girlfriends in high school. As the year went on, he caught feelings for a classmate, and it seemed reciprocated; one night, both he and she joined a large group of students walking to a house party, but they soon peeled off on their own. They'd been drinking earlier, but at that point they went to a restaurant and ordered milk shakes. Later, they went back to Oliver's dorm, where they watched a racy film on his laptop: *Moulin Rouge,* a musical about burlesque dancers at a Parisian nightclub. (I did not reach out to the other student for comment.)

Oliver alleged that they began kissing, and she asked if he had a condom; he usually didn't, but his friend had given him a Trojan earlier in the week in case he got lucky. He told her he was a virgin. Then he put on the condom, but he couldn't get an erection, which embarrassed him. He said that he took it off, and she gave him head. Once he got hard, they had sex. He never put the condom back on.

Oliver hoped the woman was going to become his girlfriend. But he said she wanted to leave quickly after sex, saying her roommate was worried about her. He claimed that he offered to walk her home, but she said no. The next day, she allegedly texted him that she was upset and wanted to take a Plan B pill. He clicked on Venmo and sent her fifty bucks for the pill, then asked when he could see her again. She said maybe after spring break, but then he received a letter from their university saying that he was being brought up on sexual-misconduct charges.

When I talked to Oliver, he was frightened. He hadn't told his parents and didn't know what he had done wrong. He told me he had "photographic evidence" that she wasn't drunk, plus "time stamps of everything" and backups of where he'd been from his phone's GPS. Most important, he said, "There wasn't a stipulated agreement that I had to wear the condom"; he was using a phrase that he'd probably heard from the lawyer he'd contacted a few days before we spoke.

Well, was there an agreement or wasn't there? Oliver told me he was an eighteen-year-old virgin. Should he have known that once asked to wear a condom, it stays on for the duration of intercourse? I would assume the act took a minimal amount of time. Maybe he got excited and rolled on top of her without thinking about what he had to do, then, seconds later, it was over. "I wasn't about trying to do it without a condom," he said in his own defense. "I was just hoping that she had fun."

By Title IX rules, the university could (and did) bar him from attending lectures of the science class they shared, Oliver told me. He studied his friends' notes, but he was finding it difficult to keep up with the lab work because he was allowed in the building only during certain hours. "I don't want to drop a class I'm doing really well in," he said, sounding distraught. "This is practically ruining my life! This has been going on for two weeks already."

I hung up the phone, knowing it would be going on for a lot longer than that.

Risk of Accusation

The next few chapters will consider intricacies of assault that haven't entered our discussion. Even with these imperfections, which are many, I believe the new system has more upside than down.

When an assault is reported to a college, there's often an explosion of violence, anger, and lawyers in a short period, and then the losing parties put Kenmore fridges and mountain bikes up for sale and move on to the next phase of their lives. But not everyone can let emotions go after a decision about culpability is made. "Being accused is very debasing—if someone [says] you're a sexual predator, it doesn't get much worse than that," says a recent graduate, a lonely, fiercely intelligent fellow with black eyebrows. "I almost would rather someone said I embezzled money or I was a drunk driver who killed someone. As a man, I have a deeply ingrained instinct that I want to protect women, not hurt them. This strikes right at the heart of my identity."

The relative of another accused boy puts it more starkly. "This is a witchhunt, no different than the Salem witch trials or McCarthyism," she says in a raspy voice when she calls me from a state far away. "A fear has been sold to the country, that every man is a potential rapist. This is now an American truth, just the way the Communists infiltrating and taking over our country was a truth of McCarthyism. For our American boys today, it's guilty before innocent."

Chloe and the Wesleyan radical cohort—and, actually, Zoe Ridolfi-Starr and the Columbia group too—liked to call themselves "the witches." They not only possessed the sorcery to upend societal orders but were unfairly victimized. But accused boys wanted this sobriquet too. After Yale expelled Jack Montague, a basketball captain who brought its team to its first NCAA tournament bid in fifty-four years, Montague's high-school coach published a letter in a Tennessee webzine that compared the boy to a man killed for witchcraft during the purges in Salem. "He was 'pressed' to death—forced to lie under large wooden boards while rocks and boulders were piled on to squeeze the life out of him," the coach wrote, adding that his protégé was "the victim of a Title IX witch-hunt, where his dreams, reputation and future employment are being 'pressed' out of him with the same cowardly, irrational piety shown by those Puritan zealots of an earlier New England."

If I told you every friend of mine who has a son confided she is scared of him being accused of sexual assault in college — and some of these sons are toddlers — would you be surprised? It's a deep fear, and maybe it's born of a reverse Oedipal complex. But the risk of being accused of assault is minimal — and, obviously, far, far less common than being sexually assaulted.

In 2014, roughly 12.2 million students attended nonprofit four-year colleges. Just under 5.5 million of those students were male. That same year, according to the National Center for Education Statistics, students at these universities across the country reported a total of 6,314 sex offenses to school authorities. This is triple the number of sex offenses reported in the early 2000s, but it's still vanishingly small. Assuming a one-to-one ratio of reported offenses to male students, 1 in 871 is reported; since we know some guys will be reported for more than one offense, it's fair to spitball something like one in a thousand will be accused.

"Survivor of False Accusation"

So how do they defend themselves, these boys? As I mentioned, they all say the charges aren't true. This seems ridiculous, since in the criminal justice system, repeated studies have demonstrated that just 2 to 8 percent of all accusations are false. But one can reasonably assume that a university environment, with lower stakes and administrators who are generally more sympathetic than cops — more on them later — invites more shaky accusations.

The definition of *false*, though, is fairly broad in this group. Some said that women were outright lying, that ex-girlfriends, mentally disturbed young women, gold diggers were wielding these charges as weapons. (Governments might use them as well; a well-known conspiracy theory involves the United States pushing two women to accuse WikiLeaks' Julian Assange of misconduct in hopes that he would be imprisoned, after which he could be extradited.) This logic puts women in a catch-22 — they don't want to be seen as vengeful exes, crazy people, or gold diggers, but if they say nothing about the assault, then nothing changes, and more women suffer.

This rape victim's conundrum (one of many, as I've explained over the past few chapters) didn't occur to these boys. But they were very aware of the catch-22 that they themselves were in — they could insist they were innocent, but no manner of exoneration would ever remove the stain.

A former hockey player from Boston University's Terriers, a couple of years into the pros, tells me, "From athletes' perspective, girls make these accusations because they're looking for lottery tickets." Two of his friends were accused of sexual assault in the mid-2010s. Reporters descended on the campus and splashed the guys' pictures across the *Boston Globe*. He says they were innocent. "I used to hear stories about college rape on TV and be like, 'What an asshole that guy is,'" he continues. "But when I hear the news now, I'm wary. When you live through a scandal, you have a different perspective." (The charges against one student were eventually dismissed, and the other pleaded guilty to a lesser charge.)

Post-accusation, all the Terrier players were obligated to attend sexual-assault workshops, which did not always help clarify matters. "We were doing these exercises to figure out what is consent, and I remember thinking that the law was so crazy — I couldn't even figure it out," he says. The reform effort did change the players' lifestyle of super-casual sex, though. "We'd go out to bars and go home ourselves," he says. "We pretty much stopped taking girls home, and within a semester, all of us got steady girlfriends."

The hockey player was quiet and measured in our conversation, as was Joshua Strange, a South Carolinian with the coloring of Ben Affleck. In 2012, way before Sulkowicz began carrying her mattress, Strange was expelled from Auburn, a public university in Alabama with about twenty-two thousand undergrads. When I spoke with him on the phone, he was working as a cold-caller for a business-to-business telemarketing firm near Spartanburg, his childhood home. "It's a temporary job," he told me, describing the way he called around with prepared monologues, or scripts. "I've sold appointed sales systems for restaurants, I've sold school districts in Ohio on a new telephone-answering service . . . and, hmm, something else I can't remember." He let out a short, bitter laugh at the brain-numbing effects of a job that required no college degree. "That's why they give me a script, so I can remember."

Strange, who votes Republican because there's not a box for conservative, intended to major in political science at Auburn. The summer after his freshman year, his roommates drifted away for vacation, and he stayed in a condo. Early in the summer, he met Charlotte,* a nineteen-year-old student. Within weeks, she essentially moved into his apartment, her puppy tagging along. (She did not agree to speak with me, and this account represents Strange's recollection of events.)

At the end of June, the couple went to a bar to celebrate a friend's acceptance to law school. "I only had twenty dollars in my pocket . . . so I knew how many I could have without running out of money," he explained. "When I left the bar, I was intoxicated, she was intoxicated, and I still had money in my pocket. I don't know where she was getting all the drinks from."

At the condo, a female friend helped Charlotte change for bed while Strange took the puppy for a walk. Not long afterward, the two passed out. Strange alleged they woke up in the middle of the night and started having sex, during which he accidentally penetrated her anally. "All of a sudden, she just starts melting down. As soon as she got upset, everything in the room just stopped. Like, *everything* stopped . . . you say, 'No,' I'm going to stop."

Strange said Charlotte started phoning her friends, one of whom was an off-duty cop who may have called his precinct. Shortly afterward, he was handcuffed and in a cruiser. He was released after several hours and made his way back to the condo's living room, where he said he sat in the dark, frightened and unable to move. His phone rang. It was Charlotte, and she wanted to come over. He said when she got there, she apologized, explaining that she never meant to get him in trouble. "She asked, 'Are we okay?'" said Strange. "I said, 'Uh, yeah, I guess so. I guess we're fine.' Then she says she's really tired and goes to my bedroom to go to sleep."

Strange continued to live with Charlotte for a little while, but he was suspicious about another guy coming into the picture. He confronted her, they argued, and she stormed off—terminating the relationship, as far as he knew. He deleted her number from his phone. He decided to hang out with his friends for a while and stop thinking about girls. Charlotte had been his first girlfriend.

A week later, while he was grocery-shopping, his roommate called his cell phone. "I said, 'Hey, man, I'm at Walmart. What do you need?' And he said, 'Um, I don't know why, but the police are here and they're looking for you.'"

The warrant was for Strange slapping Charlotte outside a frozen-yogurt shop — an allegation he flatly denied. "During the night [we've discussed], I practiced poor judgment, and I freely admit I did, but I did not rape someone," he said, adding that on the night of the yogurt-shop incident, "I wasn't even in the same zip code."

Strange received criminal charges, according to a report, and Charlotte filed charges with Auburn. He alleged that she made photocopies of the police report and began distributing them on campus, even at his frat house. "It didn't take three or four days before I would walk across campus, and people would point and whisper and glare at me," he said. "I was a pariah."

Strange and Charlotte's adjudication hearing was held in Auburn's student center. "Everyone knows what's happening, because you've got a group of people [waiting to go in] sitting over here all dressed up, another group sitting over there all dressed up," he recalled. The room was divided in the middle by a long PVC pipe with a black sheet duct-taped to it so they couldn't see each other. A panel sat in judgment: two students, a fisheries professor, a liberal arts professor, and a librarian. Both Charlotte and Strange brought along lawyers, but when Charlotte's introduced herself, Strange's attorney was shocked: she was the prosecutor for the city of Auburn. "My lawyer grabbed my arm, spun me around, and said, 'That's the city prosecutor that's going to try you later.'" He was perhaps talking about the non-campus charges; anything Strange said here could be used against him then. "You don't say a word, understand?"

The university's panel found for Charlotte, not only expelling Strange but also banning him from Auburn property for life. The criminal charges were dropped. Still, his frat brothers turned their backs. A massive depression came next. Unsure of whether he should move cities or schools or what, he packed up for Spartanburg. "Except for a vacation to the seventh circle of hell, there was no reason for me to be there," he said.

Like college assault victims, Strange calls himself a survivor — he uses the phrase *survivor of false accusation*. "I have triggers, like an Auburn sticker on a car or a contact name on my call sheet similar to hers," he said. "It's little things, and you never see them coming."

"How Dare You Say *Only* Two Percent?"

As it happens, the accused have their own national support group. On a warm spring afternoon in 2015, I traveled to the Donovan, a Washington, DC, boutique hotel less than a mile from the White House, to meet members of this organization, which includes both Joshua Strange and his mother, Allison, and goes by the fairly neutral name of Families Advocating for Campus Equality, or FACE. Few of these young men allege that their accusers are fabulists or gold diggers or that they stated the accused was present at a yogurt shop when he was far away. What they say is the sex, or sexual misconduct (one mom says amiable ribbing led to Title IX charges), was consensual.

While most families practice anonymity—or what they call "shielding their sons"—Allison Strange, a paralegal with a brunette bob, clear blue eyes, and a genteel Southern manner that masks a deep stubbornness, is an exception. "Josh has always wanted to go into politics, so I said, 'Son, if you ever want to run for office, you better own this like your best suit.'" She adds, "'You put this on and wear it like your seersucker suit with a bow tie.'"

Although those attending the FACE event in Washington have inverted the catechism of young activists—not "Believe survivors," but "Believe boys"—the groups have some traits in common. In both, an angry solidarity serves as a bulwark against powerless grief. Both offer numerous reasons for the other side's failings and for their own side's grievances. There's also a deep sense of puzzlement about their adversaries' utopian goals. What do college girls want? To neuter men? Or banish them to Mars? Have kids via parthenogenesis?

This DC event, the second of its kind after a meeting in Minneapolis the previous year, seems to have more moms of accused students around than the students themselves. In the Donovan's lobby, which is decorated with smoky mirrors and in dark purple hues, I meet a few moms along with Allison Strange's co-organizer, Sherry Warner-Seefeld, who says her son Caleb was falsely accused by a student at the University of North Dakota. A fifty-eight-year-old high-school teacher and the former leader of her Fargo teachers' union, she calls herself a renegade, and when I ask about her husband, she shoots me a quick "Don't have one" with a look that closes the topic. Petite with a short, peroxide-blond hairstyle that would suit an alt-rock band singer,

Warner-Seefeld wears deep red lipstick and has an ankle tattoo of a dove and heart. Each earlobe bears what look like half a dozen diamond studs. "Oh Lord, have mercy," she says when I ask about the diamonds. "These are fake ones."

Warner-Seefeld is unique in another way: She says she managed to overturn the university's decision in her son's case. She couldn't stand by after her son — who "alternated between rage, and then he would just absolutely collapse down on the floor and just sob, and sob, and sob" — was found guilty. She pursued contacts in her state capital. "Going to the board of higher ed, going to the legislators, going to attorneys, going to alums," she says. "I don't know how else to say it, but my goal was to shame or humiliate them into making it right. And making it right was to reverse the finding."

Caleb now works as a truck driver for a major delivery company. "He makes more money than I do, and he's very happy," says Warner-Seefeld. "Except when anyone asks him about this." When he was giving interviews to bring attention to his case, he found reliving the experience much as Liz, the high school survivor who wanted to be anonymous, described — traumatic, unhelpful. "He said to me, 'I just replay it over and over in my mind, she said, I said, I did, she did, did I misinterpret?'" says Warner-Seefeld. "'I can't live that way, Mom. I was sad, I was angry and I can't live that way.'" He won't attend gatherings like this one or talk to reporters.

When Warner-Seefeld reads a story about a case like her son's, she understands his lack of faith in the media. "The picture on the article is a very sweet girl on campus, and at the bottom there's one or two paragraphs, sometimes, of false accusations," she says. "And then the journalist includes the statistic 'only two percent of rapes are false accusations.'" She shakes her head, mentioning her anger at the use of the word *only*. "How dare you say *only* two percent?" She adds, "That's a lot of kids. And one of them's my child." Caleb is a changed man. "These boys don't just lose their education or have careers jeopardized. They lose lives. They lose marriages. Themselves." She looks into the distance. "Grandchildren . . ."

Allison Strange adds to this point. "These are great young men," she says. "We raised them right. Josh is an Eagle Scout!" She looks me square in the eye. "One rape on a campus is too many. One rape gets huge publicity, and everybody rallies the troops. One false accusation is too many, but nobody gives a damn."

We talk about what they've been up to this weekend. Strange and Warner-Seefeld booked speakers to talk to the group, and they came yesterday: a psychologist who works with grieving men and a journalist who tends to side with the accused. The psychologist discussed men's pain as a cultural taboo that Americans have been taught to ignore at all costs. He gave this example at another event: When a woman cries in a restaurant corner, "You look over, and [think] 'Poor dear. She must have just broken up with someone. How can I help?' But what happens if there's a man sitting there? 'There's something wrong with that guy—he must be drunk!'"

Warner-Seefeld was particularly moved by the journalist who discussed her difficulties in interviewing accused men, their inability to open up or share what they were feeling. "What sells papers?" she says. "Crying girls. We have estrogen, we are made differently in the womb, plus we have a whole life of socialization saying it's okay to cry." Boys don't cry. "Their emotions go totally inside, and they shut down. Their faces are blank, their tones are blank." And no reporter wants to write about that.

An accused boy I talk to elaborates on these points, saying he did cry, eventually, but most of the time during the disciplinary process he simply felt angry. "But when you're in the process, you cannot show a hint of that, because angry is bad," he tells me. "I had to present myself as an absolutely passive, docile creature, even though there was an injustice going on and the inclination is to be angry. Not [angry] like 'I want to find a woman and bash her head in,' but angry as in 'This is wrong.'"

What possible motivation does a female student have to make up a false charge? I ask. One mom offers a lengthy list. "Speaking from the collective calls that we get, they range from her grades were bad and she was about to lose her scholarship, so she needed an excuse," she says. "Or her high-school boyfriend was coming the day after and she had a hickey on her neck and had to explain it. Regret. There was no serious commitment from the guy the morning after. Or she changed her mind and was embarrassed. Her roommate says, 'Where were you last night?' And she says, 'I had something horrible happen to me.'" She sighs. "The girl might discuss it with someone like an administrator, and the administrator will decide, 'Oh, yes, you were assaulted.'"

She continues, "I don't know of a single nineteen-year-old female who cannot be a drama queen. I have never met one. They can turn it on when they need to. And now they desire to be part of a greater cause. 'Oh, I'm a victim, I'm going to rally with my sisters in this, and we're going to get back at all the evils of the world.' It gives them a purpose. It's something they feel is mature, something that brings them to the forefront, something trending at this time. And they don't realize that what they're saying is a serious accusation that has repercussions for the person on the other side. It's like, 'There's nothing to see here, move along. I was assaulted and you're going to get kicked out of school, no big deal, move along.'" She gestures around the lobby. "And that is not what happens. That is not the experience of it *at all*."

In many cases, when boys are accused of misconduct, say Warner-Seefeld and Strange, they are too confused or embarrassed to call their parents, just like Oliver was. That's another behavior they share with the other side. Girls wait to go to the hospital or to tell the school, and Sulkowicz and others I met didn't tell their parents for a while either. "We know lots of young men who never call their parents until it's all over," says Warner-Seefeld later. "When it's too late."

Strange clucks. "Actually, not 'when it's too late,'" she says. "Because from the get-go, it's too late."

Unfair

Boys who are accused of assault may be quietly advised by adults on campus that university politics have shifted, and they will likely be suspended or expelled. The best thing to do is simply withdraw from the university. No harm, no foul. Transfer somewhere a bit down the food chain, go from, say, the University of Michigan to the University of Indiana, because losing a case may mean enrolling at local community college.

Today, experts told me about half of American college boys who remain on campus to fight university charges are found guilty. At least a hundred students, nearly all male, are now suing their universities for unfair disciplinary proceedings and, in some cases, what they call reverse discrimination.

(Lawsuits against universities have intermittently been a tactic of young activists, some of whom turned to celebrity attorney Gloria Allred several years ago. But settlements with confidentiality clauses mean sealed lips, which is definitely not what they were after.) Many boys note the sex in question occurred when both parties were extremely drunk, yet only one party—the male—was held responsible under Title IX's gender-neutral statute.

The girls get the Obama-promoted accommodations: repeating courses for free, extra time on tests, psychological and emotional support, advocates with advice in their corner. The accused is out in the cold. And for what? "An indiscretion," says Allison Strange. "I don't think [our sons] wouldn't say, 'You know what? That may not have been my best judgment.' But there's a huge difference between lacking judgment when you're eighteen, nineteen, twenty years old, and intent to harm."

It's not convenient for me to admit this, but she has a powerful argument. After reading about twenty legal complaints resembling soap-opera scripts with a cast of postadolescents pawing each other in the dark, I can report that these boys' position that they're innocent—if not by the letter of university codes, then by the spirit—is strong. Two caveats: Most of the documents contained only the boys' side of the story. And one shouldn't conclude that these cases are representative of most American campus-assault scenarios, because those willing to press the issue in court are likely to have strong cases.

In many of the cases I read, consent—what we were discussing in the last chapter—is the issue, which seems most unfairly problematic for the boys (it's certainly the most common hotly disputed case, though as I said, boys dispute almost every case). In the moment, on a mattress, students may not interpret signs and signals as easily as Columbia's Suzanne Goldberg, promoter of the traffic light, imagines. Kimberly Ferzan from the University of Virginia put it this way: "Reformers say, 'What's the big deal, you stay at the red light until you're sure you have the green,'" she explained in a lecture. "But that's not what's going on here. What's going on here is that you have to think of our population reaching the level of red-green colorblindness where we can no longer rely on red and green lights, and so we decide we're going to change the rules and have orange and purple. All of a sudden it's orange and purple, and you think, *I don't know what that means, does it mean stay or should I go?*"

I'm thinking about consent as half a dozen new arrivals in the lobby drift over. They are meticulously dressed and have gym-toned bodies and real diamonds in their earlobes. In some cases, their sons, men in their early twenties dressed in cargo pants and slouching sheepishly, trail after them.

I meet with Scott,* from a small school outside of DC; Jackson,* from a large school in the South, and his mom Annabel*; and moms of accused boys from two large universities and a small northeastern university. Later, I talk to a soft-spoken, willowy woman in a neon-green shirt who says her son is "John Doe from Occidental." That's a famous case, and it made news from *Esquire* to Fox News to the *Daily Beast*. To recap: John Doe, eighteen, so drunk that another student quantified his inebriation as "shitshow," and Jane Doe, seventeen, so drunk that a witness said she was having a hard time walking, started making out in John's room. Jane's two friends tried to remove her from the room. I say *tried* because after her friends brought her home and put her to bed, John texted Jane: *The second that you're away from them, come back.* Jane agreed, texted her friend, *I'mgoingtohavesex now*, wound her way through the dorm's hallways, paused briefly to vomit in a trash can, then entered John's room. After sex, she sent a smiley face emoticon to friends. The next day, she woke up with zero recollection of what had happened, and, since she'd lost her virginity, she was deeply upset. But John, who pieced it together from finding her belt and earrings and a used condom in the room, claimed he didn't recall the sex either. He was expelled.

At one point, the moms compare how much they've spent on attorneys. Since the odds of recovering damages are so slight, attorneys don't work these cases on contingency. Nor will they sue accusers for defamation or damages, most likely because nineteen-year-old female college students tend not to have assets. Also, one mom firmly adds, "Lawyers see it as politically incorrect."

Scott says his parents paid almost $100,000 — "Lawyers rounded bills to the nearest thousand as a courtesy discount," he says, shaking his head — and the university reimbursed him five grand when they found him innocent. A cross-legged mom says she's spent $90,000. The Southern student's mom, $135,000. At last, one mom, who asks for anonymity, chimes in: "We are one million dollars into this stupid trial."

Everyone gasps.

"We were down to our last dime," she continues. They blew through the 401(k), the savings, everything. But her husband sold his company, and now there's so much money it's like funny money. "He said, 'We live to fight another day. We will get justice.'"

Female Dominance

After we speak for a while in the lobby, Warner-Seefeld protests that this is far too public a place to discuss sex and rape. She suggests moving to her hotel room, and we head to the elevators, boys trailing behind. "Come on," Warner-Seefeld says to the boys. "There's no need to be worried. I'm just taking you up to my bedroom."

In her room, an empty wine bottle rests on a countertop near an ironing board, which has a crumpled blouse on it. "Come hang out in bed with me," she says to Allison Strange, and they giggle as they sit down on her bed, backs resting against the headboard, legs out in front of them.

We talk for five hours straight about men and rape, about their sons. The sadness, frustration, and anger at being unheard for so long is palpable. Like true victims, which they may or may not be, they become breathless while relating their side of these stories, and, possessed of a privilege culturally off-limits to their sons, some begin to cry. "Everybody in my family is male —brothers, sons, a great husband," says a mom from the West Coast. "They handle this differently than I do. These people have been enormously supportive to me, because I don't have anyone I can talk to about this."

They are focused on bonding even as Scott makes an odd comment. "You look at other people, and they do things that cross the line," he says, then he adds something that disturbs me. "Man, I wish I could have gotten some of that sexual assault. Not really violent sexual assault, but I wish I could have done the sort of borderline." I am shocked to hear this, and I say so. But the moms quickly huddle around him, offering their support, declaring that it's good for him to express his feelings.

I thought that these moms would want to talk about what they'd done wrong as parents to have raised sons who might be villains, or at least knaves. But is there a mother alive who would not take her son's side? Instead, they want to talk about what is wrong with girls. Gender stereotyping is rife. "One thing none of us can deny is we were all made a boy or a girl, and there are certain hormonal things we can't fight," says a mom. A girl thinks she's so empowered, hooks up, has a DF, a drunk fuck, or a FF, a finals fuck, or whatever they call it. The next day the boy goes, "See ya, not into you"—well, all of a sudden she feels horrible about herself. She adds, "It is the human nature of the female to not feel good about that." A girl's feeling that she has been sexually assaulted may come from this essential difference between men and women, they say, not from the complex PTSD-like chain reaction described by Rebecca Campbell.

The feminine psyche is complex, say the moms in this room, and women often emotionally manipulate men to get what they want. In this counternarrative, the girls are in control, even when they're out of control. One of the moms talks about how women know how to get guys at a bar to buy them drinks if they're low on cash; Charlotte might have been flirting with a guy at the bar in Auburn who bought her some drinks while Joshua was there, unaware. She talks about the way adolescent girls can reel in boys in middle school with flirty talk before most boys are ready for anything sexual, and that's a decent point.

These moms have a strong sense that pop culture is arrayed against their sons in particular and young men in general. They see Taylor Swift shifting from a romantic teenager pining for her Romeo to a knife-wielding girl-squad chieftain and Katy Perry no longer shooting whipped cream from her breasts like a fun California girl but singing about fuck-boys who pretend to be Tarzan when she's the real Jane—all the stuff that orthodox feminists look down on and smear as "pop feminism" but that has clearly created significant changes in the outlook of college girls—and they are anything but amused. These pop idols appear to them as Kali-like destroyers of the male ego, and the men around them are cast as simpering fools. Look at the popular sitcoms like *Everybody Loves Raymond* or *Modern Family* or *The Simpsons*, where the husbands are always bumbling stupid idiots and the wives are sharp, witty women, explain these moms. We're dumbing down the image of man. We're telling society that men are secondary and irrelevant. It's a whole mental shift, and college girls don't even necessarily realize it. Brainwashing.

These women are good storytellers, and they're self-confident. They're mostly fifty to sixty. This fight has deep personal meaning, coming as it does at an uncertain time in their own lives. Not only are they processing their sons' sexual humiliation and, in some cases, long-term depression, but many of them are caring for sick, aging parents and having daily fights to secure good home aides or elder-care facilities.

Their troubles surprise them after lives of relative mastery, including formative years during the era when the sexually empowered college woman suddenly became the new normal. "We went to college in the 1970s during 'Make love, not war,' and 'I should be able to have sex and not be thought of as a slut,'" says one mom. "We come from a time, our generation, where we wanted a seat at the table and an opportunity to soar."

Again, it's not convenient for me to mention this, but I relate to this too. Gen X professional women often dislike advertising ourselves as victims (bosses don't respond well), dwelling on negative experiences (there are antidepressants for that), or even thinking of ourselves as vulnerable (our mantra: "Suck it up"). We are superwomen: strong, stoic, confident. In college, our messy interior lives were shared with close friends and our journals, which we hid under pillows when we left for class. My formative years were also spent at the frontier of hookup culture. Young people in the 1990s were its pioneers. Hookup culture was considered a good thing for us back then, not only creating sexual parity with men but also unknotting us from demanding relationships so that we could concentrate on other parts of life, like getting ahead in our careers.

These moms, whatever they did in college, consider hookup culture a lie —a lie based at least in part on denying women's innate ability to enjoy no-strings sex. And quite a few other American women agree. "[College] girls want full sexual equality"—to meet a guy at a party and then have sex and even drink as much as he does—"it almost sounds like gay-male-bathhouse culture, have sex with whomever," Caitlin Flanagan, an essayist for the *Atlantic* who often favors a return to conventional norms, declared on a podcast. "But young women are having a tremendous problem with this . . . and they're turning to adults, saying, 'Sort this out!'" Saying we can't look at this in terms of hookup culture and alcohol is wrong, and we'll never get to an honest point. She further added, about assaults on campus in general, that these incidents "are minor!"

Yale activist Alexandra Brodsky, a guest on the same podcast, was aghast. "[Students] want to engage in the sexual life of campus," but the cost is you go home with someone, and someone can do anything to your body, she shot back. Isn't that too high? When I talked to Brodsky several months later, she'd developed a talking point: "Young women want access to the bathhouse but know that they can only enter if the price of admission isn't rape."

These moms wanted equality in college, had perhaps successful careers, produced families, drive nice cars, own diamonds. Are they still feminists? "No way," a radical activist said to me about this group. "This 'Hell, I've been triggered too,' and bootstrap shit about girls getting privileges instead of boys is deeply conservative. These women will never say, 'My boys should learn to become sensitive to girls' needs,' because that's simply not in their worldview. They make fun of liberal snowflakes and yet their whole worldview is 'my poor precious snowflake son.'" I tried to explain that their hurt struck me as genuine. "You're holding up their trauma because you see their ruin as a tragedy, whereas the violation of woman *isn't* a tragedy, because bodies don't belong to women, since sex is what we're made for," she spat back. There may then have been a mention of my "internalized misogyny."

So perhaps they're not feminists. "I experimented, sure," a mom from the West Coast tells me later. "I even woke up in college one morning next to two guys!" Her face darkens. "And now I'm bringing up my son in the most repressive atmosphere imaginable."

Grievances pinball around the room. "My son has to sign up for Selective Service, and if you don't, you don't get financial aid," says one woman. "If women want equal rights, why aren't they out there?"

She adds, "It shouldn't be Take Back the Night. It should be Take Back the Responsibility!" She tries to psychoanalyze the situation: "Maybe these girls who are going after these guys have an issue with not having a dad in their lives," she says. "They want to gravitate, and once they develop feelings, they don't want to let go. When that guy doesn't reciprocate the feelings, they strike out."

Jackson looks at it differently. "They just want all the power," he says, fiddling with a shoelace. "Most of the time, the girls are raping the guys."

Sensing the depths to which this experience has brought them, I ask if any mom has weeks when the subject isn't on her mind. Strange turns to me, her eyes blazing. "You don't get it," she says, dropping the Southern sweetness from her tone. "Four years since it happened, and I still wake up in the middle of the night and cry. It will be three o'clock in the morning, and I'll wake up and begin to think about the college experience that my son was robbed of. The friends that he lost. The homecoming football games, enjoying stuff with friends. There is a part of him that will never get over this." As she talks, tears stream down her face. "I lost a part of my child, and I grieve the death of that part of my child every day. So you don't get past it." She gestures around the room. "Then you get involved with these women in this room, because it's so wrong." New parents call their hotline at least four or five times a week. "They are in the throes of 'Oh my God, we got served with this, and we Googled and found your name. Please help us.' The moms are crying and the kids are suicidal and the dads are in shell shock." She shakes her head. "You do the best you can to try and guide them. But every time you talk to them, you are right back there."

The room goes silent. One or two women sit and breathe. A few start gathering their things. One rises, says she needs a long shower before they reconvene for dinner. Then the mom who talked about DFs and FFs kneels next to my seat. She scrolls through photos on her phone, showing off pictures of her twenty-two-year-old, who is absent this weekend. There he is at a concert; there he is smiling on the steps of European medieval churches. "He's such a good kid," she tells me, wiping away a tear.

I don't agree with these women's take on pop culture or with most of their opinions about gender relations. But I agree that we, as a society, are terrified to look at boys as boys rather than men and give them a break as such. And we're equally scared to tell girls that they too bear responsibility for their sexual behavior and safety.

8

Guilty

Periodically, I'd think about who was guilty.

Alec Cook, a twenty-year-old University of Wisconsin student resembling a *Pineapple Express*–era James Franco (shoulder-length brown hair and soulful eyes that telegraph lazy afternoons making girls herbal tea post-rock-climbing class) — he could be one of the guilty ones. In 2016, according to a report, over a dozen women accused him of sexual assault. Cook had twirled and dipped a student at the gym. He'd slapped the butt of a woman in ballroom-dancing class. He'd made grotesque comments in the grocery store. In the middle of sex with a student, he asked, "Do you like that," then kept pounding away after she'd answered, "No." Another student, who'd gone home with him after a study date in the library, said he kept her in a "death grip," raping and choking her until she was almost unconscious. Law enforcement also alleged that he kept notebooks about where he met the women and the color of their eyes, along with a check box next to the question "killed?" Yet his attorneys explained that Cook was only flirting, same as guys through the ages have done. Some of his bad acts were "more Arthur Herbert 'Fonz' Fonzarelli than felony," they said, talking about the star of the feel-good sitcom *Happy Days*, set in nearby Milwaukee in the mid-1950s.

What about Elliot Rodger, who killed six near the University of California at Santa Barbara in 2014 before shooting himself in the head with his SIG-Sauer? In a 137-page manifesto entitled "My Twisted World" that he wrote before the rampage, Rodger said that sexual jealousy was primarily what turned him into a monster. "I felt like such an inferior mouse whenever I saw guys walking with beautiful girls," he explained, complaining that, like a loser, he couldn't get one college girl's number to plug into his cell phone. In the months before the shootings, he began to angrily toss Starbucks coffee out of his car at happy couples or at hot girls waiting at bus stops, and then, contemplating whether he was going to be a virgin forever, he made his choice. "I knew that I would rather die than suffer such a fate, and I knew that if it came to that, I would do everything I can to exact revenge before I die," he wrote.

Rodger was a murderous psychopath, of course. Brock Turner, the Stanford swimmer, is a more typical campus predator. We know he went to the frat where he met a student's older sister with the intention of hooking up; he was grabbing other girls at the party, including her younger sister, and kissing them. In fact, he pounced on the older sister only when the younger sister left to take a drunk friend home — and by that time, the older sister was so deep in a blackout that when she dialed her boyfriend's number and left a voice-mail, she was no longer speaking English. "I was the wounded antelope of the herd, completely alone and vulnerable, physically unable to fend for myself, and he chose me," the victim wrote in her extraordinary letter to the court.

Somewhere between that voicemail and twenty minutes later, when she was found motionless behind a dumpster — unconscious, her long necklace wrapped tight around her neck, bra pulled out of her dress, stripped naked from the waist down — Turner spotted the victim alone, kissed her too, and left the party with her by his side. Perhaps he planned to bring her back to his dorm. Perhaps he was always planning to get his rocks off wherever was easiest. The choice was made when she fell down some paces outside of the house under a set of towering pine trees. A dumpster stood nearby. This was the heavenly Stanford campus. Even dumpsters enjoyed a bucolic setting.

What happened under those trees? They didn't have intercourse, but he fingered her, and he may have sent a photo of her naked breast to friends via a group text conversation that someone had allegedly given the gross name "Bonessss." When the Swedish graduate students happened to cycle by, he was dry-humping her with his pants on.

Whatever Turner did, he did it without regard to her choice in the matter, or her humanity. What's harder to know is what he would have done if the Swedes hadn't pedaled past. Turner has insisted that he didn't realize the girl had passed out, that if he had, he would have stopped the hookup. This declaration did not convince his victim. "You say that, but I want you to explain how you would've helped me, step by step, walk me through this," she wrote. "I am asking you; Would you have pulled my underwear back on over my boots? Untangled the necklace wrapped around my neck? Closed my legs, covered me? Pick[ed] the pine needles from my hair? Asked if the abrasions on my neck and bottom hurt? Would you then go find a friend and say, will you help me get her somewhere warm and soft?" We don't have answers to these questions. But given the way he had comported himself so far that evening, I can't imagine he wouldn't have left her under the trees, lying still in the night air.

Like many victims, she experienced the act as only the first insult. The press treated Turner like other celebrities facing sexual assault charges, noting his A-student, homegrown-hero-bound-for-the-Olympics persona. He was the important one, not she; the authorities hadn't even told her his identity. "I learned what happened to me the same time everyone else in the world learned what happened to me," she wrote: after reading an article about her case. "That's when the pine needles in my hair made sense, they didn't fall from a tree. He had taken off my underwear, his fingers had been inside of me. I don't even know this person. I still don't know this person." The same article that graphically reported her state of undress at the scene also listed Turner's swimming times. "She was found breathing, unresponsive with her underwear six inches away from her bare stomach curled in fetal position. By the way, he's really good at swimming. Throw in my mile time if that's what we're doing. I'm good at cooking, put that in there, I think the end is where you list your extracurriculars to cancel out all the sickening things that've happened."

Before the victim's letter went public, the central question posed by the press was why Turner would do such a thing when he could doubtless have found a willing sexual partner. And his family and friends defended Turner the way fans rally around celebrities accused of similar crimes, part of our culture's odd pattern of first splashing men accused of rape across headlines to shame them and next systematically shaming the accuser: they extolled his high moral character and insisted he was incapable of such an act. When the letters of family and friends were leaked — along with discrepancies between what he'd claimed in court (for example, that he'd never been exposed to party culture before) and his real life (his phone included texts about candy-flipping, slang for alternating doses of Molly and LSD) — the writers were publicly shamed, as Turner himself had been. Turner ultimately did only three months of jail time, but his accuser's openness and eloquence about the night in question and its effects on her brought her some measure of justice.

Predators, Serial and Otherwise

For a decade, it was a rumor in the fashion world that photographer Terry Richardson took off his clothes and misbehaved with unknown models during shoots — or, as a friend of mine put it, if you worked with Terry, there was going to be jizz. For decades, Roger Ailes was allegedly asking broadcasters who wanted jobs at Fox News to wear garters, in one case videotaping a woman and then saying, "I am putting [the tape] in a safe-deposit box just so we understand each other." For three decades, the rehab doctor for the U.S. women's Olympic gymnastics team was allegedly sticking his fingers into the vaginas of teenagers with hip and back problems, calling it a necessary medical procedure (it wasn't). And for many more decades, it was an open secret in the comedy world that pudding-pop-hawking, dad-sweater-pioneering, African American morality guru Bill Cosby, married for over fifty years to a wife Oprah Winfrey described as possessing "the kind of splendor attendant with royalty," was a serial predator. But it took until the 2010s for some elite magazines to ban Richardson, for Ailes to fall from his perch atop the news business, for *60 Minutes* to expose the coach, and for the planet to turn its back on Cosby, accused by about sixty women of luring them into bedrooms, slipping "herbal supplements" in espresso or Grand Marnier, and attacking their unconscious bodies in incidents lasting over at least half a century.

In the mid-2010s, the combination of Obama's progressive politics and a press inclined to push the fear button to the max promoted the view that most campus rapes were committed by a few repeat offenders acting out a set pattern — jizzed on at the shoot, fingering with a vague medical purpose, garters, "herbal supplements." And students adopted this rhetoric too. When Sulkowicz said that Nungesser was a "serial predator" at the campus rally, she was echoing sentiments that had already been made in Columbia's bathrooms. Like my peers at Wesleyan twenty years ago, some students had posted a list of offenders on campus there: a fencer headed to the Olympic team, a DJ, a campus-blog staff writer, and Nungesser's name next to the capitalized phrase SERIAL RAPIST. When Sulkowicz is asked her opinion about this list, her eyes flick up briefly. "Whoever wrote it was probably tired of seeing these guys," she says. "I don't think it was a bad thing."

It makes sense that survivors believe those who have attacked them are serial rapists. When one is badly treated by a doctor, one wants to prevent the doctor from mistreating other patients, because one assumes many are suffering harm. Survivors brought this up often. "I was very vocal about my case, and one reason I was very vocal was because I knew four other girls who had been possibly assaulted [by the same guy]," one told me, mentioning a girl who told her the guy had targeted her when she was "very, very drunk and alone."

But is telling Americans that campuses are full of serial predators, as Callie Rennison would say, "180 degrees from the truth"? The notion was based on a single 2002 study conducted by University of Massachusetts clinical psychologist David Lisak that found that over 90 percent of rapes and attempted rapes were committed by 4 percent of the male student body, with each offender committing an average of nearly six rapes. In a reenactment of an interview Lisak said he did with one of the predators, the boy, whom he called Frank, described his attacks as premeditated. "I had this girl staked out," he says on the video in a low drawl. "I picked her out in one of my classes, you know. I worked on her. She was all prepped. I was watching for her, and, you know, the minute she walked into the door of the party, I was on her."

Lisak's evidence was a good counterpoint to "he didn't mean it," and it was comforting to think that we could solve the problem of college sexual assault by raining harsh justice down on a few felons. "It's a little more palatable, I think, to say that a small group of people are doing this horrific crime, rather than saying that sexual violence is happening all over the place," explains Kathleen Basile, a violence prevention scientist at the Centers for Disease Control and Prevention. But as the years went on, it became clear that Lisak's study had cut corners. His survey consisted of 1,882 men on the campus of the University of Massachusetts Boston, but that's a commuter school, with many part-time students and no campus housing. Plus, his subjects ranged in age from eighteen to seventy-one — about 20 percent of them were over thirty years old. And it turned out that interviewers conducting the study hadn't even asked the subjects if they were students; they could have been passing through the UMass campus on the way to an office job. A critic hunted down Lisak's dissertation at Duke University and claimed that he had created Frank's monologue from a hodgepodge of interviews — interviews she said showed scant evidence of premeditation.

In 2015, another theory began to take hold. Researchers led by Georgia State University's Kevin Swartout published a study in *JAMA Pediatrics* that contradicted some aspects of the serial-rapist theory. In their study, they discovered that 11 percent of male college students had engaged in rape since the age of fourteen. But of all men surveyed, only 1 to 2 percent fit Lisak's profile.

Controversy exists in each corner of the sexual assault universe, it seems, and sociologists are no exception. Lisak, displeased by this new study, hired an independent researcher from Wellesley College who appealed to *JAMA* on the grounds that Swartout's study was not only methodologically unsound but also undercounted serial rapists by assuming that a student who offended during one academic year wasn't offending many times that year. *JAMA* re-reviewed Swartout's paper and, with small exceptions, called it a fair piece of work. And I agree with its premise. Of course there are premeditated serial predators in college, but it's unlikely that there are more of these guys on college campuses than elsewhere in America; 1 to 2 percent of men who assault are likely serial rapists, perhaps the same proportion as off campus.

The Red Zone Revisited

For the most part, the college guys that I interviewed said that they understood that pushing girls into sex was wrong. A student at the University of Texas at Austin tells me, "You know, I read something the other day, a bunch of suggestions for how to be a real man. 'Shave with the grain the first time, always buy tools you don't have to replace, don't aim a gun at someone unless you intend to shoot them.' And it said, 'Don't have sex with anyone who doesn't want to have sex with you.'" He pauses. "That made me think — those are good words to live by."

And yet they also said that they felt the expansive definition of sexual assault used by many colleges today is casting far too wide a net. The concept of them as the aggressors and girls as the passive targets is outdated and false, they say. "Men are the dominant force in society, it's true, but some girls that you're talking to are crazy horny and come after you no matter what you do," a Syracuse student tells me. Another points out a girl to me one day outside the campus center: "That girl booty-called me, and then she never talked to me again," he says, half smirking, half hurt.

So if both students are drunk, is it the man's responsibility to figure out how into it the girl is? I ask the UT Austin student. "That's a tough situation — uh, I mean, a tough question," he says. "The man should be the big person and figure out if this is a good situation to be in or if he's taking advantage. But there is some responsibility on the female as well." Another student, also at a Texas school, puts it more frankly. "You go to a frat party on a Friday night, and everyone's going to jail," he declares, recalling the comment I heard from the hot metal guy's friend. "It's not like the girls are only prey, and we're only predators."

Is that guy telling the truth or is that a cover because he's a predator? These are the mind-twisters one encounters when contemplating predation, which some sociologists — though not Swartout and Lisak — say is profoundly difficult, if not impossible, to quantify. No one likes owning up to his or her own misbehavior, sexual and otherwise, on surveys.

He could also be the specific type of college offender that Swartout's research also identified. Swartout says that about 8 percent of all male students only commit rape while in college. This is fascinating. We've established that girls are vulnerable to assault earlier in their college careers and also earlier in the school year. The Golden Gophers alleged rape occurred on September 2. Karmenife says her assault happened early in her freshman year. Molly Morris was a new transfer student. With Sulkowicz and Nungesser and with Syracuse's Jacqueline Reilly, the semester hadn't started. But males also commit these assaults earlier in their college careers — a different kind of red zone, if you will. Perhaps it's because they're more susceptible to peer pressure early on or because they have arrived at college with a distorted idea about how to persuade girls to have sex. No one thinks you can change the behavior of the 1 to 2 percent of serial predators. But this 8 percent might be a different story.

Who's the Predator?

How do we identify potential perpetrators, whatever kind they are? Is the "hot metal" guy a perpetrator? What about playful players like the Bid Day boy who talked about the "talent" in the freshman class, or his friend, the one who threw the rolled-up paper at him? Experts offer a wide range of predisposing factors: personality traits like impulsivity, narcissism, lack of empathy, adolescent delinquency, enjoyment of casual sex, perceived peer approval or pressure, and—a key factor—hostile attitudes to women. A friend's abusive boyfriend struck me as possessing these traits. In a dream, I imagined him constructing a jungle gym and imprisoning her inside.

In my reporting, administrators presented different versions of the campus rapist. One Title IX officer compared them at two campuses where she's worked. At a private northeast university, these guys had a greedy mentality: "She led me on, so I deserve her, because I'm a winner, and I'm entitled to this girl." At a lower-ranked Bible Belt school where her fellow staff members' husbands wouldn't let their wives travel, some offenders seemed autistic and believed that women were inferior to men. She paraphrases this variant as "She led me on, so I deserve her, because she's only a woman, only a vessel, on this planet to serve my needs." Though she's describing two very different types of men and rationales, the undercurrent that unites their thinking is misogyny.

There's one other common denominator: alcohol. "Most of the guys don't use weapons or physical force or even threaten physical harm, but they'll use alcohol. They'll use it to alleviate external barriers; they'll exploit a woman's drunkenness to commit rape," Swartout says. "They'll also use alcohol to silence their internal barriers that say it isn't the right thing to do, and the next day, they'll say, 'Oh well, I was drinking, we were both drinking,' as an excuse." Wesleyan's Karmenife puts it this way: "The way they think is, 'If I'm drunk, I have no control over myself, so nothing I do is my fault.'"

Although a majority of college offenders and victims report drinking the night of the assault, drinking doesn't *make* anyone commit rape. What it can do, according to Antonia Abbey, a professor of psychology at Wayne State University who has extensively researched the topic, is lower inhibition in men who are already predisposed to sexual aggression, increasing their focus on immediate feelings of anger, frustration, sexual arousal, and entitlement while decreasing their morality, empathy, and anxiety about consequences. In other words, alcohol doesn't turn men into rapists, but it can be the tipping point when added to other underlying factors.

This isn't a surprise. But alcohol and sexual assault also have another powerful cultural connection: in America, drunk women are perceived as sexually promiscuous, and men tend to overestimate the women's sexual interest. A 2001 study published in the journal *Experimental and Clinical Psychopharmacology* tested this theory by asking one hundred and sixty college men — some drunk, some sober — to listen to a tape of a date-rape scenario, then flick the tape off when the male character's behavior became inappropriate. In the tape, a woman agrees to kissing but starts to protest when the man touches her breasts, then loudly protests at an escalation of verbal and physical force. Not surprisingly, the intoxicated participants rated the woman's sexual arousal higher than their sober counterparts did and allowed the man to continue for longer before hitting the stop button on the tape.

So here are the risk factors we've identified so far: free-flowing alcohol and misogyny. Where does one find them on a college campus? I'll give you one guess, and it's not the library. Fraternities have to enter our discussion at this point, and after that, athletics. Both of them have become vastly more powerful on campuses over the past decade.

During our country's last major student upheaval, the late 1960s, fraternity membership, which ritualizes and legitimizes both of those behaviors, took a nosedive. In 1968, over a thousand Syracuse men pledged allegiance to frats, but two years later, half as many remained. In 1970, not one Syracuse sorority gathered enough pledges to fulfill its quota, and a couple of years later, eighteen of fifty-six Greek houses closed down. "Not rushing was cool, and the Greeks were parodied by student radicals as arrested adolescents who could only survive college by living in the protected environment of a house," explains a multivolume history of the school.

The Greek system today is on spectacularly different footing. It's catnip for millennials and is alive and well today across the country. Membership in frats and sororities is up more than 50 percent over the past decade. They're popular even at Harvard and Yale, where residential colleges, which most students identified with strongly, have long been at the center of social life and such a robust construct that frats were seen as peripheral if not laughable relics. At Yale, DKE was understood to be a repository of future power, but nobody who wasn't in DKE cared about DKE.

Why are Greeks so much more popular today? "This points to record numbers of undergraduates specifically seeking opportunities for leadership, academic support, and personal growth through the brotherhood and fellowship of men," a representative from the North American Interfraternity Conference, an association of sixty-nine frats, told me in a statement. But there are other reasons too. Wealth and class markers have never been easier to acquire, thanks to low-APR car loans and H&M's note-perfect twenty-dollar couture — therefore, true status is that much harder to discern. A prestigious college degree is America's top marker of social status for students as well as parents, but the Greek system — with its monolithic social media power and its many parties — provides a sense of elite access.

What kind of access? Well, in the long term, in an uncertain economy and ever more competitive world, professional access. If you want to maintain your status as a striving middle-to-upper-middle-class member of society, having been part of the Greek system in college is a sure way to do it. To land a six-figure job, it's not enough to have gone to Duke; you have to be a Sigma Nu from Duke. And in the short term, something very nonprofessional: access to friends and sexual partners. To be frank, it makes it a lot easier to hook up, to find someone to blindly fumble around with on a mattress, if you're going to frat parties where this is pretty much the goal.

Along with these advantages, however, comes an institutionalized gender imbalance. Gabriela, a sorority sister, complained about Syracuse's "culture of frat-boy worship." She described the way a frat with hot guys can host a week of events, like dancing for a panel of frat-boy judges, that girls will fall over themselves to go to. "You wouldn't bother dancing for Sig Ep, because they're not hot enough, but the hot frat boys get to sit there and watch the girls shake," she says. "Or they'll tell girls to cook for them in a cooking competition, and the boys decide who made the best dish. Or there'll be an event where brothers will wear hats, and you need to get their hats for points, so you'll see girls running after boys trying to get their hats, just chasing after them. Or they'll sell women's T-shirts at their charity events, but only smalls and mediums, with no larges."

Gabriela says some guys look down on her sorority because they're not attractive enough for them. "We had an event with one of the hot-guy fraternities, and the next day I heard they sent out on their chapter listserv something like 'Never saw panties drop faster in my life,'" she says. "It drives me crazy. These guys love to think we all love them. They love to think we all want to have sex with them."

Is it detrimental to campus culture that sororities can't have parties at their houses or any alcohol in their chapters at all, ever? Those are America's official National Panhellenic Conference's rules, meant to provide a safe living space for girls — but, in practice, perhaps not as useful as the middle-aged wizards who preside over the national Greek system presume. Party and alcohol rules are not necessarily bad, Reilly and other sisters said. The girls don't want students vomiting on their floors and wrecking the good china. But the reality on the ground is a skewed social scene in which the guys get to sit back and relax at home, and the sorority sisters have to come to them dressed up like bunnies or Little Mermaids or whatever the invitation dictates. "The new fad is just bras," says Lianna, the tall student who went to Buckingham Palace. "Girls wear miniskirts and then bras decorated with the theme of the party, like leopard print for jungle theme." She sighs. "[Bras can work] for all themes, unfortunately."

Dead Meat

The truth is that predators come in all stripes — serial and not, frat brothers and not. I heard a story about a couple of DJs at one school assaulting girls. I even heard that about some student leaders of sexual-assault orientation programs. At Ohio State, the marching band was accused of sexualized hazing that involved naked midnight sprints in the football field; of distributing nicknames like "Squirt" and "E Row Vibrator"; and of printing a "Boys of T Row" calendar featuring flirtatious trumpet players in stages of undress. There was also a byzantine story about a tuba player in a conflict with another tuba player about who got to dot the *i* in the *Ohio* formation, apparently the most prestigious honor for a member of the band. When I talk about this with the University of Michigan's Elizabeth Armstrong, she doesn't seem surprised. "Schools can be so particular," she says. "This is about which group of men are given a pass."

But that's true only to a point. Frat brothers and athletes aren't hugely overrepresented as assaulters, although most assaults happen after frat parties or parties in general. They are, however, overrepresented as gang rapists.

For "single perpetrator rape" in the United Educators' report, 15 percent of the students were athletes and 10 percent were members of a frat. But these proportions were reversed for gang rapes. Gang rapes were 10 percent of United Educators' claims. But many of them involved athletes (40 percent) and frat members (13 percent). (Interestingly, according to NYU's Jessie Ford, female athletes have some of the lowest rates of assault on campus; she believes they're protected by their social capital via their connection to activities the school values or possibly because the forty-eight-hour rule stops them from drinking many nights.)

According to Heather McCauley, an assistant professor teaching human development at Michigan State, data conflicts about whether athletes overall (the track team, volleyballers) are more likely to offend than the rest of the student population. Two sports stand out as exceptions: basketball and football. There's a duh factor here, I know. Amy Schumer made this point best in her popular 2015 parody of TV's high-school-football drama *Friday Night Lights;* in it, an upstanding coach declares a new rule of "No raping," prompting cries of outrage at this attack on football tradition. The coach insists football is not about rape. "It's about violently dominating anyone that stands between you and what you want," he yells.

Both the most vicious and the saddest case of rape I came across — somehow emblematic of the whole issue — occurred in 2013 at Nashville's Vanderbilt University among four Commodores football players and an unconscious student who'd passed out after a night of heavy drinking. These postadolescent men transformed into monsters, ruining their lives and their victim's in the process.

Being unconscious, the woman, whom I'll call Lisa, shared a characteristic of gang-rape victims: they're usually passed out, underage, or mentally disabled. This case also defies standard assumptions in ways I've explored, suggesting the messier, more confounding reality represented by Swartout's

research. The boys committed these acts not because they were serial predators (at least, that evidence hasn't come to light), and not because of volatile
norms of postadolescence. The acts happened as result of coincidental factors that exist only on a college campus, with its ritual camaraderie and peer
pressure. It wasn't the beginning of the semester, but it was another beginning: the football team's summer practice session, which included the arrival
of new students. All involved may have been completely blotto. The boys also
expressed uncertainty in the moment or afterward about what had happened
and whether a line had been crossed.

Vanderbilt, which is nicknamed the "Harvard of the South," isn't a football
school. For years, it ended its seasons at the bottom of the Southeastern Conference rankings, but in 2010, the school hired coach James Franklin, who
brought ferocious recruitment efforts along with him. The year before this
June night, the team had had its most wins since 1915.

At Vanderbilt's Gillette Hall, the dorm where football players were bunking, Brandon Banks, Jaborian McKenzie, and Cory Batey—three African
American redshirted freshmen, now on their way to becoming sophomores
—were hanging out. The youngest son of thirteen children, Batey, the main
actor in the unfolding events, was an uber-playful player, a handsome boy
with dreds and dreamy eyes on whom many girls caught crushes. He was
raised by a phlebotomist mom who had worked at Vanderbilt's clinic for over
thirty years. After losing his father to cancer at nine years old, he excelled
in football, track, and basketball, winning scholarships to a Nashville prep
school and, later, Vanderbilt. Batey was the first member of his family to attend college. "We were best friends," McKenzie said of the trio. "Whenever
you saw one of us, you saw all of us."

These three had been joined on the team by someone they knew only by
reputation: Brandon Vandenburg, an immense six foot six and 260 pounds,
who had just landed at Vanderbilt from the California desert. ESPN had him
pegged as the nation's top junior-college tight end. On a social media account, Vandenburg introduced himself thus: "Honors Student. Aspirations
to go to the NFL. Praise God! #IAMSECOND #GODFIRST."

These four men had never interacted other than on a football field before
this night in late June, when the first three began their evening by drink-

ing honey Jack Daniel's and "going with the flow, just drinking, wherever the night was taking us, that's where it was going to go," according to Batey. He was well on his way to getting wasted, consuming, by his (perhaps inflated) count, six to eight shots of the whiskey, four to six shots of vodka, and four to six Bud Light limeritas, or "beer margaritas."

Meanwhile, Vandenburg and Lisa were at the Tin Roof bar in town, enjoying a tab a football booster had opened for the team. They'd met when Vandenburg was recruited; she was one of the pretty girls on the pep-rally dance team to whom he was introduced. A neuroscience and economics major with an infectious smile, Lisa wore her black tank top bearing Vanderbilt's white starburst *V* with pride. "Hostess programs," wherein pretty girls on pep-rally dance teams are specifically selected for introduction to recruits, are not permitted in college football, but was Vanderbilt running an official hostess program? Certainly not, said Coach Franklin when asked about this.

After midnight, the couple left the bar together, both profoundly drunk. The two of them stepped out of a cab at Lisa's apartment complex, and she lost a single black high heel, then couldn't figure out how to unlock her front door. Vandenburg, who allegedly had a mix of alcohol and cocaine in his system, fared little better with the key. Locked out, they climbed in Lisa's black Mercedes, and Vandenburg piloted it to Gillette Hall. By the time they arrived, she was passed out in the passenger seat.

By coincidence, the three friends, two of whom had walked to Qdoba to pick up Mexican food, were passing through the parking lot at that moment. Vandenburg called out, laughing, and showed off the drunk girl in her car. He hefted Lisa's dead weight on his shoulder and carried her to the elevator while they followed. As this new crowd exited on Vandenburg's floor, he let her inert body slip out of his grasp. Her skirt rode up, exposing her underwear-clad butt. The boys snapped photos of the spectacle on their phones. Then, in an ominous move reminiscent of the Steubenville football players, two of them picked her up, not by her waist, but hands and feet, like hunters bearing a piece of fresh game. They dumped her in Vandenburg's room, and the selfie-snapping took a turn toward Abu Ghraib.

Unlike most rapes committed during the course of history, the following events have not have been lost to the creaky mechanism of human memory.

The perpetrators, true millennials, documented most of it themselves on their cell phones. According to news reports, which chronicled the movements of the actors in the room without establishing an exact sequence of events, as Vandenburg's roommate pretended to be asleep in the top bunk, they took Lisa's clothes off. A boy took close-up pictures of her vagina. Vandenburg took out a box of condoms and handed them around. Batey took off his jeans, stripping to his boxers, which were patterned with the American flag. "You're not even hard, bro," Vandenburg told him while surfing Internet porn. He was allegedly coked up and didn't achieve an erection. Instead, when someone inserted a water bottle into Lisa's anus, Vandenburg egged him on, giddily laughing, saying, "Squeeze that shit, squeeze that shit" in a hoarse whisper.

According to the *Tennessean*, Batey also stuck his fingers in Lisa's vagina and his penis in Lisa's mouth, sat on her face, and raised his middle finger. And after he and Vandenburg slapped Lisa's face to see if she'd come to, Batey peed on her hair, reportedly announcing, "That's for four hundred years of slavery, you bitch."

"I Think We Messed Up"

Of all participants, Vandenburg was the first one to realize that a serious line had been crossed. That same night he sought advice from the team's wide receiver and other players; the next day, he told his roommate that what had happened wasn't funny, and it was best if all involved tried to put it behind them. He'd texted photos to a friend in California, whom he'd previously texted thoughts to under the hashtag #penisproblems; his friend, appalled, told him to stop immediately — or, more precisely, to "drop kick that bitch out of the room." (Soon, Vandenburg would fly to California to try to destroy photos and videos by tossing a friend's phone into a lake.)

The day after the incident, he strove to reassure Lisa, inviting her back to his room and painting another version of the night. She had woken up at eight the next morning, feeling rough and hungover, plus something was off with her hair: "I knew immediately that my hair had been wet the night before," she explained. "I know my hair." She stumbled across the hall to the room of a football player she'd dated a while before, crashed there for a few hours, then hit the Pancake Pantry with friends for brunch. Later, Vandenburg invited her to his dorm room, the site of the attack. "He told me that I had gotten sick in his room, and he had to clean it up, and that it was horrible, and he had to spend the whole night taking care of me," Lisa said. "I apologized. I was so embarrassed." The two of them talked for a while. "He was extremely kind, nicer than usual," Lisa recalled, and initiated sex.

The incident might well have been written off as another blasted night if campus police hadn't been looking into which group of athletes at Gillette Hall, doubtlessly also wasted, bent a set of doors off their hinges. They reviewed the evening's security video, and their jaws dropped when they saw the football players carrying a comatose girl into a room and shutting the door.

In the days that followed, stories started flying around the Vanderbilt football scene that a few players might be in terrible trouble. Batey texted his brother: *I think we messed up and I think they're going to charge us with rape.* The boys were most afraid of losing their scholarships: "My scholarship put a roof over my head, food on my table," Vandenburg explained. "It's basically my job, my livelihood." Of the friends and classmates who worried this might cost the boys their scholarships, one of the most concerned was, of all people, Lisa. To her mind, these boys faced dire consequences for no reason — nothing had happened in that room that night other than her embarrassing herself by getting too drunk.

Some texts:

> LISA: are you okay I'm worried?
>
> VANDENBURG: No I'm not . This is all so messed up, I didn't do anything and I feel like I'm getting blamed for stuff that didn't even happen. I just want to cry.
>
> VANDENBURG: Me and a bunch of my teammates are probably going to get kicked off the team unless something changes.
>
> LISA: I don't want anyone to get in trouble because of me.
>
> LISA: I'll do everything I can to clear your name.

When Nashville's deputy district attorney Tom "the Thurmanator" Thurman wanted to indict the boys on multiple counts of aggravated rape, Lisa still didn't think anything had happened. But the pictures told the story: a penis in Lisa's mouth, fingers near her butt. "Image after image of my genitalia covering the entire frame on the screen" is the way Lisa described it later. "These stark, alien-looking fingers all over the flesh were moving from frame to frame, with multiple hands reaching in." As she scrolled through, she saw herself. "At one point I saw what I first thought was a dead woman's face. I was suddenly overwhelmed by my memory of a family member's corpse, and then I realized that it's me. They had taken a picture of my face during the rape."

These men would not be among the large majority of rapists who remain uncharged, though black men (and there were three of them here; Vandenburg and the victim were white) are much more likely to be prosecuted. What kind of defense could be brought? Not much, and when Vandenburg and Batey went on trial in January 2015, in a high-ceilinged, wood-paneled courtroom—a painting of a bald eagle draped in the American flag in one corner, TV news crews staking out their positions on the perimeter—the jurors appeared aghast from the beginning. Still, for nine days, the jury watched a parade of perfect specimens of humanity, these gorgeous American heroes (Vanderbilt football players, Vanderbilt cheerleaders), give their testimony about an unconscious victim, lack of intercourse, racial overtones, a boy who allowed others to assault his own date while abstaining from sexual contact himself, whether other men in the room were homoerotically performing for him, and the production of "rape selfies."

One side of the gallery was packed with supporters of the accused, their family members clucking and grimacing at each piece of evidence. Most benches on the plaintiff's side were empty, apart from the one where Lisa sat stone-faced between her mother and a few victims' advocates, one of whom had a book, *Managing Cultural Differences,* open on her lap. Lisa was now studying neuroscience in a graduate program in Houston, taking time off to fly to Nashville for the trial. Her hair was darker and lightly styled. She wore a boxy black business suit.

On the stand, the boys minimized the act. "It was funny at the time," McKenzie said. "But looking back on it, it wasn't funny." Batey's texts to a friend show no sign of remorse, lumping the event into a string of academic and personal failures. He texted his friend Tiny, a three-hundred-pound football player, *Over the past year I've just been fucking up, I failed a drug test, missed class, and now they tryna say I raped a bitch with some other teammates.*

There was a bumbling attempt by Batey's lawyer, a friend's dad from prep school working pro bono, to blame Vanderbilt for the assault, portraying his client as, in a sense, a victim himself of a corrupt American college culture: "A culture of sexual freedom, a culture of sexual experimentation, a culture that encouraged sexual promiscuity . . . [and] social media, like Twitter and Facebook and Snapchat, which glorifies sexual freedom and glorifies alcoholic behavior, and also TV shows like *Jersey Shore,* and *The Bachelor,*" he said haltingly. Near the end of the trial, Batey took the stand in an aubergine tie, sweating and trembling and even breaking into tears, *The Bible Promise Book* with a mahogany-colored cover between his hands, and he blamed alcohol for his actions. "I was drunk out of my mind, and this is nothing I would ever have done in my right state of mind," he said. "I wish I could take it back." Later, he called the event an "unintentional tragedy."

Vandenburg's lawyers relied on a centuries-old strategy: they prosecuted the victim's sexual history, assigning behavior to her for which they had no evidence except Vandenburg's word. "[Brandon] had reason to regard [Lisa] as a party girl," explained one of his attorneys in a pretrial hearing. In an exchange that defies logic, they also encouraged Vandenburg to claim he had Lisa's consent.

> VANDENBURG: Well, while at the bar she [Lisa] was handing me drinks, saying: "You need to relax and get ready for tonight . . ."
>
> VANDENBURG'S ATTORNEY JOHN HERBISON: And it's okay to say what words she used.
>
> VANDENBURG: Okay. I'll be as verbatim as I can . . . It is pretty explicit. She said: "I can't wait to F-you tonight. Your body is so sexy." She grabbed me in my genital area; she grabbed my butt; she kissed me, all while at the bar.
>
> HERBISON: The "can't wait" comment, did she truncate that word to just the letter F, or did she use just the full word?
>
> VANDENBURG: She used the full word.
>
> HERBISON: Okay. The word being.

VANDENBURG: Fuck . . . She got sexual[ly] aggressive in the cab. She grabbed my hand and placed it on her genital area, started rubbing it. She, basically, said "I can't wait to have sex with you, I'm so wet," and "Let's get back," like "hurry and get back to the apartment already" . . . walking to her apartment she was grabbing me. She was grabbing my genital area, my butt, and whispering in my ear, kissing my ear, things of that nature; and, saying that she was wet and couldn't wait to have sex.

The prosecutor began his cross-examination.

PROSECUTOR THURMAN: . . . she said she wanted to have sex with you; right?

VANDENBURG: Yes. She said she wanted to have sex all night long. I guess, I could take that as me. She said it to me.

THURMAN: Not with anybody else. You . . . Did she consent to sex in that room that night?

VANDENBURG: I guess, I couldn't speak for her. I know she consented to me.

THURMAN: To you, when?

VANDENBURG: Less than a half hour beforehand. Less than twenty minutes beforehand . . . she told me she wanted to have sex all night long. It's very ambiguous as to who she wanted to have sex with. She just said, wanted to have sex all night long. That could mean any number of people. Anyone, specifically, that's ambiguous.

When this scheme didn't work, Vandenburg's lawyers stressed that their client never touched the girl; his culpability lay only in inciting, encouraging, and failing to stop the abuse once it began. But when the foreman read his name in the list of the guilty, his father let out a long scream, and Vandenburg's look of confusion suggested he'd never imagined he'd be severely punished.

After two guilty verdicts and one mistrial, the Nashville judge, an elderly black man with a reputation for even-keeled verdicts, sentenced Batey to fifteen years in prison without the possibility of parole. Because Vandenburg incited the crime, he received seventeen years. "It is one of the saddest cases that I have ever encountered," the judge said. "And I have been in the legal business for thirty-two years." In a highly unusual move unsuccessfully challenged by a media coalition that included the *Tennessean* and the Associated Press, certain records related to the case were sealed. No one needed to know anything more about that terrible night.

Part III

THE MAN

Interlude 2

Ceci N'est Pas un Viol

The Vanderbilt incident was unique in terms of its volume of unambiguous evidence. In many other situations, there were competing narratives and wisps. And, as the weather turned cold after Columbia students' major October rally at the *Alma Mater* sculpture, the public began to learn that this might have been the case in the most famous alleged assault of all—Emma Sulkowicz and Paul Nungesser.

At least, that's what Nungesser wanted people to think, on the advice of his wily attorney Andrew Miltenberg, whom he called after my article came out in *New York* magazine. I heard that Nungesser's father had flown in from Germany to visit his son, and when he arrived in the city, he saw Sulkowicz and her mattress peering out from newsstands. This story was much bigger than he had realized, and his son required help.

Miltenberg is a nice fellow, freckled, with an earnest manner that covers up a deeply emotional side. Our breakfast in the backroom of a swanky restaurant was set up by his publicist—I chuckled thinking about an attorney with a publicist, but Miltenberg is a New York character with the media-savvy of bold-faced Gothamites from nightclub owners to Donald Trump. Campus rape gets lawyers' names in the papers, and that's good for their businesses and good for their self-image.

Though he represented a man accused of overpowering a woman, Miltenberg positioned himself as David fighting a university Goliath (much like the campus activists, come to think of it, though their point of view was diametrically opposed). "Look, I'm not a senior partner at Blank, Blank, and Blankety Blank—I'm just Andrew Miltenberg with an office across the street from Penn Station," he explained to another reporter. "But if you dare question the motives of an Ivy League school, you're suddenly trapped in a room with a bunch of white-shoed guys with Roman numerals after their names. And they're all harrumphing about the audacity of questioning anything they do. Well, we're questioning them."

On Columbia's campus, there were whispers that Nungesser's side of the story was worth hearing, though the vast majority of students seemed to favor Sulkowicz's interpretation. After all, when students wrote in the bathroom that Nungesser was a serial rapist, they were both gesturing to Lisak's research (which had been seared in their minds via Obama's promotion) and the multiple cases that had been opened against Nungesser. Sulkowicz was one of three women who had accused him of improper behavior — and, it was later revealed, one man did as well. One of the female accusers, a girl who had been in a long-term relationship with Nungesser, believed he was emotionally and sexually manipulative. The other said he'd offered to help her restock a bar at a party, then grabbed her and tried to kiss her. The guy said that while he was hanging out with Nungesser, Nungesser massaged his back and crotch.

Why didn't Columbia take these cases seriously? Well, they may have. But the first student dropped her case (the demands for interviews and paperwork became time-consuming, she said); Columbia found in favor of the second student, but when Nungesser filed an appeal, she chose not to subject herself to a new round of questioning. The university did not find the man who'd accused Nungesser credible.

Facing a torrent of accusers, Nungesser seemed like he wouldn't tell his story publicly. But he was angry that he'd become radioactive on campus. "They have a process in place, which I followed to the letter," Nungesser said of Columbia later. "I had everything to lose in it. And it's been worth nothing. Absolutely nothing."

In the weeks before Christmas, the scoop was delivered to the *New York Times*, which dubbed Miltenberg's client "one of America's most notorious college students." The tale he told about Sulkowicz, here and in legal documents, was about his innocence. She was a young woman who was initially confused and later perhaps became vengeful. If she was in touch with the other students who brought claims, was she charismatic enough to have persuaded them; could she have helped them reevaluate acts with which they were previously comfortable? He suggested that she might have been desperately in love with him.

Beyond this, Nungesser wanted to make clear he was the moral one, not she. At Columbia, he was an upstanding member of campus society: a lightweight rower, a stage designer for campus theater, founder of a student film production group. Radical students might have imagined him as White Patriarchal Privilege Embodied, a stereotype. But while he might have come off as aloof and arrogant to those who didn't know him well, he was (a) an architecture major, and aren't they like that?; and (b) from a different country. In Germany, he insisted, he'd been raised to recognize his own entitlement. He was the only child of middle-class parents who shared responsibilities of work and home life. His father was a schoolteacher. His mom was a journalist who "raised me as a feminist," he said. He attended high school in Swaziland, taught literacy to fourth-graders, and managed a soup kitchen, and, in a detail doubtlessly meant to impress, he let it be known that he had once assembled a CD of a school choir performance to raise funds for a classmate with leukemia.

Nungesser said there was a simple explanation of why Columbia's administration failed to find evidence of his wrongdoing: he hadn't done it. The major assaultive act alleged in their otherwise consensual sexual relationship was forced anal sex. And, he claimed, it was Sulkowicz who had initially introduced him to that particular behavior; she'd suggested they try it months before the alleged assault (Sulkowicz has said this was not the case). Plus, he wasn't physically capable of forcing sex in the missionary-style position she described, with her legs up against her chest, Sulkowicz said he argued. She was a fencer, and her legs were the strongest part of her body; as a lightweight rower, he didn't have the strength for that maneuver.

Drawing on old texts that Sulkowicz had sent him, Nungesser tried to establish that she was smitten. Before the encounter in question, she'd sent him messages like *I want to snuggle with you, I miss you more than anything,* and *I love you-so much.* Although he admitted he received fewer texts after the incident, none indicated any change of feelings that he could detect. After all, two days after the alleged rape, when he messaged her on Facebook, *Small shindig in our room tonight — bring cool freshmen,* she responded, *lol yussss,* then added, *also I feel like we need to have some real time where we can talk about life and thingz because we still haven't really had a paul-emma chill sesh since summmmerrrrr.* Later, when he sent birthday greetings, Sulkowicz wrote, *I love you Paul. Where are you?!?!?!?!*

These messages certainly made Sulkowicz seem more immature than her image as a mattress-bearing Joan of Arc. But her description of what she was doing — trying to keep the atmosphere light, trying to get him to talk to her — made some sense. "I love you" is a bit of a strange thing to say to a boy she called "my rapist," but it could be evidence of the loving feelings that Campbell said victims sometimes direct toward offenders. At the least, she had told me earlier, "I didn't really get how rape worked at the beginning of all of this. I was like, maybe I should talk to him and see if we can sort things out, because I thought that was how you're supposed to deal with rapists. I'd say part of this whole thing is that I'm very naive."

But Nungesser had more to say. He soon produced messages from far before the night in question, raising more unsettling questions.

SULKOWICZ: fuck me in the butt

NUNGESSER: eehm

maybe not?

jk

I miss your face tho

SULKOWICZ: hahahah

you don't miss my lopsided ass?

NUNGESSER: i do

just not that much

good I am actually too tired to choose a movie

*god

also to tired to spell apparently

When I read these strange comments, I took a sharp breath. But Sulkowicz, again, explained them as part of a larger picture. *Fuck me in the butt* was an all-purpose curse about being tired, not a coarse invitation: "Back in freshman year, I used to say the phrase 'Fuck me in the butt' to mean 'OMG, that's sooo annoying,'" she explained to *Vice*. "We all said stupid shit fresh-man year. Over time, I worked that kink out of my lexicon, but now and then I still say stupid things. We all say stupid things! I hear people say things like, 'That test raped me' or 'I raped that test,' when they don't actually mean that a rape occurred."

In these messages, *fuck me in the butt* was meant as a complaint about not getting enough sleep. This was Sulkowicz's explanation. That's highly pos-sible, but the phrase wormed its way into the media's consciousness and un-dercut her story. In the world outside campus walls, the conversation about Mattress Girl shifted, recasting her from victim to villain. Those who histori-cally argued against rape's prevalence, like Camille Paglia, were ebullient: "[If I had Sulkowicz for a student,] I'd give her a D!" she said. "I call it 'mattress feminism.' Perpetually lugging around your bad memories — never evolving or moving on! It's like a parody of the worst aspects of that kind of grievance-oriented feminism."

And whatever Sulkowicz had meant in that exchange, one thing seemed clear: She and Nungesser were misunderstanding each other, at the very least in these messages and at the most when they were together in her room that night. Because Nungesser was, on some level, uncomprehending, generating a different response to her question about missing her lopsided ass: *Maybe not, jk, I miss your face tho.*

Whether Nungesser was being truthful about his perspective will remain a mystery. I would have liked to interview him myself, and when a top Ger-man newsmagazine asked me to fly to Berlin to speak to him, I accepted the assignment. But his parents apparently stood in the way. I was told some-one had contacted the editor and insisted they find another writer because I had previously authored an article sympathetic to Sulkowicz — a demand the magazine met. The activists weren't the only ones who knew how to play hardball with the media.

If Nungesser meant to shock Sulkowicz into silence with his tactics, he failed. As the weather turned colder, she began executing a difficult art project, one in which she would turn the digital medium that had captured her text mes-sages to Nungesser to her advantage. Through Marina Abramović, one of the high-profile artists impressed by the mattress protest, she met a video director with whom she began collaborating. She told her friends that she had something big in mind but didn't say exactly what; to the ones with orthodox ideas about assault and political messaging, she said, "It's going to be great, but I don't know if you're going to like it."

Sulkowicz arranged this new project on a website. *Ceci N'est Pas un Viol,* or *This Is Not a Rape,* retasks the famous caption René Magritte put below his painting of a pipe in 1929's *The Treachery of Images;* it has been paraphrased by countless artists and intellectuals and become shorthand for all things meta — commentaries on language versus meaning, representation versus reality. Under the title *Ceci N'est Pas un Viol,* three components made up one artwork: an essay, a video, and a comments section in which she encouraged the audience to let her know what they thought of the project.

The essay was not as clear as carrying a fifty-pound mattress. In fact, I found it to be a confounding mix of request, admonition, politesse, and demands. First, there was a trigger warning, letting everyone know she was about to discuss sexual violence. This was followed by an inclusive gesture verging on retraction ("However, I do not mean to be prescriptive, for many people find pleasure in feeling upset") and a strange presumption that others could, or would, know her intentions and honor them: "Do not watch this video if your motives would upset me, my desires are unclear to you, or my nuances are indecipherable." Then she voiced a more expansive, though somewhat confusing, thought. "You might be wondering why I've made myself this vulnerable," she wrote. "Look — I want to change the world, and that begins with you, seeing yourself. If you watch this video without my consent, then I hope you reflect on your reasons for objectifying me and participating in my rape, for, in that case, you were the one who couldn't resist the urge to make *Ceci N'est Pas un Viol* about what you wanted to make it about: rape."

Shot by four cameras simulating the split screen of security video, the flawlessly executed film opens on a dorm room in the midst of beginning-of-the-semester moving-in chaos, much as Sulkowicz's room had been on the night that now dominated her life. Boxes are strewn around, and plastic and department-store bags are heaped on a navy couch. The wooden dresser matches the wooden bookshelf matches the wooden bed frame, all in dorm-room light oak. The bookshelf is bare, as is the shiny, blue Columbia-issued mattress.

Sulkowicz plays herself, and an unidentified male actor takes the role of Nungesser. Her hair is cut in a long bob, dyed blue, and she wears jean shorts with strings hanging off the bottom. He takes off her black tank top, and she doesn't have on a bra. She takes a condom out of a small black purse. The Nungesser character is wearing a black T-shirt and jeans; he takes his pants off, and his penis is long and thin, perhaps half the length of a hammer. They're naked. He eats her out. She gives him head while he sits on the bed. Then she's up on top, having intercourse with him, and then he's on top, missionary-style, except her knees are pushed against his torso.

The actor gets more excited as he pumps away, going faster and faster, then slaps her face with an open hand. He pulls out, rips off the condom, holds her down firmly, and anally penetrates her. In his grasp, she can't move. She says "Ow" and "Stop." Then, as quickly as he started, he stops, sits up on the side of the bed, grabs his clothes. Without a word, he exits the room.

The choreographed movements of the actors captured exactly what Sulkowicz said happened that night. (To be clear, they appeared to be having sex, not pretending or secretly wearing Spanx, like actors in an R-rated movie.) Perhaps this wasn't a pipe, but it wasn't unlike a painting of a pipe.

The fact that the icon of the movement made a tape reenacting her rape — I'm somewhat unclear about why admitting this means I didn't "resist the urge to make *Ceci N'est Pas un Viol* about what you wanted to make it about" — pushed things far beyond college feminism's neo-Madonna-ist stance on sexual self-exploitation and toward culturally uncharted territory. At the same time, the video functioned as an effective sex-ed seminar in the difference between consensual and nonconsensual sex, because that anal penetration didn't look like the clearly consensual sex that preceded it.

What came back to Sulkowicz in the comments section of *Ceci N'est Pas un Viol* was a roar of Internet id. *Unsurprising*, I thought; *what a masochist to do this to herself.* Still, she was right to display this terrifying illustration of the unregulated world beyond campus walls. To some men who were not at college being schooled in new sexual norms, nothing in that video looked like rape, or if it did, the fact that it did excited them.

"I masturbated to this," wrote one commenter. "Fuck your consent."

9

The Fixer

One spring morning, I traveled to the heart of the contemporary American dream. Malvern, Pennsylvania, near Philadelphia's historic Main Line, is an aspirational middle-class suburb where everything is about the kids and the grand futures of those kids, with college as the capstone. Malvern's a little rural, a little suburban; what's the big deal about forty more minutes on the freeway if you get a huge house for less than what it would cost in Philly? Malvern is close to the fabulous King of Prussia mall. The schools, both public and private, are solid.

I came here to meet Brett Sokolow, a man with one of the oddest jobs in America—he's the nation's top university sexual-misconduct adviser. He gave me the address of the type of mini-malls common in bourgeois areas today (a spin center, sushi, a boutique named Bedazzled) and told me to meet him in the cozy coffee shop. I peruse the trinkets for sale, most designed to appeal to moms: hand-painted ceramic lockets on chains, patterned skirts for little girls, paper roses made from vintage books of "the greatest love stories" (*Romeo and Juliet; Pride and Prejudice*). Behind me, two mothers trade gossip about college acceptances—"Alice applied to ten schools, and got in everywhere!"—and nearby, graduating high-school seniors in green plaid skirts loudly discuss how good one of the girls' houses smells. "People keep telling me my house smells so good, but I can't tell because I'm there all the time. I'm excited to go to college so I can come back and smell it," she tells a friend, slightly deadpan.

Sokolow saunters into the café a few minutes late, wearing khaki shorts, flip-flops, and a blue polo shirt with a tuft of gray chest hair poking out the top. He has deep brown eyes fringed with heavy lashes, a Pat Buchanan–size head, and a brash confidence at odds with a voice that he may purposely keep soft and unthreatening in one-on-one conversation. A typical suburban dad taking a casual Friday he is not; he has done more than any other person to influence university protocol on sexual assault. Sokolow says he has trained three thousand Title IX coordinators, eight thousand investigators, and eight hundred college-hearing boards; written a hundred campus codes of conduct; and personally led more than a thousand college investigations. He was on the roster to testify as an expert witness for Florida State University football player Jameis Winston's alleged victim; his services were reportedly called on at Wesleyan, where sources shared his seminar workbooks with me; he has been the University of Virginia's hired gun. He tells me that his employees have, on occasion, referred to him as the "Moses of Title IX," though perhaps a better comparison is to the TV show *Scandal*'s Olivia Pope, the high-level fixer and presidential inamorata played by Kerry Washington who swoops in to solve thorny problems and saves countless compromised careers.

"We're in a superheated environment right now, and if a school screws up a little bit this way or that way, someone is going to have their ass," he tells me after taking a seat holding an oversize ceramic cup. "So a lot of campuses are interested in 'What does the right bowl of porridge taste like — not too hot, not too cold? . . . How do you find the perfect pitch?' Because if you don't, somebody will write a book or an article about you, someone will file an Office for Civil Rights complaint about you, you'll get sued by one side or both — and it's going to be everlasting hell."

The people I had encountered so far had their sides of the story, from Blackout Blonde to Lianna, Karmenife, Joshua Strange, the moms who say that girls are manipulative because they are manipulative too, Vanderbilt's Brandon Vandenburg and his declaration that his victim consented. They may have all had their own set of beliefs about gender and sexual dynamics before there was even a story; certainly, their involvement in sexual-assault scenarios enhanced and solidified points of view that they held, at least subconsciously. Those beliefs were logical, at least to them, and one could sympathize with their side, or not, as one wished.

But someone has to be the referee for sexual disputes between students, both the girl with the boy's hand under her parka and the boy in American flag boxers who urinates on a girl in retaliation for slavery. The midwestern state university student losing his virginity who doesn't put on the condom the second time. This referee has to handle their advocates too, like the attorney with a publicist, and the young activists dumping stories to the media. The radicals who insist all survivors are believed. The parents with the fat bank accounts who say their sons have done no wrong. The famous student who bests carrying a fifty-pound mattress with *Ceci N'est Pas un Viol*.

Sokolow is the unofficial overlord of the university system that decides the fate of all of these characters. This system isn't quite the American justice system. It's an alternative justice system, and, yes, as the girls at Wesleyan would say, that's very cool. But campus discipline is also a system of gaps, where fellow undergrads and fisheries professors may adjudicate rape cases while accuser and accused are usually separated from each other, either by videoconference or even Auburn's flimsy curtain taped to PVC pipe. To hear affected families tell it, the universities' bureaucratic schemes — no-contact orders, canceled hearings, policies that change midway through a case, a ban on cross-examining witnesses, and "picking and choosing evidence, discarding other evidence, I've never seen anything like it," says one mom of an accused boy — are elaborate. "It sounds like the DMV," I say to one accused boy ticking off harms, whereupon he shoots back, "Maybe a Nazi DMV."

Though much effort is being put into making this system fairer, right now appeals are allowed on both sides, and a host of Nazi DMV–like rules piss off everyone involved. But without these campus courts, not only would many rapists get away with their crimes, but the myriad types of sexual assault that are, as Chloe, the Wesleyan activist, called them way back in chapter 1, "not illegal but unethical" would also persist.

Whether these courts work comes down to one question: How good are the university employees running them? They are the arbiters of justice, even though they have a stake in the matter: self-protection. They themselves admit this can be a problem. "I'm very bothered by the lack of sophistication on the part of administrators," says Jason Laker, a San Jose State University professor of counselor education who was previously its vice president of student affairs. "The practice of avoiding saying anything of substance based on being sued or losing your job is ridiculous to me, and in my experience it's more likely to generate a lawsuit, because you're disrespecting [students] and making them feel like they're talking to a wall." Laker summarizes the psychology of administrators judging sexual-misconduct cases this way: "They prioritize the career, the university brand, the legal and reputational issues . . . and they get wigged out."

Sokolow gives those who do this work, called Title IX officers, a de-wigging by giving them tools to do their work and calming them down, plus he provides something for them to aspire to: a glossy image. He is a curious type of person; he shoots from the hip, but he's also an ace word-mincer. It's the combination of these two characteristics, I'd imagine, that makes him appealing to college presidents meeting him on the ninth hole, perhaps alongside partners from Blank, Blank, and Blankety Blank, for straight talk about "nonconsensual sexual intercourse." That's a term Sokolow is credited with introducing to colleges. School justice loves bland terms, ones that downplay the reality that they're operating as de facto courts outside the legal system and that avoid emphasizing the particulars of various cases. University officials corrected me when I used words like *judging* and *guilty*, and even *sexual assault*; they prefer *sexual misconduct*. *Adjudicating* is the right word, not *judging*. "He's *responsible*," not "He's *guilty*." A victim is a *complainant*. An offender is a *respondent*. The disciplinary process is an *educational experience*.

On one occasion, I overhear Sokolow on the phone giving some advice to a university administrator about, presumably, the wording for an e-mail about a possible drugging and assault. "I don't think you could withhold the sexual-assault part of the warning now that you know that that's credible . . . Say, 'A student brought to our attention an allegation of drug-facilitated sexual contact' . . . An allegation . . . Originating at an off-campus . . . you know, whatever you want to do, in terms of identifying location . . . Sure, if it's a bar, then I would say so . . . Then I would sort of go into 'Students are cautioned when going out there for drinks.' Then I would sort of say, 'The college is making further inquiry, and we'll provide an update if any new information arises' . . . Well, I'd rather not disclose any additional information now . . . Yeah, say you are making further inquiry. It's true. And you can say local police have been alerted . . . Well, we don't know really what it was — you can say that the student suspects that maybe the drink was drugged? . . . Good, I like that. All right, good luck!"

Though Sokolow has many nuanced views of the system, he insists that the post-2011 climate is a vast improvement over what came before. Universities react in one of three ways to reports of nonconsensual sexual intercourse, and before 2011, there was "ten percent at the bottom that were corrupt," meaning that they'd sweep cases under the rug and not help victims, he tells me at Malvern café. "Eighty percent in the middle who were indifferent. Ten percent who were proactive and caring." He smiles as he gives today's improved figures: "Fifteen percent of campuses are indifferent, sixty percent are trying their asses off, and twenty percent are excellent." Not so fast. His help is still needed: "Five percent of campuses are still corrupt, and even within campuses that are not corrupt, there are still corrupt athletic departments that throw off the whole environment." These improved stats are not unrelated to his influence, of course. "In 2011, overnight, I became a prophet when I had been a voice in the wilderness!" he says, laughing a little. "And that's still weird."

Such radical shifts come with a price tag. The federal government drove the push to eradicate sexual assault on campus, but they never said they'd pay to fix it. Calling his work "systems-level solutions," Sokolow created several organizations, including ATIXA (Association of Title IX Administrators), NCHERM (National Center for Higher Education Risk Management), NaBITA (National Behavioral Intervention Team Association), SACCA (Student Affairs Community College Association), and SCOPE (School and College Organization for Prevention Educators). A flurry of lower-level options on his websites — trainings, videos, and audiotapes "essentials for the busy higher education professional" — include courses like Consent and Blackouts: The Legal, Psychological, and Prevention Perspectives, and Mandated Reporter Training for Employees: Reporting Sex/Gender Discrimination, Harassment, and Campus Crime. There's also six pages of template language to satisfy new disclosure requirements ($249); a series of Title IX training videos ($379); and four sixty-minute modules on paths to "good decision-making" in sexual-misconduct cases ($599). For $299, he sells a kit called Investigation in a Box — everything from models of proof to a list of what's protected under FERPA to a "template letter to a reluctant victim."

In fact, when we start talking about affirmative consent, he uses cash as a metaphor. "Have you seen any of the videos where I do the wallet thing?" he asks me eagerly. Leaning forward, he extracts his wallet from his pocket to demonstrate how the common concept of money can be applied to sexual currency. "We've established it's mine, I can show you my ID in it, my wife gave it to me, anniversary present — my property," he says, turning it over in his palms like a magician performing a trick. "Do you have any right to my property?" I shake my head no. "So given that you don't have a right to my property, how do you get it?" I say I'd, you know, ask for it. "Right, you'd have to ask for consent."

He tugs at a hundred-dollar bill. "Occasionally, with sexual permission we do licentious things," he says. "We leave our Benjamin hanging out, we wave it around — and it's very tempting. But you know this is *my* Benjamin, right, and if you grab it, you're engaging in a theft?" I agree. Now a twenty-dollar bill comes out, and he says, "So when sexual property comes into it, sometimes I'm offering my Jacks, I'm perfectly comfortable with you touching my Jacksons, but my Benjamin is right near it, and everybody knows that, but I was pretty clear it was only a Jackson." People who touch Jacks think they can also grab the Benjamin, and what kind of idea is that?

He puts the wallet back in his pocket. "So [sexual consent] isn't that radical a concept." He chuckles. "And the thing that's so wild about the focus groups and studies going on right now on campuses is that today's students *want* this definition of consent. This is their thing!" He shakes his head. "Like they invented it."

My Moral Compass

Sokolow knows when consent rules were invented. In the 1990s, he met Katie Koestner, a William and Mary student who one could say became America's first date-rape poster girl, a Gen X Emma Sulkowicz. Koestner, who said a date pressured her into sex a few weeks into her first semester, made the cover of *Time* magazine in 1991; in the photo, she's wearing a ribbed turtleneck and small pearl earrings, giving the camera a look equal parts vulnerable and shocked. HBO made a film of her story, *No Visible Bruises*. Yet William and Mary students were so incensed by her story and the loose definition of rape it seemed to encourage that twelve hundred of them signed a petition demanding HBO depict the accused's side too. "Although I cared very deeply that people hated me, I kept telling myself, 'It doesn't matter, you must believe in yourself,'" Koestner says now, adding, "I didn't have any role model at all."

At the time, Sokolow was planning a career in international law. "I had never given a thought to sexual violence in my life until I met Katie," he says. "But when she didn't get what we considered a fair shake from William and Mary, we searched around for a way to get her relief. What do we do to force the universities to deal with this problem? How do we leverage her powerless position?"

While traveling to American campuses with Koestner, who began a formidable lecture career and later founded the Take Back the Night Foundation, Sokolow tried to pique administrators' interest in a fledgling consultancy business. "[I was] putting out articles, talking theory at conferences, and there was a hundred percent pushback," he explains at the Malvern café. Universities told him, "You're full of shit, this is never going to happen. Title IX doesn't mean what you say, although we know you want it to." They accused him of using scare tactics to get business. "And, in fact, things turned out to be far scarier for them than I ever told them it would be," he says.

Today, Sokolow says he is married to a survivor, and they have two preteen children. Later, they'll head to their home at the shore and spend the weekend doing "kid things," he says. But for now, he looks me square in the eye. The core of the campus violence problem is malignant masculinity, he implies, and as a man, he'd be included in that. "I remember being at a urinal on a campus fifteen years ago, going to the bathroom with a sign above the urinal that said, 'You hold the power to prevent rape right in your hands,'" he says. "And as crass as that message is, that's the message we need . . . 'It's my penis, and I have to put it where it's supposed to go, and not where it's not.'" He later talks about his wife. "My wife is my moral compass, and my everything. She tells me how to stay victim-centered, how to address victims, because I don't really know. She sees everything through that lens. She is my true north."

These sound like the thoughts of the private Sokolow, but I can't be sure. He's actorly in the extreme and in fact tells me later he's created a costume closet of sorts for campus visits, which makes me wonder if the casual outfit he's wearing for our interview is planned too. When he does focus groups with students, he wears a sweater and an open-collared shirt. During a Title IX investigation with students, he puts on a jacket and slacks. "So I don't project the power of the institution," he says. "A large-scale training, [add] a tie; and a meeting with the president or board of trustees, a suit and tie." He pauses. "I'm pretty intentional about it."

To say that Sokolow is controversial, especially with faculty, is vastly understating the case. He is just the individual that they do not want in their sanctums of higher learning; to them, he is a creation of well-fed bureaucracy that is feeding off their bones — dropping their salaries, wasting time with mindless meetings, issuing endless memos. From progressive faculty, he gets grief for not being hard-nosed enough about rape complaints. Danielle Dirks, the Occidental College professor, calls his companies "an acronym army," adding that he is the reason that school response to sexual assault is "highly patterned."

Despite the prevalence of liberal faculty on campus — up to 90 percent of humanities professors identify as Democrats — other professors have found themselves in the strange position of regarding regulations around sexual assault on campus with skepticism, and it's because they don't trust the university itself. They smell bureaucratic overreach into students' private lives as well as into what professors can and can't say about sex and violence in their classrooms; about whether the Nazi DMV can sort out which party in a student sexual-assault scenario is truly at fault, they are faithless. To a one, professors I talked to were horrified by Obama-era rules that prohibited them from speaking in confidence with students about assault, insisting incidents were to be reported to the school's Title IX office. "As a professor who teaches violence against women classes, it's so common — for all of us in this area — to have students come in and tell us what happened to them," says Callie Rennison of the University of Colorado Denver. "They aren't looking for anything. They just want to tell their story. And now, because of Title IX, when you see it coming, you have to say 'Stop, I must tell you, no matter where this happened, and if it happened when you were seven, I am required to report this to the university.'" She's the professor who has devoted her life to enlightening kids; administrators are paper pushers. "Is this helping students who have been victimized? Not a bit. And I don't like it. I'd like to give them resources. I think it's the worst thing you could do."

Sokolow, however, says he's just the kind of impartial observer universities need at this moment. He tells me that in some rape cases he believes the accusers, in others the accused. He speaks of "hundreds, literally hundreds" of cases "where I thought the guy was a slime bag, he was definitely guilty, and he was definitely somebody I was never going to let my daughter near. And I still found him not responsible because the evidence wasn't there to find a violation. As much as I knew deep down that he was scum, it didn't matter. It mattered what I could show."

Sokolow also has an understanding of one of the deepest, most paradoxical problems with college rape, proof that he understands quite a bit more about the scene as it exists than his critics imagine: he acknowledges the possibility of true-but-also-not-quite-true accusations at universities. He connects these to what he calls "hypersensitive millennialville."

Affirmative consent "reflects the values of who they are, because they actually want to talk about sex — they *want* to communicate in those situations," he says. But these traits, the communicating and wanting to talk about sex in particular, are double-edged when it comes to assigning victimhood and blame. Sokolow thinks that compulsive sharing combined with millennials' sheltered lives before college is producing a lack of resilience, an absence of coping skills, and susceptibility to mental-health crises. "And that plays into our cases, because what you have now is a number of women, empowered by . . . [survivor] groups who are going around claiming victimization for something they absolutely *believe* happened, for which they *are* experiencing trauma, [and yet] did *not* occur — because they don't have contact with reality the way the rest of us do." He takes a sip from his ceramic mug. "And I wish I could figure out why that's happening, but it is happening a ton."

Interestingly, Sokolow stops short of calling such complaints baseless. A woman who feels violated still needs to be taken seriously, at least at first. "They're not false complaints," he says. "It's not false to *them*."

Winning

And yet despite many of the things I've just said, after spending many months studying the campus justice system, I have become convinced that universities and Sokolow are equipped to handle assaults among students, and they're getting better at it all the time. Criminal justice doesn't work for the reasons we explored in the Gophers' case, and it also doesn't work because the *law* part of *law and order* doesn't want anything to do with it. "People pick up the newspaper and they read that Baylor's getting sued because they were bringing young women in as sex objects to the football team; your average American sits there and thinks, *What the bejeez is happening on college campuses, better get law enforcement involved,*" says Peter Lake, director of the Center for Higher Education Law and Policy at Stetson University College of Law and a thought leader on campus safety issues. But law enforcement isn't desperate to be involved, says Lake: "Prosecutors tend to shy away from these cases because they don't get the conviction, and that hurts them, politically." And a criminal case can take years, which isn't fair to the victim, who may graduate from college by then.

I began to come to this realization when I attended the most important meeting of Sokolow's brood, held annually in Philadelphia. Title IX officers from across the country descend on the city for this meeting of one of his entities, the Association of Title IX Administrators. Sokolow founded ATIXA in 2011 and now counts thousands of members, five hundred of whom are here for the next three days learning to navigate the murky stew of objectively and subjectively traumatic college experiences, of consensual and nonconsensual sex, of personal belief in tough individualism and caring compassion.

The Office for Civil Rights post-2011 requires each university to hire one Title IX officer. But the nature of bureaucracy is to expand. In the wake of the Sulkowicz-Nungesser scandal, Columbia upped its related staff to eleven and now funds attorneys to represent both alleged victims and alleged perpetrators. As of 2016, Yale had thirty part- and full-time Title IX administrators. Harvard had fifty. While I was reporting this book, I stayed in touch with a handful of these folks, and I had to keep updating their contacts; they were constantly being promoted or jumping to a new university or, even more lucratively, turning freelance, a new class of salesman crisscrossing the nation to dispense sex and rape advice at five hundred bucks an hour.

In the Sheraton hotel's ground-level corridors, I fall into step behind two middle-aged women in blue blazers, casual tops, and flat shoes, one of whom carries a heavy book entitled *Diagnosing and Changing Organizational Culture,* third edition. "Shared governance is great and all, but then faculty takes off for three months, and I'm twenty-four/seven," one says. "I was on the plane this morning when the president called asking, 'How many sexual assault trainings have we done for students, and how many for employees?' He said, 'I need to know right now.'"

The other waves a hand. "Oh well, you do the best you can do."

Amid the colonial flourishes of the city-block-length ballroom — colonnades, sconce lamps, a geometric rug in a citadel blue, mustard, and brown — blue-blazered professionals munch on pastries at circular tables draped with white linen. The room's cohort fits demographics represented in ATIXA's survey, which I flip through as one of Sokolow's assistants fiddles with AV equipment: 78 percent white, 75 percent female. Residential schools employ three-quarters of them. Forty percent have been in their positions for under a year. Seventy percent have obligations in addition to Title IX duties — equal-opportunity, human resources, student affairs; universities "voluntold" them to manage sexual-misconduct cases or compensated them with an extra $10,000 in annual salary. These are the less fortunate. The more fortunate are very fortunate indeed. Most salaries for Title IX officers who possess no other role are upward of $75,000, and 40 percent receive $100,000 a year — on par with most tenured professors.

These folks' job is, essentially, to circle the consent question, to figure out who had it and who didn't, even if they have to use a bludgeon when a scalpel is required. They interview the students who are willing to talk to them and file investigative reports that often run to a hundred pages chronicling John Doe's alcohol intake on the night in question and providing the unexpurgated text messages of Jane. Who is to blame? Is he or she (almost always a he) deserving of punishment?

To be successful, these officers must understand the cultural environment in which students swim. In the Sheraton's ballroom, a large mounted screen begins to play the music video for Taylor Swift's "Blank Space." Blond curls to her shoulders, Swift, boogying in front of a fairy-tale castle, falls in love with a guy and then destroys him, cutting the pockets out of his Paul Smith shirt, setting his clothes on fire, and hitting his car with a golf club. "'You know I love the players, and you love the game,'" she sings.

This, the speaker at the lectern explains, is negative relationship modeling. "It's all around us," the speaker says. "Our movies, our music, our TV shows. And let's not even talk about the influence of social media . . . I encourage you to put the apps your students are using on your phone. One of the apps took a picture of me when I downloaded it, and I went into panic mode thinking my students would be able to see me, so beware of that."

This is a group of Gen Xers, most of them around my age, who are devoting themselves to analyzing millennial sex. Sokolow is offering an impressively well-rounded program: an opening keynote from Rebecca Campbell on the neurobiology of trauma and a closing keynote from the number-two officer at the Office for Civil Rights, who urges paying more attention to discrimination against transgender students. (The year after I attended, he invited Laura Kipnis, author of the anti–Title IX manifesto *Unwanted Advances*, to deliver a speech.) There's a panel of defense attorneys who represent accused students. "We get that you're dealing with literally a sexy issue, the zeitgeist has caught up with you, and you're under pressure from all sides," says one. "Relax, and breathe." I also attend Understanding Sexual Assault Risk Factors in Fraternities and Sororities—"This generation trivializes sex in a way that no generation has ever before," the lecturer complains—and Managing the Risk of Liability to Students Disciplined for Sexual Assault led by Title IX expert Erin Buzuvis, which draws so many attendees they move to a room three times the size. "Can university adjudicators be found *personally* liable in Title IX cases?" a man asks nervously from the audience. Buzuvis laughs and then assuages his fears: "Very unlikely."

At a panel on "building a comprehensive Title IX investigative team," three sleekly groomed Texas Women's University administrators in lightweight suits use football analogies: BARRIERS TO THE END ZONE, reads one slide; BUILDING YOUR FANTASY TEAM; SCORING A TOUCHDOWN. "The word we're told is to be *objective*—well, this isn't objective at all, so I have a problem with that word," say the women, some of whom are from the Fitness and Recreation department, addressing the packed room with surprising frankness. "Let's do what we need to do: understand what winning is at our institutions, and then win."

A question from the audience: "What do you do about compensation for deputies in your office?"

"Wait, I thought I was only getting softball questions!" she says, laughing. "Well, they're not paid extra for the work. And there is friction over that."

"May I ask the room: Is this typical?" the audience member says.

A hoot goes up. "All right, I was hoping to hear differently . . ." he says, shaking his head.

Chatter at the Sheraton suggests that Title IX administration is neither a scintillating nor rewarding job. Beside me, a student-affairs officer surfs the web on his phone looking for health supplements. Another taps out an e-mail to her home college: *Are we willing to lose a student over a parking pass? Many of us understand the need of being sensitive to parking permit needs of students who don't on face value meet the criteria. The exceptions committee is not necessarily in line with this thinking . . .*

But one on one, these folks come across as very engaged — careful listeners, astute observers. They believe themselves to be in a fascinating existential position, and a critical one, as they seek to shape America's young population in an important stage of life. I'm impressed by a lecture from Jyl Shaffer of the University of Cincinnati (she's now at Montana State University), who describes her own experience of growing up in a "not very good home" and notes that it led her to develop the priceless intuition that serves her well in her current role. "Victims feel a lot of guilt and shame," she says. "For the average person, if something bad happens, he blames someone else, but who do victims blame? Themselves. Because we're a culture that tells them it's their fault. And all of us in this room don't get to be exempt from that." She waits a beat. "I love Taylor Swift," she says, then, referring to "Blank Space," "I know that song. I can sing that song."

Shaffer advises conference attendees against *expecting* trust from a student who needs their help — "I'm from Appalachia," she says, lapsing into a piney drawl, "we don't trust nobody unless they grew up next door to us" — and then tells them how it can be earned: gestures of caring and kindness; invest in a Keurig coffee machine; treat accused students with dignity too, get their moms a parking pass, maybe even a mattress from facilities if they're staying over at the dorm. Students should not be "surviving your processes," she explains. You need to make sure you are not traumatizing them. Have a soft blanket in your office for the students to touch or hold when they're sharing traumatic stories, or maybe even a stuffed animal. "I have a sea turtle named Wally who is the right size to cover anyone's abdomen, and he has arms so people can play with his arms while we're talking — and he's funny, because who has a sea turtle in Cincinnati?" she says. In a blue blazer today, she tells us that for interviews, she takes it off, and she shows off her array of tattoos, including one of the Roman numeral *IX.*

She also reminds Title IX officers that they have to care for themselves. Shaffer suggests Internet pictures of cats, funny memes, anything to buoy the spirit. This is hard work. "If I do an interview, I need four hours: two for the interview, one hour to type notes, and one to walk away." Most important, she recasts their occupation as far from ancillary in today's college environment. "When people come to your office, they're not talking about sex—they're talking about control," she says. Sudden loss of control is a prime cause of PTSD, and these students may suffer from it. "They're saying, 'Someone took away my control. Someone made a decision about me and I didn't get to make it' . . . And now you have the opportunity, because of your institutional authority and power, to give control back. And that may look like an investigation, and it may look like a cup of coffee." She gazes into the crowded ballroom. "We are definitely altering the future of this country."

Feeling Raped

Not all officers are as thoughtful as Shaffer. A leading administrator says as much to me: "I think the people who choose the job, who apply for investigator positions, want to do it, and my experience is they do a good job. They're people who are curious by nature, and have flexibility in their thinking. But if they're designated by the school, I think that's the other side of things." She pauses. "I don't know if I could say the same thing about those people."

But when I strike up conversation with half a dozen other folks here, I'm impressed. "Law school, that shit was not exciting, but now I love my job, and I am never bored," one tells me, talking about connecting with students in his off-hours. Without self-deprecating irony, he also shares what's actually quite a common sentiment. "These young people have problems because they live unattended! They must be *guided.* We must *guide* them."

Another talks about an anonymous tip she got about a fraternity's annual awards party "celebrating" the female student who'd bedded more frat brothers than anyone else; they shoved the prize in the girl's face in front of the entire group. The administrator thought, *Hmm, maybe I'll knock on the door, say, Hey, guys, what about this prize?* She did, and at the frat house, she could tell by their terrified faces that they knew what she was talking about. She told them what would happen if they awarded it again: an investigation at the school, "and this shit will definitely get you kicked off campus, and we do not care how much money your alums bring in. But that's not all. It will be front-page news, and future employers will Google you, and they will know exactly what you did. Now, do you still want to do this shit?"

This story receives a multitude of vigorous nods. That's the way to do it, they tell me. "Sometimes you need to hold the hand, be the parent. And other times, you need to say, 'I'm going to whip your ass.'"

They also confess to taking certain borderline actions in the line of duty, actions that they'd prefer not to publicize. "It's unconventional," says one. "But the best thing to do with Greeks is go to a dinner or a small function and hold a glass of wine. Now, I don't mean doing shots. Hold on to that same glass. Let them drink and talk. Then you establish trust."

I'm surprised to hear a lot of sympathy for the accused boys. "It breaks my heart to see the boys that come before me," says another officer. "I have to tell them, 'I'm kicking you out of school,' or 'I'm suspending you,' and this boy is not a rapist. He is part of a sexual-misconduct case, yes." She feels that if she had been able to step in earlier, she could have educated this student, and he might not have done a bad act. "No one at my university wants learning about sexual assault to be mandatory—'Oh, read this webpage, do this, do that,'" she says. "It needs to be like when you were a kid and your mom said, 'We're getting your shots.'"

What's the truth about accused boys who say they're falsely accused? Should I trust them? The officers identify the same problem that Sokolow does: There are students out there who are claiming assault when they haven't been assaulted and then claiming trauma from the assault—and they appear to be telling the truth about the trauma. Are they mentally disturbed? Are they mirroring their friends who have been assaulted? Has there been so much discussion on blogs and in the news and on campus about assault that—as always happens when a particular crime hits the news—victims are coming out of the woodwork, and some of them haven't been victimized?

How often do college accusers say they've been traumatized? I ask Justin Dillon, one of the lawyers on the defense attorney panel, the panel on which an attorney talked about the zeitgeist and breathing slowly. "Every single time," he says. "It's part of the playbook now." He ticks off the buzzwords: "*Trauma. Trigger. Frozen* . . . It's the twenty-first-century version of double-speak, a substitute for rational discourse. You get to say the words instead of making an argument about how they apply."

An easy way to understand why female students are doing this is developmental (they're copying friends), but another one is political. It's fair to say that many progressive female students are creating this pickle. I heard often from this type of student about the need for historical justice: Victims have for too long been disbelieved, silenced, shut up, gaslighted, even committed to psychiatric wards for believing their experiences were real. And they're right about that. But extrapolating from one's individual assault experience to a wholesale renovation of history seems a little over the top.

As early as 1987, Catharine MacKinnon insisted, "Politically, I call it rape whenever a woman has sex and feels violated." Some progressive students may agree with this too—part of the way toward gender equality involves calling these feelings rape. At the same time, *feeling* violated can be the same thing as being violated, and even these officers who are devoting their lives to this topic have a hard time saying where the line falls.

Athletic Elite

I heard that word—*political*—with particular frequency during this conference. I thought officers were referring to the pressure put on them by politically radical activists. But when they say, "Title IX cases can sometimes get political, and there's pressure," they mean something totally different. A trustee's son is accused, an important athlete is accused. It's your Title IX case, and you supposedly have the authority to decide it. But suddenly you're getting calls and pressure from the chancellor or someone in the top ranks pushing for a certain outcome. Political.

Now, there is reason to suspect that this doesn't happen as much as one might imagine (and if you read the news, you probably imagine it happens a lot). Buzuvis, the Title IX expert, says that as the OCR has made its way very, very slowly through those three hundred and fifty Title IX complaints, they've found mostly "ho-hum violations," like investigations that last for ninety days instead of sixty. "I don't want to discount the importance of violations about bad policy—who knows how many students would have reported rape but didn't because you had a crappy policy—but it's not a very splashy story to say that the only thing they found wrong was on paper," says Buzuvis. Peter Lake, of Stetson University, agrees: "Everyone wants to read about failure and redemption, but the end of this story is the most boring book ever written. After years of fuss and thunder, they were doing a pretty good job."

Still, these people I'm talking to right here know where the bodies are buried, and some of them are telling me that some investigations get political. What's left unsaid is that with political cases, justice is not always served. This is most often an issue with college football, the least well-kept and by far the dirtiest secret of administrative coverups at universities. These high-revenue-producing teams are ever more isolated and sequestered on campus, a privileged class of indentured servants who bring in about as much income as pro sports teams like the NBA and NHL. The power dynamic among players, the university, and female students is problematic, to say the least. These boys make millions for the university. The university doesn't pay them. You could argue that universities know payment comes in a different form—women's bodies.

Football players are campus celebrities, and like celebrities, they can get laid as often as they want. They're not that different from rock stars with groupies. Groupies have always meant group sex, and group sex always has the potential to cross a line. And when it does (along with premeditated rape), that's when the gnarliest form of rape culture clicks in. With the financial stakes of college football sky-high, and given the belief on some teams, as the BU hockey player explained, that women frequently lie—athletic directors and universities often shame and blame the victim and protect and defend the players.

I'll briefly describe a classic of this genre. It's extreme in some respects because of the fame of the accused (he was a Heisman Trophy winner), but it clearly shows the common themes in these situations. This is the case of Jameis Winston, Erica Kinsman, and Florida State University. Kinsman, a premed freshman, accused Winston, soon to become the team's star quarterback, of raping her after he and some friends picked her up at Potbelly's, a bar. Although she went directly to the hospital after the alleged incident, and the university was immediately informed, delay after delay meant that Winston was never charged. Did the Tallahassee police act in concert with FSU's football program to cover this up? Kinsman's lawyer Baine Kerr says, "There's phone records that link everyone up at critical times."

Kerr calls the Florida State case an anomaly because Winston was such an important player. When a player is just a member of a college team, they'll get plenty of protection, but nothing like this, he explains. "They have the same routines." The local police protect the team. The players are tipped off so they'll get their stories straight. The coaching staff retains lawyers. "And it's so easy to discredit the women; they're not lying, but there's something in their story they're getting wrong, because they've been traumatized, and that scrambles memories." Florida State paid Kinsman $950,000 to end her litigation at the same time they issued a statement denying wrongdoing. Winston settled for an undisclosed sum.

As corrupt as some athletic departments remain — or as "challenging," to use the Title IX lingo — by 2017, there was some indication that those who acted similarly wouldn't get away with it easily due to a mix of empowered Title IX departments, legal challenges, and survivors' willingness to turn to the media. Not only was the coach of the University of Minnesota's Golden Gophers fired, but the curtain was ripped off Baylor University, the country's largest Baptist school, in Waco, Texas. The university wanted a winning football team and a big new stadium on the banks of the Brazos to bring the school to further prominence, and female students bringing sexual-assault allegations against players might have been obstacles to this goal. A lawsuit by an alleged victim, a client of Kerr's partner, claims that from 2011 to 2014, thirty-one players committed fifty-two sexual assaults, some of which were ignored, even graphic ones against the defensive end Tevin Elliott. Two female students told ESPN that Elliott raped them. He pushed one's tampon up during forced intercourse, and another said that when she said no, "He fed off that energy. To him that was yes. He liked that energy." Elliott was brought up on criminal charges and sentenced to twenty years in prison.

What did Baylor chancellor and president Ken Starr know, and when did he know it? Yes, that's the Ken Starr who acted as independent investigator of the Monica Lewinsky affair — the sanctimonious scold who ordered Lewinsky to turn over her semen-stained blue dress, the moral policeman who made sure President Clinton was impeached. Starr claimed he had no idea, though in retrospect, he declared that the teachings of the Bible might have made it inevitable. "Even in the best of programs, horrible deeds are done," he explained in *Bear Country*, his 2017 book about his tenure. "We are a fallen race."

In a stark symbolic shift, Bill Clinton's bête noir tumbled from his perch. The Big Twelve football conference also announced that they'd withhold part of $30 million in conference revenue from Baylor until receiving evidence that the school changed its policies toward survivors.

Hunting for a Feather

Sokolow has been putting out fires and missing for some of the conference, but he arrives early to lead a basic Title IX training session, held in a small but packed conference room with silver jugs of water sweating on each participant's desk. Over sandwiches with names like the Thomas Jefferson (grilled chicken) and the Ben Franklin (roasted turkey), the audience takes in a free-associative download by Sokolow and his associate Leslee Morris, the Title IX investigator for the San Diego Community College District. They talk in a loose, tangent-friendly fashion about best practices, shortcuts and pitfalls, methods of proficiency, and professionalism.

The best administrators can do, Sokolow tells the room, is be impartial, fair. An equitable process can withstand scrutiny. "Your work will be reviewed by some administrator or panel. It will then potentially go to a hearing, then potentially to an appeal," he says, his head bobbing at the front of the room. "Then your president and your board of trustees, even though that's not an official level of appeal—they'll have something to say about it if it's controversial. Then the front page of the newspaper, OCR, the judge and the jury. They are your audience—no pressure." He spreads his arms wide. "If at the end of day, they look at what you did and say, 'Hey, I see where they came to that conclusion. I agree with it,' then you've done what you needed to." Now he becomes serious. "If they find anything that makes you look like a fool, well, we're not going to want to be made to look like a fool."

Sokolow's tips are largely Investigative Journalism 101 and Private Investigation 101, which tend to be the same thing: Be thorough, reliable, impartial, prompt, and fair. Get off your butt. Visit the location of the alleged rape, check out the acoustics, the lighting, "and pray something happened during study-abroad in Rome." Arrive early to interviews with students, because there's only one chance to establish rapport. Leave no stone unturned, no witness un-interviewed. Document everything. Type up notes promptly. Print every e-mail, and put it in a folder. "Paper trail," says Sokolow. "I know it's a lot of work. But it's a lot more work trying to defend [yourself] in federal court four years later when you don't remember what you've said to whom."

Step one is a search for proof. An administrator must put biases aside and accumulate evidence, even though this can be difficult, because students wait an average of eleven months to report sexual-assault incidents. Morris tells me later that surveillance, texts, and social media data increasingly factor into cases; video monitors on a dorm floor showing the Vanderbilt victim slumped over in the hall, "outcry" social media messages like the one Erica Kinsman posted on Twitter after she left Winston's apartment. "Someone texted someone something," she says. "There was an Uber driver. There was someone checking IDs at the door. There was a phone call someone made. There's usually something."

At the same time, Sokolow admits "smoking guns are really few and far between." He recommends looking for a "feather" to tip the scales over fifty-fifty. Fair enough; in many cases, like Sulkowicz and Nungesser's, strong arguments exist on both sides, and a feather is enough to tip the scales. (By the way, Columbia had a rule about not mentioning the existence of other cases, and Sulkowicz's panel never heard about Nungesser's other accusers.) "If you look at the *Maxwell* [*Law*] *Dictionary*, it says that preponderance is fifty percent plus a feather," he explains. "So that's what we're doing. We're looking for that feather."

Sokolow also gives great pointers about applying affirmative consent in a white paper his firm put out explicating the concept. It's centered on a graphic case study of two female roommates playing around with a vibrator and cunnilingus. After another student in their dorm hallway makes one of the students uncomfortable and embarrassed about lesbian acts, that student reports her roommate, in part for not asking before she went down on her and not stopping right away when she told her to. Should she have? "Sure," Sokolow wrote. "But is it a sex offense that she didn't?" No. Consent is an imperfect concept, and Sokolow believes some manner of sexual reciprocation should play into it; I think he might not punish Yale's Kai for reciprocal oral sex either. Looking at the totality of the evidence and the context of the relationship, a reasonable person would see these events as consensual.

Step two is punishing provable acts to the full extent of university law. On this, Sokolow holds the line. "I am the hanging judge on sanctions," he says, taking on the unforgiving tone of a vigilante. "For those of you student-affairs folks in the room, spouting Abraham Maslow or Adventures of This and That, encouraging students' maturation . . . so that their behaviors align with values, I get what you do. And I respect it deeply. But you have to stop trying to educate and rehabilitate sex offenders. Because that is not your job. That is not developmental." If an officer still wants to be soft and let a student back in after a suspension, that's okay with him as long as that officer meets one requirement: he agrees to set the student up on a date with his daughter first. "Because that's what you're doing. You're setting them up on a date with somebody else's daughter."

Keep these guys out, he tells the audience. But some audience members can't do that; they work at open-access community colleges, which means, Sokolow says, they're "where the prestigious schools send their rapists when they screw up — the dumping ground. Lobby your legislatures so that you can be an institution [off-limits] for certain off-the-charts offenders." He gives a half-smile. "I will say a sex offender should get a college education. But I think it should be online."

There are also a lot of dirty words this afternoon. "As a forty-four-year-old guy, I get blown away by millennial sex every day. I don't think I could survive in college today. And if you don't know how different it is, it's enormously different," says Sokolow. He offers an example: "I remember the first time I interviewed an African American guy, he said, 'Well, yeah, I hit that.' My Title IX bells went off, right? He didn't mean he was hitting her. He was having sex with her." He laughs. "Because that becomes popularized in music, then the lame white kids adopt it too, because it sounds cool. They always talk about hitting that and tapping that, nutting here, nutting there. They're not eating cashews." He adds, "Dancing is grinding, and it's probably further than [I got] in my sexual experiences." Earlier, Sokolow told me he found some of this sex "icky," and when we discussed condoms, he said something that reminded me of Oliver at the state university in the plains, though he also could have been describing jerks who take off condoms partway through sex, claiming they can't feel anything. "They don't use condoms!" he says about students. "Half my cases are 'He came in me and I didn't want him to.'"

"Does anyone know what FOMO means?" asks Morris.

The room is silent, and Morris's face takes on a horrified look, perhaps for real, perhaps for show. Sokolow tells the audience that they must build "cultural competency" and explains the acronym: fear of missing out. He tells a ribald story about a "blowjob-giving Catholic" at a college in Texas who accused a student she called her "backup fuck buddy" of rape. "When I went to college, we didn't have fuck buddies, let alone 'backup fuck buddies,'" he says. He scans the crowded room. "Go back to your room tonight, stand in front of a mirror, and say, 'Penis and vagina' over and over again until it's not a big deal. Please do. Because if you're awkward about it, the students will sense it, and they'll be awkward about it."

Sokolow chuckles. "I used to not be the kind of guy who'd sit in front of fifty people and say 'backup fuck buddy.' But now it kind of feels fun."

10

Adult Supervision

One unseasonably warm winter afternoon while reporting at Columbia, I was sitting on the steps of Low Library, site of campus rallies, drinking in the sun alongside students poring over textbooks. It was quiet, at least until a student docent in a blue windbreaker led a group of prospective freshmen and their parents up the stairs and paused before the grand sculpture of *Alma Mater*.

She talks about clean fun on campus, like a Christmas-tree-lighting ceremony with a cappella groups performing carols before counting ten-nine-eight to an Instagram pic. She mentions visiting food trucks, and the school's annual Bacchanal music concert. "The stage is set up right here, and students pack the steps," she says brightly. "We've had Lupe Fiasco and the guys who did the #Selfie song"—the Chainsmokers, via Syracuse, at the top of the charts—plus Kanye West, Snoop Lion, and Vampire Weekend. She puffs up a bit. "You know, the four members of Vampire Weekend went to Columbia. We're very proud of that."

The docent doesn't mention the word *rape*. But she does say that if a Columbia student is followed or "feels unsafe from a man on the street," she or he should look for red stickers in windows of the restaurants and shops nearby, which have been designated Columbia University Safe Havens. "You can tell the manager to shut down the entire store, kick everybody out, and wait for public safety to pick you up," she says, adding, "Now, I've never heard about that being used." She also mentions Columbia's blue lights, tall kiosks lit by high-wattage blue bulbs with a direct line to authorities that American universities have strategically placed around campus for two decades. "Again, I have never heard of a blue light being used except by a skeptical mom on a tour one time," she says, "and then we had to deal with a very angry public service officer!"

It's an awkward whitewash, and I chuckle a little as I head to a dorm lobby to conduct an interview. There, a very different scene awaits me. Goldberg's traffic lights are here, but they're lost in the blizzard of sexual-assault literature spread among stickers and flyers. Video-monitor messages announce the rape-crisis center's hours and demand "enthusiastic consent." I don't see any mention of food trucks or the Bacchanal, which, in fact, Columbia reportedly canceled over concerns that a drunken, rowdy rock concert might engender a sexually threatening atmosphere — a risk the institution can't take with Sulkowicz still schlepping her mattress around.

CONSENT IS SEXY, CONSENT IS BAE, KEEP CALM AND CONSENT ON. These are slogans on thin, low-cost T-shirts sold around the country in universities' bookstores — well, with the advent of online shopping, they're not bookstores anymore, just boutiques filled with swag in school colors. What else did I see? Signs in common rooms for early-evening showings of films like *I Never Thought It Was Rape* and *It Was Rape*. All-weather sandwich boards, temporary tattoos, shoelaces decorated with an 800 number for crisis centers. Water bottles decorated with the phrase "know your part, do your part" and round cardboard "awareness coasters."

Much of this swag comes from the Colorado Springs–based company PSA Worldwide ("Promotions. Solutions. Awareness"). I flipped through its eighty-plus-page catalog one afternoon, checking out the Sexual Assault Awareness Towels, No Harassment Lip Balm, and a squeezable green rubber stress reliever spelling out C-O-N-S-E-N-T? The sales copy tried to clarify the product's intent — "word-shaped stress reliever relieves tension and helps spread the message of obtaining consent before sexual activity" — though it didn't explain why the tension-creating question mark had been added. For orders of over one thousand, they're available for $1.91 each.

I never saw this tension-creating tension reliever in the wild, nor have I seen any of the other higher-tech options now in development or already available for purchase online. There's Undercover Colors, a type of nail polish designed by four male graduates of North Carolina State University's College of Engineering — dip it in your red Solo cup to detect if your drink's drugged

—and a plethora of "smart jewelry" options: the Athena, a half-dollar-size pendant in black, antique silver, or rose gold with a button that sets off a loud alarm and sends text messages with a GPS location to a list of loved ones; the First Sign Hair Clip, a ponytail holder that triggers cell phone cameras and microphones to record an encounter; and the Safelet bracelet, whose online video ad depicts Little Red Riding Hood fleeing a pack of wolves. "The Safelet creates a community that surrounds and protects, a network I can rely on," Little Red Riding Hood says, and her terrified face transforms into a grin.

Consent . . . isn't there an app for that? Well, yes. We live in a world with digital-phone apps like We-Consent, which provides an easy means of recording a yes from a prospective sex partner. On Consentgear.com, one can even buy an affirmative-consent kit, which contains breath mints, condoms, and a ready-made sex contract—"YES! We agree to have SEX!"—that's a perfect prop for selfies.

Blue lights, Consent T-shirts, the wolf attacking Red Riding Hood—all of it draws ire from young activists. Blue lights are "security theater." The CONSENT IS BAE T-shirts are offensive because "it's far from time to be cute on this subject yet." And those wolves and Red Riding Hoods promote outdated images of stranger rapists.

Still, it's easy to imagine these items finding their way into the luggage of a daughter heading off to her first year at college.

Consent Ed

If there's anything Americans know how to do, it's create a marketplace. Figuring out how to change students' hearts and minds and actions is much harder, particularly about an issue that can be subjective. My personal point of view is aligned with the sociologists who believe that adults are going to have a difficult time changing mores for students and that the changes have to come from the students themselves. We know that postadolescents don't care about anything except what their peers think of them, and programs against binge drinking or for safe sex in this age group are almost never effective. In most twenty-one-year-olds, the prefrontal cortex, which controls impulsive behaviors, still isn't fully developed; students are likely to engage in risky behavior, are not very concerned with the repercussions of that behavior, and don't want anyone telling them what to do. Blackout Blonde is going to ease her insecurities by getting drunk; she wants to loosen up and relax and feel confident. Students are not going to be deterred from partying or drinking; let's try to accept that. "You want to help people achieve pleasure through getting drunk, dancing, being on Molly, but not so fucked up they get so vulnerable that they have sex they don't want to have" is the way a sociologist puts it to me.

At the same time, there's a chance that colleges can figure out how to reach that 8 percent of guys whom Swartout identified. This is the group that may commit rape sporadically in college — not before, perhaps not after. And even if colleges can't figure out how to remold that 8 percent, they might succeed in teaching other students to avoid them.

Broadly speaking, American universities offer students three types of anti-sexual-assault programming, and experts say that offering all of them together would give schools a decent chance of changing some behaviors. (They note, however, that offering programming during orientation, when students are disoriented by the campus map and setting up social connections, is a waste of time.) No set of programs can be expected to do more than that because many students' attitudes about sex and consent are already set by the time they reach college. The Centers for Disease Control and Prevention has stated strongly that consent programs need to begin far earlier, maybe in middle school, maybe even earlier. Marybeth Seitz-Brown, the Know Your IX activist, talks to me about teaching little kids at camp about body autonomy: "I like to talk about different models of consent — you don't have to hug Grandma; you can wave. You can dress yourself, and no one owns your body. You can put on your own pants. You can take a bath yourself."

Many experts — and the State of California, which has mandated this for high schools — agree that education needs to start earlier. "What the federal government wants us to do right now in college with prevention is an impossible task, and I don't think anybody understands this," says Brett Sokolow. "A student arriving on campus at eighteen is already socialized in the norms and problematic beliefs of America. And in a short four-year period, colleges are supposed to reprogram students? There's no such thing. You can't overcome every TV show they've ever watched and every movie they've ever attended, their friends' beliefs, their parental attitudes." A CDC evaluation of

140 sexual-assault-prevention strategies found that only *three* of them significantly reduced sexually violent behavior, and two of those were middle- and high-school programs. Nevertheless, many students and parents demand that colleges actively create an environment that protects women, reduces assault, and enforces consent rules. And again, the three approaches mentioned above can have some of these effects when schools combine them. But partly for funding reasons, and partly for political reasons, which I'll explain, no university uses all three together.

Let's begin with the program that's noncontroversial, apolitical, and cheap — and hence the most popular. Bystander education trains students to step into a couple's business in places that adults won't go, like cruddy frat basements. More abstractly, it encourages students to spread positive social norms and messages among peers. In many ways, the term *bystander education* might be considered code for "raising awareness." The University of Kentucky–developed Green Dot, one of the most popular programs of this kind in the United States, emphasizes this. "Even before I see a concerning behavior, there are things I can do on campus to help set the norms that we don't tolerate violence here," explains Jessy Lyons, Green Dot's associate director. "When I have a conversation with a friend about this issue or I post a story on Facebook encouraging people to stop violence — that's still an intervention. It's doing something to set a new norm on my campus that decreases the likelihood that people will get hurt."

Bystander education had boosters in the Obama White House. On a November afternoon in 2015, Vice President Joe Biden's motorcade swung onto the 'Cuse campus, part of his extensive national tour giving speeches about sexual assault. As it happens, he knows the school well. Biden was a law student here in the late 1960s, and it's where he married his sweetheart.

The theatrics in preparation for the visit were precise. In the school's biggest auditorium, the same one as the Bid Day event, AXiD sisters Jacqueline Reilly, Caroline Heres, and dozens of other Syracuse student leaders took the stage and formed a neat line behind a podium, all of them in orange T-shirts. Biden strode out shortly after, his blue suit paired with a bright orange tie. "It's good to be home!" he said, smiling broadly. "Frank Sinatra once said, 'Orange is the happiest color.' Now, he must've been thinking about Syracuse."

That was the first and last joke the seventy-three-year-old bard of the everyman made before cutting to the point. He connected his crusade against college sexual assault to the American project — "When historians look back to see what kind of nation we've been . . . [they will look to see how] we treated the most defenseless among us, and within that they'll question how society dealt with sexual violence against women and men" — and also to ethical community standards. "This is a *community,* no matter how loosely knit it is," he declared. "Each of your individual attitudes has a profound impact on your classmates . . . the quickest place to change culture is to change it on the college campuses of America."

Biden also added a personal touch by talking about his son Beau, who died from brain cancer in his forties. Beau stopped a sexual assault and was later beaten to a pulp by the offender. His son was a man of character, Biden told the audience of several hundred, and he knew about victims' non-virtuous cycle of self-blame. "'If I *knew* you, there must have been something *I* did!'" said Biden. "The *victim* did! 'I should have somehow known better!'" He paused, shook his head. "What a sick standard."

Then, turning his attention to the men in the audience, Biden's voice became a howl of rage. Gramps was now an angry God. "Guys, it's not complicated," he declared. "You're an upperclassman at a frat party, a lovely young girl gets drunk, like too many of them do, and she's nearly passing out, you see your fraternity brother walking her upstairs" — he began yelling — "have the *gumption to step in. Tell* him! *Expose* him! *Save* him! . . . Have the *nerve!* Look at that young woman as if she were your sister or your mother. You know it's wrong! You know!" He said earlier: "There's nothing abstract about this. It's not complicated. It's like the famous Supreme Court decision about pornography: you know when you see it."

The room was riveted. "We have to change the standard of decency by which we measure ourselves," he continued, scanning the audience. "Any time consent is not given or cannot be given, we understand, we make no mistake, we make no excuses: *It is rape.* Or it is whatever form of sexual assault it has taken. And it's a crime. That should be the measure of our decency." He stepped back. "Guys, look in the mirror, and ask yourself — just you: Are you living up to the standard that you think is required of you to be a man?"

A Matter of Honor

Of course, sexual assault is more complicated than Biden portrayed it in this speech. And yet, the way that he talks about honor and ethical sex could lead some college guys to reassess their goal of getting laid at any cost. I'd put money on one big change eventually coming out of such ideas: a shift in the rates of incapacitated rape (rape that happens when a student is on her way to passing out or is passed out). Male students are going to realize it's uncool to take advantage of someone who's wearing beer goggles. Even a poster produced by the University of New Hampshire's Prevention Innovations Research Center, a leader in the anti-rape-programming field, seems effective. That poster shows three boys at a lunch table with speech bubbles hovering overhead. One boy says, "My friend Jeff is the man. He got this girl passed out drunk and then nailed her." His two friends look at him with disbelief. "You've got to be kidding," says one. "Your friend raped her." The other says, "Your friend's pathetic."

But bystander education's basic premise seems a bit flawed. Stepping in to create a distraction and possibly stopping an assault before it happens is hardly a new idea — girls have been pulling their friends away from creepy guys at bars' last calls for decades. And its effectiveness is limited, given that most assaults, around 85 percent, experts say, happen behind closed doors. (Personally, I like the idea of students being scared straight, like the BU Terriers teammate described, but experts told me that deterrence, or punishing others to frighten the rest, doesn't work.) But these seminars offer a constructive and subtly effective message about being a Good Samaritan, a standup member of the community. That's an easy standard for most college students to embrace because it plays into their idealism — another common feature of this developmental period — and their school spirit. Experts say this type of education has a side benefit: it teaches guys that they can settle conflicts over girls, which is what telling a guy not to take someone home can turn into, without using their fists.

At Syracuse, the administration didn't do much after they received the number-one-party-school ranking. Nor did they reopen the standalone rape advocacy center as activists had requested. But they did spend a great deal of time creating a new center as well as a significant network of interrelated administrative bodies, a deeply rethought resource system that portends a more serious attitude toward sexual assault. Time will tell.

Syracuse also majorly embraced bystander ed on a university level and among the students. Jacqueline Reilly and Caroline Heres of AXiD ramped up an extracurricular group they named Girl Code, after the jokey feminist show on MTV. They organized a walkathon and created social media campaigns, posting #cockblocktips on Facebook and Twitter: "Cock Block Tip #1: Trust Yourself and Trust Your Instincts. If You Feel Unsafe or Uncomfortable, Leave the Party." "Cock Block Tip #2: The Girl Code Is About Sticking with Your Friends: Arrive, Stay, & Leave Together."

Some nights, Girl Code's dozen or so members step in to help students. "I'm such a grandma," says Reilly, explaining that she usually leaves parties early but has walked "multiple girls" home. Her friend Julie Gelb puts it this way: "It's not like I walk around with a giant pad and promote abstinence. But I like the idea of bystander intervention: Trust your gut, and if you see something sketchy, say something. If your friend is drunk on the couch at a party, and a bunch of guys are making fun of her, poking her, taking pictures of her, step in. *Duh.*"

Gelb falls into the category of repeat survivors, which I mentioned back in chapter 5. Unaffiliated freshman women are vulnerable to begin with, but women who have been assaulted before are more likely than others to be assaulted. No sociologist I spoke with could explain why this is. One of them suggested that these girls repress the memories but act out the same behavior by placing themselves in vulnerable situations. Gelb says she was raped twice, once on a high-school ski trip and again outside a subway station while studying abroad in Madrid. She says that at Syracuse, she once stopped something she's pretty sure would have become an assault. A friend of a friend was visiting for the weekend, and at a frat, she began to go upstairs with a guy. "She had only meant to go to the bathroom, and then she was intercepted by this guy, and they were talking, and he was kind of pulling on her, trying to pull her over to him," says Gelb. "So I went up to see if they were both in a fine state of mind to have sex — which, again, fine if they want to do that. I couldn't find her. I had to kick down some doors, and when I finally did, it was actually the case that he was being super-aggressive."

She took the girl out of the party, and the two clattered down Syracuse's darkened paths. "We ended up going back home and making cupcakes. And eating ice cream. Yeah. There was a happy ending."

Less than a year after I had this chat with Gelb, Girl Code's ideas began to percolate through campus. Heres told me, with pride in her voice, that some girls from a sorority higher in the pecking order than hers had asked her what to do about a friend who'd said she was assaulted — "These girls who are so cool," she says giddily, "and they asked me for my advice!" They weren't sure exactly what had happened and what part the girl herself might have played. "I told them, 'Whoa, whoa, you *must* believe her.'"

One Syracuse frat was derecognized after a kid who was hazed in the snow allegedly lost four fingers to frostbite, and another had the same thing happen, reportedly because of action by Reilly, Heres, and Gelb's sorority. At a mixer with AXiD, a guy allegedly pulled his dick out and ran around shoving it at a bunch of girls. The sorority reported his behavior to Syracuse administrators, and they punished the frat, something they might not have done several years prior. Some sorority sisters thought that it was cool that the frat got in trouble, but others thought AXiD had overreacted. One of them sighed when she told me about it. "It's a fake scandal," she drawled.

Sigma Alpha Epsilon, the frat that put on *The Penis Monologues,* is not currently recognized by Syracuse University. The frat's national leadership told me that ΣAE lost its recognition due to "violations [of] their health and safety regulations." The rumor among the kids was that some brothers were caught having a competition about who could sleep with the most girls. Or they were caught keeping a blacklist of girls not to sleep with. Or they videotaped a brother having sex with a girl without her knowledge. The undergrad rumor mill worked overtime on that one, so I can't say for sure.

Toxic Masculinity

The second type of campus anti-assault programming, which has a much smaller slice of the pie, involves masculinity seminars. These are led by guys, many influenced by daytime-nighttime Stony Brook sociologist Michael Kimmel. Toxic-masculinity seminars unpack the way men's fear of appearing tender leads them to assume tough, dominating, and toxic personas. This overcompensation, sociologists say, leads to a vicious cycle; these men make other men feel inferior, so they overcompensate too. The resulting behaviors might be benign, like obsessively pumping iron, or malignant, like sexually assaulting women.

In April 2016, I attended an event called Party with Consent at St. Joseph's College, a four-year Catholic-affiliated university with a heavy enrollment of childhood-education and criminal justice majors, and mostly black and Latino students. The seminar was led by Jonathan Kalin, a young graduate of Maine's Colby College, who remarked to me that people say he resembles Adrian Grenier from *Entourage*. Those people are right — he's a dead ringer for the actor, with curly black hair and dreamy eyes. Kalin's father died in a car accident when he was twelve, and he took on the role of the "man of the house," he says. "I cohabitated with my mom, who, because of some traumas in her past, very much didn't want to look for another partner. And I actively chose to be celibate in high school and much of college, maybe because of weird reasons — Freud proves everyone right . . ." he says, trailing off. "I had to be able to say to my friends, 'Well, I've never had sex with a woman' and be okay with that. Versus a lot of guys who feel like they need to say to their friends, 'Yeah, I've had sex with fifty girls.'"

At Colby, whenever students received student-conduct handbooks, with rules about consent, in their mailboxes, the mailroom guys put recycling bins nearby because they knew there'd be a lot of trash. "So I know students aren't reading what their schools give them," he says. "I've become interested in 'What is going through the male mind, how do you get in touch with these guys? How do they understand power? How do they understand their position if they're physically stronger than women? Do they want to be someone, sexually, who is aware of a woman's interests, be mutual about it, or do they want to be psychopaths about it?'"

Today, as lunch hour begins at St. Joe's, about a hundred students shuffle into the chapel for Kalin's talk, grabbing ham-and-cheese sandwiches and Welch's grape juice from a neatly arranged buffet in the back of the room. Normally, this is time for a "fast-focus" lunch prayer, and Xeroxed reminders to attend the twenty-minute session tomorrow rest on the seat of each black folding chair. I sit next to a twenty-one-year-old named Rob, who takes out his retainer and stuffs it in his shirt pocket before wolfing down his lunch and then goofing around with his friends.

Striding before the crowd, Kalin is delightfully charismatic. He shares his own story about his mom and dad and how he later became the captain of the basketball team at Colby, which gave him purpose and a sense of belonging. Although we're at a Catholic college, he says he wants to create an "authentic space," so he screens video clips from *Superbad,* the 2007 movie starring Jonah Hill and Michael Cera as high-school virgins desperate to get laid before college. When Emma Stone, playing a cute classmate, invites them to a party, Hill tells Cera, "She wants to fuck me, she wants my dick in and around her mouth," then insists, "Just come with me on this voyage, and stop being a pussy for once, and we can fucking fuck some girls already . . . You know when you hear a girl saying, 'Ah, I was so shitfaced last night, I shouldn't have fucked that guy.' We could be that mistake!"

The room is silent when the *Superbad* clip ends. Kalin says, "In college, I was watching *Superbad* and all this messaging telling me that this was the reality about sex. But let's juxtapose that with St. Joe's definition of *consent.*" He picks up the college handbook and turns to a dog-eared page. "So, 'Consent can't be given if someone is unconscious, asleep, incapacitated due to drugs or alcohol, or a minor.'" He nods. "This was written by the people who are authorities here at this school. If something was to come up, *this* is where we look for our definitions, not *Superbad* and Jonah Hill."

The next part of Kalin's speech involves audience feedback, engaging the guys. It's called the Man Box exercise. Kalin tells the students to shout out whatever they see as the defining characteristics of a man and he'll write them down on a large white pad set on an easel at the front of the room. "Confident! Tall! Muscular!" yells one of Rob's friends, then nudges him. "I guess you're not a man," he says, laughing.

"What kind of car does a real man drive?" asks Kalin.

Now Rob knows what this exercise is about, and he'll take the opportunity to make fun of it. "Corolla!" he yells. "Prius!"

Kalin looks a little annoyed. "What kind of dog would this man have?"

"Labradoodle," says Rob. "Chihuahua!"

"What kind of drink?"

"Mike's Hard Lemonade!" says Rob, cracking up.

For the next exercise, Kalin asks students to explore what guys have to think about in terms of assault when they go to a party. That question elicits few responses. Then he asks what women have to think about. The girls in the audience start shouting out immediately: "Don't go alone!" "Watch what you wear." "Text when you leave, and when you get there." "Be on the phone with someone if you're walking home alone." "Keep keys between your fingers." "Walk in the middle of the street, not a dark sidewalk." "Don't go anywhere alone with a guy you don't know." "Yell 'Fire,' not 'Rape' — you're more likely to be helped."

One of Rob's friends nudges him again. "Wow, girls do have a lot to think about," he says, and Rob nods. At the end of the seminar, when the student-body president asks for a few students to come up and take a picture with Kalin, Rob volunteers for the photo.

Earnings per Share

Although the girls at Kalin's event were largely talking about avoiding stranger rape, which is far less common than acquaintance and party rape, the fact that they shared those experiences caught Rob's attention, such as it was. And in my interviews around the country, many boys mentioned that girls opening up to them — as lovers or even as friends — is what changed their minds about how misogyny and sexual assault can damage the female psyche.

"The fact is that women and men do not inhabit the same city," says Henry, the philosophy student from Vermont. "We do not walk the same streets, have the same banal interactions with cashiers and waiters and strangers in elevators . . . this is my knowledge gap to be filled in, the gap of what it is like to walk through the streets as someone other than me." Hearing his female friends talk to him about being harassed and seeing them "become visibly upset," he says, "is enough for me to consider my eyes."

What Henry means by *my eyes* is the way men assess women as sexual objects on the street or at college parties without thinking twice about it. He's keeping himself from doing this now and wants to hear more about the way women feel. "When we talk about 'oppression' and 'power,' no one really wants to hear the perspective of my demographic," he says. And he's fine with that. "Women have not been given adequate time with the microphone."

This is a new trend — boys as part of the movement, not as survivors, but as allies. Rob's enlightenment may be temporary, but I met more woke guys in the colleges I visited than I expected to — sex-positive, intense, intelligent, speaking with the zeal of the newly converted. (Some of them were probably virgins; I sometimes chuckled to myself that I was getting schooled about rape and sex by virgins.) Kevin Carty, the Brown University frat brother, says he too came to the cause after a female classmate shared an assault experience with him, but then he kept peering further into a woman's perspective on life. "Finding feminism is one of the best things that happened to me . . . the philosophy I found in college that said, 'You've seen this stuff, here's why it's happening,'" says Carty. For him, it was a way of reassessing what he'd observed in his all-boys high school: "The worst bullying, the worst fighting, the worst male gender roles, hardcore homophobia, sexism, misogyny." Those classmates are the ones who taught him how to treat girls. He talks about what an older boy advised him to do at a freshman dance: "'When you're grinding with a girl, start moving your hands toward her chest or crotch, and if she's down, she won't stop you. If she's not down, she'll stop you. Then you can decide if you want to keep dancing with her or give it another try later.'" Carty pauses. "Like, that was his advice, in all seriousness. The thing is, a fifteen-year-old, I absorbed this as totally normal, as what confident guys did to get girls."

At Brown, Carty became a student leader. He emphasized to other boys that sex didn't have to be an acquisitive endeavor, about reaching bases. "If you approach sexual encounters with the right . . . I don't want to say *tool bag*, because that sounds kind of fucked up, but . . . the right language, being comfortable talking and thinking about [sex] in a critical way, then you can ensure that you don't hurt your partner. Then you can ensure you don't miscommunicate." Sex needs to be thought of as a "conversation, a mutual involvement, a reciprocal encounter."

Carty means *conversation* in both a metaphorical and literal way; the words should be used for consent too. He doesn't think getting verbal consent for sex is that big a deal. "How many times have [my friends and I] played Never Have I Ever and talked exclusively about sexual stuff?" he muses. If talking about sex is easy in a parlor game, he says, "then it's easier to talk about sex when you're having it." He calls this a "generational switch."

Andrew Brown '15 is another leader from Brown University. A male student assaulted him the first week of freshman year in his dorm bathroom.

During the national day of solidarity with Sulkowicz, he carried a heavy, metal bathroom-stall door around campus to represent his experience. Some students were confused and didn't step in to help the way they did with the ones carrying mattresses. "Was it their own discomfort, or their own . . . impotence in not knowing how to meaningfully help me, or their indifference, or something else?" he wonders.

Brown points out a key distinction between himself and female survivors: his story is readily believed. "If I had it in for another man, the idea that I would allege he had sexually assaulted me is ludicrous, because that's supposed to be more humiliating for me than the person who did it," he says. But he points out that young gay men who have been assaulted are often silenced by their own community. He chalks this up to gay Gen Xers sweeping assaults under the rug because they crave the respect of mainstream society. "[They want to] look perfect to gain a lot of people's sympathy and empathy, and what rights and respect, frankly, we're entitled to," he says of older gays.

It's one thing to ache under the weight of a bathroom door or lecture guys in a peer-education seminar, and it's another to talk to them outside of Brown University's bubble — and many guys I spoke with couldn't quite figure out how to change minds in broader social situations. A UNC student who attends the university's men's project meetings describes spending an evening in an apartment with some guys he didn't know well. The group had the Victoria's Secret fashion show on TV and made misogynistic comments about flab and boobs. "I felt so uncomfortable in that space . . . but I didn't want to alienate or lose these friends," he says hesitantly. "They weren't men's rights activists who were super-political. These were average guys who say sexist shit. How do you talk to them without coming off as elitist? How do you talk to a guy like that without shitting on the way that he sees himself as a human being or a man?" He stayed silent at the time and is ashamed. "I felt like I let myself, and other people, down."

Women's Work

What makes bystander education and toxic-masculinity seminars more popular than the third strategy, risk reduction, isn't only their price and acceptability. It's also that they answer the question young activists have successfully implanted in our minds: Whose task is it to prevent sexual assault? Is it the woman's duty to avoid it? Or is it the man's task to prevent it, as a matter of ethical responsibility and, perhaps, fear of accusation? You can't possibly say it's the woman's, not only because that's obnoxious, but also because that makes stopping rape a woman's burden. But if you don't, you could be missing out on a chance to deter assault.

The most stunning manifestation in how colleges address sexual assault is that women's self-defense programs—popular in the 1970s, and a brief blip in the 1990s—are on the wane. When I looked into offerings through the country, I found a bizarre hodgepodge. The most popular class is RAD, for Rape Aggression Defense System. Founded by a former Marine with a third-degree black belt in karate, it is, as the young radicals would say, a bit patriarchal. Women practice punching, kicking, and deflecting blows with an instructor or volunteer wearing a trademarked full-body Aggressor Simulation Training Suit that resembles police riot gear. On the website for a self-defense group using the RAD method, text explains that the world is made up of three types of people: prey (sheep), predators (wolves), and sheepdogs. "Women are mostly sheep. Predators are mostly wolves." RAD will turn women into sheep*dogs*, the type of people found in the military who meet violence with violence.

Jocelyn Hollander, head of the sociology department at Oregon State, has been studying women's self-defense since 2000. She says that research is clear that in a physical assault, forceful strategies (kicking, striking, running away, yelling) are better than pleading, begging, or crying. But she reminds me that most attacks aren't physical or perpetrated by strangers. "Women are generally reluctant to use damaging physical self-defense strategies against someone they know and in situations they expect to be social, so the strategies taught in RAD classes may not help women deal with the vast majority of situations they are likely to face," she says. The most effective programs, "empowerment self-defense," focus on the full range of violence against women, from harassment to rape. Jujitsu techniques like framing—using arms and legs to create and preserve distance between your body and an opponent's—are often taught. "It sounds simplistic, but setting clear boundaries with your body language—putting your hands over your head and saying 'Back off' or 'I don't want to do that' or 'You're getting too close to me' — can be very effective," she says.

What percent of university programming is centered on self-defense? "It's minuscule," says Hollander. Here and there, university police, phys-ed departments, or local martial arts studios offer classes, and some women even organize them for themselves. I went to one of these at a boxing gym in 2016. This was definitely not a feminine environment. The first thing I noticed when I showed up was a graffiti-splattered door. The second was the aggressive décor: a poster of Sid Vicious, Al Goldstein's *Screw* magazine with the headline "Oriental Sluts Open Their Slits," and a collage of photos of women's bare butts with their Instagram handles at the bottom of each.

A dozen punching bags were lined up in the main room, there was a boxing ring at the back, and through the gym, college-age women were jabbing with all their might. "One, two, one, two!" a trainer yelled at them. "Ba-sic! Ba-sic!" was another taunt to get them to hit harder. A stereo blasted songs like Drake's "Controlla," about a woman who plays him like a joystick but who also likes it when he dominates her in bed: "You like it when I get aggressive."

Some attendees were concerned about risk; a twenty-two-year-old urban college senior told me she keeps pepper spray in her purse and carries it in her hand when she walks home alone at night — at least, she did until the other night at a nightclub, when a security guard searching her purse confiscated it. Some were here for a workout; a seventeen-year-old with the looks of Willow Smith told me she mostly was hoping to be inspired to eat healthy. All of them were interested in the female-self-empowerment aspect of self-defense. "Now's the time for women to rise and men to chill!" Sophia, a twenty-three-year-old grad of a Catholic university, told me.

Three trainers — female boxers who were tough, muscular, and beautiful — taught the girls some unofficial moves. Afterward, they sat with the girls in the ring and answered questions. The conversation could only have happened in the mid-2010s, and not only because of the strange confluence of Instagram butts and female self-empowerment and the sudden confession by one of the trainers that she became involved in boxing because of rapes in her childhood. The organizer also initiated an au courant discussion of shame, declaring, "We are in pursuit of a culture that is shame-resistant! When we talk about shame, we destroy it."

Questions were also asked about the boxers' "self-care methods," a phrase the trainers had clearly never heard before. "Uh, wine?" one of them answered, laughing.

Another question: "How important do you think it is that women learn self-defense?"

"Feeling weak, feeling like you can't do nothing — I think that's the worst feeling ever," said one of the trainers. "You should always know how to throw a punch." She added, "We know men are stronger than us, but don't think you're going to come and *take* it."

"Mm-hmm," went the girls.

She said, "You're literally going to have to fight for this" — *this* meaning her body. Grab the balls, elbows, bite, do whatever you have to. "We are too precious for people to just be taking advantage of us."

Afterward, the girls took photos of each other in front of punching bags. They straightened their sports bras and made mean mugs — sexy mean mugs — then checked themselves out on their phones. "That one's it, that one's lit, post that," a young woman with a Rapunzel-like braid told her friend. The friend laughed, then took a playful swing at her face. The first girl punched back pretty hard.

O Canada

Risk reduction has always focused on women, but when assault is men's responsibility to stop, the focus on women is considered insulting and retro. The notion that rapes are perpetrated by a small percentage of college men — Lisak's study — also plays into this shift. If you believe Lisak, you think it makes little sense to train women to stop rape when a serial attacker will find another target if one well-trained woman fends him off. But as we've seen, his research is hardly conclusive and was an unsteady foundation on which to base an educational strategy — one that now dominates nearly all American campuses.

Over the border in Canada, they've taken a different approach. I learned about this when I spoke with Charlene Senn, an applied social psychologist at the University of Windsor and one of Canada's top experts on the subject. Windsor has historically been that nation's Sin City—at Leopard's Lounge and Broil, one of the city's strip clubs, Mötley Crüe still blasts out of the speakers during the occasional Saturday-night dwarf-tossing—though it's mostly cleaned up now. To get there, you fly into Detroit, cross the world's longest suspension bridge, and voilà.

In Canada, the word *rape* doesn't exist in a legal context. They banished it in the 1980s in favor of the catchall term *sexual assault*, which covers acts from kissing to penetration. Affirmative consent has been the law of the land since the 1990s, when it was codified by Canada's highest court; the court rejected a forty-nine-year-old man's story that he assaulted a young woman who'd applied for a job selling his woodwork at the mall only because she didn't resist. Alas, none of this has changed punishment much; like the United States, Canada has low rates of victims reporting sexual assault to the police and low rates of prosecution and conviction. But Canadians like the consent standard nonetheless. "When too much is left up to interpretation, *that's* when cultural ideas about yes and no in male and female relationships reflect normative ideas and make rape invisible," says Nicole Pietsch, a coordinator at the Ontario Coalition of Rape Crisis Centers.

Senn, the Windsor professor, is a superstar in the anti-rape-education world. In 2015, the *New England Journal of Medicine* published the results of a nine-hundred-woman trial of a program she created. This was the first time the preeminent medical journal addressed an anti-rape program. Lasting twelve hours in total, the program is made up of four sessions designed specifically for female first-year college students. Groups contain no more than fifteen people, and leaders must be under thirty years old, Jonathan Kalin–like peers. The results are astonishing: One year after the program, compared to a control group who read leaflets about rape, the students were half as likely to have experienced rape and nearly three times less likely to have experienced attempted rape. (For purposes of the study, Senn used the word *rape* to mean penetration, so her results were translatable in the U.S.).

Senn is understandably proud and speaks with a firm manner on many matters having to do with sexual assault. Her profile isn't that different from that of the young activists today, just thirty-five years removed. As a student at the University of Calgary, she was abused by a man she lived with.

She worked as a hostess for stag parties—well, this part is different—serving drinks among strippers, though she herself remained clothed. Women's studies classes gave her a new perspective, though, and with friends, she began a radical protest group like the one Sulkowicz and her cohort pioneered at Columbia. They called it Theodora, named after the Byzantine empress who punished rapists with death, and it focused mainly on combating pornography. Though she was once a hostess, she railed against the strip clubs that dotted her city at the time, and when Windsor chose to slap taxes on dancers, she called the city "a pimp."

Among sexual-assault researchers, at least in their public comments, Senn is nearly alone in her fierce anti-porn stance. Social scientists have demonstrated that the number of low-level violent acts in porn, like slapping, spanking, and hair pulling, have increased as porn has become easier to access and more violent—and also more glamorized, as culture pornifies itself. But since the 1990s, they've largely maintained that porn has a negligible effect on offline assault—that, essentially, "pornography wasn't causing people to go out and rape other people," says Emily Rothman, a professor at the Boston University School of Public Health. These days, inquiry focuses not on a "one-to-one connection," she says, but on a "more general question about society, which is: If many people are consuming sexually explicit media that denigrates certain people or promotes the idea that it's okay for sex to be nonconsensual or for people to get hurt who don't want to be hurt, is there a larger net effect where sexual violence is more normalized?"

Results of research probing this question have been mixed. "Longitudinal studies show that use of pornography is predictive of some kind of negative behavior . . . but we don't know what is causing what," says Rothman. "The type of person who frequently uses certain kinds of pornography may also be the type of person who holds particular undesirable attitudes, or even participates in undesirable behavior." She adds, "But that's like saying that the person who buys junk food has negative attitudes about exercising. Well, is the junk food causing those negative attitudes? We don't know. We can't get there with social science."

The effects of porn may be hard to gauge, but Senn's longstanding, forceful opposition to it seems prescient. She is similarly definitive in her stance about the purpose of her program, which she calls "rape resistance" rather than "risk reduction" to make clear that she is not teaching women to avoid risk, but rather to resist coercive behavior.

I spoke with Senn while she was finishing a rough draft of a chapter for a book about rape-resistance courses for women; she was writing it with Christine Gidycz, an Ohio University professor who developed her school's program, and Jocelyn Hollander, who created a successful thirty-hour self-defense program at the University of Oregon that shares some characteristics with Senn's. "We know that longer programs work better, but still, even for my program, which is twelve hours, one of the most common questions I get is 'But could you make it shorter?'" Senn says, somewhat ruefully. That's the first of her several complaints about the current rape-education scene on campus, which she sees as woefully wrongheaded.

Senn wants to be sure I understand the drawbacks of the United States' current programming syllabi. Bystander education doesn't work in mixed-gender groups, only in single-sex groups, and it doesn't have an effect on perpetration either, though it can have a positive effect on attitudes. Lectures centered on toxic masculinity, like Kalin's, haven't been shown to change the rate of perpetration, though they can have a slight effect on men's attitudes, which may be a first step (most men don't like misogynistic talk about women but tend to think that other men do, and changing men's minds on that score can be meaningful). Consent education — elaborating on the White House's PSA — is good sex ed but hasn't been shown to deter sexual violence. Researchers studying men's and women's responses to subtle sexual cues have found that both genders can, and do, read nonverbal signs like turning a head away, stiffening, and rigidity as a lack of sexual interest. Senn is not at all convinced by my stories about the accused boys who believe they had consent when they didn't. "University students don't necessarily know what the legal definitions of consent are, that is true," she says. "But a misunderstanding about consent is *not* what leads to rape . . . If you say, 'Okay, a woman is unconscious, is she consenting to have sex with you?' everybody, no matter what their definition of consent, knows there cannot be consent under those circumstances, yet" — and now her voice rises — "all over North America, men are having sex with unconscious women!"

In Senn's course, peer leaders take freshman women on a painstaking (but fun!) tour through the emotional, cognitive, and behavioral challenges of identifying that they're in a bad situation and then taking action to protect themselves. As in Girl Code's first Cock Block Tip, getting out early is key. "We know from research that there's a whole lot about the beginning of sexual-assault situations that doesn't look anything like we've been socialized to expect," she explains.

What are the red flags? Senn talks about stepping away from men who control women, who speak negatively about them in general, or who purposely try to get them drunk or high. She reminds girls that they should be wary of guys with traditional gender-role expectations, because research shows that those expectations can mask inappropriate beliefs such as women "owing" men for buying them dinner. Such men might insist on driving, might get angry when a girl wants to pay, and often interrupt when others, especially women, are talking. Be wary, too, she says, of a guy who is persistent in trying to get what he wants when he knows it isn't what you want, even if the situation isn't sexual.

During her sessions, leaders point to a poster headed OUR PERSONAL RIGHTS. There are four of them: to defend yourself; to have the sex you want; to not have the sex you do not want; to speak out when you do not like what someone is doing. Although Senn emphasizes that women should focus on gut feelings and perceptions of danger so they can remove themselves before physical actions are needed, she incorporates self-defense maneuvers that are likely to work in an intimate setting, such as breaking wristlocks and chokeholds. Participants also learn about the after-effects of sexual assault so that they understand that "Let's just get this over with" isn't the best move when sexual assault can led to depression, PTSD, and dropping out of college, the very place they've worked so hard to reach.

The most innovative part of Senn's program is the last unit, entitled Relationships and Sexuality, most of it from programming developed by the Unitarian Universalist Church. "The problem with so much focus on sexual violence is that we tend at times to make it disappear women's own positive sexual desires and their own right to initiate the consensual sex they do desire as well," Senn says. "We make it about reacting, yes or no to someone else's interests."

Part of her solution is a game called With Whom Would You Do It? Presented with a series of notecards, freshman women consider what kind of sexual behavior—kissing, cunnilingus, anal sex—they want to explore and with whom they'd be interested in exploring it; options range from a fuck buddy to a long-term partner to a life partner to "no one." For some young women, this will be the first time they've considered in the abstract whether they'd be interested in engaging in a particular sexual act.

A doctoral student found a remarkable outcome when looking at these exercises and others. "Young women who came into the program thinking that they had it all going on sexually, very engaged, and sort of cool—many of them reported decreasing their sexual behavior post-study because they realized that a lot of the sex they were having was not for their own pleasure," says Senn. "And young women who came in . . . I'll use the language of 'closed' as sexual beings—very conservative, definitely not sexually active, 'This may be for later but definitely not now'—came out of the program much more open to seeing themselves as sexual people, even if that involved being a sexual person on their own, increasing autoerotic and not partnered activity."

So this works. But to embrace Senn's program, we need a reassessment of the current thinking in the United States, which is that men need to be retrained. In 2016, Florida Atlantic University was the only American university offering the course. The CDC hasn't supported it, which is surprising, given that no other program has made its way into the *New England Journal of Medicine*. The logic is that Senn's program isn't primary prevention—it isn't interrupting a perpetrator's behavior, because if one woman fights off a man, he can assault someone else—and thus the overall risk of sexual assault won't go down.

There's another reason Senn's program isn't popular; this is an open secret in the prevention world, and several experts mentioned it. "Programming that's more focused on reducing women's risk gets a lot of backlash from the feminist community," says Katie Edwards, a professor of psychology and women's studies at the University of New Hampshire. But "we have to deal with what the data shows—and the data shows that Charlene's program is very compelling, with rigorous methodology."

We should think of Senn's program as a way to achieve a short-term goal, and bystander intervention as a way to achieve a long-range one. Edwards adds, "If we think of why sexual assault happens, it's a combination of things

—community norms that perpetuate it, people being apathetic and not taking bystander action, *and* [not telling] women who are confronted with those situations that to physically resist or act assertively are more likely to thwart a sexual assault. For me, from a science perspective, why not focus on all of these?"

11

Phoebe

T he young people involved in assaults in this book, just like Sulkowicz and Nungesser, never admitted that they could see the other party's side. But growing up a little puts one in touch with complexities. The story I'll tell you here is typical of how these attitudes are moving out into the world and maturing as college students themselves mature.

In the summer of 2016, an old assistant e-mailed me out of the blue. A twenty-three-year-old Georgetown graduate, Phoebe accompanied me to Wesleyan on an overnight trip when I broke my knee. Her silent little sister, a high-school junior with a long blond ponytail and braces who needed to start touring colleges, tagged along. We were a motley crew, us three, walking (or hobbling; I was on crutches) the campus paths together, interviewing students as they passed.

On this trip, Phoebe and I got to know each other. She'd started off her university experience at a big university, but it was too fratty, and when she transferred to Georgetown, she found refuge working at the *Hoya*, the campus newspaper. One night, a fellow *Hoya* journalist left a party with her under the guise of offering a friendly walk home. When they arrived at her dorm room, she went in, and he began to push his way in; she held the door shut as he threw his body against it. This experience put her in touch with survivorhood, she said, using the favored collegiate vocabulary: "I feel very privileged to have had that experience, so I can sympathize with survivors' feeling of powerlessness."

Phoebe pulled some research on sexual-assault statistics for me and conducted a few interviews. Soon, she became busy, and we lost touch. It was a surprise to hear from her a year later, with an e-mail that dropped into my inbox like kryptonite. "Suggestions for a Tinder rape story pitch?" read the subject line. What was inside roiled my stomach so completely that, unlike my chiropractor, I ran to the toilet and vomited.

Phoebe was looking for a place to pitch a personal essay, that much I understood. The story also had something to do with her profession; she'd been trying to move into podcasting. She'd put up a photo on Tinder with a caption saying *funny and feminism are turn-ons.* She thought a funny podcast could be made out of a taxonomy of "Guys on Tinder" — Topless Bathroom Selfie Guy; Guy Who Tells You What to Do in his profile, like "Don't be drama"; Guy with a Gun; Guy with Solo Cups because he hasn't taken any fun pictures since he was at a frat party; and Dog Guy, who wants you to cuddle his dog. A bunch of guys swiped right, including Dog Guy, who soon texted: *When can you join us — us* meant him and the dog — *over wine, laughter, cuddles, feminism, stories and happiness?*

She showed me their text messages, the flirty banter. They texted for a while. When it came time for them to meet, it was sort of an interview and sort of a date.

> DOG GUY: Id send you an uber we would drink laugh play with the puppy have meaningful conversation and continue to enjoy each people's company

> PHOEBE: Hm not sure about going to you and your wingman's lair first time I meet you

> DOG GUY: We'd be going to a bar until im sure youre not a serial killer slash want to harvest my kidney slash steal my dog

> PHOEBE: See women in new york with no pet leases are so starved for animal interaction all you have to do is send them pictures of your dog and their hormones skyrocket and they turn into chemical zombies on a mission for cuddles and I know im not above that . . .

So they were supposed to meet at a bar, but at the last minute he told her to meet him on a street corner because he was out walking the dog. She did so. When he told her he needed to put the dog back upstairs, she went up with him. In his apartment — an Airbnb rental, impersonal and with clean sheets — they had beers on his balcony. He started talking about sex, what she had tried, if she liked BDSM. She offered the thought that she was curious about it. Then he asked her to sit on his lap, and she said no; she strode back into the apartment, ready to leave. He said sure. But first he wanted her to cuddle the dog.

As she said no over and over, he pinned her down. When she struggled, he handcuffed her. Then he stripped her naked. As she began to realize what was going to happen, odd thoughts floated through her head, the sort of thing that Rebecca Campbell, who wrote about the neurobiology of rape, described. "In that moment," Phoebe wrote in her e-mail, "I was thinking about how I hadn't shaved, wasn't wearing cute underwear, and did not want this person to see me with my pants down. I wasn't thinking that he was going to try to rape me. I was just thinking about how I could be more clear to this person."

Phoebe and I talked for a while on the phone, but she needed to get back to the office. The next time I talk to her is at her subterranean studio on the fringes of the city. "I have the greatest apartment ever!" she tells me, quickly pointing out the leafy backyard with a fire pit. Her mom's pink pointe shoes from girlhood hang on a nail on the wall across from a mirrored mantel on which Phoebe has placed the cover of the Beatles' *Sgt. Pepper* album, a photo of Susan Sontag, and a self-affirming note from her ex-boyfriend about how she "overwhelmingly [exemplifies] what it means to be a good person." A couple of friends live upstairs; I overhear some of their conversation, and it's about buying a plastic bin to make Jell-O shots, a first threesome, babysitting a guy who was tripping too hard, and "I'm on my parents' insurance until I'm twenty-six, though can you believe that if I die, they'd have to pay my student loans?"

Phoebe, in a blue Hoya sweatshirt and jeans shorts, pours me a glass of water, gently places it on a coaster decorated with a picture of Frida Kahlo, then takes a seat on a low-slung couch. As we talk, it becomes clear that what happened at Dog Guy's apartment was more complex than I thought. She had told him that she was interested in exploring BDSM—that, she'd told me already. "It's intriguing, because it seems like what I'm interested in, what I like in sex," she says. "I've even put a book in my Amazon shopping cart, like, 'I'm going to read this before my first BDSM interaction.'"

On the balcony, he had pushed her to sit on his lap, to have another beer, to kiss him—and each time, she said, "No," or "No, let's wait," or "Next time, not this time," but he never respected those boundaries, just kept trying harder. Still, when she was handcuffed, then blindfolded, she found herself becoming a player in events. "It very much became a porno," she says. She let him eat her out, and she thinks she might have had an orgasm. And after that, she told him to fuck her. "Just to get it over with," she says.

Her eyes brim with tears. "It's frustrating to me in retrospect — just get out! Tell him, 'Fuck, no,'" she says. "It just wasn't in my vocabulary at that time. It didn't come to me in the moment . . . and it feels *problematic*, in my head, in that way." She adds, "I guess unless you're passed out behind a dumpster, you had autonomy in some way. But . . . in the moment, when I was being led by handcuffs, it didn't seem like I had any autonomy, so I didn't kick and scream."

When he penetrated her, he put her legs up close to his head — she was "just a hole in which to put his dick," she says. She started to scream in pain. "I'm pretty vocal during sex, but I realized I'm screaming in pure pain, no pleasure in this. I remember thinking this must be what I'd sound like if I was being attacked or murdered. I've never broken bones or been hurt badly. The sound was new. I didn't know my body could make it. I felt like I had all of eternity to watch myself, and underlying everything was the thought in my head, *When will this be over, when will you get out of here."* She adds, "I focused on the pain and drifted in and out of hoping it would reach an end, wondering how I ended up here when, just an hour earlier, I had almost flaked on meeting him."

I wish I thought the way that Charlene Senn does; I wish I believed that no one ever thinks he has consent when he doesn't. But the stories of Oliver at the midwestern university and John Doe at Occidental made question this idea, which I held as a shibboleth before I began reporting this book. And now here's Dog Guy — one of the most extreme characters I'd come across, possibly a serial predator, because logic dictates that if he had an Airbnb rental and handcuffs ready for Phoebe's Tinder date, he probably had it ready for others.

And yet the question remains: Did Dog Guy possibly think he had consent with Phoebe? From the beginning of the situation, he was clear with her about what he wanted — sex. The forbidden can be desired — that's why Phoebe was interested in buying a book on BDSM, even if she had a different vision of what that sex would be like. She's the one who met him even though she'd thought about flaking. She's the one who wasn't sure if it was a date or an interview. She went to his apartment when she said she wouldn't. She sat on the couch and cuddled the dog. She had an orgasm.

But she also says she said *no* in various different ways at least twenty times. "While it was happening I was thinking, *How did I get here,* and with the [emphasis] on *I—How did I get here?*" She blithely walked into a dangerous situation, which is still not at all like "asking for it."

Just tell him, "Fuck, no." But she didn't. Simply stating that she should have been strong enough to say it isn't going to change anything. Maybe if she'd put her hands up, pleaded, and then said, "Back off," he would have stopped, but I'm not sure. I *am* sure that Senn's program could have helped her. She would have recognized the clues: Dog Guy's insistence on having her come upstairs. His giving her alcohol even though they were on the way to a bar. His persistence in the face of no. For all the discussion of whether schools should be involved in the intimate corners of students' private lives, this seems to me to be exactly the type of teaching a university should do.

What about a "yes means yes" standard here? Well, clearly, it would have been useful. Affirmative consent is not going to change the fate of woman-kind, something that the redoubtable Catharine MacKinnon, the radical feminist legal theorist, has made clear. "If a woman can be made to suck an employer's penis to keep her job, or to have sex with a dog while being pimped, presumably she can be made to say yes," she wrote. "Consensual is a fall-back stand-in for 'it wasn't so bad' in societies in which sex by definition fulfills rather than violates women, because sex is what women are for." In such a society, MacKinnon said, "a lead pipe over the head or its equivalent can sincerely be believed to produce consent to sex."

But Phoebe would not have said yes if she had been asked the question point-blank. "Yes means yes," boundaries, good judgment, recognizing patterns of male behavior, men not making excuses for these behaviors—this is part of what will change sexual assault on campus. Punishment via the Title IX system is a piece of it, but it's only a reaction to the problem, not a solution. All we can ask of students is to talk and participate, listen to their friends' stories on social media, go to the seminars and take them seriously, as clichéd as they may be.

The other part of the solution is what the culture has already presented us with: Sharing stories. When I wrote this chapter, I was worried that simply by sharing her story, I was exploiting Phoebe or that I might embarrass her, and she wasn't the only young subject for whom I felt responsible and whose intense experiences I felt conflicted about sharing. There aren't a lot of secrets in this generation, and this is not only because of the Internet. To Phoebe, sharing what happened to her was not embarrassing. It was healing and morally correct. If she swept this experience under the rug, didn't broadcast it or reach out to others — just tried not to talk about it — it would hurt worse. And it would hurt not only her but others too.

Sharing sexual-assault stories is our culture's latest and greatest upwelling of truth. But we need to be able to hear the guys' point of view too, not to excoriate them, but to educate them. In my reporting, girls honestly sharing their stories of sexual assault with their guy friends — Kevin Carty, Brett Sokolow — was the number-one reason that guys decided to take sexual assault seriously.

What about sharing your feelings with the guy who assaulted you? Well, then you might end up like Sulkowicz, with a series of flirty text messages that you claim were your way of getting an offender to meet up and talk about what happened but that he insists he interpreted as clingy. And college survivors who are bringing cases to universities don't often want a mediation. "I don't think I've ever had a complainant who wanted that," says Leslee Morris, the San Diego uber-investigator. "More typically the response is, 'I want them to know it impacted me. I don't want it to happen to someone else.' They don't want to sit down with the person. They want them to know it was impactful, but they don't want to have a tête-à-tête."

Restorative justice schemes could be helpful, and some young activists, particularly those associated with Know Your IX, have looked into them. "It's a very small and not super-dominant community, the restorative justice community," says Marybeth Seitz-Brown, the Columbia grad and Lutheran pastor's daughter. "Some people in it don't even want to use the word *perpetrator* because once you do that, you can never be transformed and mend the harm you caused — and, also, it ignores the fact that people can be survivors *and* perpetrators." Seitz-Brown was planning to apply for PhD programs in sociolinguistics when we spoke, and we discussed terms like *accuser* and *perpetrator* — she's not a fan of them, and I agree that they can be difficult words to stomach for the individuals to whom they're applied. And, as she notes, some people are both.

Seitz-Brown says that we must stop advocating for sending campus offenders to prison or expelling them and stop thinking that locating a scapegoat and casting him out is the only way to establish peace. Options could be put on the table and the survivors asked, "What do you need from your community to feel like you can be safe here? How can you heal from this experience and hold people accountable?" The power would be put back in their hands. "My father ends up in the same place that I do about violence," she says, "and that's that the violence you do goes back to you."

So restorative justice, yes; mediation, no—and figuring out the difference between these two is an entirely new set of training sessions for the Title IX bureaucracy. For now, let's talk about what happened when Dog Guy asked Phoebe for another date. Unlike many women, who would have ghosted him, she told him she felt violated. And he protested that he'd done nothing wrong.

Phoebe's best friend, a high-school teacher in Connecticut, had recently gotten engaged. They were constantly on the phone talking about plans for her wedding and, now, about this. The friend convinced Phoebe that the way to move on was to sit down with Dog Guy and tell him exactly what she had experienced. This, too, was partly professional and partly personal for Phoebe. "I want to experience things that other people don't and convey them in media in some way," she explains to me. "I've never heard of people talking to their rapists—can you convince them [of what they did]?"

Dog Guy agreed to meet her in a park one afternoon. "I wanted to make clear that I wasn't going to accuse him of anything but that I was going to explain what happened to me in each moment," says Phoebe. She says she wanted to say, "I get that I didn't behave perfectly as far as victims go. But that doesn't negate all these other feelings I have."

He approached and offered her a cigar. "I'm going to have one," he said. "Would you like one?"

"No," she said.

"No?"

"Okay," she said.

Persistence; everything from asking her to smoke a cigar again when she'd said no to pulling her pants off when she resisted. "Someone who doesn't listen to you and your needs in one context often won't listen in another context either," Senn explains.

They shared their cigars in silence for a moment. "Are you shaking?" he asked.

"Yeah, I'm scared," responded Phoebe.

He shifted in his seat. She was scared — of him? "We clearly have different perspectives on that night," he said. He was talking to a woman who, in his eyes, came over to his apartment, drank alcohol with him, and said, "Fuck me." "You loathe me, and I found you charming."

"I am charming," she joked, a bit coyly.

"The dichotomy on our perspectives — 'Oh, this girl's awesome, let's go to Mexico' — is so broad, a chasm," he said.

She shot back, "I didn't know you! I knew you for half an hour . . . I was in an apartment with a strange man who was pulling my pants down when I pulled them up, who I said no to. I said, 'I don't want to have sex now because I want to see you again,' giving you the promise of sex in the future, thinking that's enough for you to say, 'Okay, next time.'"

He reeled back. "Did you ask me to fuck you?"

She stiffened. "I don't know!" she said. "And to be honest, if I said no that many times, it doesn't matter. Because no doesn't mean keep trying until you get a yes."

They went on this way for a while, but Phoebe kept pressing her point, and soon he started to cry. "I'm not crying, it's onions," he said. "I really thought you were having fun." He glanced down. "I'm trying to navigate feeling really disgusted with myself and also trying to replay clues I mixed. And also feeling" — now he looked at her — "I feel a lot of things, and I know you do too."

Soon, he delivered what Phoebe deeply wanted, what might have made her feel better than taking him to court or writing his name on a bathroom wall: an apology. "I'm sorry," he said.

And she believed him.

12

Down with the Frats

T here is one extremely obvious action that would make an enormous difference in ending, or at least stemming, college assault. Destroy the frats. Or coeducate the frats. One or the other, and they may go hand in hand.

Young activists ding universities for mishandling sexual-assault claims, but they're aiming at the wrong target. Universities are perhaps not as bad on this score as they once were. They're increasingly run by women, and, as I learned at Brett Sokolow's conference, officers dealing with sexual assault are overwhelmingly female. But there's somewhere on campus the true patriarchy persists — the fraternity.

The central role frats play in college sexual assault has been understated. As I said earlier, there's no evidence that the majority of predators are frat brothers. But on Planet College, the Greek system dominates social life, and deforms it. I believe sexual assault happens in large part because of cemented gender norms that tell guys they must pursue girls at all costs, and many girls don't know how to say no but don't want to say yes. So having institutions with cemented gender norms controlling social life on campus seems like a really bad idea.

What about athletics? Do I want to shut down sports teams, make students sit around all afternoon playing Super Mario Brothers instead of whipping balls during baseball practice? No. Bigtime college athletes are campus celebrities, yet in terms of personal interaction, they have little truck with student culture; at Syracuse, I rarely met a student who had even been to a party with the members of their powerhouse basketball team. So while there's no question that sports culture at a university like Baylor is a repository of malignant ideas about women, in terms of sheer numbers, there simply aren't enough athletes to influence campus life.

Fraternities are a uniquely American creation and closely tied to the production of young American masculinity. In *The Company He Keeps*, a fascinating history of historically white fraternities (which make up a majority of frats nationwide, in a system that is still highly segregated), University of Northern Colorado professor of history Nicholas Syrett ties these two entities together, beginning with the establishment of the first frat at tiny Union College in 1825.

Syrett identifies four distinct types of young men dominating four eras. The initial fraternal ideal was the original, unreconstructed scholar and a gentleman, a stoic, stellar academic with a code of chivalrous restraint that served his own emotional repression as much as female virtue. But after the Civil War, this began to change. In the late nineteenth century, scions of wealthy industrialists refashioned the ideal into a more youthful and vigorous figure, a young man who also excelled in athletics and politics, leading staffs of both the yearbook and the newspaper. In the 1920s, as Victorian standards eased, Jazz Age decadence went mainstream, and enough colleges went coed for male competition to express itself in *l'amour*. The ideal frat brother shifted again: metrosexual *avant la lettre*, this man was dashing but not quite carnal. He participated in a new consumer culture of pomades and lady-killer Gatsby suits and excelled in attracting the fairer sex. Fewer than half of his brothers made whoopee, and those who did so did it strictly with social subordinates like waitresses and prostitutes.

The fourth and final type, Syrett argues, arose in the 1950s, when GI Bill undergrads returned from foreign wars with notches on their belts to face Eisenhower's moral strictures at home. Enter the Hawaiian shirt, panty raid, and pursuit of coitus. With some percentage of their female classmates now potentially their willing partners, sexual congress became the paramount goal. Closet virgins would compensate by projecting outsize virility, and a display of machismo also distinguished the fraternity brothers' tribe from the other young men known to share close quarters, chiefly Communists and homosexuals. Secret hazing and pledging rituals took on multifarious forms of sexual humiliation; by surviving, pledges became members and earned the right to exhibit the same behavior — sometimes discreetly, sometimes not — toward women.

Syrett marks this era as the one when date rape metastasized at America's universities. Sociological studies of college sexual behavior in the 1950s records that 50 percent of female students felt uncomfortable with male sexual behavior, and 20 percent were the victim of forceful sexual intercourse (a familiar number). College men believed that a female student who presented herself as a "bad girl" or had a reputation for putting out had an obligation to be sexually available, a duty that was suitably enforced.

Universities benefit from the Greek system. It's a tool for the recruitment of high-school boys; a strong emotional tie for contributing alumni, who can pull up at the house when they visit campus and crack beers on the front lawn; and, at a time of high anxiety over the legal liability of alcohol on campus and in dorms, the primary location of unsupervised drinking. The frats also remain a magnet for a valuable economic tier — students who pay near or full freight. These kids tend to make fewer demands of faculty, have fewer learning disabilities (or have gotten a decent primary education that's helped them develop coping skills), and, overall, have higher GPAs. Universities are also deeply reliant on the Greeks for housing. "They're hotel-motel-Holiday Inn — if the fraternities and sororities closed, students wouldn't have any place to sleep," says Peter Lake of Stetson University; he calls them a sprawling hospitality industry within the ivy-covered walls. "They've killed it on a lot of campuses. They outcompete university housing."

But this isn't enough of a reason to keep them, or to keep them single-sex. It's also true that the more power that frats exert on campus, the higher the rate of unseemly, unhealthy, and even criminal behavior. We know from insurance companies that cover frats that claims about sexual assaults are filed more frequently than any other kind except those concerning physical altercations, like fistfights. By the way, the sheer number of claims across the board is why insurance rates for fraternities can be as high as they are for companies performing toxic-waste removal. Frat members abuse alcohol more than any other group of students, and most fraternity-related crime occurs when these members are rather less than compos mentis. In 2000, 175 chapters of Phi Delta Theta went alcohol-free and have since reported a sharp decline in the insurance rates that fraternities pay to cover rape, hazing abuses, and accidental death in their houses. As a USC grad muses, "White man is drunk, and where does it start? College. Why does it start? Tradition."

When I asked Sokolow for his prediction about the Greek system, he said that he believed disbanding frats could potentially chase the most sexually predatory members into other organizations, like sports teams, where they'd find shelter and camaraderie. "You can eliminate the structures, but it's always going to be more effective to try to shape the culture," he said. But he also added, "I think the Greek system is weakened. Whether it will survive depends on the forces trying to reform it from within, but if they succeed, the Greek system will not retain its current form anyway. Evolve or perish is the choice they are facing. I predict they will evolve."

"The Rape Factory"

At Wesleyan, the evolution has been particularly sudden.

As much as the new radical chic at Wesleyan felt unfamiliar to me, with the students' talk about genderqueerness and *The Shmagina Monologues*, it's certainly an outgrowth of the way a slice of students were acculturated when I was there. What I was more surprised to find was that, much as Syracuse and other big universities were having an upsurge of activism, Greek life at Wesleyan had also grown more robust even as campus politics in general had become more incendiary. Hundreds of students belonged to one of the school's three all-male frats, which have been housed in mansions at the center of campus since the nineteenth century. Like many frats these days, they're associated with specific sports, creating another level of comradery: Beta Theta Pi is lacrosse, soccer, basketball; Delta Kappa Epsilon is football, baseball, ice hockey; and Psi Upsilon is rowing and cross-country.

The centrality of the frats to Wesleyan's contemporary social life was not just my impression. President Michael Roth told me that he, too, was shocked at how popular the frats had become. When he took office at Wesleyan in 2007, he assumed they were vestiges of a minor tradition that would continue, quietly, to endure through his tenure. "I'm a historian," he said to me. "I take seriously things that have been around for a long, long time — be careful when you change them."

But Wesleyan's millennial student body embraced frats. "I was very surprised," Roth told me. "I spent my career, up until coming back to Wesleyan, in California, at a women's college for twelve years and then an arts school that didn't have frats either. If someone brought frats up, it would have been part of an arts installation and very ironic. So it never crossed my mind. Partly, I thought it was probably just a very tiny group of people who like that thing."

At Wesleyan, not everyone wanted to be a brother or sister, but the frat parties were attended by most students on campus, even radical elements — even Chloe, the middle-class student from New Jersey turned campus's uber-activist, which blew my mind. I doubtless would have gone if I were a student. Big parties, live bands, Molly, a hot room, the crush of bodies; it's popular now because it's fun but also for the same reason that live tours are ever more lucrative even as streaming services put successful musicians below the poverty line — we're human and we crave other humans; we can't be on the Internet every minute of the day.

The fraternity story at Wesleyan began in 2010 when John O'Neill, a visiting high-school lacrosse teammate of a Beta Theta Pi brother, raped a female student from Maryland at the frat's Halloween party. The alleged details astonish: O'Neill, living in his mother's basement and recently arrested for selling pot out of an ice cream truck, cornered the woman, pushed her down on a couch, and forced her to give him oral sex. When she bit his penis, he called her a bitch, then initiated intercourse, saying, "The more you try, the faster you are going to get out of here."

This news wouldn't have made its way out of Connecticut if the victim hadn't retained Doug Fierberg, the nation's top anti-frat lawyer. "I don't care if you've got a tradition that started a hundred years ago with white men smoking pipes, guess what, you've got an inherent management structure that promotes dangerous circumstances and doesn't reasonably dissolve risk of injury and death — right there's your fucking problem," he told me during a phone conversation in 2015. He was speaking from his office in Lake Leelanau, Michigan, during a week of media speculation about the perils of modern frats. The debate this time had been sparked by a surreptitiously taken video of the University of Oklahoma's ΣAE chapter on a bus to a formal, the boys in their black tuxedos chanting, "There will never be a nigger at ΣAE /

you can hang him from a tree, but he'll never sign with me" to the tune of "If You're Happy and You Know It, Clap Your Hands."

Fierberg asserted a campus nickname for Beta, the Rape Factory, that put his client's $10 million suit against Wesleyan and the frat in the national glare, even with scant evidence the epithet was in circulation at school. Beta bros are rowdy lacrosse players in pastel Vineyard Vines polo shirts, with the lean bodies of Westchester and Greenwich, Connecticut, moneyed elite. A brother from another frat glosses the membership as follows: "Beta's very 'my father works in finance, I've got arrogant machismo, and I only want to mingle with other people like me.'" And in the graffiti that students use to mark rebel sentiments here and there on Wesleyan's campus — *Whose walls? Our walls!* reads a common scrawl — Beta's, as allegedly copied down by an aghast summer boarder, display witless sexual menace (*She said stop, I said Hammer Time*), casual racism (a slit-eyed caricature's speech balloon: *"I have a ver smarr penis"*), and puerile frat affirmations (*Things That Are Gay: 1, Reading; 2, Books; 3, People Who Don't Like Hawaiian Shirts*).

The parties settled with O'Neill's victim, and peace reigned on campus for a while, but as it happened, the 2010 case only set the stage, and the next student to be assaulted by someone she met at Beta would pursue a different avenue of justice. As a junior, Chloe shared a two-bedroom apartment with a friend in Wesleyan's ugly, super-max-ish dorm High Rise. One night, she says the two of them were dancing together at Beta. "So this kid came up behind me while we were dancing, and he started groping me like I've never been groped before — not your usual low-level grope," Chloe says. Nonetheless, she and her friend tried dancing with the boy, an athlete, after which she trudged down frat row to DKE, hung out with friends, then headed home to High Rise.

In her apartment, she put on sweatpants, lay down in bed, and tucked a red Indian-print comforter under her chin. She called her long-distance boyfriend at Boston College and turned off the light. Asleep, Chloe didn't hear her flatmate come home from Beta, nor did she realize that she'd brought along their former dancing partner for a hookup. In the middle of the night after going to the bathroom, the guy made his way into Chloe's room. She says she came to consciousness as he was groping her crotch.

This type of event has long been a staple of college life — a classmate one hardly knows, perhaps one with unrequited affection, slips into one's bed at the end of a long, drunken night. Whoever did anything about that? But this is also textbook sexual assault—a victim so "incapacitated" that she's actually asleep. What was Chloe's reaction? "I was like, 'Oh, we're doing sex right now?'" she says, her forehead wrinkling at the recollection. Was she terrified? She responds with typical bravado. "I was more thinking, *Get out of this apartment, get out forever, bye. And get out of school, maybe.*"

Armed with the knowledge of her Title IX rights, Chloe filed a report, and the boy soon faced a campus hearing. It can be hard to get the full story in cases like these because student records are not accessible. Still, leaks happen, and in this case I received handwritten notes recording some of the campus proceedings.

These documents demonstrate that the boy admitted he was in her room, though he claimed to have thought she was her sleeping roommate. "The event was a scary one for both of us," he wrote in a statement. "Waking up to a frantic person with my hand in her underwear when I believed I had consent was frightening for me as well." He added, "Alcohol did play a role in this incident. In no way am I using alcohol as an excuse for my actions, but to put it in perspective, when I was with the roommate who had invited me in, I fell and chipped my two front teeth that same night." (The boy did not respond to requests for an interview.)

Chloe says that to assess her case, the panel asked her if the boy penetrated her with his fingers or not. "I was thinking, *I'm going to kill myself right now,*" she says. If his fingers were around, not in, it wasn't rape, but sexual assault. The notes show that Wesleyan disciplined the boy, and he appealed.

Policy Changes Concerning Greek Organizations

Chloe and her clan of bitches did all the things that the young-activist network advised students to do. She talked to End Rape on Campus, the organization started by Annie Clark and Andrea Pino, about filing a Title IX complaint against Wesleyan with the Office for Civil Rights. They began holding rallies and storming offices, handing out flyers about sexual assault to prospective students, and projecting art on building walls. They learned about the tactic star—the eight tools, from strategy to message to tone to timing, that activists must master when putting together a campaign.

Chloe studied the early history of ACT UP. The slogan "Silence = Death" inspired her group to name itself "Silence = Violence." She began to understand that the playfulness of mutable gender identities had a political reason behind it (along with genuine desire, of course). It wasn't just dumb kid stuff or adolescent identity-transformation stuff, like the girl standing behind me in line at a college Chipotle and explaining to her friend that she was now a pescetarian (yet Chipotle doesn't serve fish). It was part and parcel of fighting against the cis-white-male norm that warps non-white-male Americans' sense of themselves, making them feel inferior and giving them fewer chances in life. It was about fighting disgusting gender norms, both traditionally male and traditionally female, that were promoted by frats.

When Chloe had this realization, she saw another path forward. Since the frats posed the biggest threat on Wesleyan's campus, she would fight that fight locally. "How cool would it be to have art majors in there paint these frats, make them look incredible?" she says to me at one point. "We are going to pry them out of their cold, dead hands."

Chloe was a student government leader, a bit of a wonk. She was interested in promoting coeducation at the frats, even though of the three all-male ones at Wesleyan, only Psi U could possibly coeducate, since the national chapters of DKE and Beta prohibited it. Upon coeducation, those two would have to either shut down or give away half their rooms to women who weren't in the fraternity, and who wants boarders in a clubhouse?

Stealthily, Chloe and friends wrote a resolution, "Recommended Housing Policy Changes Concerning Greek Organizations," then brought it to the weekly student government meeting on a Sunday night. "Radical reform is realistic," she pronounced. "Sexual assault happens everywhere, but it does happen more in some places. Radical reform is the only reform appropriate for this situation." She added, "I'm in the mood for a Hail Mary."

The immediate reaction in the room was shock and disbelief. A frat brother named Brian* argued back. "Rape is repugnant," he said, but this resolution was "unrealistic, because sexual assault exists in female and coeducational spaces on campus . . . [And] we can't ignore the issue of historical precedent and tradition. It is real, and must be considered."

Brian turned out to have a complicated public profile. He was the same guy who allegedly sent one of Chloe's friends nasty texts one night, even though they were only platonic friends, texts like *I kinda wanna do dirty things to slut; Are you okay, hoe?; I wanna sleep with you babe.* Brian also allegedly grabbed a girl at a party and kissed her when she didn't want to be kissed. "It's true that he is basically the biggest environmentalist I know, and the biggest socialist I know—for a frat bro he is definitely way on the left of the spectrum," says a female student. "But I had people say to me, 'That means he's not a misogynist,' and no to that. Manarchists can care about raping the environment or the minimum wage. The Weather Underground was a hugely sexist organization. Those things don't correlate."

The clock ran out, and the government meeting adjourned for the evening. But other girls on campus heard about what was happening. "I'd had so many experiences in high school with victim blaming and catcalling, 'You're asking for it, you're doing this or that,'" says Sally, a junior. "I was like, 'I'm here for this.' I'd recruit my friends, and we all squeezed into the meetings."

At the subsequent meetings, the radical sisters and the frat brothers—who also recruited their friends—turned out in force, as did administrators, including President Roth, who might have seen an advantage in the escalating clash. Brian wasn't in attendance; as he emerged as an opponent, the girl who'd received those drunken texts obtained a no-contact order from a Wesleyan dean, which meant that he was forbidden to be in any room she occupied—a censure one frat brother called a "political assassination."

Reps from both factions came out swinging. According to several students, to start with, a black female student rose up out of her seat and launched into a screed against frats, claiming she'd been manhandled at DKE.

At this, a DKE member stood up and said, to the best of their recollection, "You were not—we told you to get out of the house!" He said he didn't like the way she was dressed.

This brought a chorus of female boos. *Please, I don't think DKE has ever told a white girl to leave their house for dressing too slutty,* one girl thought.

Equally tumultuous Sunday-night student government meetings followed before a vote was scheduled for Easter, even though the frat brothers argued against a vote on a Christian holiday, which, they claimed, they were the demographic likeliest to have family obligations away from campus. They noted that when Wesleyan's pro-Palestinian students scheduled a vote about divesting the campus from Israeli companies for Holocaust Remembrance Day, the vote was delayed in deference to Jewish students — but the student government wouldn't extend the same courtesy to white Christian guys?

The Beta brothers were frustrated, and one composed a rap and posted it to his SoundCloud account for Wesleyan students to hear. "For the Boys" is an impressive piece of work, actually, even if I don't agree with the composer's sentiments. He begins with the student government's dramatic mise en scene, talking about tempers flaring so hot that they built the frats a pyre. He himself was licked by flames, lost in damnation and surrounded by hypocritical women. Addressing Chloe's band of bitches, he asked: "I still need to clarify, do you not drink or smoke? Do you roll, dance, grind or do lines of coke? Do you curse, listen to rap music, watch HBO shows?"

Nevertheless, on Easter Sunday, Wesleyan's government leaders held the vote. There were ten abstentions, mostly from students out of town for Easter, but the vote was fourteen for coeducation of the fraternities, twelve against.

Even as the radical sisters claimed their victory, there were significant distortions in the realm of moral thinking. Following up on an anonymous complaint, Wesleyan's campus police called the producer of "For the Boys." They asked about intentions behind the music, what specific events inspired him, and whether a threat of violence lurked in the lyrics. Charges were not filed.

Brian, too, would be the target of an anonymous complaint after he moved to DC to begin his career in the U.S. government with a staff job at a congressman's office. The unidentified caller wanted the congressman to know that he was employing an individual with a sexual-misconduct record. Four days later, Brian was fired. He hired Andrew Miltenberg, Nungesser's lawyer, and filed suit against Wesleyan, claiming to suffer from "great anxiety, depression, fear, distress, and apprehension, as well as shame, shock, embarrassment and sadness." The parties settled.

In the coming year, when her assailant returned to campus, Chloe would press her point. Wesleyan had created a no-contact order, meaning that they couldn't come within a certain number of feet of each other. She hung a whistle around her neck to alert him if he approached. One day in a cafeteria, she saw him and blew it — and he didn't leave. A sanction was imposed. "I find the expectation that I should be conditioned to respond to the sound of a whistle in public to be incredibly dehumanizing," he wrote in an appeal letter. "Instead, I see the blowing of the whistle as potentially an 'act of contact' in itself." The leaked paperwork further shows that Wesleyan denied his appeal.

And after a summer break, Karmenife, the Jimi-Hendrix-meets-Rihanna-styled student I interviewed in the Indian restaurant, returned to Wesleyan. She performed a piece of theater in which she printed out pictures of Roth and the top members of his administration, had a friend pour what looked like blood on her, talked about how they bled her out, then ate their pictures. She and Tess collaborated on a photo project for which she dressed up like a dominatrix and led guys in shirts reading FRAT FILTH with ball gags in their mouths around on a leash.

The idealistic romanticism that I had glimpsed over roti is gone. And as we're talking one day, she points to her calf, where there's a new tattoo. In big black letters, retasking a decades-old slogan, are the words KILL YOUR LOCAL RAPIST.

Karmenife tells me about an experience she had on the train after getting the tattoo: "I was at a stop, in my shorts and Timberland boots, and this guy kept coming towards me, so I put my leg up on the seat, pointed at the tattoo, and he ran away." She continues, "I want to tackle my issues by destroying everyone who tries to destroy me and reclaiming my space on this campus, not as a victim but as a vicious, powerful person. I want people to know, 'This bitch is serious.'"

Advantage: The President *and* the Radicals

That was a highly dramatic, scary, slightly goofy, only-at-a-liberal-arts-college story. But imagine being the college president responsible for these individuals.

A university president's role with regard to frats is particularly fraught. As a liability and reputational issue, and as a matter of ethics, the president could do without the jeopardy the Greek system represents. But the president also bears the brunt of attacks when they're banned. In the late 1990s, when Dartmouth president James Wright, a historian and ex-Marine, demanded an end to single-sex housing to force coed membership on his Greeks, a thousand students protested outside his home. A frat flew the banner JUDAS, BRUTUS, ARNOLD, WRIGHT — classifying him as a traitor to his gender.

Wesleyan's Michael Roth was aware of these dangers. "Most of my [fellow college presidents] are grateful for having succeeded people who did it, because those people got run out of town," he says to me. Yet he had become increasingly enthusiastic about shutting the frats down since the Rape Factory incident. The student government coeducation vote wasn't binding on his administration, but he had to admit he found it interesting.

Like radicals and university presidents through the ages, there was no love lost between Roth and Chloe's crew, even if Roth took their concerns seriously. Chloe found a complex essay Roth had written about Freud in which Roth observed that while it was important to cogitate about patriarchy and its power, there was a downside to too much thinking: "Now we know not only that sex must be deeply consensual but that it should be *really* healthy — so safe that it is, well, less than desirable," he wrote. She put that quote on a banner and hung it in the campus center, making sure everyone knew who had written it.

Yet perpetuating patriarch and college feminist soon became bedfellows. A female student whose charges against an athlete were not resolved in her favor tells me that Wesleyan, under the radar, paid for her mom to fly to Connecticut from the West Coast to console her. (Roth says he does not have knowledge of this, and regulations prevent him from commenting on specific cases if he did know.) He invited Chloe's circle to lunch to air their concerns, and he didn't shy away from conflict with her at another luncheon, this time for trustees. After receiving a text from a friend that her assailant might be there, she strode up to Roth. "I said, 'I don't like seeing my rapist at events,'" she claims she told him. "'Is there a check — are we checking to make sure we're both not invited to the same university events?'" He told her that he didn't understand what she was saying and that she hadn't been raped. "He said, 'Were you raped?'" Chloe explained, telling me that she thought he wanted her to say "No. I was sexually assaulted." To her, President Roth was "the kind of person that fights trauma with semantics." (Roth confirms that he spoke with her, though in limited comments he remembers the conversation differently. "I think I said, 'Who?' because she'd said, 'My rapist,' and that's such an odd [construction]," he tells me.)

Roth and Chloe were never going to see eye to eye, but perhaps he could live with that—and achieve a major goal in the process. The sexual-assault issue and the student government's resolution made an excellent cudgel against the frats. It just had to be wielded carefully. Waved around too wildly, in a manner that attracted too much attention, it would become a rallying point for donors. "C'mon, Wesleyan frat brothers are among the most liberal in the country," says Adam Diamond, head of Beta's Wesleyan chapter. "And we think it benefits Wesleyan to say, 'We're such an open school that we're open to everything, even fraternities.' Stifling us just contradicts the free and open Wesleyan attitude."

Shortly after the student government's vote, alums with links to frats began mobilizing, aware of where Roth's thoughts were likely to lead. "There is a long list of esteemed alumni from the Gamma Phi chapter of DKE at Wesleyan—none of them are criminals," read one letter Roth received. "These men are all pretty successful people who enjoyed part of their adult development sitting around a table [there]."

DKE also rebutted the girls' characterization of frat row as a seat of privilege, claiming that its brothers received more financial aid than any group on campus. "We're all very close knit from blue-collar families, people who wouldn't have gotten into Wesleyan, but got in because of blue-collar sports—football, ice hockey, baseball," a member of DKE explains. "We keep to our own. We feel like, these other kids are cool, but they come from families we don't connect with. We don't fit in . . . I can honestly say I've never seen a guy force a girl to hook up with him at DKE—that shit wouldn't fly. There's a macho feeling there about protecting women because men are stronger, and that's a masculine thing to do."

The characterization of financial-aid packages at DKE may be true—I was provided evidence to this effect—but then this boy says something that makes me raise my eyebrows. "Coeducation . . ." He trails off. "A girl flushes a tampon down a toilet, and what happens? We like girls but we need alone time. And fraternities are disgusting, the bathrooms are disgusting, we have a party, someone vomits on the floor, and no one cleans it up for a week. With girls at DKE, we'd have to be a better, improved version of who we really are. It would be like living with our mothers."

Soon, forty-seven prominent Wesleyan alumni, including major donors, told Roth coeducation would make them very angry. They'd finance an effort to combat sexual assault if he wanted — fund a raft of new prevention programs, funnel frat brothers into them, and voilà. Also, Roth should be aware that analysis of sexual-assault cases in one school year seemed to demonstrate that only a couple of reported assaults occurred at frats, with most in Wesleyan's coed dormitories, which some of them long ago argued against anyway. They also dug out some Facebook posts from queer Wesleyan students. "To me, the DKE house is a patriarchal space beyond redeeming," read one. "We need to evacuated it [sic] and burn it down." "WE SHOULD JUST THROW ROCKS THROUGH ITS WINDOWS." Now, weren't *those* violent threats?

Roth had to convince these folks that the coeducation of Wesleyan's Greeks was not about kowtowing to radical elements. His partner in this project was trustee chair Joshua Boger, a biotech executive who'd flown out of his company on a golden parachute and was now often in the Fiji islands practicing underwater photography. "I am not alone in finding the term 'Greek Life' cloyingly annoying," Boger wrote to Roth in a series of notes about introducing fraternity coeducation to Wesleyan's donor class. "There is nothing 'Greek' about it apart from the letters, which most members could not identify. It is precisely similar to 'right to life' and other movement monikers that try to take ground nominally."

Over a summer, both men on vacation, the two discussed how to present the coeducation of the three all-male fraternities. Roth's anxiety over the issue seemed to manifest in their sign-off, which ended with talk of fish. "The hammerhead isn't scary if you know its intentions, which are very far from eating gassy, chewy, noisy us," Boger told him at one point. Roth responded, "Is it frightening to see a fish like that? I was just swimming on my own in the early morning, misty lake and was anxious about being next to a loon."

Roth, at first, wanted to emphasize inclusion along with sexual assault. "Will Wesleyan be a stronger university ('dedicated to providing an education in the liberal arts that is characterized by boldness, rigor, and practical idealism') with or without Greek life?" he wrote in a draft memo. "This position is not about 'political correctness' any more than the decisions to integrate schools (rather than support the 'choice' of state rights) or the decisions in NYC to outlaw restricted social clubs (rather than just offering women 'their own clubs') were made to be 'politically correct.' This is about equity, choice and the tensions between them."

Boger wanted to sharpen the point. He advised not alienating alums ("we are not trying to re-classify their college years as proto-criminals; 'Orange is the New Red & Black'"), but at the same time, he insisted Roth emphasize the "unifying theme between the sexual violence and frats at the root cause, which is all about male power structures." Roth needed to "paint frats into a corner ethically and morally. All your probative options remain open."

Roth recast his memo but Wesleyan's emeriti trustees were enraged anyway. One earlier quoted Nobel Prize–winning physicist Niels Bohr: "'There are trivial truths and great truths. The opposite of a trivial truth is plainly false. The opposite of a great truth is also true.' The draft policy proposes a major shift in the balance of two great truths at Wesleyan: successful co-education and liberal freedom of association." The trustee said a unilateral decision, even if Wesleyan's bylaws permitted it, was unprecedented; nearby Trinity College, a Wall Street feeder school, took a board vote before coeducating the Greeks. (Then again, Trinity's president's head soon rolled, and the college reestablished frats quickly thereafter.)

Boger's strategy of punching frats in the gut had backfired. In fact, sexual assault was the claim that most angered donors, which took Boger aback. "Those disquieted by the memo continue to be upset at the (unwarranted in their view) conflation of fraternities and sexual violence & drinking," he wrote to Roth. "In any case, the 'how we got here' historical approach to the issues is probably unwise and unnecessary, as it does inflame those wounds, whether that is unreasonable or not."

Is That a Mattress Protest?

As summer wound down, students filtered back into Middletown. Only trustees and donors knew that Roth had made his mind up about coeducation; he hadn't yet presented it to the student body. Summer Elbardissy, a sophomore with Kardashian coloring — her Egyptian parents bestowed the name Summer on her because it's easily pronounced in both English and Arabic — came back early. The Rape Factory scandal was a few years past, and when she entered Wesleyan, she wasn't aware of it. As a freshman, a Beta brother asked her to come over to the house. "He said, 'I have a dog, you want to come meet my dog?' Me and this other girl were like, okay, and we went to Beta to hang out with him, and then my roommate was texting because it was one of those group-from-the-hall-goes-out-together-at-the-beginning-of-school things, and when I said [I was at] Beta, she was like, 'OMG, get out! We heard it's the rape factory!' . . . I cannot describe the level of fear. 'Er, your dog's so cute, we got to go!'"

Elbardissy changed her mind about Beta. She was a terrific student in high school (on her résumé, she underlined *High School GPA: 3.81*), but her college grades slipped to Bs and Cs. She became "that frat biddie," she says. "I stood out so much in high school . . . involved in several different clubs, mentoring programs, plays, musicals, sports, had really good relationships with my teachers. I went to college and I was like, 'I'm going to slip under the radar for a little while, because I'm tired.'"

On this warm September night, Beta was throwing a jock-themed party. Elbardissy put on a backward baseball hat and an old election T-shirt with Barack Obama slam-dunking while standing atop John McCain. She bummed a cigarette and crawled out a window to Beta's second-floor "porch," which was just a bunch of plywood that the guys had put on top of some tresses — highly dangerous, but wasn't everything about Beta called dangerous these days? The porch wasn't that far from the ground; she'd seen people jump off it.

This was an all-campus party, a before-the-reality-of-classes-sets-in party. Even Karmenife was there, in a fishnet ensemble approximating a net athletic tee, smoking up in a bedroom on the second floor. At some point Elbardissy's best friends may have thought she was pretty messed up and needed to chill. She said they put her in a room on Beta's third floor. Elbardissy would be safe in there, or at least they'd be safe from her.

It was 1:09 a.m. She doesn't recall what happened next, but it's probable that she crawled out the third-floor window, thinking it was the second-floor window that led to the porch, but she was thirty-five feet in the air. She fell, first quickly and then slowly, through the branches of a tree and down into the bushes. A student ran over. "I heard something come down in the bushes behind me," he said at the time. "When I checked on what it was, I found an unresponsive girl."

Elbardissy fractured her skull and pelvis and suffered a traumatic brain injury. She spent weeks in a hospital, breathing through a tube, and months at a subacute-care pediatric facility. "It was a children's facility, which is weird, because I'm at the age where I'm kind of a child and kind of an adult," she tells me, and she talks about having hallucinations, like her bed morphing into a rocket ship. "I was obsessed with the idea of escaping," she adds. "I was in the ICU yelling, 'I'm going to school tomorrow, you can't keep me here!'" There was also a lot of shame. "My mom said that I kept saying, 'I'm such a loser.'" In Middle Eastern families, respect for the father is paramount. "I would see [my dad] and think, *I can't believe he has to be in this hospital because his stupid daughter fell out a window.*"

Soon after a Life Star helicopter had whirled Elbardissy up in the sky, Beta was shut down. Roth presented the dictum for coeducation as a matter of general student safety, not safety from sexual assault. In fact, the term *sexual assault* didn't make it into his public announcement, which was printed in the *New York Times* and for which he and Boger received hearty congratulations. "Wow, Josh, bold move!" a venture capitalist and Dartmouth trustee e-mailed Boger. "I am chair at Dartmouth and we are thinking similarly . . . but you only have [3] frats, we have 15!"

The Beta brothers threw their stuff in garbage bags and moved to reassigned housing in tiny apartments and even in Wesleyan's sober-living house, never to return. "Suddenly Beta's closed, and someone posted, 'Not sure if there's a mattress performance piece about sexual assault happening right now, or the Beta boys are just moving their mattresses out of the house,'" says Chloe, shaking her head. "It was too real."

Dinner with Folks

Shutting down the frats probably won't work, as Lake and Sokolow have explained. But coeducation is a savvy tactic to bring growth under control or ultimately force national chapters to include coeducation in their bylaws. A year and a half after Wes's frats went coed, Harvard ordered their frats and final clubs to do the same. A sexual-assault-prevention task force had found that nearly half of Harvard women involved with final clubs experienced "nonconsensual sexual contact," compared with 31 percent of all female seniors at Harvard. Whopping numbers on both counts, but with a meaningful divergence. "I've been groped at those clubs, and had a guy expose himself to me — not *rape*-rape, but there's a lewd atmosphere," a young female Harvard graduate tells me. "A friend of mine was fooling around with a guy at a club and he suddenly flipped her over and jerked off on her back. It's just a weird sense of entitlement to women's bodies. And these are the cool guys on campus, so no one wants to say anything."

It should not come as a surprise that pro–final club arguments at Harvard resulted in the usual cycle of public shaming and hasty apologies. For officers of the Porcellian, founded in 1791 and the oldest club, it was a point of pride that the club had not given on-the-record statements to the press since inception. But now the alumni president dashed off a letter to the *Harvard Crimson* claiming the victim mantle. Sexual misconduct was not an issue at the Porcellian, he explained. And the university's push for coeducation would backfire, because "forcing single-gender organizations to accept members of the opposite sex could potentially increase, not decrease, the potential for sexual misconduct." As usual, backlash was unforgiving, and he apologized later the same day, writing, "I chose my words poorly." He soon announced his resignation.

Harvard tried to require these clubs to admit women in 1984, and the clubs broke official ties with the university rather than accede to the demand. But now the university upped the ante; beginning with the class of 2021, student members of organizations that refused to become coed were barred from leadership positions on campus — the type of positions intrinsic to Harvard students' self-worth and career momentum. Want to be the captain of an athletic team or receive an official recommendation from Harvard for fellowships like the Rhodes and Marshall Scholarships? As part of a single-sex club, you're out of luck.

At Wesleyan, DKE fought the school, winning a lawsuit and flying a plane over homecoming with the banner WES PICKS OUR BROS? FASCISM. LOOK IT UP. Today, their doors are shut along with Beta's. The campus is quieter, and no one much notices they're gone.

Psi U, however, began coeducating. On the first night of coed pledging, I showed up with Chloe, her chunky boots crunching on the snow as we approached the looming English manor.

A lectern with the list of pledging names is set up at the door. The brother standing at it gives Chloe a weird look, then swiftly marks her off. "You can put your coats in there," he says, gesturing to a closet, "or take them upstairs if you want." We opt for the coat closet, though hangers aren't to be found. We fold our coats neatly and set them on a bench.

A steep set of stairs leads to the second floor, where we'll hang out with guys in their rooms — Psi U is on probation and supposed to be dry, but the risk of getting busted while drinking in bedrooms is low. Down a ratty hallway, a friendly English major waves us into his room, where another brother wearing a black blazer and, oddly, black leather driving gloves hands me a red cup containing cheap Dubra vodka and tonic. *I can't believe you're a grown-ass woman drinking Dubra*, Chloe texts me, then winks. She turns to one of the boys. "What kind of girls are you looking for to pledge?" she asks. "I think we're looking for girls who are herb-y," he says absent-mindedly, messing with a laptop to put on some music. "You know, into herb?"

We're the first women here, but soon a Korean American junior is ushered in. "I called my dad in Korea tonight to tell him I'm pledging a fraternity," she tells us. "He couldn't believe it!" She takes a sip of the drink she's carrying and shudders. "There are, like, seven shots in this drink."

In another room, a few guys are drinking Miller Lite around a coffee table topped with a glass vase that's filled with a disgusting concoction of what looks like far-past-their-prime wasabi beans and dried banana bits. They tell us that they're relatively psyched about coed rush, though two brothers have "de-pledged" over it. "No one wants anything forced upon us," one says. "That's the whole thing — fraternities are self-autonomous fucking groups."

Post Malone's "White Iverson," about loving basketball and the basketball lifestyle, comes on: "I'm with some white girls and they lovin' the coca."

Another room is more relaxed, with a *Cool Runnings* poster over a bed and a copy of *Where the Wild Things Are* on a side table alongside a stuffed white llama. A blonde pledge in knee-high boots talks about an econ class one of the guys has signed up for that she took last year. "It's hard, but you can do it all at the end — three days of Adderall, color-code the lectures, and you're done." He winces. "But I just got back from a semester in Prague," he says. "I did no work at all. Emphasis on *none*. Negative work!"

This is boring, so Chloe and I wander the common rooms, like the enormous dining room, where a couple of filthy mops rest against a wall covered with wallpaper printed with iconic Wesleyan buildings, including Psi U, and the words *O Ivied Walls, O Storied Halls*. "We have a chef for lunch and dinner, and this is where we have dinner with the guys," a short blond brother in a blue wool ski cap tells us, gesturing broadly. "Not 'dinner with the guys' anymore," Chloe corrects him. "Now it's 'folks.'"

An oddly anticlimactic evening, I thought to myself, but I heard that the rest of coed pledging went well. But a couple months later, eleven Wesleyan students were hospitalized after what seemed to be a Molly overdose, and soon after, individuals connected to Psi U were involved in some sort of drug scheme. President Roth ordered the fraternity closed for a year. At publication, it was back open and fully coeducated.

Chloe and some of her friends graduated soon after the Molly overdose, and once they left, the furor about sexual assault on campus began dying down. The cycle of radicalism will ebb and flow; universities should be ready for that too. But in late 2016, the *Boston Globe,* in a searing article about sexual behavior between teachers and students at northeastern private schools, Wesleyan learned that an administrator who often chaired their Title IX panels had been fired by his former employer, the Vermont Academy, for allegedly propositioning a sixteen-year-old female student in lewd text messages.

Two hundred students called for Roth's resignation, organizing a series of protests on Wesleyan's busiest prospective-student day. Outside the colonnaded library, a rotating cast of students lay nearly naked on the lawn. A flyer nearby explained, in part, WE ARE ONE UPSET BITCH IN NOTHING BUT HER UNDERWEAR / WE ARE A LOUSY PAIN IN THE ASS MILLENNIAL.

13

Battleground

I n 2017, those involved in the sexual assault issue at universities received the shock of the decade. Donald Trump, along with his reactionary ideas about male domination, was elected president. Many campus survivors went into a tailspin, having already been shocked at his "I moved on her like a bitch" and "I just kiss" comments to Billy Bush, followed by a raft of accusers telling their stories to the nightly news. "I don't want to say I'm past what happened to me — I've never had a relationship that's lasted longer than two or three months, which I think might be about not being comfortable with sex for years — but I usually don't feel triggered," says Liz, the high-school survivor who chose not to reveal her university. But then she watched the Billy Bush videotape. "I listened to it over and over. There was something about the way Trump said it. The entitlement in his voice. That's how people sounded when they were touching me when I was younger. Even though I could rationalize it — he's a star, he's probably bragging, we don't have any idea if he did or didn't — something about the way he said it made me stay awake all night and feel terrible."

Trump reached the White House for reasons historians will be debating for a century; among them were his skills as a speaker and performer and his well-honed mobster-in-a-back-room persona, which was not unrelated to an alpha-male appeal. But campus politics, and particularly those connected to sexual assault, played a part too. The alt-right's ideological stance against political correctness — most vividly rendered by sneers about the campus left — gave intellectual fuel to conservative churchgoers who were on the fence about Trump. And now the new conservative administration can roll back much of the work of Obama and the young activists with a swipe of the president's pen. The executive branch controls the Department of Education, source of the game-changing 2011 Dear Colleague letter.

Does the campus court system have ambiguities and the constant possibility of injustice? Yes. But if Trump tries to shut it down, will we abdicate our responsibility to girls in terms of their safety and sexual self-confidence and tell them that they must report to the cops or they won't receive help? I believe the answer to that is yes too. Perhaps one in a thousand boys at four-year universities will be accused of sexual assault. And something along the lines of one in five girls will be victimized over the course of college — you can revise that to an outside limit of one in ten if you want to narrow it to penetrative rape. Should we prioritize fair punishment of the one in a thousand over the need for justice of the one in five or ten? Solving this moral equation is precisely why college sexual assault is such a difficult problem.

Which isn't to say that progress isn't possible. The most fruitful avenue is to change social norms — something that's already happening in many places, albeit fitfully and sometimes a bit ridiculously. We're talking about a moral shift. In the real world, when you put a deposit on a house, someone might offer a higher price and steal the house from under you. That doesn't happen when you're reserving a dorm room at a university, or even an off-campus house. Conduct rules on Planet College now include honoring other students in the bedroom and even regulating the way students deal with each other as sexual objects outside the bedroom. No, it's not realistic. Yes, it is happening.

I believe the intense focus at schools on sexual assault should lead to soaping and scrubbing of the greater environment of misogyny on campus. Let me tell you a story that's not about assault, per se, but sexual speech or, as Yale put it, "conduct of a sexual nature that created a hostile environment" in which the Title IX system worked well.

In her sophomore year at Yale, Dahlia* was invited by a member of Sigma Alpha Epsilon, a frat of rich international students, to a formal hosted by a Yale secret society. You may recognize the Yale ΣAE chapter from the news; in 2015, they were cast as a premier example of racism at elite universities when a story broke that the brother presiding over the door at Halloween announced the party was open to "white girls only." A Yale investigation turned up scant evidence of this comment, and given that the names of ΣAE members read like a speakers' lineup at the UN, anger directed at them as an American old boys' network seems misplaced.

"You're the most beautiful girl at this school," the ΣAE brother said to Dahlia when he approached her on campus. Dahlia is almost comically privileged. A then nineteen-year-old with looks that suggested a blond Brooke Shields, she'd attended an all-girls' prep school, played on Yale's polo team, and was considering a career in international law "like George Clooney's wife, Amal," she tells me at a café over lemonade. She had her first kiss at age sixteen, and lost her virginity the next year to her steady boyfriend. "I had experience with sex before college, but in terms of knowledge of how the world works, I had no idea," she says.

The night of the formal, the boy escorted her to a mansion near professors' homes. Dates were dressed in heels and Chanel, boys in suits and ties, drinking expensive whiskey and smoking cigars. Dahlia had a cross-country race the next day and refused a drink. "My date was like, 'No, no, it's not even a question. Everyone is drinking.'" And on a porch, he leaned down and kissed her. "I remember thinking, *Oh my God, I've only kissed three people ever, this is so strange!*" she says. "I'd never had to say no to a guy before. When I had sex, there was always an initial conversation, 'Do you want this? Are we ready?' But I was here at the party on his invitation, and I was young, and I was drunk. I felt uncomfortable saying no. It felt wrong, and I felt it would have been rude."

The two of them had sex in an upstairs bedroom — "I don't think it was nonconsensual; it was consenting," she says — but afterward, she quickly realized that they weren't going to date exclusively because he was hooking up with other girls. "I thought, *Oh, okay, this is how college works. You get with a ton of people.* And I figured if guys can get with girls and not be in relationships, then girls should be able to get with guys and not be in relationships too."

So when the president of ΣAE approached Dahlia at a party and said he was attracted to her, they became fuck buddies. Then there was a polo-playing ΣAE brother soon after. He lived in an apartment with two other brothers, and eventually, she slept with all three, on different occasions. She was still hooking up with the ΣAE president, who introduced pillow talk about the bedroom habits of his brothers. Dahlia didn't realize that once she left the president's bed, he razzed the other bros about what she'd said.

On ΣAE's pledge night, these private confidences were officially betrayed. The traditional night involves limericks about Roman goddess of wisdom Minerva, ΣAE's patron, but this evening, the fraternity chaplains told a legend about another female spirit — Dahlia, the girl who had allowed the brotherhood to spread their seed. She was a sight to behold. They'd enjoyed her company, even though she thought one of them was too cuddly, and another was too into oral sex, and another had pubic hair like Osama bin Laden's beard.

This was not the kind of story that could be kept quiet on a college campus. When she returned from the library one night, her friends were waiting. They sat her down on her twin bed. "I started laughing when they told me, because that's what I do when I'm uncomfortable," she says. "I said, 'Okay, no big deal. I'll talk to the SAE president.' I texted him in a mad-at-a-friend kind of way: 'Let's talk about this. I'm kind of pissed at you for letting this happen.'"

Over pizza, she says he dismissed her anger, suggesting that she'd brought their shaming chorus on herself by sleeping with guys who had sworn oaths of brotherhood. Her cheeks burning, Dahlia, who was particularly upset about the Osama bin Laden reference, which she'd never uttered, shared her friends' advice to report the incident to Yale. He warned her that doing so would expose her private life to public scrutiny. "I said, 'Wait! Any privacy regarding my sex life you completely got rid of,'" Dahlia tells me, almost chuckling in retrospect.

Trying to decide what to do, Dahlia told her mother, who was taken aback, underscoring the generational divide on these issues. "She asked me, 'Why would you have sex with five people?' then waited for an answer," says Dahlia. Her mother said she'd become a CEO by keeping her head down: "You're putting yourself at risk! Why fight when anyone else would accept that this is the way the world is, and move on?" she'd said. Dahlia tried not to cry. "You should be questioning the boys and not your own daughter," she told her mother, thinking at the same time, *I'm in college and I'm talking about sex that happened over the course of six months — five guys isn't a shocking statistic among the people I know.*

Yale's Title IX machinery got into gear, with an administrator clocking dozens of hours assembling accounts of the night. The chaplains didn't deny making the speech but insisted it was short and meant more to roast their own sexual prowess than to humiliate Dahlia. No, they didn't have a copy the investigators could read.

Yale decided Title IX had been violated. After their decision, the chaplains, who were seniors, graduated with marks on their transcripts. The school put the president, a junior, on probation for a year and recommended that he receive training on leadership and sexual harassment. The fraternity itself was barred from conducting activities on campus, including recruiting, for two years.

While these punishments didn't erase the defamation, Dahlia took solace in Yale's recognition of a vulgar, casual cruelty that rarely comes with consequences. "At least at universities, there's a system in place that takes care of these things," she tells me with a look of resolve. "Otherwise, when will these boys ever be held accountable?"

The Title IX War

Otherwise, when will these boys ever be held accountable? That's the crux of the issue, right there, and the ball we need to keep our eye on. Because in the larger society, even if celebrities are being disgraced, many regular folks aren't held accountable. And there are seismic forces that want to keep it that way. This chapter will explore those forces and the political fight that has been going on for the past few years that exploded into view with Trump's election.

Sexual assault at universities is tied to some major American social issues of the day. Feminism. Intersectionality. Privilege. Factual feelings. Campus liberalism. The alt-right backlash. Transgender bathrooms (some have argued they must be shut down to protect women from being assaulted by libidinous perverts). Guns. Yes, even guns. "If these young, hot little girls on campus have a firearm, I wonder how many men will want to assault them," is the rhetoric a pro-gun Nevada assemblywoman used to argue that concealed guns should be allowed on campus. A Florida state representative upped the ante: "If you've got a person that's raped because you wouldn't let them carry a firearm to defend themselves, I think you're responsible." Young activists argued that this was not only exploiting their cause but also promoting rape myths, since guns aren't much use defending against an acquaintance, but in 2017, Arkansas became the ninth state to allow concealed firearms at universities, joining Colorado, Idaho, Kansas, Mississippi, Oregon, Texas, Utah, and Wisconsin.

In this polarized environment, liberals thought it best to solidify the Obama-era protections around Title IX. Kirsten Gillibrand, who, upon inheriting Hillary Clinton's Senate seat in 2009, made fighting rape a high-profile piece of her agenda and who is a "true believer" on this issue, says a source close to her, led the charge. Her military assault bill that would have taken cases out of the jurisdiction of the chain of command proved too divisive to prevail in the Senate, but now she'd joined with one of her opponents, Missouri senator Claire McCaskill, to create the Campus Accountability and Safety Act, a campus rape bill that would create severe fines for Title IX violations, up to 1 percent of a university's operating budget — which, for a school like Columbia University, could come to tens of millions. It would also make some of the 2011 Dear Colleague letter's recommendations into federal law.

Over a series of breakfasts and luncheons, Gillibrand formed a coalition of thirty-six senators that included even Republicans Joni Ernst, Charles Grassley, and Marco Rubio. The bill was so popular, in fact, that South Carolina senator Lindsey Graham, another cosigner, would later joke, "In a polarized political environment, this bill would get 90 votes. I'm just assuming 10 people won't show up." Senators liked this issue. "Educated females — largely the beneficiaries of Title IX — have become a massive political force, and it's just blisteringly clear where they stand on this," says Peter Lake of Stetson University.

A politician retailing legislation is always more successful if there's a cultural product like a film, dramatizing a bill's central tenets, and the release of *The Hunting Ground*, the campus-rape documentary featuring Los Angeles activists Annie Clark and Andrea Pino, was coordinated with Gillibrand's office. Soon, the previously free-range duo, with their Craigslist apartment and cardboard desk, began working on state- and national-level policy reform. Though articles on the shortcomings of the film, including what was perceived as a one-sided depiction of an assault case at Harvard, poured forth, *The Hunting Ground* made it to nearly a thousand American campuses.

When Lady Gaga's "Til It Happens to You," the film's theme song, received an Oscar nod, young activists seized the moment to put on a memorable performance. First, Biden took the stage and called on the audience to "change the culture," and then Gaga, with her Donatella Versace–esque blond mane and a tight white pantsuit covering a wealth of non-Versace-esque tattoos, began pounding on a white grand piano. Midway through the song, fifty survivors standing behind her, including Clark and Pino, joined hands and raised them in solidarity, some with the phrase *We believe you* in black marker on their forearms. The A-list audience gave them a standing ovation, cameras panning to a teary Rachel McAdams, Kate Winslet, and Brie Larson, who later made a point of giving every survivor a hug. After the show, Gaga, who says she was raped by a mentor-producer early in her career, headed to a tattoo shop and had the design of one of the onstage survivors' — a thin, black-outlined rose on fire — inked on her left shoulder.

This was not Sulkowicz dragging a mattress across a campus quad; these were the most famous women in America. As the issue exploded among female celebrities, they began to support one another, like girls on campus were supporting their friends. In 2016, when Kesha struggled to exit a recording contract with Dr. Luke, her furious peers launched a Mount St. Helens–size eruption. Demi Lovato, Ariana Grande, Lorde, Kelly Clarkson, and Janelle Monáe tweeted support almost instantly. Fiona Apple, raped in her teen years by a stranger, took a pic of herself holding a sign reading KESHA — I AM SO ANGRY FOR YOU. THEY WERE WRONG. I'M SO SORRY. Adele, accepting an award, declared, "I'd like to take this moment to publicly support Kesha." Taylor Swift even donated $250,000 for her legal fees.

This was more than a sign of the burgeoning solidarity among female celebrities, with their air-kiss superficiality; it was a new Bat signal, summoning girl power. Lena Dunham took up the cause in her online magazine *Lenny*, writing that "it wasn't long ago that women in the public eye didn't have a loose-enough leash to reach out and support one another, for fear of losing all they had worked so hard to create. Instead they quietly watched on their televisions, hoping they wouldn't be next." She issued a whoop of victory: "Those days are over. They are fucking done."

Rolling Stone and UVA

Not quite.

Even as Gillibrand and female celebrities were holding court in front of cameras, a multipronged attack on college survivors was percolating behind the scenes — one in which victory was within the counterinsurgency's grasp. This movement began quietly at the end of 2014, when an opening was offered by *Rolling Stone* magazine's lurid tale of the University of Virginia.

As anyone who turned on a TV or read a news blog then knows, *Rolling Stone* told the story of a UVA freshman named Jackie from a rural town. One night on a date at Rugby Road's Phi Kappa Psi frat, clad in a high-necked, blood-red dress, Jackie found herself in a pitch-black room where she was pushed into a glass table, then attacked by seven boys in what seemed like a pledge ritual. "There was a heavy person on top of her, spreading open her thighs, and another person kneeling on her hair, hands pinning down her arms, sharp shards digging into her back, and excited male voices rising all around her," wrote the author of the piece, Sabrina Rubin Erdely. "'Grab its motherfucking leg,' she heard a voice say. And that's when Jackie knew she was going to be raped."

After the boys had their way with her — including a classmate in her anthropology discussion group who penetrated her with a beer bottle — Jackie, in Erdely's telling, passed out. Later, she "ran shoeless from the room" at three a.m., a "disheveled girl hurrying down a side staircase, face beaten, dress spattered with blood." She dialed a friend's number and screamed, "Something bad happened. I need you to come and find me!" The trio of classmates who appeared at her side, though, were no help. They didn't take her to the hospital: "Her reputation will be *shot* for the next four years." They thought the social price of reporting rape was too high: "She's gonna be the girl who cried 'rape,' and we'll never be allowed into any frat party again."

Jackie may have escaped Phi Psi's house of horrors, but Erdely had more to say about rape at UVA. She quoted a student lobbing the idea that the school's sexual-assault stats were "one in three" rather than one in five, said students had nicknamed the school "UVrApe," and claimed the university withheld some data about sexual assault because, according to a dean, "Nobody wants to send their daughter to the rape school." She wrote that the school hadn't meted out punishment even when a student, angry that Jackie was disrupting the order of Thomas Jefferson's university, threw a bottle at her; even when, the bruise from the bottle "still mottling her face," Jackie proclaimed that two other women had been gang-raped at Phi Psi, one of them a girl who said she'd been assaulted in a bathroom at the frat by four men while a fifth watched and then had run back to her room without any pants.

In hindsight, it's hard to read this account as anything but fiction. But when *Rolling Stone* published the story, it rocked the campus. Vandals spray-painted on a wall next to Phi Kappa Psi's house *UVA Center for RAPE Studies* and *Suspend Us!;* faculty organized a massive rally named Take Back the Party: End Rape Now! down Rugby Road. President Teresa Sullivan closed all frats until semester's end, declaring, "I think the Greek community needs to do some serious soul-searching about the way that it has behaved, about the behavior it's tolerated, about what its future is going to be."

Yet within weeks, it became clear that Erdely had fallen into a trap of her own making. Jackie had spun at least some part of the tale out of her imagination. The boy she'd named as her companion, Haven Monahan, was a pure invention, albeit one with his own e-mail account, which she apparently established herself.

I've written for *Rolling Stone* over the years. I'm aware of the way their fact-checkers worry the details in stories prepared for publication; a conversation about whether Julia Louis-Dreyfus has dark brown or medium black hair when I filed an article about her comes to mind. But Erdely was a trusted *Rolling Stone* reporter with a track record of hits. The staff took her declaration of faith — *I believe Jackie* — to heart, as well her contention that they were dealing with a deeply traumatized young adult who refused to allow them to vet her story because she was terrified of the prospect of retaliation at the hands of Phi Psi. The dazzle of printing a blockbuster must have come into play too — the story was exactly what Erdely and her editors had been looking for. Caught up in the drama that they themselves had scripted, they never suspected they were dealing with a fabulist.

Rolling Stone, with its progressive politics and muckraking zeal, was inclined to view UVA as an authoritarian hotbed of corruption and misogyny; this was the magazine's confirmation bias. The article's author was knowledgeable about the neurobiology of trauma, which created yet another layer of complexity. When Erdely encountered a friend of Jackie's who told her that Jackie's original story involved oral sex rather than being penetrated, Erdely interpreted this wavering story as a symptom of genuine suffering. "To the contrary, I found this to be entirely consistent," Erdely said. "In my experience writing about trauma victims and sexual assault victims, I know that their stories can sometimes evolve over time as they come to terms with what happened to them and work through their own shame and self blame."

This willful abdication of journalistic skepticism led to its inevitable conclusion: Erdely, her editors, and the magazine were disgraced, along with Jackie, and the movement was dealt a heavy blow. But it's worth pointing out that by publication, there had been a yearlong barrage of articles about universities' malicious treatment of rape survivors, and few outlets double-checked survivor stories.

Should they have? Discussing the UVA case, prominent activists pushed back against this idea. Wagatwe Wanjuki, a Tufts survivor, said, "I've been able to share my story over various media outlets without having any of them reach out to my assailant." On *BuzzFeed*, she added, "Realistically, how does talking to a rapist confirm that a rape occurred? Do we really believe that a rapist would admit, 'Oh yes, I was there and I raped her' if a journalist approached them? . . . Demanding that we *must* hear both sides when we talk about sexual violence plays into the tired 'he said/she said' framing often used to dismiss sexual assault." This was connected to the activists' top commandment: Believe survivors. "We should believe, as a matter of default, what an accuser says," Zerlina Maxwell, another activist of note, wrote in the *Washington Post*. "Ultimately, the costs of wrongly disbelieving a survivor far outweigh the costs of calling someone a rapist." She added, "This is not a legal argument about what standards we should use in the courts; it's a moral one, about what happens *outside* the legal system."

This is the advocates' role in the sexual assault ecosystem; investigators might probe, and police might ignore, but they must believe. But publicly accusing a specific fraternity of raping girls in a pledge ritual without evidence cannot lie within the media's purview. The fact that *Rolling Stone* hadn't sought confirmation and then defended itself by blaming Jackie for its own lapses — "we have come to the conclusion that our trust in her was misplaced," it said — is part of why the magazine was scarred by the scandal and later sued by Phi Psi, which asked for $25 million in damages. A jury awarded the dean maligned with the "rape school" comment $3 million.

This failure upended the media game around campus rape. Stories in progress, some about well-known figures, were sent to a permanent purgatory. "A great number of people are gleefully celebrating *Rolling Stone*'s retraction because now they can hold on to their fervent belief that rape is not epidemic," author Roxane Gay wrote in *The Toast*, adding dryly, "Their glee provides quite a display."

But Jackie wasn't completely abandoned. The National Organization for Women called Jackie a "sexual assault survivor" and, when the dean's attorney requested access to her texts and e-mails, demanded President Sullivan "put a stop to what we regard as a re-victimization of this young woman." Critics of the anti-rape movement were aghast at this rhetoric. "Frankly, I find the refusal to let go of Jackie to be chilling," one of them tells me.

Meanwhile, the University of Virginia, which has a strict honor code that includes expulsion for cheating and plagiarism, had not expelled a single student for sexual assault in the decade prior to the *Rolling Stone* story. In the fracas over the article, they claimed victim status, even though at the same time Erdely was following Jackie around campus, they were under what Peter Lake calls an "almost unprecedented Office for Civil Rights review." In 2016, OCR released a report about UVA's litany of ills, from slow-footing cases to a wonky informal review process to not "evaluating steps necessary to protect [the] safety of the broader University community." Lake offers this analogy for Erdely's reporting: "I once got food poisoning in a Texas restaurant, and I called the Texas Department of Health. They said, 'We just got a hundred calls from that restaurant but it's too bad because they're from the chain's other location, so you've got no complaint.' Sometimes there's something in the air, and you almost get it."

As of 2016, two UVA students have been expelled for sexual assault. This isn't a surprise; the Harvard Business School study that analyzed *U.S. News and World Report*'s college rankings vis-à-vis scandals revealed that such scandals force schools to correct the underlying problems quickly. Within five years, however, another scandal usually rears its head. Five years; a little longer than it takes a class of students at a four-year college to move through the institution, gazing back through the nostalgic haze of homecoming games and alumni weekends. Without new students maintaining pressure, institutional memory becomes fuzzy. It's anyone's guess whether the University of Virginia will remain on the straight and narrow.

Undue Process

In the wake of *Rolling Stone*'s retraction and the career damage to those involved at the magazine — not to mention Teresa Sullivan's eventual resignation from UVA — treatment of campus rape perceptibly shifted in tone and content. For the first time since the revelation about Duke's falsely accused lacrosse team in the early 2000s, mainstream media assumed a skeptical posture, and articles contained a criminal paper trail — police reports, affidavits, and so forth. This void was filled by conservative and libertarian outlets like Reason, Fox News, and the *Washington Examiner*, which flooded the media with stories about false accusations. On the social media side, memes and GIFs flew to and fro, like the one showing a smirking young woman in a tiara above a caption reading, *False rape accusation: America's fastest-growing hobby*, and a ghastly Photoshopped illustration of the OCR assistant secretary in farmer's suspenders milking a cow branded with the words *Title IX*. The cow's udders spurted dollar bills, some making their way into her pocket.

These new stories were driven by the burgeoning movement I mentioned before, a surprising coalition of libertarians, Harvard and Yale attorneys, the national Greek system, and even the mothers of the accused boys whom we met in chapter 8. Merging forces gave this coalition authoritative voices, ideological backbone, and ready access to media outlets. What most of them wanted was no less than the closure of the Title IX sexual assault system.

At Yale, professor Jed Rubenfeld — husband of *Tiger Mom* author Amy Chua — was the most outspoken. At Harvard, two high-profile law professors — Janet Halley, a sixtyish longtime antagonist of mainstream feminist ideologies about power and gender, and her younger, soft-spoken protégée Jeannie Suk — demanded that the government admit that the campaign against sexual assault on campus was a bait and switch, having little to do with rape as it had previously been defined, an act of physical brutality. A predator doesn't ask permission of his prey. "Would there have been political will to pass the

'Good Sex Act of 2013' or the 'Healthy Sexual Desire Act of 2014'?" Suk wrote with her husband, Jacob Gersen, in the *California Law Review.*

Suk performed persuasive spadework to further her points, generating a damning list of policies that have amplified consent standards in new and unnerving ways. In her essay, she quoted Gordon College's kooky definition of *consent* in 2014 ("voluntary, sober, enthusiastic, informed, mutual, honest, and verbal agreement"); tracked down a University of California at San Diego brochure advising students that "consent is not only necessary, but also foreplay"; and listed the University of Wyoming's tips on how to "Make Consent Fun" for confused students, including "Baby, you want to make a bunk bed: me on top, you on bottom?" and "Would you like to try an Australian kiss? It's like a French kiss, but 'Down Under.'"

The Foundation for Individual Rights in Education (FIRE), a respected nonprofit that says it's nonpartisan but seems quite libertarian, dedicated to fighting censorship and legal overreach in American colleges, also jumped on the issue. Founded in 1999, the group was inspired by a Jewish freshman at the University of Pennsylvania who was disciplined when he called a knot of carousing African American sorority sisters "water buffalo." The student argued that any offense he caused was the product of a translation issue; though he used the English word, he said he was referring to the Hebrew word *behema*, which means both "ox of water" and a "thoughtless, rowdy person" in that language, but Penn processed the comment as racial harassment. The student sued and received damages.

FIRE's office building is in Philadelphia's Old City across from the Liberty Bell; the lush lobby's features include marble benches, elaborate wrought-iron chandeliers, and a movie-screen-size Maxfield Parrish mosaic of a garden rendered in Tiffany glass. "We're not fat cats, but to some extent it helps us to have offices like this when people come to visit," says legislative and policy director Joe Cohn when he greets me in the reception area. In fact, the list of donors to FIRE includes fat cats like *Playboy* founder Hugh Hefner, the Koch brothers, Donors' Trust (an organization of anonymous individuals who contribute to conservative think tanks and media outlets), and Betsy DeVos, our new secretary of education.

Wearing thick eyeglasses and an impish smile at odds with the formal environment, Cohn walks me down a series of hallways, past a framed copy of the twelve amendments to the Constitution, the 1789 predecessor to the Bill of Rights. On another wall, I saw a striking poster of a student whose lips were not taped shut like *Alma Mater.* Her face had been photo-altered to leave only flesh between her nose and chin, like a character in a David Cronenberg body-horror film. *Censorship on Campus,* read the caption. *Worse Than It Looks.*

In a sunny office, Cohn explains that he joined FIRE's staff in 2012, planning to do "free-speech stuff, and perhaps a bit of campus due process stuff," he says, then he shoots me a semi-ironic look. "And now, seven days a week, I don't have one day where I don't talk about rape." FIRE's mandate as a free-speech organization doesn't seem like it should extend to sex or sexual assault in college dorm rooms and frat houses — it's hard to consider sex speech — but the lack of due process in campus tribunals motivates them. On Planet FIRE, young activists aren't called gender-justice activists, as they'd prefer, but rather anti-due-process advocates.

Caleb Warner, son of North Dakota mom Sherry Warner-Seefeld, was the first student with a sexual-assault charge in whom FIRE took interest. "Caleb caught our eye because of the amount of exonerating evidence, and the way he was treated on campus despite it — and Caleb is still driving a delivery truck to this day," says Cohn.

Cohn hooked Warner-Seefeld up with a couple of moms; when I asked why the moms didn't go to the ACLU, one of them said, "Ha! The ACLU doesn't care about us. They only care about the civil liberties that they care about, and then they care big-time." They met in FIRE's offices. "I helped them with questions like 'How do you use the photocopier,'" says Cohn, which may or may not be all that he did.

"We were naive," is the way that Warner-Seefeld describes her mom group. "We thought, *We are going to educate people, we are going to get laws changed, we are going to make changes on campus and we are going to support families.* But then you get to, how do you actually do this?" She still teaches high school, but now she devotes "five minutes before class, the prep period, and every night and weekend" to her cause. "All the time. It's a parallel life."

Cohn, sitting behind the desk, tents his fingers. "There are a lot of factors that go into whether people will take their lumps and move on," he says. "Long enough timeline, the more you abuse people's rights, someone will fight back—particularly when so much is at stake."

Attack of the Moms

If you're the mom of a boy accused of rape, you can't just do nothing; that doesn't work in the mid-2010s, our age of political hand-to-hand combat. You don't take your son back home and lick your wounds. You must organize; you must fight publicly.

When I met Jackson and Annabel at the Donovan, they were both quiet. Standing over six feet, Jackson was a three-sport kid in high school, dyslexic, on Adderall, had a steady girlfriend. Now, he wears owlish glasses and a Grateful Dead T-shirt and has a downcast turn to his mouth. The old life is still the one that he shows the world. When I poked around his Facebook page, I found a normal college guy in his prime: in a tux at a formal, drinking a bright drink the same shade as his bow tie; with his frat brothers at an EDM music festival, in mirrored sunglasses with festive primary-color tints; on top of a snowcapped mountain, hooting at the gods.

A couple of months later, I catch up with mom and son in their meticulously kept home in a Southern state that they ask me not to mention. They tell me the broad strokes of their story: Jackson was accused of physically forcing sex on another freshman at college in Texas, but he insists the sex was consensual, and, in fact, the girl made fun of him for his lack of prowess. The first call he made when he heard he'd been accused of sexual assault was to Annabel, who sits with him today, wearing slim jeans and sandals. When she got his call, she was standing in front of a wall of Tide in her local grocery store. She screamed at him for not keeping his pants zipped. (I did not contact the accusing student.)

Annabel's home computer is set to AOL's homepage, and within days of her son's call, an article popped up about a new sexual-assault suspect at his school. She called an emergency conclave of her seven closest girlfriends and told them what was happening; his university and her town are socially interconnected, and if rumors flew around about her son, she wanted them to help her correct them. As the university processed Jackson's charges through two separate systems — Title IX court and student-conduct court — she flew to Texas over and over, bunking at a Courtyard Marriot.

The combination of sexual humiliation and terror changed Jackson. He stayed on as an "underground" member of his frat ("But still, dues are required," says Annabel dryly), but cloistered himself in his room. He frequently woke up drenched in sweat and was afraid that every unknown number that appeared on his phone was someone calling to tell him he'd been found guilty. His fear was "triggered by the cold — if it was cold at all, I'd stay in bed, because out of bed it was cold, scary, danger, danger." He lost fifteen pounds in the space of months. "I felt like, 'I don't want to eat anything, I don't want to do anything, I want to barely breathe,' you know? I'd lie in bed, completely still, without eating, for days." A girl he liked asked him to accompany her to her sorority formal; he said no, but she persisted. "Finally I said to her, 'I'm sick, I can't go,' and she was like, 'Jackson, what the fuck? You have to come — you have no excuse.' I said, 'Okay, well, I'll tell you.' So I told her the whole story. And she said, 'Well, we probably shouldn't hang out until this is resolved.' I was like, 'Yeah.' And that was that."

Two years and five antidepressants later, Jackson has been diagnosed with PTSD. He attributes it to the helplessness he felt in the face of the charges. "I'm glad that I figured out what was wrong with me, but at the same time I've seen soldiers with PTSD and their lives are ruined and shit, and . . . my life has fucking sucked," he says. He dropped out of college with eight withdraws on his transcript ("And each of those Ws *costs*," notes Annabel); he is now taking online classes and living at home. From his perch on a couch in a small sitting room, he launches into an imagined dialogue: "'Jackson, you need to do your homework.' 'Mom, let me do my homework when I plan on doing my homework.' 'Jackson, I'm the one paying for it, you better do well.' 'Mom, I'm going to do well — just let me get to my work when I'm ready.'" He folds his hands in front of him. "It's a big circle."

As we talk, Annabel seems to vibrate with a mix of frustration, anger, and fear. "The girl made fun of his sexual performance — oh, wow, how disgusting." She adds, "He's a shell of the person he was — not that he can't get it back — but he's not the person born to this earth. My son did not go to war. He wanted to have a normal life. And now every day is parenting my adult child.

I don't want that, and he doesn't want that. I should not have to be coaxing my twenty-two-year-old son who is sobbing in his room to turn in a paper at the right time."

These are the people Cohn is talking about when he says that over a long enough period, someone will fight back. By 2016, FACE grew to hundreds of members—a veritable army of angry mothers, and some dads, like UTC wrestler Corey Mock's father, who became so outspoken on the topic that he alleges his employer, the University of North Carolina, asked him to resign. They established Twitter accounts, some under fake names; they lobbied their statesmen, sometimes with their sons. Many FACE members told me that they had found each other not through the FACE shingle on the Internet but rather via the comments section of articles about campus rape. In other words, those very articles that were frightening moms across the country— moms like my chiropractor in her tiny magenta-decorated office—were also bringing together the moms of the accused. Annabel found Allison Strange in the comments. The mom of John Doe at Occidental did the same. The next time I heard about Oliver at the midwestern state university, he had found FACE and his rhetoric had changed. He said maybe he'd drop out and join the military; to hell with the university's bullshit due process.

As the saying goes, a conservative is a liberal who's been mugged. Yes, these women are mostly Republicans, and though not all of them are Trump supporters, we can fairly say they're the type of white suburban women who voted for him despite his "grab the pussy" comments. Certainly, their sentiments aren't what I hear in my left-leaning urban circles. I bite my tongue through discussion about the evil of giving health care to illegal immigrants and the condemnation of the Southern Poverty Law Center—"They're not Southern, and they're not poor"—and when a white mom discussing Jameis Winston and Erica Kinsman says to me: "What did a girl like that, a girl like you or me, see in him? I think we'd have the same idea roughly of what was attractive in a guy, you know what I'm saying?"

And Joe Biden, too, is no sort of savior to these women, but rather the face of yet another liberal hypocrisy. "Joe Biden is the biggest sexual harasser in Washington," declares one mom. Another adds softly, "What we need to do is get a picture of him touching college women on [one of his visits to universities], because you know he is." The conservative news sites they read have pointed a finger at Biden as the "Veep Creep," "Creepy Uncle Joe"—putting his hands on girls, like Delaware senator Chris Coons's daughter and Iowa senator Joni Ernst's daughter, in front of cameras; standing behind the wife of Ashton Carter at Carter's swearing-in as defense secretary and massaging her shoulders for way too long. (Though I admire Biden and generally believe he's an equal-opportunity shoulder-squeezer of men and women, these videos also made me raise an eyebrow.)

Much of this rhetoric is alarmingly close to that of men's rights activists. I'd never considered MRAs particularly powerful; they're the Internet's troll underbelly, growing out of the early 2000s snarky and aggressive culture of 4chan, a website for teenage boys and miscreants. Now they formed a loose confederation with other angry men, like pickup artists (wimpy guys looking for tips on how to manipulate girls into sex), and father's rights advocates (dads who are angry that American courts favor moms in custody battles or who simply don't want to pay alimony). They also broke bread with white supremacists, ripping the veil off a world they saw being run by Jews and cucks, short for *cuckolds*, meaning those who have surrendered to the liberals. Some of the "survivors of false accusation" were a logical addition to this new cohort, which was rebranded as the alt-right.

This became a cool movement, a counterculture, at least for some guys, and one embodied on campus by Milo Yiannopoulos, the gay, platinum-peroxided thirty-two-year-old who dresses like a rock star (Miley Cyrus not as genderqueer but as a queer man). His trick is using the campus left against itself, jabbing constantly at trigger-warning-consumed snowflakes, making them sound more powerful than they are, because the more important they seem, the more righteous and heroic the insult crusade against them. He lectured on dozens of American campuses in 2016, traveling in a luxury tour bus decorated with his name surrounded by sparkles.

Here are a few samples of his inflammatory rhetoric:

On woke guys: "Male feminists [are] about the most depressingly hilarious creation of modern life . . . The best these guys get is an unsatisfying handie in the back of the car."

On affirmative consent: "Can you imagine anything more awful, anything more of a boner shrinker, than someone getting out a contract or an app?"

On feminists, whom he calls "a cancer": "What are we going to do for them? Compulsory chemo, but that seems harsh? But you do lose a lot of weight."

On gender-studies departments: "The roster of professors is dyke, dyke, dyke, divorcée, dyke."

On campus victimhood: "Everybody has bad shit happen to them, and you either use it to turn yourself into a star, or you become a victim . . . if you allow the bad things in your life to define you, you will only ever be a parasite."

But here's a more substantive and perhaps even more unnerving statement: "I'm happy to be raising hell on your campuses, because you know, of course, if you win on campuses, you win," he explained at UC Irvine. "Turn it into a show, which is what I try to do. Turn it into entertainment. And when you do that, you reach everybody . . . a cultural, social result. Once you've started talking about politics, you've lost. Once you start talking about policy, it's all over. Andrew Breitbart, founder of the site I work for and one of my personal heroes, said that politics is downstream of culture."

By presenting his ideas as cogent here, I don't mean to endorse them, and after a couple of hours of listening to his screeds, one begins to discern the smallness of the bag of tricks. But young followers are riveted. At Auburn University, the school that expelled Joshua Strange, a brown-haired boy rose to ask a question. "This microphone is so loud," he said, mustering up his courage. "We all kind of grew up talking about how we're not really supposed to talk about politics. I got a text from my own brother that basically said 'Leave the fucking politics alone before you alienate everyone who likes you.' Now, you do this for a living, and you're damn good at it," the boy continued pleadingly, "but for the rest of us, how do we talk about politics and social justice and anti–social justice — free speech — without losing everyone we love?"

Yiannopoulos offered a rousing defense of doctrine that was worthy of a self-help guru. If the student spoke frankly with his friends and family and they stopped loving him, he must abandon them. "Well, you won't lose everyone you love, you'll only lose the people who don't actually love you," he said, pacing back and forth. "You will lose the people who don't care enough about you to put their own beliefs and politics aside and love you regardless. You will lose the people who care more about themselves than they care about you, and that will be a *very painful process*. But you owe it to yourself to do it." The crowd erupted in applause.

The New Moral Majority

Did Gillibrand's bill, the one I described at the beginning of this chapter, have a shot? Maybe, maybe not. Senators are always likelier to say they'll do something than do it. But she was able to beat back an early conservative affront — the Safe Campus Act sponsored by Republican House representatives Matt Salmon of Arizona and Pete Sessions and Kay Granger of Texas, which would have sent campus cases back to the cops.

As the UVA case fell apart, the fraternity Phi Psi, the one that Jackie had supposedly been at that night, joined with three national fraternities to consider how they could beat back Title IX. Their thinking was aligned with FIRE, FACE, and other conservatives. According to reporting by Tyler Kingkade of the *Huffington Post,* this coalition turned to their closest DC compatriot: the executive director of the Fraternity and Sorority Political Action Committee, or Frat PAC, which lobbies to preserve all the stuff that makes the current system thrive (not only the Greeks' Title IX exemption as single-sex organizations, but Freedom of Association rights, tax breaks for charitable donations to renovate chapter houses, and stopping federal anti-hazing legislation). Trent Lott, the Mississippi senator turned lobbyist and a Sigma Nu alum, spearheaded the effort at a reduced rate of twenty-five thousand a month as a courtesy to the brotherhood.

Lott's firm's plan, in a memo leaked online, is detailed. "We understand that the public relations aspect of this situation is a serious problem, especially for fraternities," it begins. "We would work closely with your public relations team to explain the legal and policy positions needed to educate various constituencies about your rights. We favor a more aggressive outreach." Sororities, they explained, should be brought into the fold. "The visible cooperation of fraternity men/sorority women working together on these solutions is very powerful."

Phi Psi eventually left the effort, but the North American Interfraternity Conference and National Panhellenic Conference joined up, agreeing to spend up to three hundred thousand dollars on lobbying. The agenda under consideration was vast. They wanted to stop any mandate that the Greek system should go coed, as at Harvard or Wesleyan, for sure. They wanted better due-process protections for accused students, and didn't want schools to suspend chapters of the Greek system for actions of individual members. And they wanted congressional nullification of the OCR's 2011 Dear Colleague letter.

If this coalition thought they were going to slip this bomb into the tent without attracting notice, they couldn't have been more wrong. The young activists kicked into high gear, rebranding the bill on Twitter as the "UnSafeCampusAct" and gathering over twenty-five thousand signatures for a petition against it. Internal conversations among Greek-affiliated students on their way to DC to lobby on behalf of the system were tape-recorded and leaked online. And in a private meeting with the heads of national sororities, Gillibrand and McCaskill reportedly pressed sororities — to which both of them had belonged in college — to withdraw. The sororities beat a quick retreat. "We believe our sisters who are survivors should have choices in how, when and to whom they go to for support or to report their crime," Alpha Phi wrote in a statement. "They should have their own voice and the support and encouragement they need to move forward." The bill soon died in committee.

And yet, with Trump's election, fortunes were reversed. Who cares if the Safe Campus Act failed? Trump's new team handling university sexual assault possesses similar sentiments to the conservative coalition. He replaced Obama's main honcho Catherine Lhamon, a Yale Law–trained attorney in her forties — she's the one who was milking the cow whose udders spouted money — with Candice Jackson, a Pepperdine School of Law grad of similar age but radically different outlook. Jackson is best known as the attorney who strutted into a Trump-Clinton presidential debate with three women who accused Bill Clinton of sexual misbehavior. Active in the Roger Stone–inspired counter-ops machine, she is a Hillary hater extraordinaire.

Yet Jackson calls herself a feminist, or, more precisely, a libertarian feminist. She is pro-life and a conservative Christian but also openly gay and says she is a domestic abuse survivor. Her feminism, she explains, involves respecting individual women rather than cutting deals for women as a special-interest group, which so often goes along with the liberal agenda she abhors (pro-choice, pro–welfare state, pro–affirmative action). Her contempt for the Clintons is justified on this basis. About Bill's alleged assaults, she said, "[Bill] believed himself to be in power and helping women as a group, and it just didn't seem to matter all that much if he had to use and abuse a few individual women along the way." One might find this persuasive, except Jackson seems to be a rabid defender of rape victims only when the offender is a liberal. She calls the dozen-odd women who accused Trump "fake victims."

In her defense of the new president, Jackson is joined by DeVos and other members of the religious right, who are thrilled to have a philandering alleged assaulter in power, as bizarre as that may sound. In the Bible, God does not necessarily require a leader to be a godly man. His purposes can be carried out by a pagan king, like King Cyrus of Babylon, who freed the Jews after seventy years of captivity. In some religious circles, Trump is said to have "the Cyrus anointing." Can Trump deliver on the religious right's platform of life, marriage, and religious liberty (decoupling religious institutions from a creeping, tyrannical secular government)? To them, that's the only relevant question. Hypocrisy and morality have nothing to do with it.

Trump's higher-ed gurus include DeVos and Jackson—though not Yiannopoulos, who was cast out of the fold after he said sex with thirteen-year-olds is acceptable—as well as Jerry Falwell Jr., son of the televangelist Moral Majority founder and current president of Liberty University. Falwell's Liberty University in Lynchburg, Virginia, which calls itself the largest Christian university in the world (when counting its gargantuan online student body), not only has a Creationist department but its students are required to take History of Life, a creationist course. Yale decided to take the name of John C. Calhoun, America's seventh vice president and a proponent of slavery, off its residential college in 2017; Liberty, however, hosts a neo-Confederate conference organized by a foundation named for Calhoun's birthplace.

I dinged the young activists and the CDC for insisting that programs like Senn's are inconsistent with stemming assaults on campus. But I'll take their attitude on stopping assault before the religious right's, which centers on student self-control, meaning abstinence. Liberty prohibits sex outside marriage, along with most facial jewelry, shorts, and movies rated X and NC-17. Students are required to attend convocation three times a week, and the dorms have a midnight curfew. At the same time, Falwell Jr., like Ken Starr at Baylor, is growing the school via sports. He hired Baylor's former athletic director—employed at the time of their rape scandal—to lead the Liberty University athletic department. Soon after, the NCAA approved Liberty's request to move up to the football bowl subdivision, making Liberty bowl eligible for the first time.

Starr's book *Bear Country* includes a defense that Falwell Jr. could use if Liberty's football team proves themselves to be less than honorable toward women: it wasn't his fault, because universities shouldn't be responsible for students when they're not at a university-sponsored event or activity. It's students' responsibility to self-discipline.

But here's the next twist: Those moms with their real diamonds, and the rest of their coalition? They may have done the campus court system a favor, because their insistence on fixing the Nazi DMV and due-process protections will likely strengthen it in coming years.

And whether or not the conservatives override Obama's Dear Colleague letter or other Title IX protections may not matter at all. Most higher-education experts' prognostication about what will happen to Title IX regulations can be summed up as "field position football." Those Trump has tapped to lead the charge could retreat from some Title IX protections, but the next Congress and future administrations will bounce it back to where it was under Obama. Peter Lake of Stetson University also says that the vast shift on these issues in the past few years may have created an extralegal force of consumers of higher education—parents, students—who feel entitled to enhanced responses to sexual assault. "The voluntary compliance spirit is now very broadly splattered across the industry," he says, and that includes college presidents. "The narrative pressure on campuses is so strong that backing away substantially will be difficult."

Was there a rise in boys' sexually assaulting girls at American universities once Trump took office? Many people asked me this as though it would be detectable at this early date. I have doubts about a shift, although some college guys certainly found his presidency reassuring. "Yeah, I think Trump is terrible for the country, but part of me sees him as president and thinks, *The bitch is dead*," a male USC student told me, sotto voce. "We're back. We won, and we're mad."

CONCLUSION

Since we started with Emma Sulkowicz, let's end with her too, rewinding the tape to far before Trump's election back to 2015, when she was still a student, about to become an alum. As a late-spring drizzle falls across the gracious Columbia campus, she snakes toward large white tents in a loose processional along with a thousand seniors in the undergraduate college. Most of them wear khakis and sneakers, or sundresses and sandals, under their light blue processional gowns, with a rare bow tie or pumps. Columbia calls this event Class Day, and for generations its participants have brought a casual attitude to the ceremony, which happens a day before the all-university commencement, an occasion momentous enough that New York's Empire State Building will glow a Columbia robin's-egg blue and white in the skyline.

Filing into campus's South Field, students laugh, whoop, cluster tight for selfies, and fan their faces with event programs in the midmorning humidity. When a band finishes playing "Pomp and Circumstance," all face the podium. From their seats, they smile and whisper to one another as speakers address the newly launched adults. "You took risks," declares Los Angeles mayor Eric Garcetti, an alum. "You've held contrary opinions, held die-ins and sit-ins and carried mattresses." He urges them to "never stop being activists."

Soon the gathered seniors begin their march to a dais, where a handshake from President Bollinger, wearing an elaborate blue-on-light-blue robe festooned with emblems of distinction and draped in what looks to be a yard of white sailing rope, will turn them loose on the world. As the voice of advising deans boom through loudspeakers pronouncing each graduate's name, Bollinger performs this ritual with efficiency, students spaced about five seconds apart. Thirty minutes later, he hears the name of the most famous member of the class of 2015, though it takes three attempts for a dean to correctly pronounce the surname Sulkowicz.

With a cat-who-ate-the-canary grin, she marches to the steps, clearly disregarding the university's official ban on bringing along "large objects which could interfere with the proceedings or create discomfort to others," which was communicated in an e-mail a day earlier, perhaps specifically for her benefit. She mounts the dais with the mattress wrapped in plastic to protect it from the rain.

To formally congratulate Sulkowicz, Bollinger has to step forward and somehow extend his hand for a handshake over this very contentious object. The audience watches closely to see what he's going to do. He resolves the tension either by coincidence or by master stagecraft. As she approaches, he stoops, grabs a water bottle from his seat, and takes a swig, and then, when she is in front of him, he turns around to place his water bottle back on the chair, skirting a conciliatory gesture that, within moments, would have been captured by a thousand cell phone cameras, posted on social media, and spooled out to national news sites.

Despite the odds, Sulkowicz and Nungesser both reached graduation, and the mattress too. Reflecting on today's ceremonies later, Nungesser's father, who is present in the audience, calls the event a "slap in the face." The Nungessers now have their own active Title IX action against Columbia: a civil lawsuit citing harassment and defamation of character that they claim has prevented his gainful employment in the United States. By enabling Sulkowicz's art project, they say, Columbia is guilty of sex-based discrimination violating Title IX, all of it "severe, pervasive and objectively offensive." Though they haven't sued Sulkowicz, they note that she, too, is guilty of gender-based misconduct under the university's ban on "intimate partner violence," defined as "the use of physical violence, <u>coercion, threats, intimidation, isolation</u> . . . any <u>behaviors that intimidate,</u> manipulate, <u>humiliate, isolate, frighten</u>" (underscores are Nungesser's, in documents filed with the court). Citing research on violence by female Nazis, Nungesser's mother explained "that women, given the power and the opportunity, can become perpetrators just like men is nothing new for me."

But the larger assembly under this tent today hardly seems vindictive;

they are bound by a joyful, triumphant spirit. About a hundred graduates have added a symbol of solidarity with Sulkowicz to their blue mortarboards, the same symbol used in their rallies to gag Athena: a single strip of red tape. And soon, they're led in a boisterous sing-along to Columbia's fight song, "Roar, Lion, Roar!"

"'Columbia, Columbia,'" the graduates yell. "'Shouting her name for-ev-er!'"

Adulthood

I didn't mind spending three years listening to college kids, some of whom have never even had sex, lecture me about what sex and assault are all about. I found their ideas fascinating, whatever they borrowed from the 1990s and as much as the moral crusade could occasionally become tiresome.

Did I also spend much of these years deeply confused? I'd answer yes to that. The original title of this book was *Sex Ed: Heroism, Evil, and the Parameters of Consent*. It was a cheesy title but clear about what it promised — epic acts of good and evil, stories about demons lurking on campus and the angels whose halos they knock off.

Upon deeper analysis, I couldn't tell that story. As much as there is good in this book (coeducation of frats) and dreadful (Vanderbilt rapists), my thoughts evolved to encompass a far wider range of motivations, character assessments, and behaviors. I couldn't find Keyser Söze, because he didn't exist, and Sulkowicz wasn't Joan of Arc either. And in terms of covering up abuse, the American university isn't the Catholic Church.

It's tempting to chant "believe women" and simply leave it at that. But there's a mushy middle here — or a blurry middle. All of our perspectives and life experiences color what we think about assault, how serious we believe it is (whether, indeed, we would say on a survey that it happened to us). Those repressed memories that contemporary students talked about might sound like BS to some people. Yet while I was reporting this book, I could not remain only an adult voyeur; I not only rethought college sexual episodes that had always bothered me, but scraped the surface of experiences that had burrowed deep in my unconscious for twenty years.

I don't know what I'd say if someone told me the memories I just talked about weren't real. And yet at the same time, we need to accept that Niels Bohr's principle of great truths may be at work here: situations do exist in which accused and accuser *feel* they are telling the truth. I certainly came to this realization after being worried about saying such a thing, which I recognize some may find deeply offensive. As much as my brain was skeptical about the people I met, my heart wanted to believe almost everyone, at least those who were telling their own truths.

That's a cop-out, in some ways. As much as I'm interested in the way both sides can claim the victim mantle — and a victim like new OCR head Candice Jackson can even hate rape victims and perhaps scorn the accusers of Donald Trump as attention-grabbing liars — perception isn't the whole story. What's also true is we are in the midst of creating a consciousness that will protect students on both sides. Society has morphed, and sex is different than it used to be. Too much is up to interpretation, including flirty texts with vague messages, desires that are mediated by instantly accessible pornography, and finding the right balance of trusting (and not trusting) other students, which is as good a definition of *adulthood* as any.

Every person in this book, from Obama to Biden to Yiannopoulos, who said that when culture changes on college campuses, you win, was right. The whole nation is now engaged in a moral conversation about sex, one that was long overdue; a new etiquette is at hand. Of course, culture can go in cycles, and in a decade, when the cool kids may have Ivanka Trump hairstyles and bourgeois dreams, we could look back at this time with different eyes. For now, little evidence exists that the students are changing their stance on sexual assault. The survey of twenty-seven top research schools conducted by the Association of American Universities — the one that revealed that 30 percent of female students at the University of Michigan and the University of Southern California could be classified as victims, as I mentioned at the beginning of this book — also included other prestigious schools. Students at the University of Pennsylvania answered much the same way, at a rate of 27 percent; at Harvard, it was 26 percent; at Brown and Michigan State, 25 percent; at the University of Virginia, the University of Minnesota–Twin Cities, and Ohio State, 24 percent; and at Columbia, 23 percent. On the low end, schools included Iowa State (19 percent), Texas A&M (15 percent), and tiny science-oriented California Institute of Technology (13 percent).

What's with this large variation among schools? Are certain universities less safe, or are they providing an environment where some students feel more comfortable admitting their deep, dark secrets, at least on a survey? At those schools, do such surveys scoop up young people who are also a bit too interested in classifying themselves as survivors? This remains a mystery, at least for now. The architect of this study, David Cantor of the research firm Westat, tells me that this study wasn't meant to locate such patterns, though he did look into several school characteristics to compare rates of victimization—big, small; private, public; a student population of more girls, more boys. He came up with nothing in the search for clues.

A number-one-party-school ranking doesn't necessarily matter. And a school known for superb academics can have higher instances of self-reported assault. Cantor dances around my question about why this is happening but says his hunch is there's "something about socializing among the majority cohort on campuses with high numbers that is the problem." I think he means drinking, and he probably means sexual attitudes too. "It could be related to the kind of students that go to the university—who actually attends the university—and how they put themselves at risk," he explains.

Great truths aside, and the dominance of conservatives on Capitol Hill aside, universities are still taking the results from such studies seriously. And in this one, an average of 7 percent of female students answered yes to questions about whether they'd been penetrated when they were asleep, unconscious, or incapacitated by drugs and alcohol, and to the question "Since you have been attending [this school], has someone used force or threats of physical force to penetrate you (fingers, penis, object) or have oral sex with you?" These are not trick questions; there could hardly be a clearer definition of sexual assault.

The New Elite

The students in this book grew up, as I reported. Few had secured jobs upon graduation, and many spent nail-biting summers in their old bedrooms at parents' homes, but as the year wore on, one by one, they were hired in a capacity at least tangentially related to their chosen fields, either commuting in from the suburbs or moving in with roommates in a big city. Chloe began bunking with Marybeth Seitz-Brown, the Know Your IX activist, and took a job at a nonprofit research group focused on reproductive health. On Halloween, they dressed up as badass female icons: Ruth Bader Ginsberg (Chloe), and Charlize Theron's character in *Mad Max: Fury Road*, black grease smeared across her forehead (Seitz-Brown). Syracuse's Lianna put up a new description of herself on Twitter, "noticer of things," keeping up her patter about her generation's sex and dating habits: "I feel like our society is not far off from FaceTime first dates and that is both incredibly sad and extremely exciting!" she posted. The accused boy Jackson transferred to a new school, bringing along a dog to keep him company, but soon dropped back into a deep depression. When I last spoke with his mother, Annabel, she was signing him up for rapid-eye therapy, a promising if unconventional treatment for processing traumatic memories.

Today, some universities are downgrading messaging around sexual assault, and prioritizing the phrase *gender equality*, which has the benefit of being far less controversial. "As colleges are beginning to accept the Title IX brand as their own brand, the sell is that we're promoting something positive . . . [and talking about] what we're trying to accomplish that's good, versus what we're canceling out that's bad," says Stetson's Peter Lake.

With this shift in rhetoric, although not as a direct cause, anti-rape rallies on campus have become smaller and quieter. Two years after hundreds of students gathered in front of *Alma Mater* and marched to PrezBo's house, I returned to Columbia. The late-fall wind whipped through campus as a new group, far smaller at only a couple dozen students, gathered on Low's steps across from SDT sisters selling candy apples from a stall decorated with small pumpkins; the walls of the library were plastered with posters for a think-in on global populism.

The *Alma Mater* sculpture loomed large under the gray skies. A tall blonde in a black bolero jacket buttoned all the way to her neck to gird against the cold, the university's *C* stenciled on her blue baseball cap, scrambled up its length of eight feet to fix the ceremonial red tape over her mouth. She looked down, wincing. "But how do I get down now? I don't want to die before the rally!"

The rally had become a tourist attraction. Visiting parents walking by took souvenir selfies with the angry students as a backdrop. "It's, like, *injustice!*" joked one of the protesters, making a thumbs-up sign.

The speeches from participants were still moving. Princeton gender and sexualities studies professor Anne McClintock, a wool blue cap pulled down tight over her red bob, shouted through a bullhorn, "For the last four years we have been watching a global movement rise up against sexual violence, as millions of women and men break centuries of silence and centuries of stigma to shout out, enough is enough, our dress is not a yes, being drunk is not consent, and rape is not an accident. This is historic!" She gestured across the quad. "I can point at the building where a doctor violated his Hippocratic oath, and violated me, while I was a student at Columbia. I can say that without the slightest shame." Her voice rang across the campus. "Is it not an indictment of our society, that we still have to insist, there is no shame?"

Sulkowicz, Ridolfi-Starr, and peers forced Columbia to change some policies. But now the university had demanded that accusing students sign a contract promising not to tape-record university proceedings. This was the reason for today's rally, which had new chants — "Hey, hey, ho, ho, recording bans have got to go!" — and a good new trick. There were the usual cardboard signs, like RAPE HAPPENS HERE (in the corner of one, I thought I saw TM, like trademark, but then I realized it was TW, for "trigger warning"), but one sign revealed administrators' e-mail addresses, including that of traffic light aficionado Suzanne Goldberg, promoted since I met her to the university's first executive vice president for university life. A student encouraged the crowd to take a picture of that sign. "All of them have been complicit!" she explained, directing us to e-mail our photos of the protest to Goldberg's and the other addresses right away. She shouted, "Let them know we're out here, we've *been* out here, and we're not going anywhere!"

Are they not going anywhere? Is the movement against sexual assault a mid-2010s curiosity, a viral story like United Airlines dragging a passenger off a plane, soon to blow away, or does it portend a greater feminist upwelling? When I talk to Alexandra Brodsky, the Know Your IX co-founder, she says, "This has been an opportunity for a lot of young people, and mostly a lot of young women, to gain organizing skills at a very young age. Students do really care about a lot of different things, and will hopefully go to use that for many different movements." She pauses. "This has been such a weird, unexpected whirlwind, and I don't know how you re-create that. Violence against women, and I use that term purposefully, is weird because you end up with strange bedfellows. I don't know if you can tell as sexy a story about family leave as you can about hot young coeds getting raped. I believe there's a possibility of progress to grow from here. I don't think it's inevitable."

You could probably draw a line from this era's sexual-assault protests to the historic Women's March on Washington, which gathered over three million supporters worldwide. Along with Black Lives Matter, these protests ushered in an era of youth-driven resistance the likes of which hadn't been seen in nearly fifty years. The signs at the Women's March — FREE MELANIA (a play on Free Harambe); GIRLS JUST WANT TO HAVE FUN-DAMENTAL RIGHTS (off the Cyndi Lauper song); PUSSIES IN FORMATION (a reference to Beyoncé's "Formation," which she performed at the Super Bowl); BETTER BITCH THAN MOUSE (what Justice Ruth Bader Ginsburg said when she learned "Bitch" was her law-school nickname) — would not have been as funny and culturally meaningful if college kids hadn't demonstrated that political protest could merge with not only with the art world but the stream of pop culture.

Though the Women's March was as much about traditional women's issues, like reaffirming *Roe v. Wade* and supporting subsidized childcare, the idea came from the germ of "pussy grabs back." At first, I thought the cat-eared pink caps worn by many marchers were simultaneously too droll and too confrontational, but as a sea of hot pink gathered in the Washington Mall, they seemed like the perfect symbol: a surprising color, unique to this moment of protest, and often hand-knit instead of made in China, thus representing the true ingenuity of the American people. For me, it was inspirational to see Madonna at the head of the mob. The first concert I ever went to was hers, when I was in seventh grade, and now she performed a song from the album *Like a Virgin*: "Express Yourself," her song about finding true love through good sex. Singing instead of lip-synching, she threw in a line not in the original song's lyrics: "Express yourself so you can respect yourself!"

The Real Emma

While the nation was erupting in campus activism, mattress-bearing students seemed like a future staple of campus protest, a successor to Take Back the Night. In fact, the prop faded soon after Sulkowicz's graduation. Not only was it not necessary as what it stood for—boldly broadcasting your truth—was incorporated into the culture (Bill O'Reilly fired; *Game of Thrones* finally waking up about its portrayal of rape; Nungesser's suit against Columbia dismissed) but among students, word went around that Sulkowicz said the symbol had run its course. Young activists were fine with this; she didn't need to continue "to be a symbol for our movement," says a Know Your IX activist. "But Emma is a celebrity in my world, and *Mattress Girl* is still a common phrase. When I talk about my work with people who don't understand the issue in a nuanced way, I usually say, 'Do you know the Mattress Girl?' They always say yes, and then I explain, 'What I do is very connected with what she is.' And then they understand."

One year after she graduated, Sulkowicz put on her first solo show, *Self-Portrait*, in Los Angeles's Chinatown. Set on a pedestrian thoroughfare that rides the line between gritty and picturesque, the gallery has beige-and-red-checked linoleum floors, windows covered with iron bars, and fluorescent lighting. It's tiny but charming, as an alternative space in an out-of-the-way district must be.

Inside the gallery, to many art-show-goers' surprise, the artist was present—in a way, doubly so. Sulkowicz herself stood on a small white platform. Next to her, a life-size rubber replica, "the Emmatron," stood on a matching platform. The self-portrait was a dual portrait.

Both the real Emma and the Emmatron had dyed-purple hair held back in a loose ponytail. Both had pink-painted fingernails. Both were dressed casually in black—the real Emma in a black pantsuit, and the fake one in a loose black blouse and faded black jeans. Gesturing to the Emmatron, who had a welcoming if slightly surprised look on her rubber face, Sulkowicz said, "I'm still getting over, 'Is that what I'm shaped like?' You don't really know what you're shaped like until you see yourself, there."

She was twenty-three now and more composed than she was as a student, but still funny, intelligent, moody, stubborn, intractably stubborn. When

asked if she had told other activists not to carry mattresses after her graduation, she parried, "I don't control the minds of students."

During the year she carried the mattress, she spent much time off campus, where her project's rules didn't require her to bring it along. Sulkowicz
described her mood during that time as fairly dark. "*Depressed* is a clinical
term, and no one diagnosed me as *depressed*," she said. "So, no, I did not feel
depressed. But I did have a new slew of emotions that weren't pathological,
I'd say." Now she was sleeping in the back of this gallery's space and taking
showers at the local YMCA. "You know how when you're in college, high
school feels so far away?" she declared. "I feel like college is like high school
now — 'Oh my God, what the fuck happened?'"

If I haven't made it clear, I believe Sulkowicz's version of the night with
Nungesser. I know she hasn't provided incontrovertible evidence. I recognize
believing her is a personal choice, and a political one too.

Now the real Emma and the Emmatron stood in the gallery for five hours
a day over the course of three weeks, interacting with the public, though not
too closely. PLEASE DO NOT TOUCH EMMA, read a small sign hanging in
front of the real Emma. A guy came in wearing a hot-pink T-shirt with the
words THIS IS WHAT A FEMINIST LOOKS LIKE. "Emma is a she-ro, a
real-life she-ro," he said. "I understand the art piece, and it's powerful, but
it's also a little intimidating because you can't touch her." *Portlandia*'s Fred
Armisen stopped by. "We had a normal conversation, about if he lives in LA
or New York," Sulkowicz said. "He wasn't going to fan-girl over me, so, you
know . . ." She wasn't going to fan-girl over him.

If a gallery-goer had questions about Sulkowicz's mattress or her rape,
though, he or she was met with a brisk redirection to the Emmatron, who
was answering questions the real Emma was through with answering, like
"For how long did you carry the mattress?" "Tell me about the night you were
assaulted." "What happened when you and three other survivors reported
your cases to the school?" "What do your parents think of this?" Listening
to the robot give these canned, prerecorded answers on one white platform
while she stood nearby on the other, Sulkowicz said, made her feel "schizo-
phrenic. Having your voice talk back to you."

A handful of people asked the real Emma these questions anyway. One
middle-aged woman in a black leather jacket appeared on opening night and

said, "I have a question for you," to the real Emma. "How did you deal with all the shit that people gave you about your mattress performance?"

"Um, well, that's actually one of the questions on the Emmatron."

"Sorry!" said the woman.

Sulkowicz decided to answer anyway: "I didn't," she said. "I didn't."

"Oh."

"I mean, it sucks, and it's a myth, right, that we can handle all of these things—"

"But what did the administration say?"

Sulkowicz's face darkened. "Yeah, actually, now you're asking me multiple questions that are on the Emmatron."

Another man: "What is this performance about?"

"Well, um, for me, it's about insisting that people realize I'm human," she said. "So many people will come up to me and [blurt out], 'Mattress Girl,' and treat me as if I'm an object. So I'm like, 'No, the object is over there, and I'm the human.'"

Sulkowicz was an adult now, and she wanted to move on, demanded a new self-definition. But here at the gallery she was besieged by ordinary people who kept talking about their rapes. "Five of them cried," she said. When a man approached her, tears in his eyes, she said, "I just can't hear another rape story. It's overwhelming to me at this point." Bawling, the man fled the room.

Sulkowicz's corpus thus far, from the mattress thesis to *Ceci N'est Pas un Viol* to *Self-Portrait*, has built narrowly upon itself. And this does leave her open to charges, fair or not, of a slightly blinkered view of the larger world. Yet Sulkowicz's art is consistently faithful to her character: vulnerable with a touch of narcissism, strident but genuinely brave. And the central theme that connects it all is a demand for subjectivity, a fight against being objectified — whether by the male or media gaze or the larger digital apparatus that we swim in. Many girls are now musing on their sex lives, consensual and not, and themselves in a new way. In their insistence on consent, on boundaries, on clarity, they are not only litigating past wrongs but creating new possibilities for themselves and the generation of girls who come next.

APPENDIX: RECOMMENDATIONS

C ollegiate sexual assault is a complex problem with inputs from pop culture, the media, law, the federal government, competing philosophies about gender relations, and subjective perspectives. University-sponsored programs in rape prevention or risk reduction won't ever be the entire answer. Each of us can take baby steps toward change, and much of this change involves having fun, just not the type of fun that involves blackout-drunk sex or the type of sex that some students may feel violated by down the line. I'll lob a few ideas here, though you'll likely have others.

For students and parents:

Watch out for guys who exhibit toxic masculinity. Don't be friends with those guys if you're a man, and stay away from them if you're a woman. Many women may joke that this means they'd have to stay away from guys entirely, but we know there's a spectrum of what guys say in conversation in front of us. Some sociologists say that the more overtly misogynist a man's language is, the more likely it is he is an assaulter. It's convenient that these two quantities line up, and young people — both men and women — would be well served if they let their knowledge about who these individuals are direct their behavior on campus. The list of recommendations below is far less valuable if the particular crowd of men who assault aren't ostracized or otherwise made to shift their behavior.

Expand your cohort. Students need friendships beyond a tight clique. Participation in clubs raises a student's social capital, which means that someone like Brock Turner — a guy looking to hook up with someone, anyone, over the course of an evening, consensually or not — will not perceive him or her as an easy target.

And, obviously, don't do what Turner's victim's sister did. It's hard not to leave a friend at a party when you're ready to go home. She may be eyeing someone she's truly interested in hooking up with later in the night. A good rule of thumb is never leave a drunk friend at a party, and never leave a sober friend at a party if you don't know a majority of the attendees.

Beware of the in-network stranger. No, other students at school aren't your friends — they're strangers. But most of them won't hurt you. Nonetheless, it's worth being wary of an older guy who is hanging out on campus but isn't enrolled at the school. I'm talking about the friend of an RA or a frat brother's high-school lacrosse teammate, as in the Rape Factory case at Wesleyan. Why would an older guy want to go to a college party or even visit a college if he's not enrolled? There's a plethora of reasons, but one of them is definitely an attempt to hook up with younger students, consensually or not.

If you are assaulted and decide that you want to report the incident to authorities or your school, do not take a shower. An STI treatment and pregnancy test can be administered no matter what, but anything you do to clean yourself up after an assault means destroying precious evidence. Don't wash your face, brush your teeth, comb your hair, or change your clothes (or, if you want to change your clothes, bring the original ones along in a clean paper bag). Rape kits are time-sensitive. You want to get to the hospital quickly, but try to find a hospital that has specially trained sexual assault nurse examiners on site. You can find one by calling the National Sexual Assault Hotline at 800-656-HOPE (4673).

This is a better avenue than calling 911 unless you're in immediate danger; if you are, do that. If you decide to pursue criminal prosecution, the hospital will connect you with law enforcement. Trained advocates may also provide support if you encounter abrasive law enforcement officers.

Don't watch your drink; watch *what* you drink. Choosing to model drinking habits after Syracuse's Caroline Heres — making sure you get your own drink at the party, like a beer that you crack open yourself — is fine. But it's unlikely to protect from much except a hangover. Roofies and Xanax may occasionally feature in assaults, but in the vast majority of cases, the drug in acquaintance rape is alcohol.

Move the drinking age to 18. Today's universities are trying to reel in binge drinking by their "education consumers." Hard liquor's out at Indiana University frats, the University of Michigan's frats are no longer allowed to have kegs, and Stanford, beginning in 2016, decreed beer and wine were the only kind of liquor that could be served at undergrad parties, and in general, any bottle in affiliated housing had to be smaller than a fifth. Dartmouth took the hardest line. Its undergrads cannot consume hard liquor in campus-affiliated spaces, including frats, period.

Some Title IX officers told me this could go further. Attorneys could devise a way to completely remove alcohol from campus culture: "Man, I need to be a plaintiff's attorney, because these suits could get big," one of them tells me. "Universities get sued because of bad outcomes from the drinking and drug party culture, but it's like a product liability lawsuit — ten lawsuits, ten people die, whatever, it costs more money to fix it. It has to cost them enough money to tip the scale."

Personally, I wonder if half-steps won't accomplish as much as changing America's drinking age. Twenty-one puts it smack in the middle of most four-year residential students' college experience. If the drinking age were lower, it not only would move drinking out of unsupervised frat basements and into public, but might have a shot at changing our youth culture of excess, moving toward the European model of wine with dinner instead of crushing empty beer cans on one's head. Some research also shows that car accidents and deaths happen most among drinkers who have just become legal, whether they're eighteen or twenty-one. At eighteen, Americans can vote, get married, and join the military — essentially, decide they want to risk their own lives. Lower the drinking age so that the psychological rush of trespassing, of engaging in binge-drinking culture because illegality is exciting, is deflated.

Read, don't speed-read, the sexual-misconduct section in your university's handbook. Prove Jonathan Kalin wrong. You'll be surprised at how restrictive the rules around sex at your college are. And don't forget to read the handbook every year. Universities can change regulations according to recommendations of their general counsel or the government. You are subject to each year's rules, not the ones that were in effect when you started. This advice will likely mean updating sexual behavior to "yes means yes," because this is probably the rule at your school.

Advocate for "yes means yes," not "no means no." I haven't made secret my support for affirmative consent in this book, and in this, I'm aligned with universities today. You can think about it as a high-toned, righteous issue about sexual autonomy, or a new minor courting ritual. It's not that different from sending an emoji to clarify one's meaning at the end of a text message. Call it a verbal condom.

There may, however, be a cloud over this matter. "You've got to be careful creating a standard for discipline that's not consistent with human behavior and the social norms of a community," says Peter Lake of Stetson University. "A lot of people don't behave according to affirmative consent standards. It isn't how they're culturalized." Lake calls it "aspirational, not typical."

Lake wouldn't be surprised to see this issue hit the U.S. Supreme Court, which he predicts will weigh in on campus issues of due process, consent, privacy rights, and perhaps the interpretation of Title IX. "Affirmative consent is ripe for the picking," he says. "Be prepared to be surprised. The issues do not line up in obvious ways, in part because the Supreme Court hasn't touched it in a generation." He notes that the Court has historically been concerned about turning universities into judicial systems. "The Founding Fathers were very disfavorable to the idea of federally regulated higher education. George Washington wanted a national college; they wouldn't give it to him. So we're actually about a hundred and eighty degrees away from where we started, and that's not going to be lost on certain members of the Court."

Don't take high numbers of assaults at a particular school as a sign that it is unsafe. Instead, search for universities with the largest number of reports. High numbers of cases at Title IX offices, which will show up in public university records, means awareness around this issue has spread through a campus, and students feel they can report assaults to the school without fear of being ostracized by their friends. If you are serious about this issue, you might want to choose the most progressive campus available in your state, or a liberal-arts school, even if silly political sloganeering comes with it. Progressive campuses are beginning to incorporate a shift in social norms about assault. And that shift in norms may eventually reel in the behavior of a majority of assaulters: that 8 percent who generally don't rape before entering college.

Explain to your kids that the risk is *off* campus, not on. Indoor, well-lit places like off-campus apartments are far riskier than a dark path from one's dorm to the library. Students should not be afraid when they are crossing through campus, day or night.

If you don't have self-defense classes on campus, learn a few self-defense tricks. If you're confronted with physical force, the best course of action is to yell, strike back, and run away. If you are attacked by an acquaintance (or someone who doesn't use force), you may need a different strategy. You probably won't feel comfortable yelling or striking someone you know, even vaguely, but Jocelyn Hollander, the University of Oregon professor, says putting your hands over your head and saying "Back off" can be effective.

Tell your children that if they're accused of sexual assault on campus — or of any disciplinary issue, actually — they must call immediately. If you want to be proactive, locate a local attorney near the school. In some small university towns, the best attorneys will have business with the school and be unable to represent your child. This is overkill, granted. But it doesn't cost anything, and it may make you feel more secure if you are truly afraid of what might happen if your son is accused of assault. But never lose sight of the fact that the odds of a boy getting reported (unfairly or not) to his college for assault is about one in a thousand, the same odds of a man developing breast cancer.

If your son has joined a fraternity, make doubly sure that he knows to call you if he becomes enmeshed in a scandal. When a sexual-assault or hazing incident hits the radar, representatives from Greek organizations tend to sweep in and take statements perhaps before boys call personal lawyers or their parents. This may not be in your son's best interests.

Bring consent education to younger students. In 2015, the California leg-islature, in a nearly unanimous vote, required that affirmative consent — "yes means yes" — be taught in public high schools. The law, the first of its kind in the United States, states that high schools that require health courses for graduation must instruct students on preventing sexual harassment and vio-lence and on consent.

The law went into effect for school districts at the beginning of 2016 but it may be a few years before a standard "yes means yes" curriculum, or even guidelines for how to teach consent, are put in place, due to government red tape. At the moment, affected school districts (which include five of the state's ten largest) are creating their own curricula, and they may contain a British viral video that uses the analogy of making a person a cup of tea to explain the concept of consent. (No one would insist that someone who was passed out had to drink tea, and no one would force someone to drink tea if she said she wanted it and then changed her mind and said she didn't.)

Los Angeles Unified School District, the state's largest, has been teaching consent in seventh- and ninth-grade health classes for a while, but begin-ning with the 2016–2017 school year, health teachers are required to dedicate between forty-five and ninety minutes (or more, if they choose) to an ac-tivity about consent. The lesson begins with a teacher's presentation, which students respond to with role-play scenarios, visual arts projects, or story-telling. Students may also develop the theme into a school-wide awareness campaign.

At the University of New Hampshire's Prevention Innovations Center, scholars are beginning to explore programs for other states. "We're trying to stop kids from saying, 'Fuck you,'" says professor Katie Edwards, meaning that they'd blow her off from the minute she walked in the room because she was an adult talking about sexual consent. "If you roll in and say, 'We're going to tell you not to rape,' you're going to get a lot of fuck-yous."

To combat this, UNH has tailored their program to teen psychology. "Teenagers like to be subversive," she says. "You like to say eat your broccoli and they like to say no, you say put on this shirt and they say absolutely not — being a teenager is about being rebellious." Her solution is to talk to kids about consent in terms of how they've been tricked, by the media and pop culture, to think it's not cool. "We tell them the media sends messages that it's okay to talk about girls as hoes and bitches — now, do we think that, or are we being brainwashed? We make them feel the dominant, heteronormative, super-masculine, super-violent culture is something they've been *brainwashed* to do, and is it something they want to be doing?"

This sounds promising to me. If you live in a state other than California, organize at your high school to lobby for consent education on the curriculum. Teaching kids about healthy relationships and consent is not controversial, and churches should learn to accept it. This is not about methods of birth control. It's about ethics.

For schools:

Protect Title IX. DeVos and her deputies could blow up some advances at universities, perhaps by raising the burden of proof. Right now it is 51 percent, which some people think is too low. I don't agree for one simple reason: it is so hard to prove sexual assault that coming up with 1 percent to tip the scales, or the feather that Brett Sokolow spoke about, is usually enough.

There are fewer fisheries professors hearing cases today. Universities are now recruiting more sophisticated investigators, like former prosecutors and law enforcement agents. Such hires should lead to more justice. The sprawling University of Texas system has signed up the four-star military admiral who led the Bin Laden raid. And at a networking dinner, I met Amy Beckett, an eccentric redhead with four grown kids from Celine, Ohio. A former criminal prosecutor with a PhD in philosophy, Beckett wants a life change; she's even looked into a job serving as a "modern butler" for an elderly woman outside Cleveland who she imagines could be LeBron James's mom. "And get this: She's only a resident in the house five months a year, so the rest of the time I can ride my tricycle inside and write *red rum* on the mirrors." She laughs at her joke, and then says, "No, seriously, I'm pretty focused on the twelve new job postings I've seen in the Midwest for Title IX officers in the past six weeks."

Beckett agrees with the principle behind Title IX enforcement: sexual assault and misconduct need to be addressed on campus, not by the criminal justice system. "We're here at universities creating civic-minded people, ethical leaders," she says. "Frankly, we're not a democracy. We're a republic, with an elite, and we aren't sending this elite through our colleges so they can regurgitate textbooks. They need to learn how to act in a dignified manner."

Shut down pre-orientation and early-fall parties at fraternities. Schools demanding that pledging wait for sophomore year are smart, but for a school like Syracuse, which relies on the Greek scene to provide social life in a depressed town, it's not realistic. Universities can, however, ban frat parties during orientation and the red zone. Kids going to these parties, usually seventeen or eighteen years old, have just left their childhood homes. They should not be thrust into a risky party culture at the same time they're disoriented. They're signing up for classes, making new friends, letting their guards down — *and* drinking more than they probably ever have before.

Designate some faculty "confidential reporters." Not every incident needs to become a federal case. "One thing that administrators don't understand is that when students come to you asking to do something, frankly, it's more important that they're affirmed," says Jason Laker, the San Jose State University professor of counselor education. Some campus assault victims want only to be heard by an adult in a position of authority. They don't want an official Title IX hearing. Among the relationships that a student has on campus, even at a time when professors at research universities are encouraged to publish rather than teach, the professor-student relationship should be mentor-mentee, or even doctor-patient. Confidences should be permitted.

Consent apps are a decent idea. Yup, I know I made fun of them earlier. Activists dislike the way they emphasize covering one's ass rather than "showing up for your partner," as author Jaclyn Friedman put it. Legal experts say they won't work even if they include video of a student agreeing to have sex, because a user will never be able to prove that he wasn't holding a gun at the victim's head outside of the frame. But there are some reasons to use them. Even if they feel corny or silly, they may clarify students' intent. And in a country where one must consent to everything, even medical procedures for which one has already been admitted to the hospital and has obviously consented, why not?

Campuses should allow students who feel violated to time-stamp stories. Jessica Ladd, who received a master's degree in public health at Johns Hopkins, has a strong idea about how to solve delayed reporting of sexual assaults and the effect the lag has on a survivor's chances of winning a future case against an assailant. Her answer is Callisto, an "information escrow" app that allows students to create a confidential, time-stamped record of an assault. If a student later decides to tell the university, she's got backup. If she doesn't, no one but her will know she wrote it down.

The University of San Francisco and Pomona College piloted Callisto in 2015, and a handful of other schools have partnered with Ladd to use it. She's also developed a tool for automatically sending a survivor's account to the school's Title IX office if another student names the same perpetrator.

Office of Greek Life webpages must include chapter-conduct histories with all the gory details. Doug Fierberg, the profane anti-frat lawyer who represented the Wesleyan Rape Factory victim, believes that universities that promote Greek culture as an essential part of student life have a duty to tell their students (and parents) about the safety (or lack thereof) of frats. "The decision not to provide that information to the greater community absolutely flies in the face of what came out of the Virginia Tech massacre, about students being entitled to timely, accurate information about the risks they face," says Fierberg, who represented some Virginia Tech victims.

Some universities publish this information now, but Fierberg doesn't like the way they're doing it. For example, on its Greek life webpage the University of Arizona summarizes judicial incidents at frats over the past few years. But the details behind the milquetoast descriptions of what brothers have done wrong are fuzzy. What are "violations related to continued alcohol, safety, and hazing regulations," exactly? A couple of pledges with open containers stopped by a cop on the street outside the frat? Or a rape?

"Anything you and I know about frats, it's all anecdotal, but universities know everything," says Fierberg. "They're misrepresenting by omission. You're a parent and you go on this website, and everything looks fine."

Consider the Dartmouth model. I believe either coeducating the Greek system or shutting frats down entirely is the best way to prevent sexual assault. Not every university will be able to follow in Harvard's and Wesleyan's footsteps, though I expect more will try in coming years.

For a university like Dartmouth, one with a deeply entrenched Greek system, an overhaul of student housing is a good first step. In 2015, they began a radical redesign of student living. Their communications director told me that the impetus was fostering inclusion and robust student interaction, not preventing sexual assault, even though an institutional report states that "high-risk drinking, sexual assault and lack of inclusivity are inter-related problems." It's fair to assume she's using a usual public relations parry, and some lessons are worth taking here.

Dartmouth's new system assigns students to one of six houses, where they are given the option to live from sophomore year onward (the college kept its longstanding freshman-only dorms). These houses are clusters of old red-brick dormitories, with faculty advisers in residence at single-family homes nearby. Named for local streets or their geographical locations — Allen House, East Wheelock House, North Park House, School House, South House, West House — each of these clusters has a gathering space. Two houses will use preexisting common space in the dorms, while the others will rely for now on a 4,750-square-foot, tentlike building parked over a tennis court and a two-story, modular structure erected behind two dorms. These common areas, designed to look like traditional student unions, have snack bars or convenience stores, communal study areas, and large spaces to host Indian dinner night or cookies and tea for a professor's lecture. To promote the system to students, Dartmouth designed house-branded T-shirts and offers generous funding for house-based social events.

While it's too soon to tell whether this will work at Dartmouth, it has very successful historical precedents. This house system is based on the residential model used by Harvard and Yale for almost a century, one that includes professors living on the premises (one may recall reading news about the married faculty in residence who created a furor at Yale over the wife's declaration that Yale was inappropriately policing students' Halloween costumes; they ultimately resigned from that post). "This is a very complicated puzzle," says Elizabeth Armstrong, the University of Michigan expert, "but certainly if you had a residents' hall with a professor who has two kids and a golden retriever living there, that would probably create a safer climate for students. If they're going to hang out, have pizza with the professor, and pet the golden retriever as opposed to get ragingly drunk, that would probably be safer."

Although the Dartmouth system was met with some skepticism — "an unpopular, poorly orchestrated experiment in social engineering," Sarah Perez '17 grumbled in the student-run newspaper the *Dartmouth* — once students were assigned to houses, some took pride in the new arrangement. "The underclassmen are buying into it more than the upperclassmen, and eventually everyone will buy into it," says Sarah Khatry, '18. "It will take time, but it will take root."

The hard-alcohol ban at Dartmouth, while hardly followed by all students — who can be stone-cold sober through a Hanover winter? — has also led to impressive changes. "It's not like my freshman year anymore, where you were handed rum and Coke from a frat brother pretending to be a bartender behind a table in a basement, and another guy pours you another immediately," says a Dartmouth senior. "Drinking hard liquor still happens, but it happens behind closed doors on the third floor. It's easier to smoke weed at Dartmouth now than drink hard alcohol."

One year after the ban, rates of some alcohol-related incidents are down between 25 and 50 percent. But students also point out an unintended consequence of the ban. "Dartmouth's social motto used to be open doors all the time, with very few parties that were invite-only," says a student. "You could go to every frat on the map one night if you were ambitious, and no frat turned you away, whether you were male or female. That's a funny thing to mourn, but now that the alcohol is private, social life is hierarchical. It's about who gets invited to the third floor."

In the 2016–2017 school year, Dartmouth looked into the conduct of at least ten fraternities. Six were disciplined, some for drinking violations.

ACKNOWLEDGMENTS

T o all the smart, cool, and curious kids I met on the road: thank you. Thank you to my editor, Eamon Dolan, who set the bar so high I couldn't help but jump then picked me up when I fell. Thank you to my extremely cool and erudite agent, Eric Simonoff. Thank you to *New York* magazine editor in chief Adam Moss, who published the piece that led to this book, and to David Wallace-Wells, who edited it. Thank you to Graydon Carter, Jake Silverstein, Doug Stumpf, and Mike Benoist for the time off.

Thanks to my talented assistants: Lydia Dallett, Amy Crawford, Erica Schweigerhausen, Lauren Tousignant, Gabrielle Bruney, and, of course, Phoebe. Thank you for the fact-checking, Julie Tate. Thank you to Lisa Glover, Loren Isenberg, Rosemary McGuinness, Alexandra Primiani, Tracy Roe, Taryn Roeder, and the rest of the team at Houghton Mifflin Harcourt.

Thanks to my amen corner: Ruth Barrett, Toma Barylak, Judd Bloch, Zev Borow, Brendan Burke, Dahlia and Glen Caplin, Meghan Daum, Victoria De Silverio, Josh Eells, Sarah Ellison, John Fahey, Ariel Levy, Janet Reitman, Deborah Schoeneman, and Sean Woods. Special thanks to two friends who delivered the eleventh-hour real real: Adam Fisher and Sahara Lotti. Jennifer Blumin, you will always be my most loyal friend.

I am indebted to the incisive reporting of many journalists, including Katie Baker, Ariel Kaminer, Tyler Kingkade, T. Rees Shapiro, Jesse Singal, and Robby Soave. Thank you to Rachel Tabachnick and Frederick Clarkson of Political Research Associates for teaching me about the religious right. Thanks to Chris Bonanos and Nell Casey, for their early help. And thank you to the wise and generous Emily Bazelon, whose fair-minded feminism on this topic guided my own and whose advice was invaluable.

Special thanks to John Homans, who has been my mentor for twenty years, and to Maer Roshan, who taught me how to report with laughter and love.

Special thanks to the smart and wily Noreen Malone, the best young editor I know. Special thanks to Chris Norris, the unsung genius; Ann Neumann, for the empathy and love; and, for the cover inspiration, Stephen Valter.

This book was brought to you by a playlist of Bach, Beethoven, Deadmau5, and one particular Bassnectar song called "Impossible and Overwhelming." It was also brought to you by the support of my family, including my aunt Lucy, godmother Harriet, and cousins Sophia, Agamemnon, Dimtri, Maryann, and George. I am also in awe of my new family Fern, Madeline, Arthur, Nina, Tim, and Elaine Maldonado. My husband, Craig, was a meticulous reader, and my daughter, Olympia, was always curious about why I was writing a book with no pictures.

In the course of writing this book, I gave birth to a baby boy, Apollo. My mother, Mary, a feminist artist who co-founded the first women's gallery in 1972, was critical in helping me understand civil rights history of that time and in helping with my family obligations.

I lost my father while I was writing this book. He was the smartest person I knew, the most loving, and the hardest-working. I hope I have honored him. May his memory be eternal.

NOTES

"Mattress Girl"

Page

xv *"Mr. President":* Max Kutner, "The Other Side of the College Sexual Assault Crisis," *Newsweek,* December 10, 2015, http://www.newsweek.com/2015/12/18/other-side-sexual-assault-crisis-403285.html.

xvi *"should haunt all of us":* Hillary Clinton, "Speech at Democratic National Committee Women's Leadership Forum" (Washington, DC, September 19, 2014), C-SPAN, https://www.c-span.org/video/?321576-2/hillary-clinton-remarks-dnc-womens-leadership-forum&start=1180.

determination and resolve: Anna Merlan, "Posters on Columbia Campus Call Emma Sulkowicz a 'Pretty Little Liar,'" *Jezebel,* May 20, 2015, http://jezebel.com/posters-on-columbia-campus-call-emma-sulkowicz-a-pretty-1705750162.

Introduction: Orientation

xx party rape: Lisa Wade, *American Hookup: The New Culture of Sex on Campus* (New York: W. W. Norton, 2017), 205.

xxii *"the most degrading":* Alexa Tsoulis-Reay, "10 Men on What a Blow Job Feels Like," *New York,* May 17, 2016, http://nymag.com/thecut/2016/05/10-men-on-what-a-blow-job-feels-like.html.

xxiii *"the pursuees":* Sarah Posner, "Exposing the Christian Right's New Racial Playbook," AlterNet, April 27, 2010, http://www.alternet.org/story/146634/exposing_the_christian_right%27s_new_racial_playbook.

xxiv *"took our picture":* Bethany Saltman, "We Started the Crusade for Affirmative Consent Way Back in the '90s," *New York,* October 22, 2014, http://nymag.com/thecut/2014/10/we-fought-for-affirmative-consent-in-the-90s.html.

xxv *not find one picture: Columbian,* 2015.

U.S. News and World Report *college rankings had:* Michael Luca, Patrick Rooney, and Jonathan Smith, "The Impact of Campus Scandals on College Applications," Harvard Business School Working Paper 16-137, 2016, http://www.people.hbs. edu/mluca/CollegeScandals.pdf.

xxvii *remains female-driven:* Scott D. Easton, "Disclosure of Child Sexual Abuse Among Adult Male Survivors," *Clinical Social Work Journal* 41, no. 4 (2012): 344–55, doi: 10.1007/s10615-012-0420-3.

"largest undergraduate sorority": Tyler Kingkade, "College Sexual Assault Survivors Form Underground Network to Reform Campus Policies," *Huffington Post,* March 21, 2013, http://www.huffingtonpost.com/2013/03/21/college-sexual-assault-survivors_n_2918855.html.

xxviii *escalating sex act:* New York State Senate, S5965, Reg. Sess. 2015-2016 (June 14, 2015), http://legislation.nysenate.gov/pdf/bills/2015/S5965.

xxxiv *to show solidarity:* Carrying the Weight Together Facebook Page, photograph, posted October 29, 2014, https://www.facebook.com/carryingtheweighttogether/photos/a.1566490130232501.1073741835.1541424646072383/1566491273565720/.

1. Planet College, Millennial Edition

7 *expulsion if caught:* Karen Schwartz, "College Students Scrawl Names of Alleged Rapists on Bathroom Walls," Associated Press, November 28, 1990, http://www.nexis.com.

from the 1 percent: The Upshot, "Economic Diversity and Student Outcomes at Wesleyan University," *New York Times,* January 18, 2017, https://www.nytimes.com/interactive/projects/college-mobility/wesleyan-university.

8 *interdisciplinary learning:* "Biography of Michael S. Roth," Wesleyan University, http://www.wesleyan.edu/president/biography/.

need-aware: Wesleyan defines *need-aware* as considering affluence for 5 to 10 percent of the high-school students it admits.

class of 2020: Jake Lahut, "State of the School Preview: What to Expect from Roth," *Wesleyan Argus,* September 19, 2016, http://wesleyanargus.com/2016/09/19/state-of-the-school-preview/.

"competitor has more": Kevin Carey, *The End of College: Creating the Future of Learning and the University of Everywhere* (New York: Riverhead, 2015), 58.

9 *breadline:* American Association of University Professors, "Higher Education at a Crossroads: The Economic Value of Tenure and the Security of the Profession," *Academe,* March–April 2016, https://www.aaup.org/sites/default/files/2015-16EconomicStatusReport.pdf.

12 *combination of two genders:* National LGBT Health Education Center, "Providing Affirmative Care for Patients with Non-Binary Gender Identities," February

2017, https://www.lgbthealtheducation.org/wp-content/uploads/2017/02/Provid
ing-Affirmative-Care-for-People-with-Non-Binary-Gender-Identities.pdf, 5.

13 *outside the binary:* Ibid.

"being a boy or a girl": Amanda Petrusich, "Free to Be Miley," *Paper,* June 9, 2015,
http://www.papermag.com/free-to-be-miley-1427581961.html.

16 *"to become people":* Rebecca Traister, *All the Single Ladies: Unmarried
Women and the Rise of an Independent Nation* (New York: Simon and Schuster,
2016), 226.

18 *refused to put it on:* Oliver Laughland, *"Vagina Monologues* Playwright: 'It
Never Said a Woman Is Someone with a Vagina,'" *Guardian,* January 16, 2015,
http://www.theguardian.com/world/2015/jan/16/vagina-monologues-eve-ensler-
rejects-mount-holyoke-college-claims-reductionist-exclusive.

2. Number-One Party School

20 *"Number One Party School":* Allie Healy, "Syracuse University Named No. 1
Party School by Princeton Review," Syracuse.com, August 4, 2014, http://www.
syracuse.com/news/index.ssf/2014/08/syracuse_named_top_party_school_
princeton_review.html.

23 *boundaries need more attention:* Kent Syverud, e-mail message to Syracuse
student body, August 5, 2014, http://web.archive.org/web/20140808222927/
http://chancellor.syr.edu/messages/m/boundaries.html.

24 *Hookup culture "is college":* Wade, *American Hookup,* 19.

26 *twenty-one universities and colleges:* England has expanded her pool of
respondents since the publication of this paper but says the results discussed
in this chapter remain the same; see Elizabeth A. Armstrong, Laura Hamilton,
and Paula England, "Is Hooking Up Bad for Young Women?," *Contexts* 9 (2010),
http://faculty2.ucmerced.edu/lhamilton2/docs/paper-2010-hooking-up.pdf.

far more often: Elizabeth Armstrong, Paula England, and Alison Fogarty, "Sex-
ual Practices, Learning, and Love: Accounting for Women's Orgasm and Sexual
Enjoyment in College Hookups and Relationships" (manuscript draft for the
American Journal of Sociology 21), http://paa2011.princeton.edu/papers/111166.

29 *plump little sister:* Marnie Eisenstadt, "Syracuse University Student Quits
Sorority, Bashes Culture of Cruelty" (video), Syracuse.com, February 2, 2016,
http://www.syracuse.com/entertainment/index.ssf/2016/02/syracuse_univer
sity_student_quits_sorority_bashes_culture_of_cruelty_video.html.

31 *ten or more hookups:* Armstrong, "Is Hooking Up Bad for Young Women?," 24.

33 *reach orgasm:* Natalie Kitroeff, "In Hookups, Inequality Still Reigns," *New
York Times,* November 11, 2013, http://well.blogs.nytimes.com/2013/11/11/
women-find-orgasms-elusive-in-hookups/.

had tried anal sex: William Saletan, "The Ass Man Cometh," *Slate,* October 5, 2010, http://www.slate.com/articles/health_and_science/human_nature/2010/10/the_ass_man_cometh.html.

37 *One in six freshman women:* Kate B. Carey et al., "Incapacitated and Forcible Rape of College Women: Prevalence Across the First Year," *Journal of Adolescent Health* 56 (2015): 679, http://i2.cdn.turner.com/cnn/2015/images/05/20/carey_jah_proof.pdf.

3. A Boy's Life

43 *bone-chilling night at Syracuse:* I broke my knee shortly before this event. I arranged for a student stringer to cover the 2015 *Penis Monologues.* This account is based on her extensive notes.

45 *"daytime and nighttime":* Michael Kimmel, "Boys Will Be Boys: Deconstructing Masculinity and Manhood at Dartmouth," YouTube video, July 9, 2013, https://www.youtube.com/watch?v=pjA98mrJJOo.

46 *"when there is social hierarchy":* Merril D. Smith, ed., *The Encyclopedia of Rape* (Westport, CT: Greenwood Press, 2004), 167.

47 *two hours for women:* "Drinking Levels Defined," National Institute on Alcohol Abuse and Alcoholism, https://www.niaaa.nih.gov/alcohol-health/overview-alcohol-consumption/moderate-binge-drinking.

focus primarily on alcohol: Office on Violence Against Women, "Grants to Reduce Sexual Assault, Domestic Violence, Dating Violence and Stalking on Campus Program Solicitation," U.S. Department of Justice, January 10, 2017, https://www.justice.gov/ovw/page/file/923431/download.

48 *"what I would say yes to":* Sarah Hepola, "The Alcohol Blackout," *Texas Monthly,* January 2016, http://www.texasmonthly.com/the-culture/the-alcohol-blackout/.

49 *Free the Nipple protest:* David Boroff, "Fraternity Pledge Asks Co-Ed for Topless Pic for Rush Week," *New York Daily News,* October 20, 2015, http://www.nydailynews.com/news/national/fraternity-pledge-asks-co-ed-topless-pic-rush-week-article-1.2404601.

50 *instruction manual for sex:* Peggy Orenstein, "When Did Porn Become Sex Ed?," *New York Times Magazine,* March 19, 2016, http://www.nytimes.com/2016/03/20/opinion/sunday/when-did-porn-become-sex-ed.html?_r=0.

watched porn: "The Class of 2015 by the Numbers," *Harvard Crimson,* 2015, http://features.thecrimson.com/2015/senior-survey/.

51 *"molested by a family friend":* Saturday Night Live, "Weekend Update with Jimmy Fallon & Tina Fey," NBC, April 7, 2001, http://snltranscripts.jt.org/00/00pupdate.phtml.

54   *"No one cares about either":* Tess Bloch-Horowitz, "On Living in Fear of Telling the Truth: My Experience with ΣAE, Retaliation and Title IX," *Stanford Daily,* May 20, 2015, http://www.stanforddaily.com/2015/05/20/on-living-in-fear-of-telling-the-truth-my-experience-with-sae-retaliation-and-title-ix/.

55   *more often than women do:* Emily Esfahani Smith, "How Strong Is the Female Sex Drive After All?," *Atlantic,* July 2, 2013, https://www.theatlantic.com/sexes/archive/2013/07/how-strong-is-the-female-sex-drive-after-all/277429/.

58   *a political party:* Daron Taylor, "Meet the Average Millennial," *Washington Post,* video, April 28, 2016, https://www.washingtonpost.com/video/national/meet-the-average-millennial/2016/04/28/29b704e8-0d74-11e6-bc53-db634ca94a2a_video.html.

generation of do-gooders: Achieve, "The Millennial Impact Report Retrospective: Five Years of Trends," November 2016, http://fi.fudwaca.com/mi/files/2016/11/FiveYearRecap_MIR_Achieve.pdf.

59   *civic engagement:* Joanna Weiss, "Millennials Don't Believe in Voting," *Boston Globe,* August 21, 2015, https://www.bostonglobe.com/opinion/2015/08/20/millennials-don-believe-voting/cGb7sx5ZvkmDCsNd3shTDO/story.html; "2014 Youth Turnout and Youth Registration Rates Lowest Ever Recorded; Changes Essential in 2016," Center for Information and Research on Civic Learning and Engagement, 2014, http://www.civicyouth.org/2014-youth-turnout-and-youth-registration-rates-lowest-ever-recorded-changes-essential-in-2016/.

Interlude 1: Pallas Athena

63   *A tiny owl:* Julia Golia, *"Alma Mater*: Erecting the Statue," Columbia University Archives, Columbia University Libraries, http://library.columbia.edu/locations/cuarchives/resources/almaearly/almastatue.html.

64   *Alma mater studiorum:* Julia Golia, *"Alma Mater*: Early History," Columbia University Archives, Columbia University Libraries, http://library.columbia.edu/locations/cuarchives/resources/almaearly.html.

bomb exploded: Louis Dolinar, "The Strike: Victory for Liberals?," *Columbia Daily Spectator,* June 1, 1970, http://spectatorarchive.library.columbia.edu/cgi-bin/columbia?a=d&d=cs19700601-01.2.14&e=— —-en-20—1—txt-txIN— —.

ran away with her scepter: Julia Golia, *"Alma Mater*: Lore and Pranks," Columbia University Archives, Columbia University Libraries, http://library.columbia.edu/locations/cuarchives/resources/almaearly/almalore.html.

4. Carnal Knowledge

66   *thrown in the river:* Smith, *Encyclopedia,* 14–15.

prosperous marriage: Ibid., 27.

into the 1990s: Jennifer A. Bennice and Patricia A. Resick, "Marital Rape: History, Research, and Practice," *Trauma, Violence, and Abuse* 4 (2003): 231.

"against her will": Erica Goode, "Rape Definition Too Narrow in Federal Statistics, Critics Say," *New York Times*, September 28, 2011, http://www.nytimes.com/2011/09/29/us/federal-rules-on-rape-statistics-criticized.html.

trans victims: Uniform Crime Reporting Program Changes Definition of Rape," FBI, 2013, https://www.fbi.gov/about-us/cjis/ucr/crime-in-the-u.s/2013/crime-in-the-u.s.-2013/rape-addendum/rape_addendum_final.

67 *"consent of the victim":* Susan Heavey and Jeremy Pelofsky, "U.S. Widens Definition of Rape Crimes," Reuters, January 6, 2012, http://www.reuters.com/article/us-rape-crimes-idUSTRE80520I20120106.

can't give consent: Rape and sexual assault generally, 10 U.S.C. § 920 — Art. 120 (2011), https://www.gpo.gov/fdsys/pkg/USCODE-2011-title10/pdf/USCODE-2011-title10-subtitleA-partII-chap47-subchapX-sec920.pdf; Rape and sexual assault of a child, 10 U.S.C. § 920b — Art. 120b (2015), https://www.gpo.gov/fdsys/pkg/USCODE-2015-title10/pdf/USCODE-2015-title10-subtitleA-partII-chap47-subchapX-sec920b.pdf.

70 *mental-health issues:* Canopy Programs, "The High Cost of Student-Victim Sexual Assault Claims," United Educators (March 2017): 9.

72 *"state of fear":* Susan Brownmiller, *Against Our Will: Men, Women, and Rape* (New York: Ballantine, 1975), 15.

delayed reports: Smith, *Encyclopedia*, 186.

rape-crisis centers: Ibid., 184–88.

"come on too strong": Bernice Resnick Sandler, "Papers of Bernice Resnick Sandler, 1963–2008" (papers given to the Schlesinger Library by Bernice Resnick Sandler between 1979 and 2008), http://oasis.lib.harvard.edu/oasis/deliver/~sch01194.

didn't cover academia: "Sec. 702: This title shall not apply to an employer with respect to the employment of aliens outside any State, or to a religious corporation, association, educational institution, or society with respect to the employment of individuals of a particular religion to perform work connected with the carrying on by such corporation, association, educational institution, or society of its activities." Civil Rights Act of 1964, Public Law 88-352. U.S. Statutes at Large 78 (1964): 255, https://www.gpo.gov/fdsys/pkg/statute-78/pdf/STATUTE-78-Pg241.pdf.

forgettable footnote: Sandler, "Papers of Bernice Resnick Sandler, 1963–2008."

73 *"federal financial assistance":* "Title IX and Sex Discrimination," U.S. Department of Education, revised April 2015, http://www2.ed.gov/about/offices/list/ocr/docs/tix_dis.html.

legally guaranteed: Title IX: Steve Wulf, "Title Waves," *ESPN the Magazine,* June 14, 2012, http://espn.go.com/espnw/title-ix/article/7985418/espn-magazine-1976-protest-helped-define-title-ix-movement.

Linda Lovelace: "Catharine MacKinnon on Lovelace," Harvard University Press blog, August 9, 2013, http://harvardpress.typepad.com/hup_publicity/2013/08/catharine-mackinnon-on-lovelace.html; U.S. Congress, Senate, Committee on the Judiciary, Subcommittee on Juvenile Justice, Effect of Pornography on Women and Children: Hearings before the Subcommittee on Juvenile Justice of the Judiciary Committee, 98th Cong., 2nd Sess., August 8, 1984, 179.

74 *porn usage:* Christina Spaulding, "Anti-Pornography Laws as a Claim for Equal Respect: Feminism, Liberalism and Community," *Berkeley Women's Law Journal* 4 (2013): 130.

"male supremacists": Emily Bazelon, "The Return of the Sex Wars," *New York Times Magazine,* September 10, 2015, http://www.nytimes.com/2015/09/13/magazine/the-return-of-the-sex-wars.html.

"the fuck, the fist": Catharine A. MacKinnon, *Toward a Feminist Theory of the State* (Cambridge, MA: Harvard University Press, 1989), 136.

"flunking out": Ann Olivarius, "Title IX: Taking Yale to Court," *New Journal,* April 18, 2011, http://www.thenewjournalatyale.com/2011/04/title-ix-taking-yale-to-court/.

75 *"your buttocks":* "Is It Date Rape?," *Saturday Night Live,* NBC, October 2, 1993, http://snltranscripts.jt.org/93/93bdaterape.phtml.

"I swear to God": David Mamet, *Oleanna* (New York: Random House, 1992), 59.

aggression was normal: Smith, *Encyclopedia,* 144; Camille Paglia, "Perspective Needed — Feminism's Lie: Denying Reality About Sexual Power and Rape," *Newsday,* February 17, 1991, http://community.seattletimes.nwsource.com/archive/?date=19910217&slug=1266788.

"fanatical sex phobes": David Daley, "Camille Paglia: How Bill Clinton Is Like Bill Cosby," *Salon,* July 28, 2015, http://www.salon.com/2015/07/28/camille_paglia_how_bill_clinton_is_like_bill_cosby/.

"verbal coercion": Katie Roiphe, *The Morning After: Sex, Fear, and Feminism* (Boston: Back Bay Books, 1994), 68.

76 *deciding vote:* Robert Shibley, *Twisting Title IX* (New York: Encounter Books, 2016), 18.

Student-on-student abuse: Davis v. Monroe County Bd. of Ed. (97-843) 526 U.S. 629 (1999).

77 *Victim Rights Law Center:* "Colleges Slammed with Lawsuits from Men Accused of Sex Crimes," *CBS News,* March 23, 2016, http://www.cbsnews.com/news/colleges-slammed-with-lawsuits-from-men-accused-of-sex-crimes/.

Clery Act: "The Handbook for Campus Safety and Security Reporting: 2016 Edition," U.S. Department of Education, June 2016, 1–7, https://www2.ed.gov/admins/lead/safety/handbook.pdf.

fudged numbers: Jay Caspian Kang, "Ending College Sexual Assault," *Harpers,* September 9, 2014, http://harpers.org/blog/2014/09/ending-college-sexual-assault/.

"God-given potential": Barack Obama, "Remarks by the President to the NAACP Centennial Convention 07/16/2009," White House, July 17, 2009, https://obamawhitehouse.archives.gov/the-press-office/remarks-president-naacp-centennial-convention-07162009.

78 *"started being myself":* Barack Obama, "Glamour Exclusive: President Barack Obama Says, 'This Is What a Feminist Looks Like,'" *Glamour,* August 4, 2016, http://www.glamour.com/story/glamour-exclusive-president-barack-obama-says-this-is-what-a-feminist-looks-like.

Clarence Thomas: Equal Employment Opportunity Commission, "Clarence Thomas: Eighth Chairman of the EEOC, May 6, 1982–March 8, 1990," https://www.eeoc.gov/eeoc/history/35th/bios/clarencethomas.html.

"If we could get this right": Cynthia Gordy, "The Root: The Far-Reaching Teachings of Russlynn Ali," NPR, April 20, 2011, http://www.npr.org/2011/04/20/135568364/the-root-the-far-reaching-teachings-of-russlynn-ali.

college sexual violence: Russlynn Ali, "Dear Colleague Letter: Sexual Violence," U.S. Department of Education Office for Civil Rights, April 4, 2011, http://www2.ed.gov/about/offices/list/ocr/letters/colleague-201104.pdf.

first time in history: Nick Anderson, "Sexual Violence Probes at Colleges Arise from Obama Push on Civil Rights Issues," *Washington Post,* May 3, 2014, https://www.washingtonpost.com/local/education/sexual-violence-probes-at-colleges-arise-from-obama-push-on-civil-rights-issues/2014/05/03/51cf604e-d228-11e3-9e25-188ebe1fa93b_story.html.

79 *"preponderance of the evidence":* David Burt and Drew Henderson, "Univ. to Revise Sexual Misconduct Policies," *Yale Daily News,* April 13, 2011, http://yaledailynews.com/blog/2011/04/13/univ-to-revise-sexual-misconduct-policies/.

eye-popping statistic: Ali, "Dear Colleague Letter: Sexual Violence," 2.

2007 study: Christopher P. Krebs et al., "The Campus Sexual Assault (CSA) Study," December 2007 (NCJ 221153), https://www.ncjrs.gov/pdffiles1/nij/grants/221153.pdf.

nationally representative: Emily Yoffe, "The College Rape Overcorrection," *Slate,* December 7, 2014, http://www.slate.com/articles/double_x/doublex/2014/12/college_rape_campus_sexual_assault_is_a_serious_problem_but_the_efforts.html.

4 percent: David Lisak and Paul Miller, "Repeat Rape and Multiple Offending Among Undetected Rapists," *Violence and Victims* 17 (2002): 78, http://www.davidlisak.com/wp-content/uploads/pdf/RepeatRapeinUndetectedRapists.pdf.

"serial rapist": John Lauerman, "College Serial Rapists Evade Antiquated Campus Responses," Bloomberg.com, June 13, 2013, https://www.bloomberg.com/news/articles/2013-06-13/college-serial-rapists-evade-antiquated-campus-responses.

80 *serve time in prison:* "The Criminal Justice System: Statistics," RAINN, https://www.rainn.org/statistics/criminal-justice-system.

81 *hostile to women:* Alissa Quart, "The New Weapon Against Campus Rape," *Take Part,* November 11, 2013, http://www.takepart.com/article/2013/11/11/new-weapon-against-rape-on-campus.

WE LOVE YALE SLUTS: Nathan Harden, *Sex and God at Yale: Porn, Political Correctness, and a Good Education Gone Bad* (New York: Thomas Dunne Books, 2012), 127.

degree of drunkenness: Lauren Rosenthal and Vivian Yee, "Vulgar E-Mail Targets Freshmen," *Yale Daily News,* September 3, 2009, http://yaledailynews.com/blog/2009/09/03/vulgar-e-mail-targets-freshmen.

"No means yes": Sandra Korn, "When No Means Yes," *Harvard Crimson,* November 12, 2010, http://www.thecrimson.com/article/2010/11/12/yale-dke-harvard-womens/.

82 *key Title IX complaint:* Christina Huffington, "Yale Students File Title IX Complaint Against University," *Yale Herald,* March 31, 2011, http://yaleherald.com/homepage-lead-image/cover-stories/breaking-news-yale-students-file-title-ix-suit-against-school/.

revocation of their charter: Lisa W. Foderaro, "Yale Restricts a Fraternity for Five Years," *New York Times,* May 17, 2011, http://www.nytimes.com/2011/05/18/education/18yale.html.

a violation of the Clery Act: Mark Alden Branch, "Yale Fined $165,000 for Crime-Report Violations," *Yale Alumni Magazine,* May 16, 2013, https://yalealumnimagazine.com/blog_posts/1461-yale-fined-165-000-for-crime-report-violations.

Emily Bazelon: Emily Bazelon, "Lux, Veritas, and Sexual Trespass: How Yale College Investigates Sexual Harassment and Assault," *Yale Alumni Magazine* (July/August 2004), http://archive.yalealumnimagazine.com/issues/2004_07/harassment.html.

$25 billion endowment: "Yale Financial Report 2015–2016," Yale University, October 21, 2016, https://your.yale.edu/sites/default/files/2015-2016-yale-financial-report.pdf.

84 *"sexual freedom":* Lizz Winstead, "Lizz Interviews Moe and Tracie from *Jeze-bel* Clip 1," YouTube, July 4, 2008, https://www.youtube.com/watch?v=yfTB6A-3IUE.

"lots and lots of sex": Lizz Winstead, "Lizz Interviews Moe and Tracie from *Jezebel* Clip 2," YouTube, July 4, 2008, https://www.youtube.com/watch?v=13Y6aHtOPbE.

"de facto role models": Ibid.

89 *End Rape on Campus:* I have donated $200 to EROC, and collaborated with them on a story for *New York* magazine.

University of Utah: "Our Cases," End Rape on Campus, May 2016, http://endrapeoncampus.org/our-cases/.

a hundred and two: Hayley Munguia, "It Takes Years to Investigate a Campus Sexual Violence Complaint," FiveThirtyEight, May 6, 2015, https://fivethirtyeight.com/datalab/it-takes-years-to-investigate-a-campus-sexual-violence-complaint/.

investigations were pending: As of April 12, 2017, the list encompassed 229 schools, with 319 investigations pending; Office for Civil Rights, "Postsecondary Institutions Under Title IX Sexual Violence Investigation as of April 12, 2017," United States Department of Education, April 12, 2017, https://assets.documentcloud.org/documents/3559293/2017-04-12-PSE-SV-Investigation-List-319.pdf.

91 *FERPA:* "Legislative History of Major FERPA Provisions," U.S. Department of Education, last modified February 11, 2004, https://www2.ed.gov/policy/gen/guid/fpco/ferpa/leg-history.html.

"'took a little break'": Matt Rocheleau, "Williams College Roiled by Report of Rape," *Boston Globe,* May 24, 2014, https://www.bostonglobe.com/metro/2014/05/23/williams-college-rocked-allegations-that-mishandled-rape-complaint/4EmNmZQfxDDTCDcqNfcX8H/story.html.

We Believe You: Annie E. Clark and Andrea L. Pino, *We Believe You: Survivors of Campus Sexual Assault Speak Out* (New York: Holt, 2016), 322.

92 *"confers privilege":* George F. Will, "George Will: Colleges Become the Victims of Progressivism," *Washington Post,* June 6, 2014, https://www.washingtonpost.com/opinions/george-will-college-become-the-victims-of-progressivism/2014/06/06/e90e73b4-eb50-11e3-9f5c-9075d5508f0a_story.html.

"knifepoint is worse": Erin Gloria Ryan, "Thank Goodness Richard Dawkins Has Finally Mansplained Rape," *Jezebel,* July 29, 2014, http://jezebel.com/thank-goodness-richard-dawkins-has-finally-mansplained-1612746602.

"subhuman shit": Tucker Reed, "Hello. I Was Raped. I Was Manipulated. But I Am Still Here. You Are Not Alone," Covered In Band-Aids, https://web.archive.org/web/20141114194657/http://coveredinbandaids.tumblr.com/.

5. "Rape Girls"

96   *"burst out laughing":* Lena Dunham, *Not That Kind of Girl: A Young Woman Tells You What She's "Learned"* (New York: Random House, 2014), 61.

97   *"calling it rape now":* Jessica Knoll, "What I Know," *Lenny,* March 29, 2016, http://www.lennyletter.com/life/a316/jessica-knoll-luckiest-girl-alive/.

100   *defiant football players:* "Minnesota Ends Boycott, Will Prepare to Play in Holiday Bowl," ESPN.com, December 18, 2016, http://www.espn.com/college-football/story/_/id/18297065/minnesota-golden-gophers-football-team-ends-boycott-prepare-holiday-bowl.

      investigative report: University of Minnesota EOAA Investigative Report, December 7, 2016, http://kstp.com/kstpImages/repository/cs/files/U%20of%20M%20EOAA%20redacted5.pdf.

102   *fled the apartment:* Ibid., 4–12, 17.

103   *upward of a thousand dollars:* "Why the Backlog Exists," End the Backlog, http://www.endthebacklog.org/backlog/why-backlog-exists.

104   *seventy-two hours:* Teresa Magalhães et al., "Biological Evidence Management for DNA Analysis in Cases of Sexual Assault," *Scientific World Journal* (October 2015), http://dx.doi.org/10.1155/2015/365674.

      "significant" injury: EOAA Investigative Report, 14.

106   *"frozen fright":* Rebecca Campbell, "The Neurobiology of Sexual Assault," presentation at the National Institute of Justice, Washington, DC, December 3, 2012, https://nij.gov/multimedia/presenter/presenter-campbell/pages/presenter-campbell-transcript.aspx.

      "five guys right now": Amanda Holpuch, "Daniel Tosh Apologises for Rape Joke as Fellow Comedians Defend Topic," *Guardian,* July 11, 2012, https://www.theguardian.com/culture/us-news-blog/2012/jul/11/daniel-tosh-apologises-rape-joke.

107   *"I am so sorry":* Sarah Silverman, Foxwoods Resort and Casino, MGM Grand Theater, Mashantucket, CT, July 6, 2012.

      number two *university:* Nick Anderson, "These Colleges Have the Most Reports of Rape," *Washington Post,* June 7, 2016, https://www.washingtonpost.com/news/grade-point/wp/2016/06/07/these-colleges-have-the-most-reports-of-rape.

108   *one student reported a rape:* Syracuse later added several more incidents over the course of the school year of 2014 to its roster. The next time I checked the report, it had been updated, but when I asked Syracuse to confirm how many incidents happened in spring 2014, they did not comment on this subject. See "Your Safety and Security: 2016," Syracuse University, 2016, http://publicsafety.syr.edu/PublicSafety/ckfinder/userfiles/files/annual-security-report.pdf, 41.

109 *she woke with no memory:* Reilly told the outline of her story to national media; see Barbara Booth, "One of the Most Dangerous Places for Women in America," CNBC, September 22, 2015, http://www.cnbc.com/2015/09/22/college-rape-crisis-in-america-under-fire.html.

6. Rape Theory 101

112 *reduction in crime:* Michael Planty et al., "Female Victims of Sexual Violence, 1994–2010," U.S. Department of Justice, revised May 31, 2016, https://www.bjs.gov/content/pub/pdf/fvsv9410.pdf, 1.

"alcohol or drugs": Neil Gilbert, "Realities and Mythologies of Rape," *Society* 20, no. 4 (May 1992): 4–10, doi: 10.1007/BF02695305.

113 *one-in-five statistic:* Christopher Krebs and Christine Lindquist, "Setting the Record Straight on '1 in 5,'" *Time*, December 15, 2014, http://time.com/3633903/campus-rape-1-in-5-sexual-assault-setting-record-straight/.

even somewhat higher: Christopher Krebs et al., "Campus Climate Survey Validation Study: Final Technical Report," Bureau of Justice Statistics, U.S. Department of Justice, January 2016, http://www.bjs.gov/content/pub/pdf/ccsvsftr.pdf.

115 more *risk:* Callie Marie Rennison and Lynn A. Addington, "Violence Against College Women," *Trauma, Violence, and Abuse* 15, no. 3 (2014): 159–69, doi: 10.1177/1524838014520724.

sexual assault: Sofi Sinozich and Lynn Langton, "Rape and Sexual Assault Victimization Among College-Age Females, 1995–2013," Bureau of Justice Statistics, U.S. Department of Justice, December 2014, http://www.bjs.gov/content/pub/pdf/rsavcaf9513.pdf.

118 before *every sexual act:* Andrew Morse, Brian A. Sponsler, and Mary Fulton, "State Legislative Developments on Campus Sexual Violence: Issues in the Context of Safety," NASPA Research and Policy Institute (December 2015): 6–8.

119 *punished by the college:* "Sexual Misconduct Scenarios," Yale University, September 9, 2013, http://smr.yale.edu/sites/default/files/files/Sexual-Misconduct-Scenarios.pdf.

"willingness and respect": SHARE, "Sexual Misconduct Information: Consent," Yale University, http://sharecenter.yale.edu/consent.

125 *overturned the decision: Corey Mock v. University of Tennessee at Chattanooga,* "Memorandum and Order," Davidson County, filed August 4, 2015, http://www.chronicle.com/items/biz/pdf/memorandum-mock.pdf.

127 *require a yes:* "Survey of Current and Recent College Students on Sexual Assault," *Washington Post*/Kaiser Family Foundation, June 2015, http://files.kff.org/attachment/Survey%20Of%20Current%20And%20Recent%20College%20Students%20On%20Sexual%20Assault%20-%20Topline.

7. The Accused

130   *in fifty-four years:* Jill Martin and Steve Almasy, "Source: Yale Basketball Captain Expelled After Sexual Allegation," CNN, March 10, 2016, http://www.cnn.com/2016/03/10/us/yale-basketball-captain-expelled/.

"an earlier New England": Dennis King, "Letter to the Editor: A Coach's Thoughts on Jack Montague and Yale," Brentwood Home Page, March 17, 2016, http://www.brentwoodhomepage.com/letter-to-the-editor-a-coachs-thoughts-on-jack-montague-and-yale-cms-25738#.Vu2NbeIrJD-.

131   *under 5.5 million:* Digest of Education Statistics, "2015 Tables and Figures: Table 303.30," U.S. Department of Education, National Center for Education Statistics, April 2016, https://nces.ed.gov/programs/digest/d15/tables/dt15_303.30.asp.

6,314 sex offenses: Digest of Education Statistics, "2016 Tables and Figures: Table 329.10," U.S. Department of Education, National Center for Education Statistics, September 2016, https://nces.ed.gov/programs/digest/d16/tables/dt16_329.10.asp.

136   *"just sob, and sob, and sob":* "Falsely Accused, The Caleb Warner Story," New Mew, YouTube video, November 2, 2013, https://www.youtube.com/watch?v=z7eNRi3mK4Q.

138   *reverse discrimination:* "Colleges Slammed with Lawsuits from Men Accused of Sex Crimes," *CBS News,* March 23, 2016, http://www.cbsnews.com/news/colleges-slammed-with-lawsuits-from-men-accused-of-sex-crimes/.

139   "should I go": "Theorizing Consent, Session Two: Affirmative Consent and Its Complications," Thomas K. Hubbard, YouTube video, May 6, 2016, https://www.youtube.com/watch?v=sj6YcwyudrU.

140   *He was expelled:* Richard Dorment, "Occidental Justice: The Disastrous Fallout When Drunk Sex Meets Academic Bureaucracy," *Esquire,* March 25, 2015, http://www.esquire.com/news-politics/a33751/occidental-justice-case/.

8. Guilty

146   *almost unconscious: State of Wisconsin v. Alec Cook,* "Criminal Complaint," Dane County, filed October 27, 2016, https://assets.documentcloud.org/documents/3189699/Criminal-Complaint.pdf.

the question "killed?": Alice Vagun, "A Timeline of Alec Cook's Criminal Complaints, Legal Proceedings," *Badger Herald,* November 1, 2016, https://badgerherald.com/news/2016/11/01/a-timeline-of-alec-cooks-criminal-complaints-legal-proceedings/.

"Fonz": At publication, the case against Alec Cook was ongoing.

"felony," they said: Todd Richmond, "Judge Won't Toss Charges Against Wis-

consin College Student," Associated Press, January 20, 2017, http://bigstory. ap.org/article/4a4d1fcc174340c49d03a9ff81dcf0a1/wisconsin-student-wants-sex-charges-dismissed.

with his SIG-Sauer: Bill Brown, "Isla Vista Mass Murder May 23, 2014: Investigative Summary," Santa Barbara County Sheriff's Office, February 18, 2015, http:// www.sbsheriff.us/documents/ISLAVISTAINVESTIGATIVESUMMARY.pdf.

147   *"I die," he wrote:* Elliot Rodger, "My Twisted World: The Story of Elliot Rodger," May 23, 2014, http://abclocal.go.com/three/kabc/kabc/My-Twisted-World.pdf.

extraordinary letter to the court: People v. Brock Allen Turner, "Victim Impact Statement," Superior Court of California County of Santa Clara, filed June 2, 2016, https://assets.documentcloud.org/documents/2852615/Stanford-Victim-Letter-Impact-Statement-From.pdf. Journalist Katie Baker published this letter on *BuzzFeed.*

"Bonessss": Gina Mei, "Brock Turner Allegedly Photographed His Victim's Breast During Sexual Assault, Shared Images in Group Texts," *Cosmopolitan,* June 10, 2016, http://www.cosmopolitan.com/lifestyle/news/a59745/brock-turner-stanford-rape-texts-photos-breasts-assault/.

150   *nearly six rapes:* Lisak and Miller, "Repeat Rape and Multiple Offending Among Undetected Rapists," 78.

"I was on her": David Lisak and the National Judicial Education Program to Promote Equality for Women and Men in the Courts, "The Undetected Rapist," DVD, 2000, https://www.legalmomentum.org/store/undetected-rapist-dvd.

151   *an office job:* Jesse Singal, *"The Hunting Ground* Uses a Striking Statistic About Campus Rape That's Almost Certainly False," *New York,* November 23, 2015, http://nymag.com/scienceofus/2015/11/hunting-grounds-questionable-rape-stat. html.

evidence of premeditation: Linda LeFauve, "The Misleading Video Interview with a Rapist at the Heart of the Campus Sexual Assault Freakout," Reason.com, November 20, 2015, http://reason.com/archives/2015/11/20/lisak-frank-inter-view-problem-rape.

fit Lisak's profile: Kevin Swartout et al., "Trajectory Analysis of the Campus Serial Rapist Assumption," *JAMA Pediatrics* 169, no. 12 (December 2015): 1148–54, doi: 10.1001/jamapediatrics.2015.0707.

fair piece of work: "Does Posting on PubPeer Count as Prior Publication? Journal Says Yes, Rejects Letter Rebutting Campus Sexual Assault Data," Retraction Watch, April 26, 2016, http://retractionwatch.com/2016/04/26/does-posting-on-pubpeer-count-as-prior-publication-journal-says-yes-rejects-letter-rebutting-campus-sexual-assault-study/.

154   *turn men into rapists:* Antonia Abbey et al., "Review of Survey and Experimental Research that Examines the Relationship Between Alcohol Consumption

and Men's Sexual Aggression Perpetration," *Trauma, Violence, and Abuse* 5, no. 4 (April 2014): 265–82, doi: 10.1177/1524838014521031.

button on the tape: A. M. Gross et al., "The Impact of Alcohol and Alcohol Expectancies on Male Perception of Female Sexual Arousal in a Date Rape Analog," *Experimental and Clinical Psychopharmacology* 9 (2001): 380–88.

"arrested adolescents": John Robert Greene and Robert Greene, *Syracuse University: The Eggers Years* (New York: Syracuse University Press, 1998), 115.

157 *"violently dominating anyone":* Amy Schumer, "Inside Amy Schumer — Football Town Nights," Comedy Central, YouTube video, April 22, 2015, https://www.youtube.com/watch?v=TM2RUVnTlvs.

saddest case: At publication, Vandenburg and Batey were imprisoned but may appeal their cases. Banks and McKenzie were still due to face trial.

158 *over thirty years:* Stacey Barchenger, "Cory Batey Tells Dr. Phil: 'I Wish I Could Take It All Back,'" *Tennessean*, February 9, 2015, http://www.tennessean.com/story/news/crime/2015/02/09/cory-batey-tells-dr-phil-wish-take-back/23151349/.

at nine years old: Ibid.

160 *pictures of her vagina:* Stacey Barchenger, "Alleged Vanderbilt Rape Victim: 'That's Me' in Video," *Tennessean*, January 22, 2015, http://www.tennessean.com/story/news/2015/01/22/alleged-vanderbilt-rape-victim-takes-stand-thats-me/22167013/.

box of condoms: WKRN, "Victim in Vanderbilt Rape Case Testifies in Vandenburg's Retrial," June 17, 2016, http://wkrn.com/2016/06/17/vandenburgs-ex-roommate-testifies-as-vanderbilt-rape-case-continues/.

"squeeze that shit": Stacey Barchenger, "Vanderbilt Rape Trial Day-by-Day Look," *Tennessean*, January 15, 2015, http://www.tennessean.com/story/news/crime/2015/01/15/whats-happened-at-the-vanderbilt-rape-trial-a-day-by-day-look/21822873/.

penis in Lisa's mouth: Stacey Barchenger, "How the Vanderbilt Retrials Are Different," *Tennessean*, http://webcache.googleusercontent.com/search?q=cache:-L7yWMrlsScJ:content-static.tennessean.com/Interactives/VanderbiltTrial Differences/VanderbiltTrialDifferences.html+&cd=1&hl=en&ct=clnk&gl=us.

his middle finger: Ibid.

peed on her hair: Barchenger, "Alleged Vanderbilt Rape Victim."

"you bitch": Stacey Barchenger, "Cory Batey Sentenced to 15 Years in Vanderbilt Rape Case," *Tennessean*, July 14, 2016, http://www.tennessean.com/story/news/2016/07/14/cory-batey-faces-least-15-years-friday-sentencing/86953944/.

163 *"party girl":* Certain documents related to the case were sealed. The clerk's

office in Nashville gave me pretrial documents in which this quote appears, as well as documents with the exchange that follows.

Interlude 2: Ceci N'est Pas un Viol

170   *who'd accused Nungesser credible:* Cathy Young consistently broke news about Nungesser. Young, "As Another Accusation Bites the Dust, Columbia Rape Saga Takes Another Turn," Reason.com, May 20, 2015, http://reason.com/ar chives/2015/05/20/columbia-rape-saga-lingers-after-mattres/.

"Absolutely nothing": Emily Bazelon, "Have We Learned Anything from the Columbia Rape Case?" *New York Times Magazine,* May 29, 2015, https://www. nytimes.com/2015/05/29/magazine/have-we-learned-anything-from-the-columbia-rape-case.html.

171   *film production group:* Paul Nungesser v. Columbia University et al., "Complaint," United States District Court Southern District of New York, filed April 22, 2015, https://kcjohnson.files.wordpress.com/2013/08/nungesser-complaint. pdf, 3.

"raised me as a feminist": Ariel Kaminer, "Accusers and the Accused, Crossing Paths at Columbia University," *New York Times,* December 21, 2014, http://www. nytimes.com/2014/12/22/nyregion/accusers-and-the-accused-crossing-paths-at-columbia.html.

classmate with leukemia: Nungesser v. Columbia University, "Complaint," 32.

was forced anal sex: Cathy Young, "Columbia Student: I Didn't Rape Her," *Daily Beast,* February 3, 2015, http://www.thedailybeast.com/articles/2015/02/03/ columbia-student-i-didn-t-rape-her.html.

months before the alleged assault: Nungesser v. Columbia University, "Complaint," 5–6.

I love you-so much: Erin Gloria Ryan, "How to Make an Accused Rapist Look Good," *Jezebel,* February 6, 2015, http://jezebel.com/how-to-make-an-accused-rapist-look-good-1682583526.

172   Where are you?!?!?!?: Young, "Columbia Student: I Didn't Rape Her."

"my rapist": Emma Sulkowicz, "My Rapist Is Still on Campus," *Time,* May 15, 2014. http://time.com/99780/campus-sexual-assault-emma-sulkowicz/.

"spell apparently": Nungesser v. Columbia University, "Complaint."

173   *"raped that test":* Sonja Sharp, "How Campus Rape Became a National Scandal," *Vice,* May 14, 2015, https://www.vice.com/read/how-campus-rape-became-a-national-scandal-513.

"grievance-oriented feminism": Daley, "Camille Paglia: How Bill Clinton Is like Bill Cosby."

9. The Fixer

181 *pressured her into sex:* Laura LaFay, "Student's Date-Rape Complaint Jolts William and Mary," *Washington Post,* April 7, 1991, https://www.washingtonpost.com/archive/local/1991/04/07/students-date-rape-complaint-jolts-william-and-mary/f0f9511f-f108-458d-abf6-a4d35efcc925/; "An Unsilenced Voice: Katie Koestner on Rape, Reaction and Change," *Harvard Crimson,* April 27, 2000, http://www.thecrimson.com/article/2000/4/27/fifteen-minutes-an-unsilenced-voice-katie/.

185 *Harvard had fifty:* Anemona Hartocollis, "Colleges Spending Millions to Deal with Sexual Misconduct Complaints," *New York Times,* March 29, 2016, http://www.nytimes.com/2016/03/30/us/colleges-beef-up-bureaucracies-to-deal-with-sexual-misconduct.html.

192 *indentured servants:* Cork Gaines, "College Football Reaches Record $3.4 Billion in Revenue," *Business Insider,* December 17, 2014, http://www.businessinsider.com/college-football-revenue-2014-12.

193 *"He liked that energy":* Paula Lavigne, "Baylor Faces Accusations of Ignoring Sex Assault Victims," ESPN, February 2, 2016, http://www.espn.com/espn/otl/story/_/id/14675790/baylor-officials-accused-failing-investigate-sexual-assaults-fully-adequately-providing-support-alleged-victims.

twenty years in prison: "Allegations of Indifference at Baylor," ESPN, March 31, 2016, http://espn.go.com/video/clip?id=14675314.

194 *"fallen race":* Ken Starr, *Bear Country: The Baylor Story* (Colorado Springs: Book Villages, 2017), 118.

policies toward survivors: Associated Press, "Big 12 to Hold Back Millions in Conference Revenue from Baylor," February 8, 2017, https://www.nytimes.com/2017/02/08/sports/football/baylor-big-12-revenue-sexual-assault.html.

195 *some manner of sexual reciprocation:* Brett Sokolow et al., "Due Process and the Sex Police," NCHERM Group, April 2017, https://www.ncherm.org/wordpress/wp-content/uploads/2017/04/TNG-Whitepaper-Final-Electronic-Version.pdf.

10. Adult Supervision

198 *for two decades:* Valerie Lucus-McEwen, "Should College Campuses Continue to Deploy Blue-Light Phones? (Opinion)," *Emergency Management,* December 28, 2009, http://www.emergencymgmt.com/safety/College-Campuses-Deploy-Blue-Light-Phones-Opinion.html.

199 *your drink's drugged:* "More than a Nail Polish," *NC State Engineering,* October 6, 2015, https://news.engr.ncsu.edu/2015/10/more-than-a-nail-polish/.

200 *list of loved ones:* "ROAR: Smart Safety Jewelry to Reduce Assaults," Indiegogo,

https://www.indiegogo.com/projects/roar-smart-safety-jewelry-to-reduce-assaults#/.

record an encounter: "Hair Clip with Sensors," TechFaster, http://techfaster.com/first-sign-hair-clip/.

transforms into a grin: "Because Safety Is What We Do for Each Other," Indie gogo, https://www.indiegogo.com/projects/because-safety-is-what-we-do-for-each-other#/.

202   *sexually violent behavior:* Sarah DeGue et al., "A Systematic Review of Primary Prevention Strategies for Sexual Violence Perpetration," *Aggression and Violent Behavior* 19, no. 4 (2014): 346–62, http://dx.doi.org/10.1016/j.avb.2014.05.004.

205   *studying abroad in Madrid:* "Julie Gelb," Girl Code Movement, January 25, 2014, http://www.girlcodemovement.com/post/74483822155/juliegelb.

206   *shoving it:* The national leadership for this frat did not return an e-mail requesting confirmation of this episode.

210   *A male student assaulted him:* Emily Kassie, "Male Victims of Campus Sexual Assault Speak Out: 'We're Up Against a System That's Not Designed to Help Us,'" *Huffington Post*, January 27, 2015, http://www.huffingtonpost.com/2015/01/27/male-victims-sexual-assault_n_6535730.html.

212   *"Predators are mostly wolves":* Women's Self-Defense Institute, "Prey, Predator or Sheepdog?," http://www.self-defense-mind-body-spirit.com/preyorpredator.html.

215   *selling his woodwork:* Alexandra Molotkow, "Teaching Affirmative Consent," *Hairpin,* June 19, 2015, http://thehairpin.com/2015/06/teaching-teens-affirmative-consent/.

experienced attempted rape: Charlene Y. Senn et al., "Efficacy of a Sexual Assault Resistance Program for University Women," *New England Journal of Medicine* (June 2015): 2326–35, doi: 10.1056/NEJMsa1411131.

217   *resist coercive behavior:* Charlene Y. Senn, "An Imperfect Feminist Journey: Reflections on the Process to Develop an Effective Sexual Assault Resistance Programme for University Women," *Feminism and Psychology* 21, no. 1 (2010): 121–37, doi: 10.1177/0959353510386094.

11. Phoebe

225   *sex with a dog:* Catharine A. MacKinnon, "Rape Redefined," *Harvard Law and Policy Review* 10 (2016): 450–55, http://harvardlpr.com/wp-content/uploads/2016/06/10.2_6_MacKinnon.pdf.

12. Down with the Frats

231 *higher GPAs:* Caitlin Flanagan, "The Dark Power of Fraternities," *Atlantic*, March 2014, http://www.theatlantic.com/magazine/archive/2014/03/the-dark-power-of-fraternities/357580/.

toxic-waste removal: Ibid.

members abuse alcohol: Henry Wechsler, George Kuh, and Andrea E. Davenport, "Fraternities, Sororities and Binge Drinking: Results from a National Study of American Colleges," *NASPA Journal* 46, no. 3 (2009): 396, https://journalists resource.org/wp-content/uploads/2013/02/jsarp.2009.46.3.5017.pdf.

232 *death in their houses:* John Hechinger and David Glovin, "Deadliest Frat's Icy 'Torture' of Pledges Evokes Tarantino Films," Bloomberg.com, December 30, 2013, https://www.bloomberg.com/news/articles/2013-12-30/deadliest-frat-s-icy-torture-of-pledges-evokes-tarantino-films.

233 *bit his penis:* O'Neill pled nolo contendere, and was sentenced to fifteen months of prison time.

"out of here": Flanagan, "Dark Power of Fraternities."

238 *twelve against:* This account is based on student interviews and partial notes from Wesleyan's student government.

"embarrassment and sadness": John Doe v. Wesleyan University, "Complaint," United States District Court District of Connecticut, filed November 20, 2014.

239 *historian and ex-Marine:* Adam Brown, "Dartmouth Outlaws Single-Sex Housing," *Tech*, February 16, 1999, http://tech.mit.edu/V119/N5/dartmouth.5n.html.

240 *traitor to his gender:* Brad Russo, "Initiative Stuns Student Body," *Dartmouth*, August 1, 1999, http://thedartmouth.com/1999/08/01/initiative-stuns-student-body/.

"less than desirable": Roth, "Why Freud Still Haunts Us."

241 *seat of privilege:* Susan Svrluga, "Wesleyan Student: My College Discriminates Against Fraternities. We're Suing," *Washington Post*, March 25, 2015, https://www.washingtonpost.com/news/grade-point/wp/2015/03/25/wesleyan-student-my-college-discriminates-against-fraternities-were-suing/.

242 *weren't* those *violent threats:* A great deal of e-mails and notes between Boger and Roth were disclosed during a lawsuit. They form the basis for subsequent paragraphs.

245 *"an unresponsive girl":* Cassandra Day, "Wesleyan Student Stable Following Fall from Frat Window," *Middletown Press*, September 8, 2014, http://www.middle

townpress.com/general-news/20140908/wesleyan-student-stable-following-fall-from-frat-window.

safety from sexual assault: Millie Dent and Sofi Goode, "Beta Theta Pi House Declared Off-Limits, Wesleyan Beta Chapter Suspended from National Fraternity," *Wesleyan Argus,* September 10, 2014, http://wesleyanargus.com/2014/09/10/beta-theta-pi-house-declared-off-limits/.

246   *female seniors at Harvard:* C. Ramsey Fahs, "Sexual Assault Report Lambasts Final Clubs," *Harvard Crimson,* March 9, 2016, http://www.thecrimson.com/article/2016/3/9/report-lambasts-final-clubs/.

"potential for sexual misconduct": C. Ramsey Fahs, "In Most Extensive Comments in Centuries, Porcellian Club Criticizes Final Club Scrutiny," *Harvard Crimson,* April 13, 2016, http://www.thecrimson.com/article/2016/4/13/porcellian-club-criticizes-college/.

announced his resignation: C. Ramsey Fahs, "Issuing Second Apology, Porcellian Graduate President Resigns," *Harvard Crimson,* April 18, 2016, http://www.thecrimson.com/article/2016/4/18/porcellian-grad-president-resigns/.

rather than accede to the demand: Jess Bidgood, "Social Club at Harvard Rejects Calls to Admit Women, Citing Risk of Sexual Misconduct," *New York Times,* April 13, 2016, http://www.nytimes.com/2016/04/14/us/social-club-at-harvard-rejects-calls-to-admit-women-citing-risk-of-sexual-misconduct .html.

you're out of luck: C. Ramsey Fahs, "In Historic Move, Harvard to Penalize Final Clubs, Greek Organizations," *Harvard Crimson,* May 6, 2016, http://www.thecrimson.com/article/2016/5/6/college-sanctions-clubs-greeklife/.

248   *sort of drug scheme:* Bryan Stascavage, "Wesleyan's Last Remaining Fraternity Accuses School of Shutting It Down on Flimsy Drug Pretext," College Fix, August 6, 2015, http://www.thecollegefix.com/post/23670/.

13. Battleground

250   *evidence of this comment:* Michael Miller, "Yale Investigation Finds 'No Evidence' of Racism at Frat Party Alleged to Have Been for 'White Girls Only,'" *Washington Post,* December 11, 2015, https://www.washingtonpost.com/news/morning-mix/wp/2015/12/11/yale-investigation-finds-no-evidence-of-racism-at-frat-party-alleged-to-have-been-for-white-girls-only/.

253   *fraternity itself was barred:* Vivian Wang, "SAE Banned from Campus After Violating Sexual Misconduct Policies," *Yale Daily News,* February 13, 2015, http://yaledailynews.com/blog/2015/02/13/breaking-sae-banned-from-campus-after-violating-sexual-misconduct-policies/.

254   *"I think you're responsible":* Alan Schwarz, "A Bid for Guns on Campuses to Deter Rape," *New York Times,* February 18, 2015, http://www.nytimes.

com/2015/02/19/us/in-bid-to-allow-guns-on-campus-weapons-are-linked-to-fighting-sexual-assault.html.

firearms at universities: "Guns on Campus: Overview," National Conference of State Legislatures, updated March 31, 2017, http://www.ncsl.org/research/education/guns-on-campus-overview.aspx.

university's operating budget: Campus Accountability and Safety Act, S.590, 114th Cong. (2015).

tens of millions: Columbia University, Trustees of Columbia University in the City of New York Consolidated Financial Statements, October 12, 2015, http://finance.columbia.edu/files/gateway/content/reports/financials2015.pdf, 3.

"won't show up": Niels Lesniewski, "Fighting College Rape Gets Personal for Senators," Roll Call, April 27, 2016, http://www.rollcall.com/news/policy/fighting-college-rape-gets-personal-senators.

255 *Dr. Luke:* Dr. Luke denies Kesha's allegations, and a judge has dismissed most of her claims against him. She is currently appealing; see https://www.nytimes.com/2016/10/22/arts/music/kesha-dr-luke-lawsuit.html.

"fucking done": Lena Dunham, "Why Kesha's Case Is About More Than Kesha," *Lenny*, February 23, 2016, http://www.lennyletter.com/politics/a275/why-keshas-case-is-about-more-than-kesha/.

256 *"going to be raped"*: Sabrina Rubin Erdely, "A Rape on Campus: A Brutal Assault and Struggle for Justice at UVA," *Rolling Stone*, November 19, 2014, http://web.archive.org/web/20141119200349/http://www.rollingstone.com/culture/features/a-rape-on-campus-20141119.

257 *without any pants*: Ibid.

Suspend Us!: Peter Jacobs, "UVA Melting Down After Explosive Rape Article," *Business Insider*, November 20, 2014, http://www.businessinsider.com/uva-chapter-of-phi-kappa-psi-voluntarily-suspends-itself-2014-11.

down Rugby Road: Marisa Taylor, "UVA Students Protest Against Rape in Wake of Damning *Rolling Stone* Article," Al Jazeera America, November 23, 2014, http://america.aljazeera.com/articles/2014/11/23/uva-protests-sexualassault.html.

"serious soul-searching": Sharon Gregory, "UVA President Sullivan Discusses Rolling Stone Article," NBC29, November 22, 2014, http://www.nbc29.com/story/27458179/only-on-nbc29-uva-president-teresa-sullivan-discusses-rolling-stone-article.

hands of Phi Psi: "A Note to Our Readers," *Rolling Stone*, December 5, 2014, https://www.rollingstone.com/culture/news/a-note-to-our-readers-20141205.

258 *"evolve over time"*: T. Rees Shapiro, "In Her Own Words: *Rolling Stone*'s Sabrina Rubin Erdely on Experience with 'Jackie,'" *Washington Post*, July 3, 2016, https://

www.washingtonpost.com/news/grade-point/wp/2016/07/03/in-her-own-words-rolling-stones-sabrina-rubin-erdely-on-experience-with-jackie/.

"to my assailant": Wagatwe Wanjuki, "How He Said/She Said Framing Is Used to Dismiss Sexual Assault — Wagatwe Wanjuki Discusses," Matthew Filipowicz, YouTube video, December 15, 2014, https://www.youtube.com/watch?v=RrQ3aY50aqo.

"to dismiss sexual assault": Wagatwe Wanjuki, "Why I Don't Want to Hear Both Sides of Rape Cases," *BuzzFeed,* December 6, 2014, http://www.buzzfeed.com/route95/why-i-dont-want-to-hear-both-sides-of-rape-cases#.rtXZQZ2Bn.

"outside *the legal system":* Zerlina Maxwell, "No Matter What Jackie Said, We Should Generally Believe Rape Claims," *Washington Post,* December 6, 2014, https://www.washingtonpost.com/posteverything/wp/2014/12/06/no-matter-what-jackie-said-we-should-automatically-believe-rape-claims/.

blaming Jackie: Margaret Hartmann, "*Rolling Stone* Regrets Blaming Alleged Victim for Messy UVA Rape Story," *New York,* December 8, 2014, http://nymag.com/daily/intelligencer/2014/12/rolling-stone-clarifies-rape-story-apology.html.

scarred by the scandal: Sheila Coronel, Steve Coll, and Derek Kravitz, "*Rolling Stone'*s Investigation: 'A Failure That Was Avoidable,'" *Columbia Journalism Review,* April 5, 2015, http://www.cjr.org/investigation/rolling_stone_investigation.php.

259 *"quite a display":* Roxane Gay, "Bad Victims," *The Toast,* December 10, 2014, http://the-toast.net/2014/12/10/bad-victims/.

"re-victimization": Terry O'Neill, Diana Egozcue, and Tannis Fuller, "An Open Letter to UVA President Teresa A. Sullivan," NOW, January 6, 2016, http://now.org/media-center/press-release/an-open-letter-to-uva-president-teresa-a-sullivan/.

Rolling Stone *story:* UVA's communications department supplied this information.

rears its head: Luca et al., "Campus Scandals," 12.

261 *"Good Sex Act":* Jacob Gersen and Jeannie Suk, "The Sex Bureaucracy," *California Law Review* 104, no. 4 (2016): 947, http://scholarship.law.berkeley.edu/cgi/viewcontent.cgi?article=4327&context=californialawreview.

received damages: Sandy Hingston, "A History of Political Correctness: 20 Years After Penn's 'Water Buffalo' Incident," *Philadelphia,* April 26, 2013, http://www.phillymag.com/articles/penns-water-buffalo-incident-20-years/.

266 *in front of cameras:* Joe Biden, "Senate Ceremonial Swearing-In," Washington, DC, January 6, 2015, C-SPAN, https://www.c-span.org/video/?323601-1/senate-ceremonial-swearingin-vice-president-biden.

268 *"yourself to do it":* Milo Yiannopoulos, "MILO at Auburn University: 'Feminism Is Cancer for Men . . . and Women!,'" YouTube video, October 7, 2016, https://www.youtube.com/watch?v=kKFA6RKIHSc.

current system thrive: David Glovin, "Fraternities Lobby for Tax Break Without Hazing Penalties," Bloomberg.com, July 25, 2013, https://www.bloomberg.com/news/articles/2013-07-25/fraternities-lobby-for-tax-break-without-hazing-penalties.

courtesy to the brotherhood: Tyler Kingkade, "How Rolling Stone's UVA Story Sparked a Controversial Frat Lobbying Effort," *Huffington Post,* December 10, 2015, http://www.huffingtonpost.com/entry/phi-mu-alpha-gamma-delta-safe-campus-act_us_5645f573e4b045bf3deead24.

"very powerful": Ibid.

269 *three hundred thousand dollars:* Ibid.

leaked online: Kingkade, "Controversial Frat Lobbying Effort."

"to move forward": Allie Jones, "One Sorority Finally Comes Out Against Bullshit Campus Sexual Assault Bill," *Gawker,* November 12, 2015, http://gawker.com/one-sorority-finally-comes-out-against-bullshit-campus-1742159718#_ga=1.20116286.765935977.

270 *Bill's alleged assaults:* Robert Bluey, "Author: Liberalism Contributed to Clinton's Affairs," *Human Events,* June 3, 2005, http://humanevents.com/2005/06/03/emhuman-events-interviewembrauthor-liberalism-contributed-to-clintons-affairs/.

neo-Confederate conference: Ben Terris, "Scholars Nostalgic for the Old South Study the Virtues of Secession, Quietly," *Chronicle of Higher Education,* December 6, 2009, http://www.chronicle.com/article/Secretive-Scholars-of-the-Old/49337.

271 *Liberty bowl eligible:* Des Bieler, "Ex-Baylor AD Helps Liberty Move Up to FBS-level, Big-Time Football," *Washington Post,* February 16, 2017, https://www.washingtonpost.com/news/early-lead/wp/2017/02/16/ex-baylor-ad-helps-liberty-move-up-to-fbs-level-big-time-football/.

Conclusion

273 *the surname Sulkowicz:* "Columbia College Class Day," Columbia University, webcast [no longer available], May 19, 2015.

cat-who-ate-the-canary: Teo Armus, "Sulkowicz May Not Be Allowed to Bring Mattress to CC Class Day," *Columbia Spectator,* May 19, 2015, http://columbiaspectator.com/news/2015/05/18/sulkowicz-may-not-be-allowed-bring-mattress-cc-class-day.

"slap in the face": Kutner, "The Other Side."

defamation of character: Paul Nungesser v. Columbia University, "Amended and Supplemented Complaint," United States District Court Southern District of New York, filed April 25, 2016, https://cathyyoung.files.wordpress.com/2016/04/nungesser-second-amended-and-supplemented-complaint.pdf, 63.

filed with the court: Ibid.

"nothing new for me": Cathy Young, "New 'Mattress Girl' Lawsuit: Obscene Drawing of Cleared Man 'Displayed on Campus,'" *Heat Street,* May 1, 2016, https://heatst.com/culture-wars/accused-man-in-mattress-girl-scandal-files-new-allegations-against-columbia/.

275   *Association of American Universities:* David Cantor et al., "Report on the AAU Campus Climate Survey on Sexual Assault and Sexual Misconduct," Association of American Universities, September 21, 2015, https://www.aau.edu/sites/default/files/%40%20Files/Climate%20Survey/AAU_Campus_Climate_Survey_12_14_15.pdf.

University of Pennsylvania: Nick Anderson and Susan Svrluga, "What a Massive Sexual Assault Survey Found at 27 Top U.S. Universities," *Washington Post,* September 21, 2015, https://www.washingtonpost.com/news/grade-point/wp/2015/09/21/what-a-massive-sexual-assault-survey-showed-about-27-top-u-s-universities/.

280   *"you see yourself, there":* I was unable to attend Sulkowicz's solo show in Los Angeles. A stringer conducted a tape-recorded interview with her from a list of questions I provided. I also hired a photographer and videographer, who sent me photos and videos from the show's opening night. An argument transpired about the nature of some of my questions, and Sulkowicz cut short the interview with the stringer.

Appendix: Recommendations

284   *abrasive law enforcement officers:* "Surviving Rape: Time Sensitive & Important Information," Boston Area Rape Crisis Center, http://www.surviverape.org/assets/pdf/time_sensitive_information.pdf.

285   *smaller than a fifth:* "No Kegs, No Liquor: College Crackdown Targets Drinking and Sexual Assault," *New York Times,* October 29, 2016, http://www.nytimes.com/2016/10/30/us/college-crackdown-drinking-sexual-assault.html.

consume hard liquor: Parker Richards, "Dartmouth Will Adopt a Hard Alcohol Ban," *Dartmouth,* January 29, 2015, http://www.thedartmouth.com/article/2015/01/113285/.

eighteen or twenty-one: Peter Asch and David T. Levy, "Young Driver Fatalities: The Roles of Drinking Age and Drinking Experience," *Southern Economic Journal* 57, no. 2 (October 1990): 512-20, http://www.jstor.org/stable/1060627.

288   *taught in public high schools:* California Senate, School Curriculum, SB-695 (2015–2016), http://leginfo.legislature.ca.gov/faces/billVotesClient.xhtml?bill_id=201520160SB695.

violence and on consent: Patrick McGreevy and Chris Megerian, "California Mandates New High School Lessons to Prevent Sexual Assaults," *Los Angeles Times,* October 1, 2015, http://www.latimes.com/politics/la-me-pc-brown-high-school-sexual-assaults-20151001-story.html.

British viral video: "British Police Use Tea as Analogy for Sexual Consent," *Star Online,* YouTube video, November 10, 2015, https://www.youtube.com/watch?v=Gp6alIALDHA.

290   *covering one's ass:* Lux Alptraum, "The Problem with Sexual Consent Apps," *Motherboard,* September 16, 2016, https://motherboard.vice.com/en_us/article/the-problem-with-sexual-consent-apps.

291   *know she wrote it down:* "How Callisto Works," Callisto, https://www.project callisto.org.

milquetoast descriptions: "Chapter Conduct and Judicial," University of Arizona, http://greek.arizona.edu/standards/chapter-conduct-and-judicial.

292   *"are inter-related problems":* Dartmouth College, Report of the Presidential Steering Committee for Moving Dartmouth Forward, January 20, 2015, https://forward.dartmouth.edu/sites/forward.dartmouth.edu/files/final-report-web_0.pdf.

293   *"experiment in social engineering":* Sarah Perez, "Perez: Half-Baked Housing," *Dartmouth,* October 20, 2016, http://www.thedartmouth.com/article/2016/10/perez-half-baked-housing.

between 25 and 50 percent: Noah Goldstein, "A Look at the Alcohol Policy One Year Out," *Dartmouth,* March 2, 2016, http://www.thedartmouth.com/article/2016/03/a-look-at-the-alcoholout/.

INDEX